Bleiburg

Zvonimir Gavranovic

Bleiburg

Massacre of the Croatian People 1945

Zvonimir Gavranovic

Adelaide
2023

Copyright ©remains with Zvonimir Gavranovic

All rights reserved. Except for any fair dealing permitted under the Copyright Act, no part of this book may be reproduced by any means without prior permission. Inquiries should be made to the publisher.

ISBN: 978-1-922582-77-5   soft
       978-1-922582-78-2   hard
       978-1-922582-79-9   epub
       978-1-922582-80-5   pdf

Published and edited by

Making a lasting impact
An imprint of the ATF Press Publishing Group
Owned by ATF (Australia) Ltd.
PO Box 234
Brompton, SA 5007
Australia
ABN 90 116 359 963
www.atfpress.com

Table of Contents

Abbreviations	vii
Preface John Hill	xv
Introduction	xix
1. History of Croatia to 1914	1
2. Croatia Between the Two Wars	35
3. The Independent State of Croatia 1941–1945	77
4. Croatian Death Marches Part 1	133
5. Croatian Death Marches Part 2	183
6. The Suffering of the Slovene People	205
7. Graves and Burial Places	243
8. Who is at Fault?	265
9. Reconciliation, Forgiveness and Peace	315
10. Conclusion	347
Bibliography	351
Index of Names	371

Abbreviations

KSuDGiO:	Kardinal Stepinac u Dokumentima Gestapa i Ozne.
TTM:	The Triple Myth.
KGBTIS:	KGB The Inside Story.
WF:	Why Forgive.
SŽRiP 1941–1945:	Svečenici Žrtva Rata i Poraca.
PoYBMF:	Paul of Yugoslavia Britains's Maligned Friend.
NDHBJPI:	Nezavisna Država Hrvatska Bilo Joj Pravo Ime.
RJZ 7 DK:	Rat je završen 7 dana kasnije.
PPG 1934–1940:	Propovijedi, Poruke, Govori 1934–1940.
CKo GKvuH:	Crna Knjiga o grozovitostima Komunističke vladavine u Hrvastskoj.
Pis:	Pismo iz suzananjstva.
PGP:	Propovjedi, Govori, Poruke.
SBAS:	Sluga Božiji Alojzije Stepinac.
SiTH:	Slava i Tragika Hrvata.
ZJKS:	Zivot Je Kratak San.
YGADA:	Yugoslav Genocide A Documental Analysis.
TFLYaW:	Tito's Flawed Legacy Yugoslavia and the West.
ASHK:	Alojzia Stepinac, Hrvatski Kardinal.

WGiHJiGaDC:	With God in Hell: Judaism in the Ghettos and Death Camps.
SDžhvVMLgD:	Sluga Domovine život hrvatskog viteza Vjekoslava Maksa Luburića general Drinjanin.
CHiD:	Crvena Hrvatsk a i Dubrovnik.
TCiiSfFaI:	The Croatian Nation in its Struggle for Freedom and Independence.
TRWFRtPaB:	To Reason Why From Religion to Philosophy and Beyond.
TWoL:	The Web of Life.
TCoC:	The Crisis of Christendom.
JaCTCoR:	Jung and Christianity: The Challenge of Reconciliation.
TSoR:	The Sacrament of Reconciliation.
CBWaI:	Croatia Between War and independence.
RoSA:	Roots of Serbian Aggression.
TBBoCCTR:	The Black Book of Communism: Crimes, Terror, Repression.
HP:	Hrvatska Povjest.
PP1945tWtNE:	Poisoned Peace, 1945, the War that Never Ended.
PP:	Partisan Picture.
TDoEW:	Diaries of Evelyn Waugh.
TEM:	The Embattled Mountain.
TS:	Tito Speaks.
TRtS:	The Road to Sarajevo.
OtPoMI:	On the Psychology of Military Incompetence.
CwS:	Conversations with Stalin.
MoaR:	Memoir of a Revolutionary.
PoaL:	Parts of a Lifetime.
W:	*Wartime.*
RaF:	Rise and Fall.

Abbreviations

TtSfI:	Tito the Story from Inside.
Hnpk O:	Hrvatska na putu k Oslobodjenja.
PCuH:	Povjest Crkve u Hrvatskoj.
BTaH:	Bleiburg Tragedy and Hope.
CLPC:	Croatia, Land, People, Culture.
TWWL:	The War We Lost.
WCPTRaSoJ:	When Courage Prevailed. The Recue and Survival of Jews in the Independent State of Croatia.
AS PoHR:	Alojzije Stepinac – Pillar of Human Rights.
KPHZM:	Kratka Povjest Hrvatske za Mlade.
BiKP:	Bleiburg i Križni Put 1945.
BOD:	Bleiburg Otvoreni Dossier.
NGaJ:	Nationalism, Genocide and Justice.
PPH:	Politička Povjest Hrvatske.
RiZKRuH:	Reprsija i Zločin Komunističkog Režima u Hrvatskoj.
HMiŽiKV:	Hrvatski Mučenici i Žrtve iz Komunistićke Vladavine.
EHLaU:	Einstein His Life and Universe.
ŽiDKD:	Život i Djelo Krunoslava Draganovića.
U-dp:	Ustaško-domobranski pokret od nastanka do travnja 1941 godine.
EF:	Embodying Forgiveness a Theological Analysis.
HISi J:	Hrvatska Iymedju Slobode I Jugoslavenstva.
OSNDHSU:	Oružane Snage NDH Sveukupni Ustroj.
PaR:	Psychology and Religion.
ČBU:	Čuvari Bleiburčke Uspomene.
TBBoCiC:	The Black Book of Communism in Croatia.
PSiGJKZ:	Prikrivena Stratišta i Grobišta Jugoslavenski Komunističkih Zločina.
LM:	Lovrečki Mučenici.

DŽJTNHJ:	Dubrovačke Žrtve Jugokomunistički Teror Na Hrvatskom Jugu.
PB:	Paveličeva Baština.
TBZS1945-TKaG:	The Bloodiest Yugoslav Spring 1945-Tito's Katyns and Gulags.
ANHDBiHBiG:	Argumenti NDH, BiH Bleiburg i genocide.
IBSSBF:	Iskušenja Bosne Srebrene Stradanja Bosanski Franjevaca 1944–1985.
MV:	Maćekova Vojska.
FaGotS:	Fruits and Gifts of the Spirit.
UCUITBoL:	Ubuntu: Caught Up In The Bundle Of Life.
MiHN:	Muslimani i Hrvatski Nacionalism 1941–1945.
PH:	*Povjest Hrvata.*
USK:	U Suvrenom Kaosu Uspomene i Doživljaji.
SS:	Sukob Simbola Politika, vera i ideologia u Nezavisnoj Drzavi Hrvatskoj.
APiU:	Ante Pavelić i Ustaši.
UiTR:	Unstaši i Treči Reich.
PIHiM:	Pavelić Izmedju Hitlera I Mussolinija.
PuB:	Pavelić u Bjekstvu.
PE:	Prince Eugen The History of the 7 SS Mountain Division Prince Eugen.
WBTHtGP:	When Bad Things Happen to Good People.
TBP:	The Bruised Peacemaker.
IA:	Irregular Adventure.
HJSČT:	Huda Jama Strogo Čuvana Tajna.
MNSH:	Maribor Najveći Stratište Hrvata.
HBDTWSSHD:	Himmler's Bosnian Division The Waffen-SS Handschar Division 1943–1945.
PHN:	Povjest Hrvatskog Naroda.
ASHoC:	A Short History of Croatia.
BCiBK:	Bogomilska Crkva i Bosanski Krštjana.

BiHP-KI:	Bosna I Hercegovina Povjestno-Kritićno Istraživanja.
CHuspi:	Crvena Hrvatska u svjetlu povijesnih izvora.
HiSDSiRN:	Hrvati i Srbi Dva Stara i Različita Naroda.
HZ:	Hrvatske Zemlje u Prošlosti .i Sadašnosti.
ZHiHD:	Za Hrvatsku i Hrvatsku Drzavnost.
TCoDMCwtEFoO:	The Collaboration of D Mihailović's with the Enemy Forces of Occupation 1941–1944.
DMiBiN:	Draže Mihailović izmedu Britanaca i Nemaca.
MuH:	Misija u Hrvatskoj.
PNDH:	Povjest Nezavisne Države Hrvatske.
LiCSG:	Love in Chaos, Spiritual Growth and Search for Peace in Northern Ireland.
UNPLiD:	Uspomene Na Političke Ljude i Dogodjaje.
ŽiDIM:	Život i Djelo Ivana Mestrovića.
BNKP:	Bitka Na Krbavskom Polju 1493.
THfRiSaC:	The Hunger for Reconciliation in Society and Church.
KCSiP:	Katolička Crkva Stepinac i Pavelich.
ZSČiHN:	Za Slobodu Čovjeka i Hrvatskog Naroda.
JJSiNIPN:	Josip Juraj Strossmayer i Nikola I Petrović Njegoš.
SMJI:	Stepinac Mu Je Ime.
BTHN:	Bleiburgsa Tragedia Hrvatskog Naroda.
TSDuS:	Tragedija Se Dogodila u Svibnju.
BUiP:	Bleiburg: Uzroci i Posljedice.
MBPiMH:	Mile Budak Pjesnik i Mučenik Hrvatski.
ASTMAHC:	Archbishop Stepinac: The Man and His Case.
UViOsUp:	Ustaška Vojnica i Oružana sila Ustaškog pokreta u Nezavisnoj državi Hrvatskoj 1941–1945.
FYFaO:	For You Freedom and Ours.

VITCatMotUC:	Vatican I The Council and the Making of the Ultramontane Church.
VS:	Vizija Slobode.
AWPHwFRaJ:	After Words Post-Holocaust Struggles with Forgiveness, Reconciliation, Justice.
PHDP:	Putem Hrvatskom Državnog Prava, Članci, Govori i Izjave 1918–1928.
HPC:	Hrvatska Pravoslavna Crkva.
B1945–1995S:	Bleiburg 1945–1995 Svjedočanstvo.
BTaH:	Bleiburg Tragedy and Hope.
TJIK:	Tko Je Izdao Kavrana?
TUPB:	The Unknown Pope Benedict XV (1914–1922).
OS:	Operation Slaughterhouse, Eyewitness Accounts of Postwar Massacres In Yugoslavia.
TKiD:	Tragedija Kavrana i Drugova Svjedočanstvo Preživjelog.
ŽiN:	Živjeti i Nedoživjeti.
IND:	Istina Nikad Dosta.
TI:	Theological Investigations.
BiKP:	Bleiburg i Križni Put 1945.
STSoaPM:	Sarajevo The Story of a Political Murder.
SiD:	Susreti i Doživljaji.
GS:	Guerilla Surgeon.
MFTCoaBMtM:	Miss Fire The Chronic of a British Mission to Mihailovich 1943–1944.
SiS:	Svedočanstovo i Sjećanja.
BiVT:	Bleiburgska i Vetrinjaska Tragedija.
MSNH:	Moja Sječanja Na Hrvatsku.
BiH:	Bleiburg i Haag.
BoTSTPoJP:	Boundaries of The Soul The Practice of Jung's Psychology.
CaJP:	Catholicism and Jungian Psychology.
TJTuNDH:	Tko Je Tko u Nezaviskoj Drzavi Hrvatskoj.

PM:	Povijesne Meditacije.
HPudk:	Hrvatska Povjest u Devetnest Karata.
HPu DK&HPuDPK:	Hrvatska Povjest u Devetnest Karata & Hrvatska Povijest u Dvadeset Pet Karata.
KnHP:	Krsačnstvo Na Hrvatskom Prostoru.
KPSHP:	Kroz Pet Stoljeća Hrvatske Povijest.
TFSPPB:	Tito Fenomen Stolječa Prva Politička Biografija.
PPHN:	Pregled Povijesti Hrvatskog Naroda.
NDHuSD:	Nezavisna Drzava Hrvatska u Svjetlu Dokumenta.
Ei MKG:	Elementi I Metode Komunističkog Gerile.
Iri oubzH:	Izmedju revolucianarnosti i optunizma u borbi za Hrvatsku.
TSRH:	Trazijo San Radičevu Hrvatsku.
VVSH:	Vladimir Velebit Svjedok Historije.
TMatM:	The Minister and the Massacres .
ČuDSR:	Četnici u Drugom Svjetskom Ratu.
WaRiY:	War and Revolution in Yugoslavia 1941-1945 Occupation and Collaboration.
HuMJ:	Hrvatska u Monarhističkoj Jugoslaviji 1918-1941.
HoW:	Horrors of War Historical Reality and Philosophy.
TiDJT:	This is Dr Jozef Tiso.
EaE:	Exclusion and Embrace A Theological Exploration of Identity, Otherness and Reconciliation.
BSD:	Branili Smo Državu.
USD:	U Službi Domovine.
SBZPA:	S Bjelom Zastavon Preko Alpa.
PiBSHOS:	Postrojenje i Brojčano Stanje Hrvatski Oružni Snaga.

HCMGitRoS:	Hidden Croatian Mass Graves in the Republic of Slovenia.
BM:	Bleiburg Memento.
HBP 13 SS:	Handzar Borbeni Put 13 SS Gorske Divizije.
BLaGF:	Black Lamb and Grey Falcon, A Journey Through Yugoslavia.
EatJoG:	Evil and the Justice of God.
AIatBoY:	America, Italy and the Birth of Yugoslavia 1917–1919.
KPi DGR:	Križni Put i Dvadeset Godina Robije.
BPoLGHUDSRiP:	Brojidbeni Pokazatelji o Ljudskim Gubicima Hrvatske u Drugome Svjetskom Ratu i Poraću.
NTIDiDKJ:	Nasilje Tijekom Izgradnje Države i Društva Komunističke Jugoslavije (1944–1946)

Preface

Salona, near modern Solin, was capital of the Roman province of Dalmatia. Important ruins survive there, and outside its walls are the tranquil remains of a major Christian necropolis, with basilicas and martyria, where Saint Domnius (or Domninus) and others were buried after suffering for the faith during the persecution of Diocletian. Diocletian came from Salona, and chose a site nearby for his retirement palace, from which developed the city of Split. His mausoleum eventually became the cathedral of the Diocese of Split-Makarska, with the nearby temple of Jupiter as its baptistery. Domnius is buried in the cathedral now; Diocletian's remains vanished after years of plundering by invading and marauding tribes.

Diocletian set out to reform the Roman Empire and so to rescue it from implosion. His intentions were good: the Empire seemed to be falling apart, and his solution was to restore its original purity, as he saw it: one civil religion, instead of tolerating all sorts of cults and sects; an assured imperial succession, instead of frequent coups and putsches; the weakening of the powers of provincial governors, so reducing their capacity and tendency to revolt. The aim was to restore the unity which its very size imperilled. Part of the project was the persecution of Christians.

To make the Empire more manageable, he grouped the provinces, firstly, into eleven 'dioceses', and the dioceses into four 'praetorian prefectures' (*Galliae*, Italy/Africa, Illyricum and the East), ruled in practice by two *Augusti* and their two Caesars, who were to succeed them on their death or abdication. The constitutional implications of this arrangement were important, of course, but even more important were the long-term effects of the *borders* of these prefectures.

The boundaries of the prefectures left behind a political and religious fault line that persists to the present day. Succeeding emperors modified the constitutional arrangement or restored one-man rule, but the border remained and so, when the Empire was finally divided into two on the death of Theodosius the Great in 395, the border between the prefectures of Italy/Africa and Illyricum became *the border between the Western and Eastern Empires.*

These emperors were convinced that religious unity was a condition of political stability: Diocletian encouraged it by persecuting Christianity; Constantine, by tolerating and then privileging it; and Theodosius, by establishing it. Now, as the religious traditions of Western and Eastern Christianity grew apart and moved slowly towards schism, that political border became a religious border as well, between Latin and Byzantine Christianity. The Western Empire collapsed in 476 under the impact of the Germanic invasions, but on its 'revival' in 800 (with the coronation of Charlemagne), the two empires once again pushed against that border. Latin and Byzantine Christianity were now rivals for the evangelisation of the Slavonic invaders, who had begun to arrive in the sixth century. Slavs on the western side of the border found themselves in the Latin sphere of influence, and those on the eastern side, in the Byzantine sphere. When the emerging nations of Central and Eastern Europe were (for political as well as non-political reasons) adopting Christianity, they had to choose between the two versions on offer, and with them, the political spheres of influence of which they were part.

Most Slavs were evangelised from Byzantium, but those to the west of the border were evangelised from Rome. The Magyars arrived in the ninth century, and Saint Stephen was in a stronger position: he hedged his bets and adopted a policy of non-alignment; when Hungary became Christian, he avoided being dominated by either the (Latin) Germans or the (Byzantine) Greeks by obtaining the title and crown of 'Apostolic King' directly from the Pope. The Slavs, north and south of the Magyar kingdom, did not have that choice. The Latin/Byzantine border which Hungary interrupts, is otherwise a continuous line that divides Latin Bohemia, Moravia and Poland from Orthodox Russia (north) and Latin Croatia and Slovenia from Orthodox Serbia (south). Diocletian's border had become the limit of opposing spheres of influence, both political and religious.

As long as the Ottoman Empire advanced into Europe, this did not matter so much. The Habsburgs were taken up for centuries with the

Ottoman invasions and the Turkish occupation of Hungary and Slav lands. But as Ottoman power ebbed in the nineteenth century, and when the Austro-Hungarian Empire disappeared in the twentieth, the issue revived. For those far distant from the dividing line, the issue was not as live as for those nations that straddled the border. Orthodox Serbia began to assert itself; took umbrage at the Habsburg annexation of Bosnia-Herzegovina in 1908 and provoked World War I through the assassination of Archduke Franz Ferdinand; and in the aftermath persuaded its Catholic Slav neighbours from the former Empire that confederation with Orthodox Serbia was preferable to union with Catholic Italy.

Yet Diocletian's border remained, even within the Kingdom of Serbs, Croats and Slovenes, which straddled it, and which became the Kingdom of Yugoslavia in 1929. For the Karageorgevic dynasty that ruled between the World Wars, and for Tito's Communist regime after World War II, the problem of Diocletian and Constantine returned: how was one to maintain the unity of such a disparate state, especially given that it was made up, not of only the Slavic nations specified in its original name, but also of various ethnic minorities? For King Alexander I, the glue would come through the Orthodox church; for Tito, through Communism. There would be one language, Serbo-Croatian.

This long history of political, cultural and religious division had led to national identities which were also denominational. If one was a Serb, one was also Orthodox; if one was a Croat, one was also Catholic. No matter how much rulers talked about 'national' unity, in a Yugoslav polity there would be a Serbian Orthodox majority and a substantial Catholic Croat and Slovene minority.

Small minorities are not a problem in such an arrangement; substantial minorities are. The union of Wales with England in the sixteenth century was followed by centuries of effort to stamp out the use of Welsh and to impose English, along with English laws and judicial procedures. When England and Scotland were united in 1707 to become Great Britain, an effort was made to smooth over such difficulties by encouraging the use of the terms 'South Britain' for the former and 'North Britain' for the latter. It did not catch on; few Scots saw themselves as North Britons. When Great Britain was united with Ireland to form the United Kingdom in 1801, there was a similar move to promote 'West Britain' for Ireland (along with the English language instead of Irish), but 'West Britons' quickly became a term of derision for those who (it was said) supported the Ascendancy domination of the Catholic Irish majority by the Anglo-Irish Protestant minority. Catholicism was part of Irish identity; whereas Catholics had been a negligible minority in Great Britain, they were now, through the Act of Union, a substantial minority within the United Kingdom—and a nuisance. Demands for 'Repeal' (of the Act of Union) and Catholic Emancipation intensified. The successive unions had intensified equations between national and sectarian identities. To be British was to be Protestant and loyal; to be Irish was to be Catholic and nationalist (= disloyal). Despite the Catholic Emancipation Act of 1829, the Great Famine (with its genocidal dimensions) that began in 1845 and the 1848 Young Ireland rebellion showed that this was a problem that would not go away.

I draw this parallel in order to put in context what was going to happen in Yugoslavia. The Axis invasions of 1941, the dismemberment of the country and the installation of a puppet Ustaša government were followed by sectarian strife and forced conversions of Orthodox by Catholics and of Catholics by Orthodox. Tito's diagnosis was the same as Diocletian's: nothing should be allowed to get in the way of the unity of the State. He saw the Croats as Fascist sympathisers and traitors, who needed to be shown that they could not stand in the way of the Yugoslav workers' paradise. And when Croatian forces wanted to surrender to the United Kingdom commander in Austria, His Majesty's Government was not interested; the U.K. in those days was highly centralised, with a fairly uniform system of government, which had its own history of dealing with troublesome national and religious minorities, and its Resident Minister in the Mediterranean at the time was Harold Macmillan, a North Briton, Unionist and One Nation Conservative, who was closely involved in the decisions leading to the tragedy described in this book.

History is slowly restoring the balance. Croatia's right to exist as an independent nation without this desire being attributed to Fascism is now acknowledged. Many Croats were murdered during and after World War II because this equivalence was taken for granted. The Bleiburg repatriations were the result of a naïve British acceptance of the Tito version of south Slav unity and a suspicion of 'fascist' centrifugalism. As Fr Gavranovic tells this tragic story, it is plain that there is much to be said (if still unspoken) on the other side.

Reverend Dr John Hill PhD
15 October 2021
Feast of St Teresa of Avila

Introduction

When I completed the biography: *'In Search of Cardinal Stepinac,'* something in me said I should write in English about the Bleiburg tragedy of the Croatian people. I felt this strongly because even though the British are partly responsible for this tragedy, the English-speaking world is almost completely ignorant of it.

Initially, I intended my book to cover the circumstances leading to the tragic events, the horrors of the death marches and places of burial of those killed. With time, I decided to outline the history of Croatia from its very beginning right up to 1914. In this way, readers would come to realize that the Croatian people are an ancient people who inhabited the region between the Drava River and the Adriatic Sea from the seventh century onwards. Contrary to common thinking, Croatian and Serbian people were the best of friends for many centuries right up to the creation of the Kingdom of the Serbs, Croats and Slovenes after the First World War.

In this book, I tell of the circumstances leading to the formation of that kingdom; the brutality of the regime of King Alexander Karagorgevich; his antagonism of the non-Serb peoples of the kingdom, especially the Croatians; and his unlawful change of name of the country to Yugoslavia. The book also tells of the events that led to the break-up of the country following the German invasion of Yugoslavia in April 1941. Contrary to what is believed by many in the west, the Croatians were not responsible for this German invasion.

The book then deals with the creation of the Independent State of Croatia during the Second World War. It was a state that began with much hope but ended tragically, causing the disillusionment of many Croatians. I then outline the surrender of the Croatian army to the

British in Southern Austria on 15 May 1945, and the resulting death marches of soldiers and many civilians.

Mention is also made of the suffering of the Slovene, German and Montenegrin peoples of the former Yugoslavia. Some Serbian people were also returned by the British and suffered a similar fate. I regret that time and resources meant I could not do due justice to this aspect of the whole tragedy in this small book. With the hope of healing and reconciliation, I trust that others will give a more complete history in the future.

Chapter seven deals with the graves and burial places in which some of those that were killed now lie. During the forty five years of Communist rule in the former Yugoslavia, any discussion of these massacres and burial places was strictly forbidden. But I believe one's respect for the earthly remains of those who have died is an obligation of a civilized society. It will take decades to discover where the burial sites of all those who were killed are, but we must discover them, and provide the reverence that the victims deserve.

I then write of those who are morally responsible for all the suffering caused, and highlight the leading figures involved. As in so many cases of human suffering, not one single person is completely responsible, it is all intermingled, and at times the events are far larger and wider than the individuals involved.

I regard the final chapter of this book as the most important. My hope is that it will speak to the whole of humanity when it asks the questions: 'What meaning can we draw from all the suffering caused by the inhumanity of people towards one another? How can we make sense of it? What can humanity learn from it all?'

The suffering of the innocent must never be in vain and yet so often it seems to happen. I have entitled this chapter: *Reconciliation, Forgiveness and Peace,* because I believe this the only answer to a humanity that has been greatly scarred throughout the ages. When we reflect on it, reconciliation, forgiveness and peace are also important for us personally and in our own lives. If we are not working towards reconciliation, forgiveness and peace within our families and local communities, then how can we hope to bring it about within the human family?

One of the characteristics of tyrannical regimes is that they attempt to wipe out the memory of all their victims, eliminating any trace that they ever existed or of their final resting place. It is as if they were nothing, of no value or significance or importance. One such order came from Vichko Krstulovich, Minister of Internal Affairs in the Communist government of Croatia, when ordering the destruction of all graves of enemy soldiers or any sign of their location in the Republic of Croatia.[1] I am inspired by the words of the great French writer Francois-Rene de Chateaubriand, who wrote in his memoirs:

> When in the silence of abjection, no sound can be heard save that of the chains of the slave and the voice of the informer; when all tremble before the tyrant, and it is as dangerous to incur his favor as to merit his displeasure, the historian appears, entrusted with the vengeance of the people. Nero prospers in vain, for Tacitus has already been born within the Empire.[2]

I am not of the level of a Tacitus but in some small way I am bringing the truth to light. I wrote this book with the conviction that each and every human being is precious.

The purpose of this book is to serve as a memorial: it speaks on behalf of all those who had their voices silenced by terror. It will bring to light all the shameful things performed in secret and it will guard their memory. We will remember. There is a moral obligation to honor the innocent and anonymous, even though a juggernaut sought to erase even their memory. Truth is a duty to history and one of our first services to the world. We all realize that the future can be built only with truth as its foundation. Without truth reinforcing and sewn into the foundations of community, its pillars will crack and erode. The truth is essential, otherwise one is living a lie and anything built on a lie will fall to dust. As Friedrich Nietzsche wrote: 'The service to truth is the hardest service.'

Another person from whom I draw great inspiration is Grace Tame; she is the Australian of the year for 2021. As a fifteen year old school girl she was sexually abused by her mathematics teacher who was much older than herself. She courageously went public with her

---

1. Josip Jurčević, *Prikrivena Stratišta i Grobišta*, 151.
2. *The Black Book of Communism*, 29–30.

abuse. In a number of radio interviews and speeches she encouraged other victims to speak out and share their stories for each story is unique, informative, educative and creative and has the potential to create change, bringing about a paradigm shift and the key starts with conversation.

Grace Tame continues:

> When we share we heal, reconnect and grow. The lived experience, the whole truth, unedited, is our greatest learning resource. It is what informs change, we cannot fix a problem unless we discuss it. To the fellow survivors she says: It is our time. We need to take this opportunity. We need to be bold and courageous. Share your truth. It is your power. One voice, your voice and our collective voices can make a difference. We are on a precipice of a revolution.

Grace Tame is speaking not only to victims of sexual abuse but to all people who suffered unjustly in whatever way. Certainly what happened in southern Austria one week after peace was declared in Europe in May 1945 is unknown to a vast majority of the people of Britain. It is a fact that British policy towards Croatia over the last century has been very unfriendly. When Dr Franjo Tudjman was elected as the first democratically president of Croatia in 1990 British foreign policy worked very hard to prevent Croatia's recognition. In fact it supported the aggressive nationalist policy of Slobodan Milosovich. If one reads the British press of the 1990s one will see that everything written in Britain about Croatia is very negative and isn't objective at all. It is a fact that under the prime ministerships of John Major and Tony Blair British policy was very unfriendly towards Croatia, in fact Tony Blair acted as an adviser to the president of Serbia Aleksander Vuchich. This says a lot. My book, is my little voice in trying to set things right.

One of my favorite books of the Hebrew-Christian bible is that of the prophet Jonah. With four chapters it is one of the smallest books in the bible, but it holds such depths of meaning. Poor Jonah! The Good God calls him to preach repentance to the hated people of Nineveh, which he finds repugnant. He attempts to flee to far-off Tarsus, but through God's providence, he eventually obeys God and preaches a message of repentance for three days to the people of Nineveh. As a result, the king and the whole population of Nineveh repent in sackcloth and ashes, and the merciful God spares the city and its people, causing Jonah to be very resentful with God for being so merciful towards the hated people of Nineveh. The story is so relevant to each and every one of us, and encourages us to look at the lack of mercy and forgiveness in our own personal lives and at times the bitterness we carry. It all starts with us. If I as an individual am not merciful and forgiving, how can I expect my country to be merciful and forgiving? This is especially true for the Croatian and Serbian peoples, formerly friendly neighbors for centuries, but divided by deep hatred and mistrust through their experience of brutality, both prior to and during the Second World War, as well as the conflict of the 1990s.

One of the most important words in the Bible is at the beginning, in the book of Genesis: 'Let us make man in our own image and likeness, in the likeness of ourselves... God created man in the image of himself, in the image of God he created him, male and female he created them' (Gen 1:26–27). They are very powerful words, words filled with so much meaning and hope, yet as the biblical story unfolds it is one constant wrestle of the noblest qualities of the human person with the most despicable, destructive and evil aspects of humanity imaginable.

It would be true to say that no age, with all its nobility and advancement has experienced such cruelty and inhumanity as the twentieth century. In those hundred years it saw the First World War; the Russian revolution, and its tyrannical government that annihilated millions; and the genocide in which Armenians in Turkey were almost entirely eliminated.[3] Then the Second World War, with its destruction of millions. One can only weep over the suffering of the Polish, Ukrainian and Russian peoples during this cataclysm, which resulted in the Shoah of the Jewish people. The Second World War introduced humanity to the evils of racism deeper and unimagined in previous ages.

As this cataclysmic war came to its end, we saw the establishment of the United Nations, which it was hoped would be an instrument to prevent such evil occurring again. While humanity is grateful such a world body as the United Nations exists, the litany of suffering has continued: in China with the implementation of the Great Leap Forward and the Cultural Revolution; in the Cambodian Killing Fields; and in genocides in Biafra and Rwanda.

---

3. Franjo Tudjman, *Horrors of War*, 112–113.

In the fourth century St Irenaus wrote: 'The glory of God is a human being fully alive'. It would seem that twentieth century humanity has been intent on the destruction of that glory. Then we have the beautiful words of St Pope John Paul II where he reflects on the nobility of the human being and that creative restlessness which is present in the human heart and the human being's ultimate longing, he quotes St Augustine: 'You have made us for yourself O God and our hearts are restless till they find their rest in you'. The Pope then continues: 'In this creative restlessness beats and pulsates what is most deeply human – the search for truth, the insatiable need for the good, the hunger for freedom, nostalgia for the beautiful and the voice of conscience'[4]. How often has this human heart been moved with the deepest vengeful hate and inflicted the most unimaginable cruelty.

I am inspired by the words of the Jewish philosopher Eliezer Berkovits who lived through the horrors of concentration camp life during the Second World War: 'The human being, as a potentiality, and the world that he encounters, are the raw material out of which selfhood emerges. The reality of man is never given; he has to shape it for himself out of what is given to him. How he does it, that alone determines the quality of his humanity'[5] In writing this book I am more determined to go forward and affirm life every day of my life and no matter how insignificant my life or the circumstances of my life seems to be, I will work for the betterment of humankind.

Being an Australian of Croatian heritage, my aim is to reveal to English-speaking readers a cruelty inflicted on thousands of people in Southern Austria during the days immediately following the end of the Second World War in Europe. Those affected were mainly Croatian, but Slovenes, Serbs, Germans, Montenegrins also suffered, and so too did all those fleeing the Communist regime of Marshall Tito.

This was an atrocity which the west refused to acknowledge; it has avoided and concealed from the public, and some authors greatly minimized the numbers killed. Although it is unpalatable, this atrocity needs to be acknowledged and recognized, because only the truth can teach and enable us to be free.

---

4. St Pope John Paul II, *Redemptor Hominis* (Redeemer of Man), 68.
5. Eliezer Berkovits, *With God in Hell,* 62.

My big hope is that there will come a time when the presidents of Austria, Croatia, Slovenia, Montenegro and Bosnia-Hercegovina, plus the president of Serbia and members of the British Royal family, will come to the Bleiburg field. I hope they will one day acknowledge what happened there on 15 May 1945. While it's too soon to hope this will happen in any near anniversaries, it certainly could be a reality for the commemoration of the centenary. May this vision become a reality.

It took me seven years of perseverance to complete this book, and when I found it difficult, I was inspired by the words of Vaclav Havel: 'Hope is not the expectation that things will turn out successfully, but the conviction that something is worth working for, however it turns out.' I kept at it with the conviction that I am contributing to a better world.

I dedicate this book to a number of bodies, firstly to the United Nations, we all know that it needs reforming as in the words of Pope Francis: 'the need for a reform on 'the United Nations Organization, and likewise of economic institutions and international finance, so that the concept of the family of nations can acquire real teeth'.[6] The United Nations is the only world body that works for world peace, the rule of law and the development of all peoples, especially those in poorer parts of the world. I also dedicate it to the World Criminal Court, with the hope that it will be greatly improved and can truly implement justice, and to the Red Cross and the Red Crescent, two bodies very much involved in relieving the suffering of conflict.

I also dedicate this book to all those who are working to end all forms of slavery and capital punishment and for nuclear disarmament.

Finally I dedicate this book to all members of the African National Congress who were imprisoned on Robben Island and who mapped out a plan for the future peaceful development of South Africa. These imprisoned members of the South African National Congress, with Nelson Mandela as their most prominent figure, have given an example for the rest of the world to follow. This is the way forward.

There are many people I would like to thank who helped me while I was writing this book, including many friends from Croatian background whose books I borrowed for my research. I am grateful for the talks I had with Stjepan Hojt, who joined the Ustasha army

---

6. Pope Francis, *Fratelli Tutti*, 86.

in May 1941, Pavo Gagro, who joined in 1943, and Ivica Mandich, who joined the Croatian regular army also in 1943. These three men remained patriotic Croatians all their lives and they were good Australians as well, grateful to the land that gave them so much freedom and wellbeing. They all witnessed the collapse of the former Yugoslavia and the coming of Croatia's independence for which so many longed.

I am also grateful to Mate Petrichivich who was born on 30 August 1933 in the parish of Lovreć-Opanci, which was also the parish of my parents' birth. Mate remembered the enormous suffering of people during the war, and told me: 'All through the war there was only weeping and wailing. Anyone who did not live through it can't appreciate the distress people were going through'. Mate also remembers 22 July 1943, when Serbian Chetniks, dressed in Italian military uniforms and under Italian command, killed forty-two people of Lovreć village. Included in those killed were my mother's sister, her husband and two sons.[7]

I am also grateful for the day-long conversation I had with the eminent Croatian journalist, Franjo Dujmovich, at his home in Sao Paulo, Brazil in June 1992. In June 1992, in Buenos Aires, Argentina, I also had extensive conversations with the Croatian industrialist, Ivo Rojnica, and Mirko Zivkovich, who was a police official in Dubrovnik and Osjek during the war, and who saved almost all of the Jewish residents of Dubrovnik.

I am grateful to Dr Kevin McDonnell who spent fourteen years in South Africa. Kevin gave me an insight into the African National Congress members who were imprisoned on Robben Island, where they mapped out the plan for reconciliation and peace as the way forward for South Africa.

I owe a lot to the Australian political journalist Peter Hartcher, because his articles introduced me to books and quotes that I applied to the incompetent Croatian political leadership during the Second World War. Some books in the bibliography may seem irrelevant to the subject of this book, but I gained insights I applied to my reflections in the final and most important chapter of the book.

---

7. Conversation with Mate Petričević. In Lovreć-Opanci parish, 1 August 2019. Also see Fra Mario Jurišić, *Lovrećki Mučenicic*, 62–67

I use some quotes without references in the book. I did try very hard to find the source of these references, but unfortunately through my long research, I lost the sources from which I had obtained them. I hope readers will understand this and simply reflect on the truths of the statements made.

A big thank you to the Australian writer, Jenna Munro, as well as Bruce Hawthorn, Nancy Donnelly, Keith Carlon and Jayne Steer for going through my original drafts, improving the English, providing their suggestions and giving the book its final shape. My thanks also to the Australian scripture scholar, anthropologist and archeologist Dr Eugene Stockton and the Australian theologan Dr John Hill for their encouragement, support and insights. I am also very grateful to Janice and Vince Moulay for their friendship, support and hospitality, as I spent much of my free time and some holidays working on the book in their home.

This book was a labor of love. I wrote it so that the western world comes to know the history of Croatia and the turmoil that its people suffered in the years leading up to the Second World War, during the war itself and its immediate aftermath. I also wrote it so that readers would be inspired to work together to create a world with just laws and where such crimes are a thing of the past.

I am inspired by the words of the Croatian poet and writer Dobrisha Cesarich:

> My friend, I am no longer here. But I am not just earth, or only grass. For the book that you are holding in your hand, is only a part of me which is sleeping. And they who read it awaken me to life. Awaken me and I will be your awakening.

The value of a book is seen not only by how well it sells, but also by how many people read it in a hundred years' time. If someone reads this book in a hundred years' time and it inspires them to make this world a more humane and better place, then my seven years of labor were well worth it and I will be very happy.

Zvonimir Gavranovic
Parish of St John XXIII
Glenwood-Stanhope Gardens.
25 February 2021.

Map of Croatia in 1914

Chapter 1
The History of Croatia to 1914

Historians of former generations held that Croatians are of Iranian origin. However more contemporary historians dispute this, claiming that the Iranian origin of the Croatians is merely a theory with no concrete basis.[1]

A significant event for the Croatians was the Roman Emperor Theodosius' partitioning of the Roman empire in 395 into its western and eastern sections on either side of the river Drina. As a result, the Drina river divided the Latin West from the Greek Eastern cultures. Later, when the Franks, under the leadership of Charlemagne, attempted to re-establish the former Western Empire, they selected the Drina as their eastern boundary. This had a bearing on later developments, because the Serbs eventually settled to the Drina's south and the Croatians to its north. The river therefore shaped the lives of these two peoples. Those living to its south tended to gravitate towards Constantinople and Eastern Christianity. Those to its north gravitated towards Rome and Western Christianity and, in a sense, the River Drina brought about a spiritual separation.[2]

When, in the early seventh century, the Byzantine Emperor Heraclius had problems with the Avars, he invited the Croatians to

---
1. The Croatian people, according to some historians, are of Iranian origin, originating in Eastern Iran and Western Afghanistan sometime in the sixth century before our era. An old Persian inscription from circa 500 BC mentions the region Harahvatis, which was situated in present day Afghanistan. Ancient Persian literature also bears the name Horvati, Harvati, Horoathos, Horouathos, and there is evidence that the Satrapy of Harahvati existed in the ancient Persian Empire during the Arsacid and Achaemenid Dynasties.
2. Antun F Bonifačić A & Clement S Mihanovih, *The Croatian Nation*, 77–79. Fra Oton Knezović, *PH*, 12. Trpimir Macan, *PHN*, 16–17. Stjepan Srkulj, *HPudk*, 12.

these parts in order to destroy the might of the Avars. At that time, Croatians were settled in what is known today as southern Poland, Czech Republic and Western Ukraine. This permitted them to settle in the Roman province of Dalmatia, from Istria in the north to the river Drina in the south and the River Drava in the east and the Adriatic Sea in the west. The most accurate dating of the arrival of the Croatians to these parts is given by the great Spanish thinker and writer of the seventh century, Saint Isidore of Seville. He was a very informed writer in the western Church, writing at the time about the movement of peoples. In fact, Saint Isidore compiled a number of encyclopaedias, it can be reasonably said that he was the father of the encyclopaedia.

In his writings, *Chronica Maior* (Great Chronicle), Isidore stated that the Slavs at the beginning of the eighteenth year of the reign of Emperor Heraclius had penetrated the Roman province. By Romans, Isidore meant the Byzantines, who were called Romans by everyone, including themselves. Since the Emperor Heraclius was crowned on October 10, 627, the coming of the Slavs would have been some time after that date.

The eminent Croatian historian Domenik Mandich (Mandić) concluded that the Croatians came through Panonia, advanced to the Sava river and then reached the rivers Una and Krk, coming to the district of the Roman city, Salona, near modern day Split. They then went along coastal roads south, until they reached the southern-most part of the Greek province of Illyria. Others went into the mountains of Herzegovina and Bosnia which, in pre-historical times was called Basa-n and, in Roman times, Basanius.[3]

These peoples came in contact with Christianity when Pope John IV (640–642), who came from Dalmatia, sent Abbot Martin in 641 with money to save Christians who had been captured by the Avars and to return their earthly remains.[4]

---

3. Domenik Mandić, *Crvena Hrvatska*, 238-242. Domenik Mandic, *HiS,* 37–49. Domenik Mandić, *HZ,* 13–21. Domenik Mandić, *BiH,* 43–44, 165–166, 179–182. St Isidore of Seville, HTTPS://www.britannica.com/biography/saint–isidore-of-sevillia. Stanko Guldescu, *Political History to 1526* In *CLP&C,* Volume 1, 82–84. Trpimir Macan, *PHN,* 16–17. Trpimir Macan & Josip Šentija, *ASHiC,* 19–22.
4. Domenik Mandić, *HiS,* 55. Domenik Mandić, *BiH* 382–386. Domenik Mandić, *TEaRHoBaH* In *CLP&c* Volume 2, 366. Ferdo Šišic, *PPHN,* 81–82. Doctor Stjepan Krašić. 13/10/2014 & 28/7/2016. Vjekoslav Klaić, *PHN,* Volume 1, 48.

The year 679 is significant in Croatian history, because in that year the Croatian tribes made an agreement with Pope Saint Agatha that they would never conduct an aggressive war with Christian nations. This was one of the first international agreements with the Holy See.[5] During that time and for a number of centuries afterwards, there was always competition between the Latin church in the west and Byzantium in the east. Croatia finally came under the wing of the western church, when Duke Branimir (879 – 890), through an exchange of letters with Pope John VIII, expressed the loyalty of Croatia to the Holy See in 879.[6]

Croatia finally became a Kingdom under King Tomislav in 925. It was Tomislav who established a clear border, the Drava river between Croatia and Hungary, incorporating Dalmatia firmly in it, and strengthening the state.[7]

At that time, a few months after Tomislav's crowning, there was a very important church synod held in Split. It determined that Split would be the Metropolitan See, which meant that all other bishops in Croatia were to be under the jurisdiction of the Bishop of Split.[8]

Following Tomislav's death, Trpimir I, his younger brother, succeeded to the throne. He maintained the kingdom and reigned till 935, followed by Kreshimir (Krešimir) I from 935–945. These two maintained the borders of Croatia as it was during the time of Tomislav, continuing the stability of the country. A dispute followed Kreshimir's death, and the throne eventually passed to Kreshimir II. During this period there was a constant challenge from the Republic of Venice with its ever-strengthening navy, increasing control over the Adriatic; its aim was to take control of the islands and towns along the Dalmatian coast. Byzantium also relentlessly tried to extend its power over Croatia during this time.[9]

---

5. Domenik Mandić, *BiH*, 382–390. Franjo Sanjak, *KNHP,* 47, 59.
6. Domenik Mandić, *SiH*, 67. Fra Oton Knezović, *PH*, 29–30. Ferdo Šišić, *PPHN*, 113–114. 119–123. Stanko Guldescu, *Political History of Croatia to 1526*, In *CLP&C*, Volume 1, 89–90. Trpimir Macan, *PH*, 26. *Znameniti i Zaslužni Hrvati*, Volume 5. Dušan Žanko, *Svjedoci*, Essay of Domenik Mandić, 310–311.
7. Domenik Mandić, *HiS*, 70–74. Fra Oton Knežović, *PHN*, 32–33. Ferdo Šišić, *PPHN*, 119–122. Trpimir Macan, *PHN*, 28–31. Trpimir Macan & Josip Šentija, *ASHoC*, 23–26. Stjepan Srkulj, *HPudk*, 28–30. Vjekoslav Klaić, *PH*, Volume 1, 98–107. *Znameniti i Zaslužni Hrvati*, Volume 1, 6.
8. Ferdo Šišić, *PPHN*, 122–123. Stjepan Srkulj, *HPudkp*, 28–29. Stanko Guldescu, *Political History of Croatia to 1526*, In *CL&C*, Volume 1, 90–91. Vjekoslav Klaić, *PH*, Volume 1, 108–115. NZ Bjelovučić, *Crvena Hrvatska i Dubrovnik*, 13–15. *Znameniti .i Zaslužni Hrvati*, Volume 1, 6.
9. Ferdo Šišic, *PPHN*, 123–124. Trpimir Macan, *PHN*, 32–34. Vjekoslav Klaić, *PH*, Volume 1, 116–128. *Znameniti .i Zaslužni Hrvati*, Volume 11, 7.

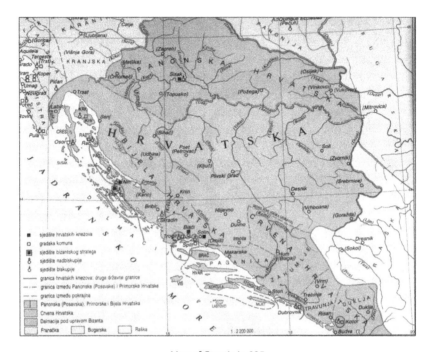

Map of Croatia in 925

Croatia reached its economic and cultural heights under the reign of Peter Kreshimir IV, traditionally known as 'The Great', whose rule extended from 1058–1075. Although territorially Croatia was reduced in size during his reign, economically it developed. Kreshimir, due to his policy of reinforcement of his navy, was able to reincorporate the coastal towns of Zadar, Split and Trogir into his jurisdiction, as well as the islands of Rab, Krk and Osor, and some smaller islands. Of all Croatian kings he was the only one able to call the Adriatic sea: *'Our Dalmatian sea'*. He travelled through his realm extensively, establishing peace and providing stability to the country, enabling it to prosper. Towards the end of his life he allied himself more closely with the Holy See, bringing Croatia closer to other states.[10]

---

10. Domenik Mandić, *HiS*, 99. Domenik Mandić, *HZ*, 27. Ferdo Šišić, *PPHN*, 131–136. NZ Bjelovučić, *Crvena Hrvatska i Dubrovnik*, 17. Fra Oton Knezović, *PHN*, 38–40. Stanko Guldescu, *Political History of Croatia to 1526*, In *CLP&C*, Volume 1, 97–100. Trpimir Macan, *PHN*, 34–41. Trpimir Macan & Josip Šentija, *ASHoC*, 29. Vjekoslav Klaić, *PH*, Volume 1, 129–136. *Znameniti .i Zašluzni Hrvati* 1X, 9.

With Kreshimir's death, the Croatian nobility and clergy, together with the support of Pope Gregory VII, elected Demitar Zvonimir in the middle of 1075 as king of Dalmatia and Croatia. He was crowned on 8 October 1075 in Salona, just outside modern day Split. Zvonimir was a pious ruler who built churches and established monasteries. He travelled through Croatia, justly settling disagreements, continuing the policy of establishing peace in the country. When he died in 1089, an ancient chronicler wrote:

> *And there remained King Zvonimir, what a just king, a son of happy memory, who was devoted to and loved the church. Who helped the good and persecuted the bad. Who was loved by all . . . And during the time of good king Zvonimir the land was blessed for it was full of all good . . .*[11]

After Zvonimir's death there was bitter division among the Croatian nobility. One faction of Croatian nobles, those in the north, wanted the Hungarian king Ladislaus to claim the Croatian throne, given he was the brother of Zvonimir's widow, Helen. In the Middle Ages the crown went to the nearest relative, but in this case some of the Croatian tribes in the south chose one of their own, Petar Svachich (Svačić), as their king in 1093. He was killed in the battle of Gvozda, attempting to drive back the Hungarians in 1097. After this, Croatia entered into a personal union (*Pacta Conventa*) with the king of Hungary, accepting King Koloman in 1102 as the king of Croatia. It was a personal union in which Croatia and Hungary would remain two separate, independent states, each living its own life. With the Hungarian king crowned with a Croatian crown as King of Croatia in the town of Biograd, near Zadar, it became two kingdoms with one king.

King Koloman confirmed he would respect all state rights within the Croatian kingdom and all privileges the Croatian nobility enjoyed. The Croatians would not pay the king any tribute or taxes, and they

---

11. Domenik Mandić, *HiS*, 81–82. Has a different quote, but in the same sense. Fra Oton Knezović, *PHN*, 42–47. Ferdo Šišic*PPHN*, 139–142. Stanko Guldescu. *Political History of Croatia to 1526*. In *CLP&C*, Volume 1, 100–102. Also, Francis H Eterovich, *Ethical Heritage*, In *CLP&C*, Volume 1, 213–214. Trpimir Macan, *PHN*, 41–43. Vjekoslav Klaić, *PH*, Volume 1, 137–144. Stjepan Srkulj, *HPudk*, 34. *Znameniti .i Zašluzni Hrvati*, X–X1, 10–11.

would administer their country and defend it with their own army.[12] From this time onwards the Croatian Sabor, which was an early form of parliament, would be the carrier of Croatian statehood and sovereignty.[13] All this meant that Croatia preserved its characteristics as a separate state with medieval Hungary. The independent Croatian state in these early Middle Ages left a strong imprint of national identity and statehood on the consciousness of the Croatian people.

At that time Bosnia and Herzegovina were part of Croatia but by 1137 Bosnia Herzegovina began to assume a vassal status in the new kingdom. By the beginning of the thirteenth century, Venice began extending its control over the Dalmatian coast of Croatia as well as hindering the naval trade of the Croatian coastal towns. In 1242, Croatia, together with Hungary and other parts of Eastern Europe, was overrun and ravaged by the Mongols, and Zagreb was destroyed. The mobility, flexibility and weaponry of the Mongols proved far superior to the cumbersome armour of the Europeans. The Mongols penetrated to the walls of Split, where the Hungarian-Croatian King Bela had sought refuge. As the Mongols had no navy, the islands

---

12. A glaring neglect of the *Pacta Conventa* was that Croatians didn't insist the Croatian Sabor had the right to appoint Croatians as Ban and other officials in the country. As nothing was confirmed in the pact, the Arpadovich (Arpadović) Dynasty would later name Hungarians as Croatian Bans, this was detrimental to the Croatian state administration and independence. (Domenik Mandić, *HiS*, 85–88. Fra Oton Knezović, *PH*, 52–53. *Pacta convent*).
13. Domenik Mandić, *HiS*, 58–60 and 89–90. Domink Mandić, *HiS*, 83–89. Domenik Mandić, *HZ*, 30–31. Domenik Mandić, *BiH*, 340–341. Ferdo Šišić, PPHN, 145–146 also 248. Dr Fra Oton Knezović, *PH*, 51–53. Stanko Guldescu, *Political History of Croatia to 1526*, In *CLP&C*, Volume 1, 103–104. Trpimir Macan, *PHN*, 43–49, 71. Trpimir Macan/Josip Šentija, *ASHoC*, 31–35. Vjekoslav Klaić, *PH*, Volume 1, 145–152. *Znameniti .i Zašluzni Hrvati*, X11–X111, 12–13. From the time the Croatians arrived in this region they developed what they called the Sabor, which was a gathering of their leading figures, including representatives of the church, in which they discussed important matters of state or region. Sabors were called periodically in order to come to a consensus. In Croatia's history they were the precursors of a modern-day parliament. At one such Sabor, held in the town of Krizevci in February 1397, a dispute arose against King Sigismund Luxemburg, who was blamed for the Christian defeat by the Turks in Varga, Northern Bulgaria. Some Croatian nobility, led by Stjepan Lachkovich (Lačković) supported Ladislav of Naples. This Sabor, known as the *Krvavi Sabor* (Bloody Sabor), ended violently. (Ferdo Šišić, *PPHN*, 219–221. Trpimir Macan, *PHN*, 110–111. Vjekoslav Klaić, *PH*, Volume 2, 325–329).

were spared. The Croatian nobles Frederik and Bartol Frankopan excelled themselves in defending King Bela. When news of the death of Genghis Khan's grandson, Batukan, reached the Mongols, they withdrew from Croatia, leaving much of the country pillaged.[14]

Throughout the thirteenth and fourteenth centuries, the Latin influence was very strong in some towns of the Dalmatian coast, with many of the inhabitants speaking Latin. Due to this cultural influence, the people naturally gravitated towards Venice, which was always trying to gain control of the islands and towns of the Dalmatian coast to assert its dominance over the Adriatic sea. Through much of this time these coastal towns possessed a certain autonomy, often competing, at times violently, for more control over the local region. Although Croatia was a sovereign state with a king whose nationality was Hungarian, parts of the country were administrated by a Ban or Vice Royal and lower levels of nobility.

In the thirteenth and fourteenth centuries, religious orders such as the Benedictines, Cistercians, Dominicans, Franciscans, Paulians and others, established monasteries throughout Croatia, contributing to the cultural development of the people. Some of them established schools, teaching reading and writing. Although the Western Church's religious services were in Latin, the coastal region of Croatia was given permission by Pope Innocent IV in 1248, to celebrate its liturgy in Slavonic, known as Glagolica. This Glagolic script originated from Saints Cyril and Methodius, the apostles to the Slavs. As a consequence the liturgical books were written in the old Croatian language that the people would understand.[15]

In 1347, King Ludovik I, handed over the administration of the town of Zrin and its districts to a part of the Bribirski family. This noble family subsequently took on the name Zrinski, and played a significant part in Croatian life right up to the seventeenth century.[16]

---

14. Ferdo Šišić, *PPHN*, 188–189. Dr Fra Oton Knezović, *PH*, 120–121. Trpimir Macan, *PHN*, 88–89. Vjekoslav Klaić, *PH*, Volume 1, 247–260. *Znameniti. i Zašluzni Hrvati*, XV111–X1X, 18–19.
15. Domenik Mandić, *BiH*, 434–449. Vjekoslav Klaić, *PH*, Volume 3, 36–46. Franjo Sanjak, *KNHP*, 79–91.
16. Ferdo Šišić, *PPHN*, 209–210. Trpimir Macan, *PHN*, 97. *Znameniti .i Zašluzni Hrvati*, XXV11, 27.

The Bogomils

During the Middle Ages, the Bogomil religion came to prominence in Bosnia. The people following this religion never called themselves Bogomils; they called themselves Bosnian Christians, the name Bogomil being given to them by later historians. Their religion derived from the Manichean Christian heresy, which had its origins in the near East, but was refined by a Bulgarian Priest, Jeremiah, in the tenth century.

The Bogomils were closely related to the Albigensians in southern France and the Cathars of Northern Italy, with whom they had a considerable amount of contact. They had their own hierarchy, with their own bishops and their version of a pope, whom they called Djed (Grandfather).

The religion's basic tenets were that creation is a form of dualism, that is, there are two principles, the good and the bad. God created the invisible world with many spirits and Satan created the visible world. The soul was created by God, but it fell away from him and entered the human body and had to be purified of sin. Christ was a greater spirit but not divine. He took a partial body through Mary, who was not a human being, but an angel. They replaced Baptism by the placing of a book of the gospels on the head of the person wishing to be received into their community and rejected Christian symbols such as the crucifix. They regarded marriage as a necessary evil. They refrained from eating meat or dairy products, nourishing themselves on grain and vegetable products. They strictly forbade the use of oaths or vows; they did not recognise Baptism or other Christian sacraments; they did not build churches for worship, claiming that one could just as effectively pray in a stable or home rather than a building specially designed for prayer. They did not reverence the dead by burying them in special cemeteries and they did not look on a grave as especially sacred. For Bogomils, the body was evil and, for health reasons, the dead could be buried in fields, forests or wherever families saw fit. Their members were divided into the 'true Christians' and 'good believers' and because they believed Satan created everything material, the Bogomils rejected all wealth and bodily enjoyment.[17]

---

17. Domenik Mandić, *HZ*, 103–111. Ferdo Šišić, *PPHN*, 180–182. Dr Fra Oton Knezović, *PH*, 303–308. Trpimir Macan, *PHN*, 83–86.

At a gathering in Bilina Field in 1203, near the Bosnian town of Zenica, with John of Casamare, a legate representing Pope Innocent III, the Bogomils recognised the teaching of the Catholic faith. This recognition did not last, and the heresy spread. Pope Honorius III in 1221 called a crusade to bring them back by force; this failed because the Bogomils saw their strong resistance as a defence of Bosnian freedom.

After the failure of the First Crusade, Pope Gregory IX (1227 – 1241) sent the Dominican missionaries, who successfully brought the ruling families into the Catholic faith, while part of the population remained Bogomil. From that time Bosnia became the first country in Europe with religious tolerance, where rulers did not impose their faith on their subjects.[18] The Bogomils became a Bosnian church, which the Roman Catholic Church tried to suppress, which was catastrophic for Bosnia because of the division which was caused.

There are a number of reasons why the Bogomils lasted so long in Bosnia and parts of Herzegovina. They practised what they preached, a very ascetic life that had a strong impact on the wider population. The medieval Croatian population of Bosnia received its Christianity by the early tenth century but it was not well established in the mountainous, scattered regions, and the people were inclined to accept Bogomilism. The Bogomils saw their Christianity as being very much Bosnian. The Bogomils were also able to take advantage of divisions between the Western and Eastern Churches and disputes between various papal claimants, which enabled them to be a prominent religion throughout Bosnia for almost five hundred years.[19]

---

18. Domenik Mandić, *HiS*, 107–109. Domenik Mandić, *TE&RHoB&H*, In *CLP&C*, Volume 2, 366–367. Fredo Šišić, *PPHN*, 180–182. Oton Knezović, *PH*, 303–308.
19. Domenik Mandić, *BCiBK*, 512–523. Franjo Sanjak, *KNHP*, 184–202. The influence of the Bogomil faith was present in the Croatian people long after its disappearance in Bosnia. Domanik Mandich remembered as a boy hearing from elderly Croatian women, that Jesus came to Mary through her ear when she heard the Angel Gabriel's greeting, and after nine months, her breasts were opened and he emerged (Domenik Mandić, *BCIBK*, 119). Doctor Domenik Mandich's book *Bogomilska Crkva I Bosanski Krstjana*, is the most thorough study of the Bogomils of Bosnia-Herzegovina in the Croatian language.

The Republic of Dubrovnik

In the political and cultural life of Croatia, there is a special place given to Dubrovnik and the republic it became. It is first mentioned in 867 when it was under the control of the Saracens. Initially, the southern section of the town was known as Ragusa, but as the town expanded northwards, certainly by the twelfth century, it was known as Dubrovnik. With the passing of time, Dubrovnik developed into a democratic republic with a people's assembly, although it wisely recognised the authority of prevailing powers such as Venice, Byzantium, the Normans and the Ottomans. All its citizens would gather and debate various issues affecting them, and make important decisions. In 1395 the People's Assembly was replaced by '*Veliko Vjece*'(Great Council), which drew its members from the aristocracy, who determined the direction of the republic. It banned slavery in 1416, stating in its statutes: ' . . . such a trade is wicked and odious, against everything human, becoming not a light burden and shame for our city . . . the human being is made in the image and likeness of our creator . . . '[20]

Due to the prevalence of plagues, Dubrovnik established a quarantine on the island of Mrkan in 1377, possibly one of the first in Europe. By the middle of the twelfth century it had established a hospital with a pharmacy. The public pharmacy in the Franciscan Monastery, established in 1317, is one of the oldest in Europe. In 1436–1438 it built a twelve kilometre aqueduct, bringing water to the town.[21]

Almost from its beginnings, due to its cultural advancement Dubrovnik had schools for the education of its youth. In the early Middle Ages there was a directive for every cathedral to have a school. The many Benedictine monasteries, both male and female, in Dubrovnik and its vicinity had schools. The first public school in Dubrovnik was established in 1333. By 1435 it was divided into lower and higher grades. The Dominicans established the first public high school in Dubrovnik in 1626. From 1658 to 1773 this school was run by the Jesuits and was known as 'Collegium Ragusinum'.[22]

---

20. Telephone conversation with Don Božo Baničević, 1 November 2020. Trpimir Macan, *PHN*, 174–175. Stjepan Srkulj, *HPudk,* 40.
21. Domenik Mandić, *HiS*, 128–129. Trpimir Macan, *PHN,* 105, 204–205
22. Domenik Mandić, *HiS*, 129. Dr Fra Oton Knezović, *PHN,* 109–115. Also in conversation with Dr Stjepan Krasić.

Dubrovnik became a centre of commerce, specialising in textiles and ship building, and trading with cities of the Mediterranean. Culturally it developed in philosophy, literature, art, music and the sciences.[23]

The History of Croatia from The Fourteenth Centuary to 1914

In the early fourteenth century a large area of Bosnia began gaining its independence from Hungary, under its Ban, Stjepan Kotromanich (Kotromanić), who left his nephew Tvrtko to rule after him. Tvrtko was only fifteen years old at the time, so his mother Jelena, who was related to the Croatian noble family of Shubich Bribirski (Šubić Bribirski), wisely advised him. Through wise policies he was able to unite Bosnia with parts of Dalmatia and pronounced himself king of Bosnia, Dalmatia and parts of Serbia in 1377. Tvrtko also sent twenty thousand Croatian soldiers under the former Ban Ivan Horvat to support King Lazar against the Turks in the famous battle of Kosovo Field on June 15 1389.

---

23. Dubrovnik's first prominent poet and dramatist was Marin Drzich (*Držić*) (1508–1567) who profoundly influenced the French dramatist FA Moliere in the fifteenth and sixteenth centuries. Andrija Chubranovich (*Čubranović*) (1480–1530) and Mavro Vetranovich (*Vetranović*) (1482–1576) were the most prominent poets of Dubrovnik in the sixteenth century. There was also Dinko Ranjina (1536–1607) a lyric poet and satirist. Other leading figures include Dinko Zlatarich (*Zlatarić*) (1558–1609), who wrote in Croatian and Latin, as well as Ivan Gundulich (*Gundulić*) (1589–1638). Gundulich's *Osman* is an epic poem, expressing the hope that, under the leadership of Catholic Poland, the Slavs would be liberated from the Turks and become a great Catholic people in Europe (Franjo Trogrančicč, *Literature 1400–1835, CLP&C*, Volume 2, 180–181, 188–189, 190–192, 197–198, 215–219. Trpimir Macan, *PHN*, 79–81. 105, Dr Nikola Zvonimir Bjelovučić, *CHiD*, 30–31. *Znameniti .i Zašluzni Hrvati*, 70, 101). After the devastating earthquake of 1667, in which 4,000 people lost their lives, Dubrovnik never reached its former heights. Due to skilful diplomacy, such as sending two ambassadors at a time to represent it, it was able to maintain its independence for a little over four centuries, losing it when Napoleon's General Lauriston entered Dubrovnik on 25 May 1806. Experiencing Dubrovnik's culture Lauriston wrote to Napoleon: 'We came as savages to this good and mature people'. On 31 January 1808 Napoleon announced the end of the Republic of Dubrovnik, incorporating it into the French empire. Due to its cultural development it has been called the Athens of Croatia (Fra Oton Knezović, *PH*, 109–115. Ferdo Šišić, *PPHN*, 482–485. Drago Matković, *Economic Development, CLPaC*, Volume 1, 175–176. Conversation with Don Bozo Baničević, Dubrovnik, Tuesday 31 July 2018).

By that time King Tvrtko extended his rule further to include parts of Croatia, and included it in his title in 1390 to become king of Bosnia and Croatia. He became the only one who was able to withstand the pressure of the Hungarians, Turks and Venetians, but fate was unkind. He died at the age of fifty, in 1391, after ruling for thirty-eight years. His death had catastrophic consequences for the Croatian people and the Christian world, because the might of Turkey was already on Central Europe's doorstep.[24]

In 1409, the Hungarian-Croatian king, Ladislav Anjou Napulski, who was based in Naples, realised he couldn't control anything east of the Adriatic. He therefore sold the whole of Dalmatia, including the town of Zadar, the island of Pag and all his authority over the rest of Dalmatia, to the Venetians for a hundred thousand gold florins. This is how Venice came to rule the coastal part of Dalmatia for the next four hundred years.[25]

In the early fifteenth century, various regions of Croatia achieved some form of vassal status for a number of years, the most notable being the region of central Bosnia and central Dalmatia. This extended from south of the Velebit mountain to include the town of Split, which was under the rule of Hrvoj Vukchich (Vukčić), who was given the title Duke. He eventually controlled the islands of Brač, Hvar, Korchula (Korčula) and later the towns of Omish (Omiš), Makarska and the area around the Neretva river and even up to Pozega (Požega) in Slavonia. Vukchich became the most powerful noble between the river Drava and the Adriatic sea, due to his skilful diplomacy towards King Sigismund of Hungary and King Ladislav of Naples, who were both claiming jurisdiction over Croatia. Vukchich's rule collapsed with his death in 1416.[26]

---

24. Domenik Mandić, *HiS*, 109–111 Ferdo Šišić, *PPHN*, 211–213. Fra Oton Knezović, *PH*, 128–131. Stjepan Srkulj, *HPudk*, 42–43. Stanko Guldescu. *Political History to 1526* In, *CLP&C*, Volume 1, 108–109. Trpimir Macan, *PHN*, 106, 170. Vjekoslav Klaić, *PH*, Volume 2, 197–198, 292–297. *Znameniti .i Zašluzni Hrvati*, P, LXXXV11–LXXX1X, 87–89.
25. Domenik Mandić, *HiS*, 153. Fra Oton Knezović, *PH*, 133–134. Stanko Guldescu, *Political History to 1526*, In *CLP&C*, Volume 1, 110. Trpimir Macan, *PHN*, 110–111. Vjekoslav Klarić, *PH*, Volume 3, 53–54. *Znameniti .i Zašluzni Hrvati*, XL, 40.
26. Ferdo Šišić, *PPHN*, 219–221, 223–224. Fra Oton Knezović, *PH*, 133–134. Vjekoslav Klaić, *PH*, Volume 2, 333–338. Trpimir Macan, *PHN*, 110–111, 114–115. Tpimir Macan & Josip Šentija, *ASHoC*, 41.

The Turks, who were continually making inroads into Serbia, were successfully repulsed from Belgrade after bitter fighting with the Christian army led by the Hungarian Prince Janos Hunyadi. This Christian army was given moral support by the charismatic Franciscan Friar John Capistrano in 1440 and again in 1456. Both the army and the Friar were determined that Europe would not experience the misfortunes experienced with the Tatars in the thirteenth century. These Christian victories greatly lifted the morale of the peoples of central Europe.[27]

On 19 October 1448, there was a second battle of Kosovo with Prince Hunyadi leading a combined army of twenty four thousand Hungarians and Croatians, eight thousand Vlahs and two thousand Czechs against the Turks. It resulted in complete defeat of the Christian armies and Hunyadi barely survived.[28]

It was a very difficult time for Croatia, with the Turks making inroads into Bosnia and Venice, eyeing the islands and towns of the Dalmatian coast and incorporating some of them within their jurisdiction.

In 1463, the Turks overran Bosnia, executing the last Bosnian king, Stjepan Tomashevich (Tomašović), and Herzegovina fell in 1482.[29] On September 28 1493 the Croatian army, led by Ban Derenchin (Derenćin), together with the nobles Ivan and Bernardin Frankopan, was defeated by the Turks near Krbavska field. Derenchin was a very courageous man, but did not know Turkish military tactics. He met the Turks on an open field, and did not listen to the Frankopans, who advised him to meet them in mountainous, rugged regions to conduct guerrilla war. The Turks defeated the Croatians tactically, and up to 13,000 Croatians were killed or taken into slavery. In this battle of the Krbavska Field, the flower of the Croatian nobility perished.[30]

---

27. Domenik Mandić, *BiH*, 277–279. 369–370. Ferdo Šišić, *PHN*, 229–232. Fra Oton Knezović, *PH*, 135–136. Vjekoslav Klaić, *PH*, Volume 3, 221–237. Stjepan Srkulj, *HPudk*, 43–44.
28. Vjekoslav Klaić, *PH*, Volume 3, 262–268. *Znameniti .i Zašluzni Hrvati*, 284
29. Domenik Mandić, *HiS*, 277–279. Ferdo Šišić, *PPHN*, 232–233. Fra Oton Knezović, *PH*, 137–139. Vjekoslav Klaić, *PH*, Volume 4, 43–59. Stjepan Srkulj, *HPudk*, 46. *Znameniti .i Zašlusni Hrvati*. XCV1–XCV11, 96–97.
30. Domenik Mandić, *HZ*, 37. Ferdo Šišić, *PPHN*, 237–238. Fra Oton Knezović, *PH*, 139–140. Stjepan Srkulj, *HPudk*, 48. Stanko Guldescu, *Political History to 1526*, In *CLP&C*, Volume 1, 112–113. Also Ivan Babić, *Military History*, 138. In same edition. Trpimir Macan, *PHN*, 120. Trpimir Macan & Josip Šentija, *ASHoC*, 42. Vjekoslav Klaić, *PH*, Volume 4, 225–234. *Znameniti .i Zašlusni Hrvati*, XL11, 42.

As a result, Croatia became a border land, so much so that in 1519 Pope Leon X wrote of them: '*Scutum saldissimum et antemurale Christianitatis*' (Strong shield and bulwark of Christianity).

The desperation of Croatia could be seen when prince Bernadin Frankopan, who was already an old man, went to Nuremburg in Germany to appeal to the assembled German nobility with King Ferdinand. He addressed them on 19 November 1522 in Latin:

> I come before you, noble princes and respected gentlemen, to tell you clearly and personally how much danger is threatened by the Turks, firstly to Croatia and then over our land to your lands which are neighbouring Croatia. I personally remind you that Croatia is a shield and door for Christianity. For this reason I ask you in the name of the whole of Croatia and in the name of the whole of Christianity, for you to provide help to this people, they alone repelled Turkish attacks from the time that Constantinople fell. We did what we could only do and we can't survive any further without your help, for we are completely exhausted. All our hope is in God and in you. Our King Ludvik, can't help us nor protect us, ever since he lost his strongest fortress of the city of Belgrade; we must therefore fear the Turk, for he has become unbelievably powerful. With tearful eyes I mention to you how this feral enemy of ours overran over a hundred of our towns, destroying some and capturing others and how in our country an indescribable cruelty was committed, which I unfortunately saw with my own eyes. Just imagine how much sadness would befall the Christian world if Croatia falls. Et tua res agitur, paries quum proximus ardet (and it is a matter of your concern when your neighbours house is burning)! Our needs are so urgent . . . I want to follow the footsteps of my ancestors, who were well respected amongst the Roman senate, who were always inclined towards your empire and who only through their heroism achieved that which they called their own throughout Dalmatia, Croatia and Slavonia. If the Turk through misfortune grabs Croatia, it would be very difficult for all the Christian armies to expel them, that's how Croatia is in its nature and that's how her towns are. We will not be begging like the important nobility of Greece, Mizije, Serbia and Albania in Rome. For this reason, not without the pain of pride, I bring before you all that is happening and announce them. May your breasts be moved by our tears; the whole of Croatia bows before you and asks your help in the name of

our Saviour and I fulfilling my mission to you, with tears in my eyes plead for help. If you abandon us and do not help us, one of two things will happen: either the Croats will accept the invitation of the Turks and thus serve them; or they will leave their inheritance and scatter throughout the world ... For this reason come to a quick decision with this urgent help.[31]

Bernadin Frankopan returned to Croatia bitterly disappointed at the lack of support from the German princes, receiving only a few hundred florins, some cannons and a promise that aid would be coming the following year. After returning to Croatia, he sent his son Krsto in early 1523 to ask for help from Pope Hadrian VI. Addressing the Pope, Krsto said:

> Holy Father! Counts, Barons, nobility and people of the Kingdom of Croatia turn to my valued father and said: You as the oldest and most eminent amongst us, and amongst rulers the most noted and respected, out of concern which you Holy Father and the Christian rulers have for us, tell them of the upheaval and misfortune, pressures and defeats, with which the Turks torture and unsettle us. Tell them how they penetrate into our land and take our people into captivity. How we, of all others, will be forced to leave our homeland, and roam as sad beggars throughout the world, or for us to join ourselves with the Turks and serve them if, Holy Father, you do not help us. The pain of my father at Nuremburg, Holy Father, is a witness, that the princes decided and promised help and as yet have done nothing. From that time it has deteriorated further, for Turkish units are penetrating deeper. Holy Father, Croatia is the bulwark or the door for all Christianity and especially for the neighbouring lands of Kranjska, Koruska, Stajerska, Istria, Furland and Italy. If she falls, please God it won't happen, all those lands will be open to the Turks. If they take Croatia then there is no stopping them, they will then easily cross rivers, seas and mountains. We have been defending ourselves already for seventeen years without any help from Christian rulers and this has not happened to any other Christian Kingdom. We can't continue any longer ...[32]

---

31. Domenik Mandić, *BiH*, 134-151. Fra Oton Knezović, *PH*, 145-147. Trpimir Macan, *PHN*, 181. Vjekoslav Klaić, *PH*, Volume 4, 358-360.
32. Vjekoslav Klaić, *PH*, Volume 4, 360-361.

Strain on Croatia increased after the massive defeat of the Hungarian army by the Turks led by Suleiman the Magnificent on the Mohackom field on 29 August 1526 and the death in battle of the Hungarian-Croatian King Ludovic II.[33] The Croatian Sabor renounced its allegiance to the Hungarian monarchy and switched to recognising the Austrian, Ferdinand Habsburg, as King of Croatia on January 1 1527.[34] Ferdinand committed himself to defend Croatia by stationing a standing army, to strengthen the defences of its towns, and to respect the constitution of Croatia and Dalmatia. In both charters, expressing their independence from Hungary, Ferdinand is called '*The King of Bohemia and Croatia*.'

This Sabor in Cetina was one of the most significant events in the history of Croatia. In this, the Croatians clearly expressed they were not a part of Hungary, but an independent Kingdom, in which the Sabor in great and decisive moments decides its fate and statehood. Through it the Croatians demonstrated their capacity as a democratic people, who settled their state matters in a democratic manner within their state Sabor. This decision in Cetina had an influence on the future development and life of Croatians for the next four centuries, from 1527 to 1918.[35] By then Croatia was reduced in size, from 120,000 square kilometres at the time of the Croatian national rulers to only 16,000 square kilometres. Croatians sadly called that area: 'The remains of the remains of the once glorious kingdom of Croatia.'[36]

It is interesting to note that in 1532, when the coastal city of Split was threatened by the Turks, it was defended by the mountain fortress of Klis. At the same time Venice was attempting to win control of Klis, given its strategic position. To strengthen the Croatian hold on Klis, Pope Clement VII and later Pope Paul III sent men and money to support the Croatian defenders, who were led by Petar Kruzich

---

33. Domenik Mandić, *HZ*, 37. Ferdo Šišić, *PPHN*, 240–241. Fra Oton Knezović, *PH*, 149–150. Trpimir Macan, *PHN,* 123. Stjepan Srkulj, *HPudk,* 49. Vjekoslav Klaić, *PH*, Volume 4. 422–427. *Znameniti .i Zaslusni Hrvati*, XL1V, 44.
34. Domenik Mandić, *HZ*, 40–41. Ferdo Šišić, *PPHN*, 268–271. Fra Oton Knezović, *PH,* 155–158. Stjepan Srkulj, *HPudk,* 50. Trpimir Macan, *PHN,* 123–124. Vjekoslav Klaić, *PH*, Volume 5, 72–77. *Znameniti .i Zaslusni Hrvati*, XLV11, 47.
35. Ferdo Šišić, *PPHN*, 268–270. *Znameniti .i Zaslusni Hrvati*, XLV11, 47.
36. Domenik Mandić, *HiS,* 160–161. Domenik Mandić, *HZ*, 42–43. Trpimir Macan, *PHN* 126, 193–196. Trpimir Macan & Josip Šentija, *ASHoC,* 43–46.

(Kruzić). The Papal support was such that Suleiman the Magnificent was reported to have said: *'That's a Papal city.'*[37]

Due to increasing Turkish pressure, Pope Paul III, in 1538, established a Holy League with the Republic of Venice and the Holy Roman Emperor Charles V and King Ferdinand, but it collapsed soon after when Venice made peace with the Turks.[38] For Venice it was more important to maintain control over the Adriatic and the Dalmatian coast than to expel the Turks from the Balkans.[39]

An epic battle to prevent the Turkish advance took place in 1566 around the Hungarian fortress town of Siget, where Prince Nikola Zrinski and up to 2,300 of his soldiers lost their lives, resulting in 80,000 Christians being taken into captivity. As a result of this battle Nikola Zrinski passed into Croatian folklore as Croatia's Leonidas.[40]

A significant event around this time was the peasant revolt of 1573, which began in Gornoj Stubice, near Zagreb. It was led by a villager, Matija Gubec, who came from Stubice, and villagers, Ivan Pasanac and Ilija Gregorich (Gregorić), who more or less led its military arm. The revolt then spread to other districts, encompassing an area of 30 kilometres by 40 kilometres, including some Slovene villages. The call of the peasants was: *'Za staru pravicu'* (For the old justice), and its symbol was a green leaf behind the peasant's hat. The peasants wanted to return to the old justice. They sought a return to the time before King Bela III introduced feudalism, when Croatian peasants were free people and owners of their properties, when they elected their own parish representatives and gave their taxes only to the King.

---

37. Ferdo Šišić, *PPHN*, 274. Vjekoslav Klaić, *PH*, Volume 5, 148. *Znameniti .i Zašluzni Hrvati*, XLV11, 47.
38. Vjekoslav Klaić, *PH*, Volume 5, 169.
39. Vjekoslav Klaić, *PH*, Volume 5, 147-148
40. Domenik Mandić, *HZ*, 42. Ferdo Šišić, *PPHN*, 278-279. Ivan Babić. *Military History*, In *CLP&C*, Volume 1, 139. Jaroslav Šidak. *KPSHP,* 61-70. Vjekoslav Klaić, *PH*, Volume 5. 329-334. Fra Oton Knezović, *PH*, 162-165. *Znameniti .i Zašluzni Hrvati*, XL1X, 49. Doctor Dominik Mandich, writing in 1973, wrote: 'The area which the Croatians inhabited with their arrival at the Adriatic and over which they ruled in the first few centuries, was larger than today's England. And the population at that time was larger than that of England. Due to the shedding of blood of the Croatian nation, due to medieval and modern-day oppression, Croatians in their homeland and diaspora number barely six million, while in England today there live up to fifty million people.' (Domenik Mandić, *HZ*, 39).

One official, Anton Vranchich (Vrančić), informed King Maximilian in 1573, that the landed gentry treated animals better than the peasants.[41] Interestingly, the peasants sought what the French revolutionaries sought two centuries later. The peasant revolt was ruthlessly put down, and up to 5,000 of them were killed. Matija Gubec and Ivan Pasanac were captured and cruelly executed in Zagreb, but Matija Gubec's name has an honourable place in the history of Croatia.[42]

As time went on, Croatians in other towns and villages also revolted, seeking freedom and civil rights. There were revolts on the island of Hvar from 1510–1514, along the Sava river in Croatia in 1653, in Dalmatia under the control of Venice 1736–1740, as well as in the vicinity of Krizevci (Križevci) in 1755.[43]

The town with the most success in withstanding the Turkish onslaught was that of Sisak, where the Croatian Christian army resisted a large Turkish army of 20,000 soldiers led by Hasan-Pasa, who was killed in battle on 22 June 1593. This was followed by another uprising near Petrina in 1596, which greatly relieved the Christian world.[44]

During the next century Croatians were dissatisfied with their foreign rulers, particularly as Vienna was centralising its authority and as the Turkish hold was weakening, particularly after the Christian victory at Saint Gothard on 1 August 1664. The Croatians and Hungarians expected Emperor Leopold to continue with the initiative to liberate Croatian and Hungarian areas. Instead he agreed on peace with the Turks at Vasvar on 10 August 1665, through which he secured his own position but left the Croatians and Hungarians deeply frustrated. The two leading figures at the time who spearheaded the Croatian desire for more independence were the nobles, Petar Zrinski and Krsto Frankopan, who initially had the verbal support of King Louis XIV of France, but nothing came of it. Petar Zrinski

---

41. Ferdo Šišić, *PPHN*, 279–282. Fra Oton Knezović, *PH,* 167–168. Vjekoslav Klaić, *PH,* Volume 5. 369378.
42. Domenik Mandic, *HiS,* 159. Trpimir Macan, *PHN,* 199–202. Trpimir Macan & *ASHoC,* 50. Jaroslav Šidak, *KPSH,* 13–60. *Znameniti .i Zašluzni Hrvati,* XL1X–L, 49–50, Also 294.
43. Domenik Mandić, *HiS,* 159–160.
44. Fra Oton Knezović, *PH,* 173–176. Jaroslav Šidak, *KPSHP,* 61–70. Trpimir Macan, *PHN,* 207–209. *Znameniti .i Zašlizni Hrvati,* L11, 52 also 99

and Krsto Frankopan began discussions with the Turks, seeking more freedoms for Croatia and recognising Turkish sovereignty. Realising that he could lose control, the Austrian emperor, Leopold, invited Petar Zrinski and Krsto Frankopan to Vienna for 'talks'. The emperor Leopold was very treacherous, for he had both men executed on 30 April 1671. Their deaths ended the influence of two noble Croatian families whose names were synonymous with Croatian freedom and independence.[45]

With the Turkish conquest of the Balkans, and especially after the defeat of the Kingdom of Serbia in the battle of Kosovo, many Serbian Orthodox families moved north, crossing the River Drina to settle in Bosnia-Herzegovina, which until then was exclusively a Croatian land. It is significant that Duke Ferdinand, at the beginning of 1526, proclaimed and crowned himself King of Bosnia, for Bosnia belonged to Croatia (*appartendo la Bossina a la Croatia*). As a result, Bosnia-Herzegovina was influenced by both the Orthodox and Catholic faiths. Initially both Catholics and Orthodox lived in relative peace under Turkish rule. Only when Catholic Croatians showed sympathy for the Croatians who were fighting the Turks in the border regions did the Turkish authorities begin to persecute them. Not wishing to be stripped of their Christian faith, some Croatian Catholics converted to Orthodoxy. According to the eminent Croatian historian Dominik Mandich (Mandić), thirty-two to thirty-five per cent of the Serbian Orthodox population in Bosnia are today descendants of the converted Catholic Croatians.[46]

The Croatian Catholic Origin of The Bosnian Muslims

Bosnia fell to the Turks in 1463. At that time Bosnia was largely Bogomil, but their numbers had reduced to somewhere between 60,000 to 90,000 due to many returning to the Catholic faith. The fall of Bosnia and its incorporation into the Ottoman Empire had dramatic effects on the Croatian nation, and it was a time of great turmoil. During the battles that continued to rage between the Turks

---

45. Domenik Mandić, *HiS*, 168–170. Ferdo Šišić, *PPHN*, 299–307. Fra Oton Knezović, *PH*, 186–194. Stanko Guldescu, *Political History to 1526*, In *CLP&C*, Volume 2, 21–23. Trpimir Macan, *PHN*, 215–222. Trpimir Macan & Josip Šentija, *ASHoC*, 54–56. *Znameniti .i Zašluzni Hrvati*, LV111, 58 also 84–85, 295.
46. Domenik Mandić, *HiS*, 205–209.

and the Croatians in the border regions of Bosnia, around 300,000 Croatians lost their lives in the space of a few short years and almost one million were taken into slavery, to be scattered throughout the Ottoman Empire.

After the Turks took over, large numbers of the Bosnian Croatian population converted to Islam. Initially, the Turkish authorities respected the faith of those under their control, allowing freedom of worship and commerce. Catholics were allowed to build new churches or replace existing ones of wood with new ones of stone. However, in 1512, the Turks began expanding beyond Bosnia into the northern regions of Croatia proper.

Around this time the Turkish authorities in Bosnia passed a law naming Catholics and their pastors as enemies of the state. The persecution reached its peak in 1524 when up to 150,000 Croatian Catholics converted to Islam. At the same time, the remaining Bogomils converted to Islam.

Further anti-Catholic laws were passed in 1530, 1539 and 1542, and the persecution became more severe. By this time the Ottoman Empire was fighting on all fronts, trying to penetrate deep into the heart of Europe.

To help meet their debt from the wars, the Turks increased their taxes on Christians to a rate higher than that which applied to Muslims. As a result there was a new wave of conversions throughout Bosnia.

A Bosnian nobleman visiting his former homeland in 1539 wrote to an Austrian prince: '*In this region there are a large number of Turkanised people who were once Christian. Because of persecution by the enemy they have now become Muslim. They are neither good Turks nor Christians*'.

The persecution and the conversion of Catholics to Islam continued in the seventeenth century. On 24 February 1612, a Bosnian Bishop wrote to Pope Paul V: '*It is difficult for the people to hold onto the true faith as every day the number of Muslims grows and the sad faithful are numerically dwindling*'.

A Jesuit, at the request of Pope Paul V, visited the region in 1612 and 1613 informing the Pope: '*Because these regions are lacking clergy and bishops, the people are being Turkanised*'.

Another observer in 1626 noted after a visit to Bosnia: 'There are far more Turks than Catholics or schematics (Serbian Orthodox) here. Very few of the Turks who work on the land speak Turkish and it is for this reason that almost all of them would become Christians knowing full well that their ancestors were Catholics.'

In 1631, Father Martin Brguljanin was nominated as the Provincial of the Franciscans, and his enemies informed Rome that almost his whole family had converted to Islam.

A similar thing happened in 1635 to another Bosnian, Father Teronim Luchich-Bogoslavich (*Lučić-Bogoslavić*). When he was nominated as the bishop, his enemies informed the Sacred Congregation that his three brothers and their whole families had converted to Islam: 'You will have a mixing of the mitre with the turban if Luchich) (Lušić is consecrated bishop'.

A Canon of Split, Petar Vukoslavich (Vukoslavić), in 1690 wrote a book on the various Bosnian Coat of Arms. When writing of the various noble families which fled Bosnia in the face of persecution, he commented: '*Overwhelmed by their love for their homeland and resolved to bear the tyrannical authority of the Ottomans . . . many neglected the Catholic faith and became the followers of the Koran*'.[47]

Many of the Bosnian Muslims regarded themselves as Croatian, seeing Croatia's salvation in Islam. Dominik Mandich quoted the poet Hasan Kaima, a Croat from Sarajevo, who wrote in the second half of the seventeenth century. His poem transcribed in the Croatian language used Arabic script:

> 'O Hrvati, ćujte me, ćujte i poćujte me
> Islamu se prignite, Allahu se dignite,
> Ne budite din dušmani, prihvatite lijep Kur'an.
> Svima nam Allah pomogao, a dušmane odmogo.[48]

(O Croatians hear me, listen and listen to me
Turn to Islam and rise up to Allah.
Do not be his enemy; accept the beauty of the Koran.
Allah will help all of us, and reject the Enemy.)

---

47. Domenik Mandić, *HiS*, 111–116. Domenik Mandić, *HZ*, 114–140.(Quote all on Muslims)
48. Quote from Domenik Mandić, *HZ*, 160.

Since the Catholic Croats were not satisfied with their position as subjects, and wanted their freedom and independence, they rebelled whenever a Christian land was at war with Turkey. There were many uprisings during 1463 to 1715. After each unsuccessful insurrection, those who took part in the upheaval were forced to leave their homes and seek refuge in Christian lands, thus causing a depletion of the Croatians in Bosnia-Herzegovina.[49]

Up to two or three per cent of present day Bosnian-Herzegovian Muslims are descended from true Turks or other Asiatic people of Muslim faith. These were administrative or military officers who came to this part of the Ottoman empire and settled there permanently.[50]

The evidence from the archives on the Croatian background of the Bosnian Muslims is clear, although Doctor Stjepan Krashich (Krašić) claims that substantial numbers of Serbian Orthodox in Bosnia also converted to Islam. Today Bosnian Muslims seem to be a nationality of their own, clearly defined by their faith. The great English historian Lord Acton, said: *'Religion is the secret of history'*.

In the case of the Bosnian Muslims, the choice made by their ancestors to convert to Islam clearly removed them from mainstream Western life and culture, creating a distinct ethnic group out of a religion.

Following the French Revolution, and with the Hungarian leadership attempting to impose the Hungarian language on Croatians, a Croatian consciousness began to develop among the people. For example, in 1813, the bishop of Zagreb, Maksimilian Vrhovac, sent a circular to his clergy, encouraging them to gather folk songs, stories and proverbs in the Shtokavian (Štokavski) dialect. In 1816, Tom Koshchak (Koščak) brought the Shtokavian dialect into Croatian school books. During this time, a number of Croatian clergy emerged as gifted writers, heightening a literary awareness among the people.[51]

---

49. Domenik Mandić, *HZ*, 114–154.
50. Domenik Mandić, *The Croatian Character of Bosnia and Herzegovina*, 128–139. In: *The Croatian Nation in its Struggle for Freedom and Independence*. Domenik Mandic's, English summery of '*The Origin of the Muslims in Bosnia & Herzegovina*' In *The Ethnic and Religious History of Bosnia-Hercegovina*, CLP&C, Volume 2, 367–381.
51. Domenik Mandić, *HZ*, 53–54. Domenik Mandić, *HiS*, 228–234. Trpimir Macan, *PHN*, 272–273.

The spirit of romanticism that spread throughout Europe in the 1830s also influenced Croatia, beginning with Ljudevit Gaj, who published the first Croatian grammar in 1830. He also started a Croatian newspaper in 1832, expanding to two in 1835, all with the hope of reviving Croatian national consciousness and beginning a new era in Croatian political and cultural life. All this was significant for Croatian literature and national life, for by 1836 all books and newspapers were written for the whole Croatian people in all regions, in the one language. Gaj gathered likeminded people around himself and, through these people, a new national consciousness penetrated all levels of society. The aim was for Croatia to ultimately achieve full autonomy.[52]

The mid-nineteenth century saw development in Croatian culture such as the building of the first opera house in Zagreb and many public libraries throughout the country, the most prominent of which was in Zagreb. Baron Janko Drashkovich (Drašković) was its patron and provided a strong impetus in the establishment of libraries. Baron Drashkovich proposed through pamphlets he published: *'the only solution to the problems of the empire was a federation of nations'*. He was the first Croatian politician who saw the importance of Croatia's economy and finance, incorporating them into political policies and also encouraged women to enter public life.[53]

The 1848 revolution in Paris brought change in central Europe. It was the spark which ignited the Hungarian politician Ludvik Kossuth

---

52. Domenik Mandić, *HZ*, 53, 57. Domenik Mandić, *HiS*, 228-231. Ferdo Šišic, *PPHN*, 403-408. Fra Oton Knezović, *PH*, 237-243. Josip Horvat, *PPH*, Volume 1. 29-34. KBK, *Literature from the Illyrian Movement to Realism (1835-1995)*. *CLP&C*, Volume 1, 244-246. Trpimir Macan, *PHN*, 274-281. Trpimir Macan & Josip Šentija, *ASHoC*, 64-66. *Znameniti .i Zašluzni Hrvati*, LXV111-LX1X, 58-59. In 1595 Faust Vranchich (Vrančić) compiled the first Croatian dictionary, and in 1604 the first Croatian grammar in the Shtokavski dialect was printed in Rome by the Jesuit, Bartol Krasich (Kasić). In 1639 the Dominican, Raymond Damovich (Damović) printed another Croatian grammar in Venice. The first newspaper in the Croatian language was published in Zadar in 1807 under French auspices. It was called *Kraljski Dalmatin* (The Kings Dalmatian), one side of it was in Croatian, the other in Italian (Josip Horvat, *PPH*, Volume 1. 50-121. *Zasluzni .i Zašluzni Hrvati*, LXX, 70. Coversations with Doctor Stejpan Krašič in Dubrovnik October 2014, July 2016).
53. Ferdo Šišić, *PPHN*, 399-401. Trpimir Macan, *PHN*, 274-275. Trpimir Macan & Josip Šentija, *ASHoC*, 67. *Znameniti .i Zašluzni Hrvati*, 68-69.

to seek Hungarian dominance over the whole of Croatia, culminating in a revolt by the Croatians. The Croatian Ban, Josip Jelachich (Jelačić), on 10 September 1848, crossed the Drava river with 40,000 Croatians and Croatian Orthodox soldiers, to save the Austrian Monarchy from the Hungarians who had revolted. By December 1848, Jelachich had finally defeated Kossuth and his rebels. Jelachich had thought Austria would place Croatia, as well as all the nationalities of the empire, on an equal footing as itself within the monarchy.[54] Although Jelachich achieved some improvements for Croatia it was not to the extent that he had hoped.[55] Unfortunately Austria did not keep its promises to Jelachich, disregarding him when it no longer needed him, causing him great disappointment and disillusionment. His own famous words best describe what he thought of his achievements: *'Moje ime pripada povjesti; ona će od mene pričati, ali od onom što san u srcu nosio za moju Hrvatsku, o tom ona će nista moći kazati'*. (My name belongs to history; it will speak about me, but what I carried within my heart for my Croatia, of that she will not be able to say anything).[56]

With the upheavals in Vienna, Emperor Ferdinand abdicated on 2 December 1848, naming his eighteen-year-old nephew Franz as his successor, who became Franz Joseph I.[57] The young

Count Josip Jelachich: (1801–1859) A capable military officer and Croatian patriot.

---

54. Ferd o Šišić, *PPHN*, 418–426. Fra Oton Knezović, *PH*, 247–255. Ivan Babić. *Military History, CLP&C*, Volume 1, 147. Vjekoslav Klaić, *PHN*, Volume 5, 687–692. 57 Trpimir Macan, *PHN*, 284–288. *Znameniti .i Zašluzni Hrvati*, 120.
55. Ferdo Šišić, 418–426. Josip Horvat, *PPH*, Volume 1, 29–33. Trpimir Macan, *PPH*, 284–288.
56. Ferdo Šišić, *PPHN*, 418–421. Fra Oton Knezović, *PH*, 266. Josip Horvat, *PPH*, Volume 1, 29–33. Trpimir Macan, *PHN*, 284–288. Trpimir Macan & Josip Šentija, *ASHoC*, 70–75. *Znameniti .i Zašluzni Hrvati*, LXV111–LX1X, 5–59.
57. Ferdo Šišić, *PPHN*, 421, 425–426. Trpimir Macan, *PHN*, 288.

emperor issued a constitution on 4 March 1849 for all countries in the Habsburg empire. In this constitution, Croatia was separated from Hungary and placed on an equal basis, although this was later rescinded.[58]

Some political parties were advocating closer union with Austria or Hungary, but at the beginning of 1860, Bishop Josip Juraj Strossmayer, the Bishop of Djakovo, tried to introduce the idea that the Habsburg monarchy be based on a federal system, in which the autonomy of all the nationalities would be recognised. When he realised that Croatia could not achieve its national rights within the monarchy, he supported the Yugoslav idea, which was akin to the 'Illyrian movement'. Strossmayer was a patron of the arts and advocate of the union of the Catholic and Orthodox Churches as well as union with the Protestant Churches. In 1867 he established the Yugoslav academy of Science and Arts in Zagreb. He also built a new cathedral in Djakovo, under the patronage of the great apostles to the Slavs, Saints Cyril and Methodius. However the Serbian, Slovene and Croatian populations of the empire did not embrace his vision of a union of southern Slavs, although it had support from some Croatian intellectuals and politicians.[59]

---

58. Ferdo Šišić, *PPHN*, 421, 425-428. Trpimir Macan, *PHN*, 306. Jaroslav Šidak, *KPSHP*, 216-220. Ban Josip Jelachich was instrumental in the abolition of serfdom, giving villagers a sense of economic equality. Through his influence, the Diocese of Zagreb was raised to that of an Archdiocese, thus becoming a metropolitan See, freed from Hungarian influence. Through his intercession, Josip Juraj Strossmayer was named bishop of Djakovo. Jelachich strongly supported the building of the Zagreb Opera House where only Croatian language musicals and plays would be performed and he supported the establishment of Zagreb University. Croatia is greatly indebted to Ban Josip Jelachich and his many achievements (Domenik Mandić, *HZ*, 54. Domenik Mandić. *Titovi Nehrvatski .i Nestrućni Napadaji na Stejpana Radića .i Bana J, Jelačiča*, 57-58. In: *Za Hrvatstvo .i Hrvatsku Državnost*. Josip Horvat, *PPH*, Volume 1, 98-154. Trpimir Macan & Josip Šentija, *ASHoC*, 70-76).
59. Domenik Mandić, *HiS*, 231-234. Ferdo Šišić, *PPHN*, 432-434, 436, 440-441, 443. Trpimir Macan, *PHN*, 292-298. Strossmayer was a friend and supporter of the great Russian theologian Vladimir Solovjev, and was also a great advocate for the union of the Christian Churches. Strossmayer was named Bishop of Djakovo because of the support of Ban Jelachich,[78] and he supported the church in developing good relations with the Protestant Churches at the first Vatican Council (1869-1870), only to be howled down by the other Catholic bishops (Fra Oton Knezević, *PH*, 263). This is why he opposed the doctrine of Papal

Croatian desire for independence continued unerringly, with Doctor Ante Starchevich (Starčević) and Eugene Kvaternik, establishing the *Hrvatsku Stranku Prava* (Croatian Party of Rights) in 1861, with the aim of achieving full Croatian independence through parliamentary means.[60] The party mistrusted and opposed Yugoslavianism in any form, and was the first political party in Croatia that stood for the full independence of Croatia, within the framework of the Austro-Hungarian state. Although a small party, it was well organised and imbued with the western liberal spirit of democracy. Its popular slogan was *'Neither with Vienna or Budapest, but Croatia for herself.'* Starchevich, who was uncompromisingly dedicated to Croatia's national independence, would often use the old Latin phrase *'Fiat justitia pereat mundus'* (Implement justice even if the world collapses).[61] The aim of the Party of Rights was to achieve independence for Croatia within the Austro-Hungarian Empire, similar to the way the British Empire was transformed into a Commonwealth. Starchevich's influence was strengthened because

---

infallibility as the Protestants would find it offensive. He was again shouted down, called and 'Lucifer', and told from the floor to relinquish the podium (John W O'Malley, *Vatican 1, at MotUC*, 172–173. Warren H Carroll. *The Crisis of Christendom*, Volume 6, 140. Trpimir Macan & Josip Šentija, *ASHoC*, 79). Strossmayer, together with Ban Ivan Mazuranich, was instrumental in establishing the University of Zagreb in 1874. During the Russian celebration of the 900th anniversary of the baptism of the Slavs held in Kiev, Strossmayer sent a congratulatory telegram to the rector of the University of Saint Vladimir in Kiev; this angered Emperor Franz Joseph, as the telegram expressed Russia's natural role in freeing the oppressed Slavs (Josip Horvat, *PPH*, Volume 1, 217–221).

60. Ferdo Šišić, *PPHN*, 440–441. Trpimir Macan, *PHN*, 297–300
61. Ferdo Šišić, *PPHN*, 440–444. Fra Oton Knezovic, *PH*, 273. Trpimir Macan, *PHN*, 298–305. Trpimir Macan & Josip Šentija, *ASHoC*, 79–83. The British author, Rebecca West, made an extensive tour of Yugoslavia in 1937 and recorded her impressions and reflections in her book: *The Black Lamb and Grey Falcon*. The very title of her book is prejudiced against Croatians, portraying the Croatians as submissive lambs and the Serbs as falcons, a courageous war–like people. The book, published in Britain during the early part of World War II, describes the Croatian Party of Rights as: *'The Croatian Clerical party . . . is a party with a long pedigree of mischief makers.'* She then mentions Doctor Joseph Frank, who succeeded Doctor Ante Starchevich as leader of the Justice Party, describing their leadership of the party as being: *'. . . violently bigoted in their pietism, and professed the most vehement antagonism to the Jews'* (which implied antagonism to liberalism) . . . *'and to the Orthodox Church'* (which implied antagonism to the Serbs, given all Serbs are Orthodox) (Rebecca West, *BL&WF*, 97).

his aims were combined with the liberal democratic aims of Western European societies, which called for equality and respect of human beings in whatever society they lived.[62] In an article written in 1883, Starchevich wrote: 'We sincerely love and hold as a brother, a Serb, a German, an Italian, a Jew, a Gypsy, a Lutheran and everyone else ... the main thing is that all work for his people and for the homeland and they may call themselves as they wish.'[63]

Culturally, Croatia developed rapidly when Ivan Mazuranich (Mažuranić) became Ban in September 1873. He was Ban for only six and half years, but he achieved significant changes by reorganising the administration and the judiciary, introducing laws for elementary education of children and the right of association and a free press. He also established Zagreb University in 1874, and a rural Cultural and Health Council.[64]

During the Chancellorship of Metternich, Austria was reluctant to antagonise Turkey. It was only after his fall in 1848, that Austria began to look for ways to take control of Bosnia-Herzegovina. In 1850 Vienna established a consulate in Sarajevo, then in Mostar, Banja Luka and Brchko (Brčko). By the 1860s Austria began an active role in protecting the Catholic population of Bosnia-Herzegovina through its diplomats in Constantinople and consulates in Bosnia-Herzegovina. With the unification of the German states in 1871, Austria received greater support. Under the chairmanship of Bismark, the Emperors of Germany, Russia and Austria met in Berlin in 1872, resulting in a triple alliance in 1873. As a result, Russia recognised Austro-Hungary's interests in Bosnia-Herzegovina.

An economic crisis developed through the onset of a revolt in Herzegovina in 1875. The Bosnian Muslim aristocracy collapsed economically and then sought support from Austria. There were factions in Austria-Hungary that were reluctant to incorporate Bosnia-Herzegovina into the Empire, because it would increase the Croatian influence, and its diplomacy worked hard to achieve this outcome. Russia's victory over Turkey in the war of 1877, in which Serbia and Montenegro took part, resulted in the peace treaty of San

---

62. Josip Horvat, *PPH*, Volume 1, 192–196. Stanko Guldescu, *CLP&C*, Volume 2, 53–54. Trpimir Macan, *PHN*, 300.
63. Domenik Mandić, *HiS*, 236.
64. Ferdo Šišić, *PPHN*, 458–459. Josip Horvat, *PPH*, Volume 1, 197–210. Trpimir Macan, *PHN*, 316–317. *Znameniti .i Zašluzni Hrvati*, 183–184.

Stefano in March 1878. This allowed for Serbia and Montenegro to become independent countries in their own right and for Bosnia-Herzegovina to become autonomous provinces under the Sultan's jurisdiction, as Serbia had been until then.

When the San Stefano peace treaty came to the attention of Austria, the Austrian Foreign Minister, Count Andrassy, called a meeting in Vienna. This meeting eventually took place in Berlin under the chairmanship of Bismarck on 13 June 1878, and it assembled the major European powers: England, France, Russia and Italy. This congress supported Austria in its occupation of Bosnia-Herzegovina, which nevertheless would remain under the sovereignty of the Sultan.

The Croatian Generals, Joseph Filipovich (Filipović) and Stjepan Jovanovich (Jovanović) led the Austro-Hungarian army to occupy Bosnia-Herzegovina, with Filipovich becoming its first administrator.[65] Croatians were dissatisfied that Austria refused to incorporate Croatian parts of Bosnia into Croatia and the Hungarians pressed to impose their language as the official language in the public service and schools in Croatian regions. At this time Bosnia-Herzegovina began to develop economically and culturally. The revolt of the Young Turks in 1908 forced the Sultan to accept constitutional government, which also brought changes in Bosnia-Herzegovina, enabling people to choose their representatives for the parliament in Constantinople. After much political wrangling and the weakening of Russia through the Russian-Japanese war of 1905, the Austrian Emperor, Franz Joseph, announced the annexation of Bosnia-Herzegovina on 5 October 1908. This outcome was welcomed by Croatians and Muslims, but greatly angered the Serbs.[66]

The Croatians always resented their subservience within the Austro-Hungarian Empire. Especially galling was the persistent tendency for denationalisation, firstly to Germanise, and then to Hungarianise by introducing Hungarian into schools and the railway system. Croatians objected to the arbitrary partition of their territories and to the economic exploitation of Croatia by Vienna and then Budapest. As a nation with a long tradition of statehood, Croatians disliked the Austrian and later Hungarian hegemony over

---

65. Ferdo Šišić, *PPHN*, 471–476. Ivan Babić, *Military History*, Volume 1, 148. Trpimir Macan, *PHN*, 317–319.
66. Ferdo Šišić, *PPHN*, 476. Franjo Dujmović, *HnpkO*, 192–193. Fra Oton Knezović, *PH*, 407–408. Vladimir Dedijer, *TRTS*, 370–374.

Croatia. In this situation the Croatians did what any freedom-loving people would do: they fought with dignity in their Sabor to maintain their traditional rights and their centuries of statehood, using parliamentary means to achieve their goals.

In 1905 Stjepan Radich (Radić), with his brother Anton, formed the Croatian Peasant Party. Their aim was to improve the lives of poor sections of Croatia and Bosnia-Herzegovina. It must be remembered that most of the Croatian population were poor villagers who struggled for their daily livelihood. Radich also worked to gain more freedoms for Croatian people within the Austro-Hungarian Empire.

During this time, some of the Croatian intelligentsia held the unrealistic dream of a large South Slavic state in which all incorporated nations would be equal partners. They were well intentioned, honest, patriotic and idealistic people, who at the time did not quite comprehend the prevailing mentality of the Serbian ruling class. Some of these Croats were quite disappointed when they saw that their well-meant efforts led to something they neither intended nor desired. Two such people were Doctor Ante Trumbich (Trumbić), a lawyer from Split, and Ivan Mestrovich (Mestrović), the world renowned sculptor.[67]

In the middle of the nineteenth century, as Serbia gained its independence from the Ottoman empire, leading intellectual figures in Serbia began dreaming of creating Serbia into a super state, recreating Serbia as it was under Tsar Dushan in the fourteenth century. This was also encouraged by the Serbian Orthodox Church, through whose influence the Orthodox populations of Croatia and Bosnia-Herzegovina began to be identified as Serbian. Serbia began in 1815 as a small principality with a certain autonomy within Ottoman rule, and then successfully extended its borders, culminating in the second Balkan war in 1913. In the middle of the nineteenth century, Serb writers began writing articles with slogans such as: 'Serbs all and Everywhere. Uniting all Serbs outside Serbia's borders with Serbia proper'.[68]

---

67. Trpimir Macan, *PHN*, 377–382.
68. Domenik Mandić, *HiS*, 221. Franjo Tudjman, *HuMJ*, Volume 1, 22–23. The most notable of these writers was Vuk Stefanovich Karadzich (Stefanović Karadžić), the Language Reformer, who supplied linguistic 'proof' that all who speak the Shtokavian dialect are Serbs, including Croatians, the Muslims of Bosnia and Herzegovina and Montenegrins. In 1836 he wrote an article: *Serbs All and Everywhere* (Božidar Čović, *RoSA*, 85–104. Franjo Tudjman. *HuMJ*, Volume 1, 22–24. Adrian Hastings, *NGaJ*, 259–260. In *Priest & People*).

For many Croatians, Serbia was a source of hope, showing that Croatia could also achieve freedom and become independent. For many Serbs from Croatia, Serbia was the mother country with which they wanted to unite.

There were a number of Serbian organisations at this time, most notably the secretive *Black Hand* movement, that were working to further extend Serbian borders, thus creating a greater Serbia.

Ilija Garashanin (Garašanin) mapped out the program for Serbian Foreign and National policy at the end of 1844 in a long article titled *Nachertanie*. According to Garashanin (Garašanin), Serbia must not remain a small country but must increase its territory without fail; expansion had to be achieved outside its ethnic and historical borders. This was not only to free the Serbian people, but also to extend Serbia to the south-east and west, with an outlet to the sea ([85] Božidar Čović, *RoSA*, 68–82. Franjo Tudjman, *HuMJ*, Volume 1, 2324. BA Symposium, 169–171). Both Karadzich and Garashanin had an enormous influence in Serbian political thinking.

Nikola Stojanovich (Stojanović) wrote a long article in *Srbobran* in 1902 entitled 'Until Your or Our Extermination', theorising on the superiority of Serbian culture and political thinking, suggesting ways that Serbians could bring Croatians over to the Serbian way of thinking (Božidar Čović, *RoSA*, article by Nikola Stojanović, *UYoOE*, 105–113).

Jovan Cvijich (Cvijić) (1865–1927) was the founder of Serbia's Anthropos-Geographic Science. His writing had a profound influence on Serbian political thinking, and included the theory that the Serbs are a race apart, being the most 'valuable' nuclear inhabitants of the Balkan Peninsula and, because of this, '*they have the right to rule over other peoples*'. When Austria annexed Bosnia-Hercegovina in 1908, Cvijich wrote: 'Serbia can't reject Bosnia, for it is her national centre and in every way its minimum demand . . . If it can't be immediately achieved . . . the Serbian problem must be solved with force . . . Europe will show the Serbian people the way of force and she will grab the first opportunity to shake Austro-Hungary with this her greatest national question.' Božidar Čović, *RoSA*, Article by Stanko Žuljić, 365–424. Franjo Tudjman, *HuMJ*, Volume 1, 82. Quoting Jovan Čvijić, *Aneksija Bosne .i Hercegovine*, Belgrade, 1908).

Serbian newspapers from the mid 1850s onwards, as well as those within the Austro-Hungarian Empire, began publishing articles claiming that territory outside Serbia proper where Serbs lived belonged to Serbia Franjo Tudjman, *HuMJ*, Volume 1, 62). As time went on, some articles became more aggressive, such as the Belgrade newspaper *Politica* which on 26 October 1908 wrote: 'Now or never has come the opportunity that we settle accounts with the medieval state which finds itself in disintegration.'

Politica carried another article on 6 February 1909 in which it stated: 'Europe must accept our aspirations or it will come to a terrible and bloody war.' (Fra Oton Knezović, *PH*, 446).

This organisation was led by Colonel Dragutin Dimitrijevich (Dimitrijević), who was also known as Apis, and who brought about a bloody coup in Belgrade in 1903, murdering King Alexander Obrenovich (Obrenović), his wife Draga and some other leading figures who emphasised Serbia's closer relationship with Austria. With Peter Karagorgevich (Kagorgević) in power as King, Serbia developed a more aggressive foreign policy, with the aim of developing closer ties with Tsarist Russia.

With the Karagorgevich family in power, Serbia was successful in the Balkan Wars of 1912 and 1913, and further extended its borders. The Black Hand movement was responsible for the assassination of the heir to the Austrian throne, Archduke Franz Ferdinand and his wife Sofia, in Sarajevo on 28 June 1914. This occurred on the feast of Saint Vitus, the anniversary of the day Serbs rose in revolt against the Turks in the early nineteenth century. This event provided the spark which ignited the First World War, a war about which a vast majority of the Croatians were unhappy and from which nothing good would come.[69] Franz Ferdinand was in part assassinated for his willingness to unite Bosnia-Herzegovina with Croatia, and grant Croatians and other Slavs an equal status with Austria and Hungary within the Empire, thus strengthening their desire to remain within it. This angered the Serbian leadership.

---

69. Bože Ćović, *RoSA*, 135–150. Domenik Mandić, *HiS*, 218–223. Franjo Dujmović, *HnpkO*, 199, 200. Doctor Nikola Rusinović, *Moja Sjećanje Na Hrvatsku*, 14–15. Vladimir Dedijer, *TRTS*, 25, 319–323, 373–374, 396–399. There were other assassinations organised by the Black Hand, which relied on radicalised youth. The administrator of Bosnia Herzegovina, Baron Vareshanin (Varešanin), was assassinated by a youth, B Zerajich (Zerajić), in 1910. Then, two radicalised proSerbian Croatian youths, Luka Jukica and I Planinscaka, assasinated Commissar Slavko Chuvaja (Čuvaja) in 1912. S Dojchicha (Dojćića) murdered Commissar Skerlecza in 1913 and V Schafer assassinated Ban Skerlecz in 1914. All these acts were planned through the organization '*Ujedinje ili smrt*' (Unity or death) which was closely affiliated with Colonel Demitrovich (Demitrović) known as Apis the head of the intelligence service of the Serbian army and key figure of the Black Hand organisation (Božidar Čović, *RoSA*, 134–150. Franjo Tudjman, *HuMJ*, Volume 1, 91–92. Relying on Josip Kljaković: *U Suvremenom kaosu*, Buenos Aires, 1952. Kljaković's 2006 edition is in 52. Ivo Ribar, *Iz Moje Političke Suradnje 1901–1963* (Out of My Political Work 1901–1963), Zagreb 1965, 93–100. Ferdo Šišić, *PPHN*, 468. Vladimir Dedijer, *TRTS*, 160–162). It all relied on the radicalised youth.

Despite all the grievances the subjected nationalities had within the Austro-Hungarian empire, it was a very multicultural empire where the ethnic and cultural heritage of the various nationalities was, to a certain extent, respected. This was especially true under the Austrian Emperor Franz Joseph I who reigned from 1848 to 1916. Although he refused to unite Bosnia-Herzegovina and Dalmatia with Croatia, keeping them separate entities, he respected national and cultural diversity. The great Czech-Australian political and social commentator of the second half of the twentieth century, Frank Knopfelmacher, had a portrait of the late Emperor hanging prominently in his living room. It was Knopfelmacher's opinion that this emperor headed an exceptionally multi-cultural Empire, where various nationalities lived in peace and harmony with one another and were quite happy.[70]

One example of this is southern Poland: it was part of the Empire yet was able to develop culturally far more than the parts of Poland under German or Russian control. For the Croatian people, the Empire was far freer than what came later. At least Austria and Hungary respected Croatian statehood; this was not the case with the Serbs.[71]

The Croatian historian, Stanko Guldescu wrote as follows of the situation of Croatia the few decades before the First World War and its experience afterwards:

---

70. In conversations with John Russell, who lived from 6 January 1943 to 6 March 2008, who was personal friend of professor Knopfelmacher and the author. It was John Russell's firm belief that. Professor Frank Knopfelmacher represented the best of European Jewry.
71. The Eminent Croatian historian Dominik Mandić wrote:
Although amongst the Croatians there existed an old and sincere love towards the western democratic people, the French and English, the Croatians for a full four years resolutely and heroically fought against the Serbs in the east and the Italians in the west to defend their Croatian homeland. That is a clear proof, that large sections, from villages and towns, did not accept the ideas of progressive youth on a national and state union of Croatian and Serbs, but they stood on the principle that Croatians are a distinct people who want their own state.
(Domenik Mandić. *H.i.S.* 241–242; The author is grateful to Doctor Stjepan Krashich (Krašić), a Dominican friar and historian, for going over this chapter with him in Dubrovnik in October 2014 and July 2016).

In the final summing up of the Croatian political experience prior to 1914 it must be acknowledged that despite the current complaints about Hungarian oppression, from 1867 to 1914 the Croatians enjoyed a far greater degree of home rule then they were ever to have during the period of 1919–1941. Or than they have had since 1945. During this period, and in fact until 1918, not a single Croatian received a death sentence for political reasons, even though attempts were made and some of them successful, to assassinate some of the most prominent personalities, including Bans Skrlec and Chuvaj (Čuvaj). Croatia's well-defined political autonomy indubitably was infringed especially in regard to financial affairs. None the less she retained enough of this autonomy to protect with absolute success the national character or national language in all of the more important domains of public life including public education, religion, justice, and internal administration. Her cultural development and educational progress were outstanding.[72]

---

72. Stanko Guldescu, *Croatian Political History 15261918*, in: *CLP&C*, Volume 2, 64–65.

Baron Janko Draskovich 1770– 1856. Writer, politician and poet

Stjepan Radich 1871–1928 The founder and leader of the Croatian Peasant Party. His assassination in the Belgrade parliament in 1928 greatly antagonized the Croatian people as well as all the democratically orientated people of the kingdom of the Serbs, Croats and Slovenes

Ban Ivan Mazuranich (1814–1890): Poet, linguistic, lawyer and politician

Bishop JJ Strossmayer (1815-1905) a strong advocate for good relations with Protestant and Orthodox churches.

Chapter 2
Croatia Between the Two Wars 1918–1941

An Introduction to Croatia Between the Wars

For English speakers from the Western world, the former Yugoslavia after the First World War with the international and internal rivalries seems very complex. This is unquestionably true of the Croatian/Serbian conflict which does not go back centuries as so many believe.

For many centuries Croatians and Serbians lived in peace and harmony with each other. They were ancient neighbours, although they spoke different languages, they understood each other completely. It was only when the two nationalities came to live together in the one state, which initially was called 'The Kingdom of the Serbs, Croats and Slovenes' that tensions developed. It must be remembered there was no referendum of the peoples of the former Yugoslavia whether they wanted to live as one. I tried to explain how this kingdom was formed and the desire of the Croatians to be fully free.

The increasing pressure of the Serbian leadership was led by Kind Alexander Karagorgevich (*Karagorgević*) over the non Serbians in the country, in particular, the Croatians, Macedonians, the Albanians of Kosovo and the Montenegrins. These matters reached their height with the assasination of the Croatian leadership in the Belgrade parliament in June 1928. Kind Alexander on the 6 January, 1929 abolished the constitution and imposed a ruthless military dictatorship causing much suffering on the people. In October 1929 King Alexander changed the name of the country to Yugoslavia without reference to the peoples that made it up.

The ruthlessness of the Karagorgevich regime caused Dr Ante Pavelich (*Pavelić*) to leave the country and establish the Ustasha (*Ustaša*) movement which worked to inform the western world of the plight of the Croatian people and also free the country by revolutionary means. The high point for the movement was the assassination of King Alexander in October 1934 when he was on an official visit to France. As a result of the assassination tensions in Yugoslavia increased. I tried to explain how the regent, Prince Paul Karagorgevich, who was the late kings cousin and a very humane man tried all he could to stabilise the country and bring about the rule of law. To show the difficult situation he was in, he had to deal with the ultra Serbian nationalists government, particularly the military, as well as, it is sad to state, the leadership of the Serbian Orthodox church.

The oppression was eased considerably when Dr Milan Stojadinovich (*Stojadinović*) was appointed Prime Minister, who established a limited coalition which brought about a significant democratization of the country. Even though it was urgent to address the Croatian/Serbian relationship Dr Stojadinovich was hesitant; Prince Paul replaced him with Dr Dragisha Cvetkovich (*Dragiša Cvetković*) with the aim of coming to an agreement with the Croatians. An agreement was signed between Dr Machek (*Maček*), the leader of the Croatian Peasant Party and Dr Cvetkovich in August 1939. This agreement brought about a considerable sense of freedom to the people of pre-war Yugoslavia which they had not experienced previously.

Europe was heading towards war, when it started in September 1939, Prince Paul and the government of Drs Cvetkovich and Machek (*Maček*) worked hard to keep Yugoslavia out of the European conflict. They were in an extremely difficult position. I show how the British intelligence service in conjunction with the ultra nationalistic Serbian element in the military worked to overthrow this governemnt for expanding the European conflict was expedient for Britain.

Croatians fought loyally for the Austro-Hungarian Empire, making up to thirteen to fourteen per cent of the conscripted army, although the population of Croatia and Bosnia-Herzegovina made up one-tenth of the population of the empire. Thus, the Croatian people expressed their main desire not to enter into a union with the Serbs.[1]

---

1. Antun Dabinović, *Hrvatska Povjest*, 154. Hrvoje Gracanin, *Kratka Povjest Hrvatske za Mlade*, 75–76. Ivan Babić, *Military History, CLP&C,* Volume 1, 148.

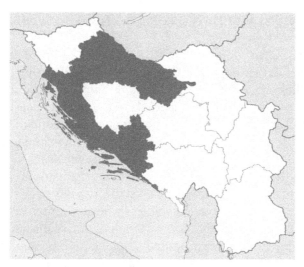

Map of Croatia from 1939–1941

The reader will see that Prince Paul and his government should have been more vigilant. The military coup on the night of 26 March 1941 came to them as a complete surprise, thus prompting Hitler to invade Yugoslavia on 6 April 1941. The reader will learn that Croatians were not at fault for this German invasion.

At this time there was a lot of movement on the international scene. Some Croatian and Serb intellectuals who lived within the Austro-Hungarian empire managed to make their way to France and England, and formed a committee in Paris on 30 April 1915. It included Pavao Popovich (*Popović*) from Serbia proper and Luja Vojnovich (*Vojnović*) from Montenegro as observers. In May 1915 the committee moved to London where it became known as '*The Yugoslav Committee*', and its main objective was to work towards a union of Slovenia and Croatia with Serbia.[2]

The committee elected Dr Ante Trumbich (*Trumbić*), a Croatian lawyer from Split, as its President. It also included the world renowned Croatian sculptor, Ivan Mestrovich (*Mestrović*), and Franjo Supilo, who was the most insightful of them all.[3] A The committee was in

---

2. Franjo Tudjman, *HuMJ*, Volume 1, 112–113. Franjo Dujmović, *HnpkO*, 202–206. Trpimir Macan, *PHN*, 384–385. *Znameniti. i Zašluzni Hrvati*, LXXV11, 77
3. Aleksa Benigar *A Stepinac*, *HK*, 46–47. Franjo Tudjman, *HuMJ*, Volume l, 112. Trpimir Macan & Josip Šentija, *ASHoC*, 89–90. In his biography of Franjo Supilo, Josip Horvat wrote that Supilo saw that Serbia was blindly following Russian

communication with Dr Nikola Pasich (*Pasić*), the President of the Serbian government.

The Croatian people, like the Slovenes, wanted their own independence. Through the Committee's influence and that of the Serbian diplomatic service, the idea of a union of these three Slavic nations gradually took hold, especially as the war was nearing its end. Because of similarities between the Croatian and Serbian languages, many people regarded the union as natural. It was often said at the time '*Croatia and Serbia are two brothers with the one soul*'.

When the Serbian army collapsed at the end of 1915, and remnants of it sought refuge in Greece, the idea developed within the committee to gather Croatian soldiers who were interned in camps in Italy to volunteer to fight for the freedom of Croatia and Slovenia. The Yugoslav Committee proposed this idea to show that the people wanted freedom from the Austro-Hungarian Empire.[4]

While part of the Committee was working in London, another movement was working within Croatia towards complete independence. A number of prominent Croatian politicians agreed that the Bishop of Krk, Dr Anton Mahnich (*Mahnić*), should approach Pope Benedict XV to request that he intervene on behalf of the Croatian people at future peace conferences. Pope Benedict XV promised to do so if he were called to participate in such a conference. When this matter was later raised with the Pope, he told the Croatians that Russia had betrayed them.[5]

On 30 May 1917, Dr Antun Korosec, a Slovene, read a declaration expressing the desire that all Slovenes, Croats and Serbs within the Empire should unite as one state under the Habsburg Crown. Most Croatian politicians proclaimed they were in favour of this declaration, as was Dr Mahnich.[6]

---

policies, which on the Yugoslav question: 'Looks through Orthodox spectacles.' She is 'Afraid of bringing in a strong Catholic element within the bounds of the old Serbian state.' For this reason Serbs will only be interested in extending their borders to the extent that 'Serbs are able to assimilate their co-nationals' and not the creation of a new democratic state (Franjo Tudjman, *HuMJ*, Volume 1, 116–117 (Franjo Tudjman, *HuMJ*, Volume 1, 116–117). Supilo came to the conclusion that it was best to work towards an independent Croatian state and for it to look for a union with Serbia when Serbia became truly democratic (Franjo Tudjman, *HuMJ*, Volume 1, 141–144).

4. Aleksa Benigar, *A Stepinac HK*, 47. Franjo Tudjman, *HuMJ*, Volume 1, 134–136.
5. Aleksa Benigar. *A.Stepinac HK*, 47.
6. Aleksa Benigar. *A.Stepinac HK*, 47. Franjo Dujmović, *HnpkO*, 210–211.

Later in August, members of the Yugoslav Committee met with the Serbian President, Dr Nikola Pasich, on the Greek island of Corfu. After much discussion, confrontation and argumentative clashes, they issued a declaration in which they declared the new state was to be given the name: *The Kingdom of Serbs, Croats and Slovenes*, under the Serbian Karagorgevich family.[7] The rights of the three nations of the new state would be respected, their flags recognised, and the faith of Orthodox and Catholic Churches and Islamic faith would be respected. It was agreed that in the *Skupshtina (Skupština) (Parliament in Belgrade)* the majority party would form a government. Dr Ante Trumich signed the declaration on behalf of the Yugoslav Committee and Dr Nikola Pasich on behalf of the Serbian Government.[8]

---

7. Right at the beginning of World War I, on 21 September 1914, the President of Serbia and its Foreign Minister, Nikola Pasich, sent a telegram to the Russian Foreign Minister, Sazonov, which included a map of the territory Serbia was claiming. It was slightly larger than the territory of the former Yugoslavia, including the northern half of Albania (Franjo Tudjman. *HuMJ* Volume. 109–110).

8. Aleksa Benigar. *A Stepinac*. HK 47 Antun F. Bonifačić & Clement S. Mihanović. In *The Croatian Nation*. Ivan Mestrović. 'The Yugoslav Committee in London.' 173–191. Trpimir Macan & Josip Šentija. *AŠHoC* 90. Franjo Tudman. *HUMJ* 1. 177–183. Franjo Dujmović. *HnpkO* 211–214. D. The world-renowned Croatian sculptor, Ivan Mestrovich, who was a member of the Yugoslav committee, related the process through which this declaration was formed and it's wrangling over Bosnia-Herzegovina. At a preliminary meeting in Cannes, France, during the drafting of the declaration, the question of the Bosnian Muslims was raised. The Serbian representative, Stojan Protich (*Protić*), who was an important figure in the ruling Serbian Radical Party, stated:

> '*Leave that to us. We have the solution for Bosnia*' Stojan Protich said.
> '*How Mr.Protich?*' asked Trumbich.
> '*When our army crosses the Drina, we will give the Turks 24 hours or even 48, to return to their ancestral faith and those who do not want to, we will do what in our time we did in Serbia. Those who refuse will be killed while those who escape may go to Turkey. Catholics of course will not be touched, nor will there be any obstacles to their being Croats if they so desire; but the Turkish minarets must go.*'

An unpleasant shock and silence followed. Tumbich's fingers started to shake and he pressed the paper which was on the table in front of him to show that he was not upset. It was a grave moment. Mestrovich and the others feared that Trumbich would get up and tear the text of the declaration to pieces.

> '*Are you serious, Mr Protich?*' asked Trumbić.
> '*Most serious Mr Trumbich. In Bosnia with the Turks the solution can't be in a European manner, but in our manner.*'

Upon the death of Emperor Franz Joseph on 21 November 1916, his successor, his nephew Karl IV, announced that his reign would be one where the equality of all nationalities would be respected, including their constitutions and national laws. The Empire would be arranged on a federal system, bringing the Slavic nations to the same level of government as the Germanic and Hungarian nations. When he was crowned as Croatian-Hungarian king in Budapest on 30 December 1916, speaking in Croatian, he promised to guard the: *'whole land and constitution of the Kingdom of Croatia, Slavonia and Dalmatia.'*[9] On 16 October 1918, he announced that the Habsburg Monarchy would become a federation of independent states.[10] It was a pity such magnanimity had not been shown decades earlier.

Dr Dinko Trinjsich (*Trinjsić*) and Dr Julije Gazzari, who were also in the room with Mestrovich, looked at one another in shock, until Mestrovich spoke. He pointed out that the King and government had promised that the fighting would continue until all the brothers were freed and united. He expressed the thought that their brothers the Muslims expect that when the Serb army arrives, it will liberate them and not slaughter them. He then went on to say, that if that was not the case, then all their work on the committee had been wasted. Mestrovich's final point was that there were large Muslim populations in the British and French empires who would revolt if the Bosnian Muslims were treated cruelly. With this, the tension subsided (Ivan Mestrović), *The Yugoslav Committee in London and the Declaration of Corfu 185–189*. In Antun F Bonifacić & Clement S Mihanović, *The Croatian Nation,* 186–190. Also Ivan Mestrović, *UnPLiD,* 64–65. This communist edition of Mestrović's memoirs' has slightly different wording to the original.
Maria Mestrović, *ZiDIM,* 121–123).
Dr Trumbich is reported to have said later: 'All my work in the Yugoslav committee was one big Way of the Cross and my Calvary was Rapallo. Rapallo was my Calvary. I had to sign it with a bleeding heart and we lost Rijeka. I had to sign it so that we did not lose more.' (Vinko Nikolić, *TsDuS,* Volume 2, 53, 68). Ivan Mestrovich also wrote in his memoirs: 'It was here that Trumbich's Way of the Cross began . . . Here he showed great tact and patience so that we would remain together.' (Ivan Mestrović, *UnPLiD,* 57).
The Rapallo treaty was the treaty between Italy and the Kingdom of the Serbs, Croats and Slovenes which Dr Trumbich as Foreign Minister of the new country, signed in Rapallo, Italy on 12 November 1920. It was a treaty which gave the Croatian region of Istria to Italy, plus the coastal city of Zadar and some of the Dalmatian Islands. Italy was promised parts of Croatia by Britain, France and Russia in a secret treaty in London on April 26, 1915, if she entered the war one month later against Austria-Hungary, but not against Germany (Dragan R. Zivojinović, *AIatBoY,* 36. Josip Horvat, *PPH,* Volume 2, 40. *Znameniti .i Zaśluzni Hrvati,* X-CXC1, 90–91).

9. Franjo Tudjman, *HuMJ,* Volume I, 158–159.
10. Franjo Tudjman, *HuMJ* 220. Franjo Dujmović, *HnpkO,* 219–221.

In June 1918, the President of the United States, Woodrow Wilson, expressed a firm resolution that:

> The free means of autonomous development must be extended . . . to the inhabitants of the Austro-Hungarian Empire. Nations and sub-regions must no longer be handed over from one state to another as if they were simply someone else's property or pawns on a chess board.[11]

The Yugoslav Committee continued to work towards its aim of separating Croatia and Slovenia from the empire, with the aim of uniting with Serbia and Montenegro. It was estimated at the time that there were 36,000 Croats, Slovenes and Serb prisoners of war in Italy, including 300 officers. Dr Trumbich visited the camps in order to establish a Yugoslav Legion that would fight for the defeat of the Austro-Hungarian Empire, to gain more freedom for their peoples. One of these prisoners was Aloysius Stepinac the later Cardinal Archbishop of Zagreb. The interned prisoners were greatly encouraged by the Wilson resolution and three quarters of them volunteered for the legion.[12]

On 29 October 1918, the Croatian Sabor, or Parliament, broke away from the Kingdom of Austro-Hungary and declared the Croatian lands, together with Slovenia and the Vojvodina region, to

---

11. Aleksa Benigar, *ASHK*, 48. In April 1918, the Emperor Karl, through his personal emissary, Professor Heinrich Lammasch, had secret contacts with President Wilson's representative in Switzerland, Professor George Herron. The aim was to establish a separate peace and transform the Empire on a federal basis, but nothing came of it (Franjo Tudjman, *HuMJ*, Volume1, 189–190). Although Wilson was deeply religious, he was a bigoted anti-Catholic, being described as: 'This Calvinist idealist, who was 'convinced of his own moral and intellectual superiority' was also notoriously anti-Catholic, though not at election time and tended to see all Europeans as parochial and unenlightened including Pope Benedict. (John F Pollard, *TUP,* 128). Woodrow Wilson did not want the existence of a Catholic Empire in Central Europe; this was the main reason for the dismantling of the Austro-Hungarian empire. Interestingly, his anti-Catholic bigotry is rarely mentioned. Pope Benedict and his Secretary of State, Cardinal Gasparri, were unhappy about the domination of two Catholic peoples – the Croats and Slovenes–by an Orthodox one, the Serbs.
12. Aleksa Benigar & A Stepinac, *HK,* 48–50. Beluhan E, *Stepinac Govori*, 53.

be an independent nation.[13] During this sitting, the Croatian Sabor did not cease to exist, but it continued to represent and carry Croatian statehood.

On 24 November 1918 the National Council of Slovenes, Croatians and Serbs (*Narodno Vjece*), which was not an elected body, but a pro-Yugoslav orientated party, declared itself in favour of a union between Croatia with Serbia and Montenegro. The Party advocated for the creation of a common state of Slovenes, Croats and Serbs and selected a committee of twenty-eight persons to bring about a union according to its instructions.[14]

As a result of the decision of the National Council, there was a significant gathering of the Congress of the Croatian Popular Peasant Party in Zagreb on 24 November 1918. It included almost three thousand party delegates from all over Croatia. Its president, Stjepan Radich (*Radić*), spoke of the previous day's decision of the National Council, which he described as arbitrary and unconstitutional. Following this, the congress of the Croatian Peasant Party unanimously passed a resolution declaring that the party was decisively against the creation of a joint state of Croats, Serbs and Slovenes. Radich stated: 'We Croatians do not want other state regulations but a confederated republic' in which Croatia would preserve her thousand year old statehood and its national and cultural individuality. The delegates approved this resolution, which was followed by supportive demonstrations in Zagreb.[15]

---

13. Dominik Mandić, *HiS*, 248–249. Franjo Tudjman, *HuMJ*, Volume 1, 223. Josip Horvat, *PPH,* Volume 2, 83–98. Franjo Dujmović, *HnpkO,* 223–225. Trpimir Macan & Josip Šentija, *ASHoC,* 92. Zlatko Matijević, *HISiJ* 32–34. *Znameniti .i Zašluzni Hrvati* LXXV,111 and 78. Ivan Mestrović, *UNPLiD*, 99–100. The Croatian political activist, cultural worker and historian, Dr Rudolf Horvat wrote: 'The Emperor Karl IV wanted to establish peace in 1917 so as to save the land from ruin which he foresaw. But his ally Emperor Wilhelm II of Germany did not allow him to do this. In this way the world war continued to 2 November 1918 when Karl IV had to establish peace. The Croats did not wait for the end of this war. The Croatian Sabor on 29 October 1918 made the resolution that Croatia, Slovenia, Dalmatia with the city of Rjeka proclaim itself an independent state, which would permanently be separated from Hungary and Austria.' (*Znameniti .i Zašluzni Hrvati.* LXX1V, 74).
14. Dominik Mandić, *HiS,* 250–251. Franjo Dujmović, *HnpkO,* 226–229. Josip Šentija, *ASHoC,* 96. Zlatko Matijević, *HISiJ,* 47–49. *Znameniti .i Zašluzni Hrvati.* LXXX1V, 84.
15. Domenik Mandić, *HiS,* 251. *Znameniti .i Zašluzni Hrvati.* LXXXV, 8–485.

This was all the unarmed Croatians could do to express their political will; October and November 1918 were very turbulent and confusing months for the people of Eastern Europe and Croatia. It was during this confusion that the National Council, headed by Serbs who lived in Croatia and by Croatians who were highly idealistic and pro-Yugoslav orientated, succeeded in undermining the Croatians' wants and established a union with Serbia and Montenegro.[16]

On 1 December 1918 the union of the Serbs, Croats and Slovenes was proclaimed in Belgrade without the approval of the Croatian Sabor, nor was it accepted by the Croatian people, but had the support of some Croatian politicians.[17] At this union, Prince Alexander Karagorgevich gave a speech promising:

> True to the example and guidance which I received from my eminent parents. . . . I will be a king of free citizens in a state of Serbs, Croats and Slovenes. I will always remain faithful to the great constitutional, parliamentary and wide democratic principles, based on the right to vote.[18]

On 6 December, just five days after this proclamation, there was a demonstration in Zagreb, held by Croatians against this union. The situation worsened when fifteen demonstrators were killed by Serb soldiers.

---

16. Domenik Mandić. *HiS* 251-253. Antun F. Bonifačić & Clement S. Mihanović. In *The Croatian Nation*. Dr George W Cesarich. *Yugoslavia was created against the will of the Croatian people*. 192-195. Franjo Dujmovich (*Dujmović*) remembers as a boy, when he was in his home town of Oriovc on 29 October 1918, how his school teacher from primary school, Ambroz Shtampar (Štampar), who was for many years a member of the Party of Rights, told him with the end of the war, Croatians would lose the little freedom they had, saying: *we have been sold to the Serbs*. Dujmovich continues: *Our Peasant Party representative Jozo Sorich (Sorić) said to me that difficult times await us,* saying 'Our enemies want to destroy us physically and economically, take our bread and break the Croatians, but the Croatians will never accept that and now there begins a struggle for existence.' Dujmovich concluded: *According to the thinking of these two elderly, sane men the future didn't look too bright.* (*Franjo Dujmović. HkPS* 22).
17. Domenik Mandić. *HiS* 252-253. Josip Horvat. *PPH* Volume 1. 382-383. Trpimir Macan & Josip Šentija. 96. Zlatko Matijević. *HISiJ* 50-54. *Znameniti .i Zašluzni Hrvati.* LXXXV, 85.
18. Josip Horvat. *PPH* Volume I. 384.

At this time, Croatia was in a state of political turmoil. It is interesting that Pope Benedict XV had particular reservations about the Kingdom of the Serbs, Croats and Slovenes. He was also unhappy about the domination of the two Catholic peoples, the Croats and Slovenes, by the Orthodox Serbs. In fact in January 1919, Pope Benedict's secretary of state, Cardinal Pietro Gasparri, dispatched an emissary to Zagreb with the task of impeding this union. By that time it was too late.[19]

The Serbian, Alexander Karagorgevich, who had become king following the death of his father, King Peter, called an assembly in Belgrade on 24 February, 1919, in order to form a government.[20] The Croatian leader, Stjepan Radich, refused to attend, protesting that King Alexander had failed to consider representation from certain districts. The Croatian people did not want to regard themselves as a 'liberated and occupied' people but rather as a nation on equal footing with any other. Radich continued to campaign for the Croatians, and his party received overwhelming support as a result.

With the creation of the Kingdom of the Serbs, Croats and Slovenes, the Serbian element, headed by the Karagorgevich family, began to exert its dominance over the Croatians and other non-Serb nationalities of this new state. The leaders of the old Serbian state became the dominant political figures in the new state and, in essence, they saw the new state as an extension of Serbia. Croatians were not proportionately represented in the government and diplomatic corps. Serbian laws were imposed all over the country, schooling was imbued with the Serbian spirit, and Croatian teachers were retired, transferred, and persecuted. High administrative posts were filled almost exclusively by Serbs, taxes were lower in Serbia than in other parts of the country, Serbian enterprises received highly profitable orders and concessions for export, and the major part of foreign loans were spent in Serbia. The economy was badly shaken

---

19. John F Pollard, *TUP Pope Benedict XV*, 145–146.
20. Beginning in 1919, articles appeared in Croatian newspapers about officers and sub-officers of the Serbian army in Croatia beating Croatian soldiers and civilians, especially villagers. This caused revulsion in the whole Croatian population as the Croatian Sabor had outlawed beatings in 1869. Many of the young gendarmes, mainly Serbs, were beating Croatian villagers, because they supported the republican arrangement of the state (*Znameniti .i Zašluzni Hrvati.* LXXXV1, 86.)

by the unjust exchange rate of the former crown for the Serbian dinar (4:1) All this had negative effects on political and social conditions as well as on land ownership in the former Austro-Hungarian parts of the country.[21] The Croatians supported various political parties, the majority supporting the Croatian Republican Peasant Party, founded and led by Stjepan Radich.[22]

Radich refused to go to Belgrade and enter the parliament with his deputies from 1919 to 1924, stating: 'We want to be with the Serbs, but not under the Serbs, we want a Serb for our brother and not our master . . .'[23] In 1922, he presented the League of Nations with a long memorandum and petition seeking Sovereign Statehood for Croatia. Since his demands would have required a revision of the treaty of Versailles, he was advised to work instead towards improving the relations between the Croats and Serbs.

---

21. Trpimir Macan & Josip Šentija, *ASHoC*, 97.
22. The Central Committee of the Croatian Peasant Party accepted the resolution of 8 March 1919 in which it stood up against all the brutality the Croatian people were bearing. It also stated:

    The Croatian citizens do not recognise the so called Kingdom of the Serbs, Croats and Slovenes under the Karagorgevich dynasty, as this kingdom was proclaimed outside the Croatian Sabor and without the mandate of the Croatian people. We do not recognise the state council of the Serbs, Croats and Slovenes (that is the provincial people representatives in Belgrade) so we revoke all legal powers of the central government in Belgrade.

    As there was a French military delegation in Zagreb at the time, Radich gave a translation of the resolution to the delegation; this resulted in Radich being arrested on 25 March 1919 (*Znameniti .i Zašluzni Hrvati*, LXXXV 1, 86).

    At the same time, three members of the Croatian Justice party, Dr Josip Pazman, Dr Vladimir Prebeg and the medical doctor and writer, Dr Milan Kovachevich (*Kovačević*), were imprisoned because the Justice party attempted to inform the international community of the political situation in Croatia (*Znameniti .i Zašluzni Hrvati*, LXXXV11, 87).

    This democratic spirit of the new state was proclaimed and signed in the treaty of Saint Germain-en Laye on 10 September 1919. In article 2 it states: 'The State of Serbs, Croats and Slovenes is committed to give all its citizens full and complete protection of life and freedom irrespective of origins, nationality, language, race or religious faith.'

    In article I of this agreement it states that this principle '*cannot be replaced by any other law, order or official measure.*' It was this international agreement that the inner workings of the new state were to be based (Josip Horvat. *PPH* Volume 1. 384–385).
23. Domenik Mandić, *HiS*, 257–258. Josip Horvat, *PPH*, Volume 2, 154.

In his attempt to gain foreign support, Radich left Croatia for England on 21 July 1923. He met with the leaders of the English Labor Party including Arthur Henderson and Ramsay MacDonald, who advised him to visit Belgrade and attempt to solve the Croatian question in the parliament. He also met with Seaton Watson and Wickham Steed, who were the leading authorities on the Balkans at the time and who 'did not approve of the policy of transforming the Kingdom of the Serbs, Croats and Slovenes into a greater Serbia or the tendency of the Croatians to separatism.' They advised Radich to come to an understanding with the Serb politicians with integrity.[24]

Leaving London, Radich travelled through Paris, where he met the French socialist Leon Blum, and then continued to Vienna, where he based himself for a number of months. He had discussions with the Austrian chancellor Dr Johann Schober. Through the Soviet embassy, he received an invitation to visit Moscow, where he met Soviet President Kalinin and Foreign Minister Georgy V Chicherin. His stay in Moscow resulted in his Croatian Republican Peasant Party becoming a member of the International Peasant Association. The leadership of the Croatian Peasant Republican Party approved the steps Radich took in Moscow, perceiving it as a way of developing relationships between the Croatian and Russian peoples and gaining support for its cause.[25]

On the advice Radich received, particularly in England, his party entered the Belgrade parliament in March 1924. Radich was an outstanding speaker and organiser who was able to communicate what the Croatians wanted. He became the champion of their rights, and on occasions attacked the Roman Catholic Church and its clergy for what he believed was their neglect of the poor. This inevitably resulted in a distance between Radich and the Church, to whom a vast majority of Croatians belonged.[26]

---

24. Franjo Tudjman, *HuMJ*, Volume 1, 398.
25. Franjo Tudjman, *HuJM*, Volume 1, 398–402. Jozo Tomasevich, *WaRiY*, 21–22.
26. Radich's attack on the Catholic hierarchy and clergy had some justification as the Church, especially the clergy, was beginning to lose touch with the lives of people. This was also related to the author by Dr John Kelly, former spiritual director at St Patrick's College Manly, Sydney, Australia. Dr Kelly had spent three months in pre-World War II Croatia and told the author: 'What I saw was that the Croatian Catholic clergy lived quite simply but they seemed to have lost contact with the lives of people, they lost touch'

In January 1925 Radich, together with key leaders of his party, was imprisoned by the regime. The party was convicted of communist sympathies and methods, although the party's leadership more than once announced that the party was against the aims and methods of the new State's Communist Party. During his time in prison, Radich changed his policy from a republican and separatist one, to one that accepted a united country of Slovenes, Croats and Serbs within the Kingdom. He also accepted the Serb-Croat agreement that he had previously opposed and changed the name of his party to The Croatia Peasant Party. The party adopted his policy changes and recognised the Vidovanski Constitution and Karagorgevich Crown.[27] The declaration of these changes meant a real turnaround for the party, causing some of its members to become disillusioned with Radich. Although the new policies were overwhelmingly approved by the leadership of the party in its special sitting on 26 June 1925, the party did lose some support.[28] Radich was released from prison in July 1925.

In September 1918 the Croatian Roman Catholic Bishops issued a statement of loyalty to the new State in which a Serbian Orthodox was Head of State. Despite this, rumours circulated that the Catholic Bishops wanted to break away from the state, and there was pressure on the Church to distance itself from Rome. In some regions, Greek Catholics, who belonged to the Catholic Church but were of Eastern Rite, were pressured to become part of the Orthodox Church. The Catholic bishops issued a protest against such pressure in April 1925, without any success.

Radich had some sympathy with Lenin's Russia as the Serbian leadership supported the White armies of General Wengle and the restoration of Tsarism. Radich supported the Bolsheviks stating: 'it is completely natural that we Croatians respect and love this Bolshevik Russia far more than the former Tsarist Russia which didn't know or care for us or was always unfriendly towards us because we were Catholics and not Orthodox.' Radich saw the socialisation of Russia as freeing the oppressed peoples (Josip Horvat. *PPH* Volume1. 384–385).

27. The Vidovanski Constitution is named after St Vitus, whose feast day is 28 June. It was on that date that the famous battle of Kosovo was fought in 1389. The date is Serbia's national holiday, and the constitution was also proclaimed on that date in 1921 (Franjo Tudjman, *HuMJ*, Volume 1, 342–344. *Znameniti .i Zašluzni Hrvati*, XC11, 92).

28. Franjo Tudjman, *HuJM*, Volume 1, 456–457. Trpimir Macan & Josip Šentija, *ASHoC*, 98–99.

The government showed its favoritism towards the Orthodox Church by building Orthodox churches in districts that lacked an Orthodox population. It also appointed Catholic civil servants in regions of Serbia because there were no churches, thus making it difficult for them to practice their faith. Furthermore, Serb Orthodox civil servants were appointed in completely Croat regions.

A number of measures, including funding, were taken by the government to weaken the Roman Catholic Church. In the census of 1921 the population consisted of forty-seven per cent Orthodox, thirty-nine per cent Roman Catholic, eleven per cent Muslim and two per cent others, yet the distribution of funds to the various religious bodies resulted in the Orthodox church receiving two-thirds with the remaining one-third allocated to the rest.[29]

Ante Ciliga, who was Secretary of the Croatian Communist Party after World War I, wrote that, with the support of the government, Orthodox churches were built in totally Roman Catholic areas, even in Slovenia which was almost completely Catholic. Ciliga wrote that at that time proselytism was seen for the first time, more due to the measures taken by the dictatorship than out of any conviction. According to the census of 1931, compared with that of 1921, the difference was four percent to the benefit of the Orthodox as against the Catholics.[30]

As increasing pressure was brought to bear on the Croatians, Radich, as head of the Croatian Peasant Party became the voice of the opposition. He also worked with Serbian Parties, who were in opposition to the centralist policies of the Serbian elite, in order to extend his party's influence in Serbia proper. He did this by gathering support from discontented Serbs and other nationalities within the new state, all of whom sought more autonomy for themselves[31]

---

29. Aleksa Benigar, *A Stepinac HK*, 91–93.
30. Ante Ciliga, *Slučaj Stepinac Simbol Vjerskog .i Nationalog Sukoba.* in 'Stepinac Mu je Ime', Volume 1, 281–282.
31. Some time in 1923 when Ivan Mestrovich was doing some sculpturing in Cavtat, south of Dubrovnik, on behalf of Stefi Rachich (Račić), an economist who was close to the Serbian ruling families, he recalls that Rachich's wife, Pava, told him of a list of several thousand Croatians whose heads were to be cut off to solve the Croatian question. On this list were the names of Radich, Trumbich and others who had expressed discontent with the Serbian leadership (Ivan Mestrović, *UnPLiD*, 149).

The Serbian leadership, in its aim to break the primary Croatian opposition, arranged the assassination of the Croat representatives in the Belgrade parliament on 20 June 1928. Paval Radich, Stjepan's cousin and Dr Djuro Baserichek (Baseriček), were killed. Stjepan Radich was also shot dying of wounds on August 8, 1928. The assassin, Punisha Rachich (Puniša Račić), shouted 'Long Live Greater Serbia'. He calmly walked through the ministerial rooms, to a waiting automobile, later announcing to the newspapers: 'That is what I wanted, that's what I completed.'[32]

This bloodshed in the midst of the Belgrade parliament, which was organised by the Serbian oligarchy, led by King Alexander, eliminated the leadership of the main opposition and the legitimate leadership of the whole of Croatia. It also meant the breakup of the parliamentary constitution. The assassination brought about a general revolt by the Croatians and a disgust in all the oppressed peoples within the kingdom.[33] As a result, the Croatian representatives left

---

Mestrovich also recalls that on 27 July 1924, he had a conversation with Prime Minister, Dr Ljuba Davidovich (Davidović). Davidovich related to Mestrovich a conversation he had with King Alexander in which King Alexander used filthy language against Stjepan Radich and the Croats, stating that he had no desire to respect Croatian rights (Ivan Mestrović, *UnPLiD*, 161-162).

He also recalls a conversation he had with Dr Milan Gavrilovich (Gavrilović), a Serb politician in Belgrade some time in November 1924, during which Gavrilovich told him: 'Radich needs to be killed. The state is more important than Radich'. Mestrović was shocked at these words and replied: 'Yes the state is more important than an individual, but don't you know that behind Radich stand almost all the Croatian people, and to shoot at Stejpan Radich you would be shooting at my father and brother?' (Ivan Mestrović, *UnPLiD*, 163-164).

32. Franjo Tudjman, *HuMJ*, Volume 1, 508-509. Trpimir Macan & Josip Šentija, *ASHoC*, 100.
33. The huge funeral of Pavao Radich and Dure Baserichek in Zagreb on June 23, 1928, turned into a general condemnation of the actions and intentions of the centralist hegemony of the government in Belgrade (Franjo Tudjman, *HuMJ*, Volume 1, 512).
   As a result of the assassination in Belgrade, the secretary of the Zagreb district Communist Party, Josip Broz Tito, issued a pamphlet calling all workers and villagers to join in a general demonstration against the coming dictatorship. On the day of the funeral, many of the demonstrators were wounded and arrested. Tito avoided capture, went into hiding but was arrested a few months later and was sentenced to five years imprisonment, which he served out in Lepoglava prison. (Franjo Tudjman, *HuMJ*, Volume 1, 512-513. Jasper Ridley, *Tito*, 97-98).

Belgrade, not to return until an agreement was made with the Serbs in 1939.[34]

---

34. Franjo Tudjman, *HuMJ*, Volume 2, 7–9. Josip Broz, later known as Tito, was born in the Croatian village of Kumrovac in 1892. He received no more than five years of schooling and rejected the Catholic faith as a teenager. While serving in the Austro-Hungarian Army he was captured by Russian troops in 1915 and sent to Siberia. While there, he witnessed the Bolshevik seizure of power and through the upheavals became a convinced Communist. By September 5, 1918, the Soviet government legalised terror with the famous decree 'On Red Terror':
At this moment it is absolutely vital that the Chekas be reinforced. . . . to protect the Soviet Republic from its class enemies, who must be all locked up in concentration camps. Anyone found to have any dealings with the White Guards organizations, plots, insurrections, riots will be summarily executed, and the names of all these people, together with the reason for their execution, will be announced publicly (The Black Book of Communism. 76).

> One can also see the ruthlessness of the Communists through what Leon Trotsky wrote in 1920 when he was the commander of the Red Army, directing the Red Terror: *As for us, we were never concerned with the Kantian-priestly and vegetaranian Quaker prattle about the 'sacredness of human life'. We were revolutionaries in opposition, and have remained revolutionaries in power. To make the individual sacred, we must destroy the social order which crucifies him. And that problem can only be destroyed by blood and iron* (Leon Trotsky, *The Defense of Terrorism*, 63. The 1935 edition has the same page references). A little further he writes: *The man who recognises the revolutionary historic importance of the very fact of the existence of the Soviet system must also sanction the Red Terror* (Leon Trotsky, *The Defense of Terrorism*, 64.)

Tito was the only leading Yugoslav communist whom Stalin trusted before the war. Tito virtually admitted this: '*In 1938, when I was in Moscow . . . we were discussing whether to dissolve the Yugoslav Communist Party. All the Yugoslav leaders at the time in the Soviet Union had been arrested; I was alone, the party was weakened without leadership; and I was there alone.*' (Christopher Andrew & Oleg Gordievsky, *KGB The Inside Story*. Milorad M Drachkovich & Branko Lazich, *Stalins Massacre of Foreign Communists Leadership*, 108).
At this time approximately 100 Yugoslav Communists were arrested, including the Croat Milan Gorkich (Gorkić), the Party's Secretary General, and former school colleague of Krunoslav Draganovich (Draganović). (Mijo Ivurek, ŽiDKD, 121. Milovan Djilas wrote: '. . . we were delighted that the Soviet Union had dealt a final blow to the emigrants. This was particularly true of Tito and Kardelj, who were more familiar with the situation in Moscow.' (Milovan Djilas, *MoaR*, 303. Dr Sima Markovich (Marković), a Serb but a real Communist idealist, was also arrested in July 1939 and shot. Markovich sympathised with the Croatians; this can be seen in his help to the imprisoned Juraj Juco Rukavina, a high official in the Ustasha movement in prison (Milovan Djilas, *MoaR*, 136).

With the collapse of Communism, the Serbian writer Pero Simic (Simić) was able to delve into the Communist archives in Moscow. He discovered that:
Tito had arrived in Moscow on 21 February 1935, immediately starting to work with the Commintern, the function of which was the spreading of Communism in foreign lands (Pere Simić, *Tito*, 66) He quickly gave the impression that he was a dedicated and faithful Communist of the Stalinist mould. (Pere Simić, *Tito*, 68–69).
On 21 July 1936 he reported on his former colleague from Zagreb days, Duro Cvijich (Cvijić), who in Moscow had the surname Kresich (Kresić): *He is sickly ambitious, thinking that only he has the ability to be head of the party. Yes, he is capable and politically very grounded, but as a Bolshevik he hasn't rid himself of petty buzva limitations.* (Pere Simić, *Tito*, 72). On 31 August 1936 he reported on Dr Sima Markovich, one time general secretary of the Communist Party of Yugoslavia: *Milich (Milić)* (as Markovich was known in Moscow) *earlier on did not gather people around him, but in recent times as is known, many of the discontented members of the right faction of the Communist Party of Yugoslavia would gather at his place.* Pero Simich adds another nine references from this section (Pere Simić, *Tito*, 73).
When Tito was again in Moscow, on 23 September 1938 he wrote a confidential document reflecting on his life, giving his impressions of some of the leading Yugoslav communist including Simo Miljus, editor of the Commentern newspaper *Strani Radnik* (Foreign Worker) as well as on Markovich. Simich continues: *Both, on the basis of false proofs, will be sentenced to death and be shot not quite seven months after Tito's negative writing of Markovich and of Miljusa stating he had 'a bad impression of them'* (Pere Simić, *Tito*, 116–117). Ivo Ivurek, drawing on the research of Simich as well as Silvin Eiletz wrote: *On the basis of opened secret archives in Russia it is clear that Tito collaborated in describing his party colleagues, bringing out 'characteristics' which often brought the death sentence. That was a means of showing loyalty to Stalin's Party and ideology, a way of surviving and climbing the party ladder. Amongst many who were so described and sentenced to death was Milan Gorkich – Tito's predecessor as general secretary of the communist party of Yugoslavia and one time school colleague of Krunoslav Draganovich* (Mijo Ivurek, ŽiDKD, 121)
Simich brings out that in the May, 1939 edition of *Proletera*, which was the organ of the Central Committee of the Yugoslav Communist Party, Tito praises the work and *'wise leadership of comrade Stalin who overcomes all difficulties before beginning his grandiose work.'* Simich adds there was a number of articles in the same edition where Tito praised Stalin (Pere Simić, *Tito*, 145). In the village of Dubrava, near Zagreb, on 19 October 1940, with up to a hundred delegates present, Tito was named general secretary of the Communist Party of Yugoslavia (Pere Simić, *Tito*, 164–165). Tito visited Moscow in the autumn of 1938, and then again in the summer of 1939 and the spring of 1940 (Milovan Djilas, *MoaR*, 303). *Tito's position in the Central Committee was exceptional: he was the only person in whom the Comintern had confidence, and they recognised the composition of*

On 6 January1929, King Alexander announced a military dictatorship, abolished the constitution, banned all associations based on national and religious affiliation and gave General Petar Zivkovich

---

the Central Committee as he envisioned it . . . his power and role were therefore exceptional, Djilas added, *His word was most decisive* (Milovan Djilas, *MoaR,* 280–284).

The Black Book of Communism States: *The fact that Tito rose up against Stalin in 1948 takes nothing away from his responsibility for the purges of the 1930s* (*The Black Book of Communism,* 306. Also Jure Vujić, *ICoC,* 130–131. In *Represia .i Zlocin Kommunistickog Rezima u Hrvatskoj).*

Tito, although biologically Croatian, he had no Croatian patriotism in him. A hardened Communist, he was an internationalist, a brilliant organiser with a brilliant mind, but extremely ruthless. He impressed people by *his powerful personality* (Jasper Ridley, *Tito,* 215). William Deakin wrote: *Tito was as always sharp to take the point* (William Deakin, *TEM,* 117)

The estimate of the number of dedicated Communists for the whole of pre war Yugoslavia varies from eight thousand to twelve thousand but they were very well organised. The Communist youth members numbered up to thirty thousand. They were mainly university and high school students, up to half of whom were ordered to join the Partisan detachments at the beginning of the war. The symbol and idol of this youth was Ivo-Lola Ribar, a highly intelligent Croat who was described as a 'dauphin' of Tito (William Deakin, *TEM,* 92. Jure Vujić, *Intellectual Crimes of Communism,* 131–132. In: *RiZKRuH).*

With the German invasion of Poland, the Communists of Yugoslavia saw Britain's and France's war with Germany as an imperialist war. Milovan Djilas wrote: *England and France, although at war with Germany, were fighting not Germany but a neutral state.* This article was published under the pseudonym V Zatarac 1941 (Milovan Djilas, *PoaL,* 130–131. Published under pseudonym V Zatarac 1941).

Stjepan Radich died of his wounds on August 8, 1928, and his death further deepened the Croatian people's disgust of the regime. His funeral in Zagreb on August 12, 1928 became a general demonstration of the people against the centralist authoritarian policies of the regime (Franjo Tudjman, *HuMJ,* Volume 1, 524–527. Also Bogdan Krizman, *Ante Pavelic .i Ustaši,* 22–23) The Croatian Peasant Party was the Croatian equivalent of the Labor parties of Australia, Britain and New Zealand.

Rebecca West writes a biased and negative opinion of Radich. The Croatian Peasant Party, which he led, aimed to improve the lot of the Croatian poor, who in the main were village people. She did not mention that when the bodies of Pavo Radich and Djuro Baserichek were taken to Belgrade railway station to be transported to Zagreb, up to 60,000 citizens of Belgrade came out to express their respect. It was a massive demonstration of the Serbian people's solidarity with Croatians and the Croatian leadership. (Rebecca West, *BLaGF,* 101–102). Dr Vladko Mačak was a Tolstoian pacifist.

(Živković) the mandate to establish a government. Zivkovich was one of the conspirators involved in the murder of King Alexander Obrenovich (Obrenović) and his wife Draga in 1903. On 3 October 1929 King Alexander issued a decree in which he changed the name of the country from the 'Kingdom of the Serbs, Croats and Slovenes' to 'Yugoslavia'. The name Croatia therefore disappeared from public usage by annulling recognition given to the Slovenes and Croatians, and only sanctioning the Serbian and general 'Yugoslav' nation.

The dictatorship created a police state and antagonised young intellectuals, especially in Serbia and Montenegro, pushing them towards communism. This move threw the people into utter confusion and greatly heightened tensions, and a dark and humiliating period of Croatian history began.

The use of the Croatian name, flag, and anthem for any public or private occasion was forbidden by Yugoslav law, and the users were punished even though the use of the Serbian name and flag was allowed. This caused the non-Serb nationalities to feel hostility towards the new regime.[35] For the first time in thirteen centuries, the institution of Bans and Sabor was completely abolished.

When Dr Ante Pavelich (Pavelić), leader of the Croatian Party of Rights, visited Belgrade on October 28, 1928 he announced that his aim was the establishment of a sovereign Croatian state.[36] Dr Ante

---

35. Domenik Mandić, *HiS*, 261–262. Esther Gitman, *ASPoHR*, 29. Franjo Tudjman, *HuMJ*, Volume 2, 10–15. Franjo Dujmović, *HnpkO*, 291–294. Jasper Ridley, *Tito*, 104–105. Jozo Tomasevich, *WaRiY*, 23–26. Trpimir Macan & Josip Šentija, *ASHoC*, 100.

36. Dr Ante Pavelich was born in the village of Bradina in Bosnia in 1889, where his father was a railway worker. He was educated by the Jesuits in the Bosnian town of Travnik and gained his doctorate of law from Zagreb University in 1915. In his university days Pavelich was actively involved in politics, becoming secretary of the Party of Rights by the end of the First World War. By the early 1920s he became mayor of Zagreb and in 1922 was elected to represent Zagreb in the Belgrade parliament. His aim was to achieve state autonomy for Croatia within the Kingdom of the Serbs, Croats and Slovenes (Aleksa Benigar, *ASHK*, 329–330). Ante Pavelić, *PHDP*, 537–540. He was the only Zagreb lawyer to volunteer to defend 26 patriotic Macedonian university students in Skopje, Macedonia in November 1927 (Ante Pavelić, *PHDP*, 246–265. Bogdan Krizman, *APiU*, 22–23). The students aimed to achieve autonomy for Macedonia within the Kingdom of Serbs, Croats and Slovenes. It must be remembered that Serbia did not give autonomy to Macedonia, regarding it as Southern Serbia and it also incorporated the Macedonian Orthodox Church into the Serbian Orthodox Church. Although

Trumbich, one of the founders of Yugoslavia, also supported this announcement, for he saw that Croatians were oppressed in this state.

there were no Serbs living there, no one could be a public servant, school teacher or a people's representative if they did not regard themselves as Serbs. It was in fact a crime to refer to oneself as Macedonian or Bulgarian (Domenik Mandić. *HiS* 253). The Macedonians were very much an oppressed people. Pavelich left Croatia for Austria on January 19, 1929 with the aim of forming a military movement named Ustasha whose purpose was to achieve Croatian independence. Its constitution was already formulated before he left Croatia. He received support from Admiral Miklos Horti's Hungary, where Pavelich's colleague Gustav Perchec (Perčec) bought a property and established a military training facility at Janko Pusti near the Hungarian-Croatian border. However Pavelich's main base of operations was Mussolini's Italy.

On 20 April 1929, Pavelich signed an agreement of co-operation with the leadership of the Macedonian exiles, the Macedonian revolutionary organisation VMRO (*V'tresna makedonska revoljuciona organizacia*) (The United Macedonian Revolutionary Organisation) headed by Dr Konstantin Stanisev in Sofia, Bulgaria. The VMROs aim was achieving independence for their peoples. Pavelich gave a number of speeches, among which he said: 'We don't fight with a prayer book in our hands against criminals. . . . If we want to see our homeland free we must roll up our sleeves and go into battle . . . ' (Ante Pavelić. *PHDP* 463, 477–478. Bogdan Krizman. *APiU* 54–58. Mario Jareb. *U-dp* 81–83). On 1 September 1929, Pavelić sent an appeal to the League of Nations in Geneva pointing out the unconstitutional means by which King Alexander Karagorgevich had imposed dictatorship on the country. Because of the terror he imposed, and the bloodshed in the Belgrade parliament on 20 June 1928, Pavelich wrote 'a common life of Croatia with Serbia is permanently impossible.' (Ante Pavelić. *PHDP* 532–536. Mario Jareb. *U-dp* 107–108). As a result of his activities, a Belgrade court sentenced Pavelich and his colleague Gustav Perchec to death in absentia (Ante Pavelić. *PHDP* 483–490. Bogdan Krizman. *APiU* 59–60. Mario Jareb. *U-dp* 83–84). In Budapest on 17 March 1933, Pavelich also established an agreement with the Albanians of Kosovo (Bogdan Krizman. *APiU* 116).

Pavelich was very active in publicising the Croatian cause, establishing a newspaper in the Croatian language which was smuggled into Croatia, plus brochures in German and French for the wider public. He also published a book in German: *Aus dem kamf* (Out of the struggle) detailing the desire and right of Croatians for an independent state, as well as a book in French on the same theme. He worked to gain support from Croatian communities in Austria, Germany and Belgium as well as in South America, where he sent Dr Branimir Jelich (Jelić) in 1931 to boost support from the large Croatian communities, especially in Argentina where he established a Croatian newspaper *Hrvatski Domobran* (Mario Jareb. *U-d p* 204–207). Pavelich sought support from North America, especially the United States, where there were large Croatian communities in all the major cities, and Dr Jelich visited these communities in 1939.

Immediately after the implementation of the dictatorship, Pavelich made the decision to achieve Croatian freedom through whatever means possible. He left the country on January 19, 1929 when he discovered he was about to be arrested. He went on to organise the Ustasha movement, which would break Croatia 'free from under the foreign yoke'. The leadership of the Croatian Peasant Party, headed by Dr Vlatko Machek (Maček), was not in favour of any revolutionary action, believing that Croatian freedom and sovereignty could be attained through peaceful means. He was arrested on 22 December 1929, but through a court decision, was released on 14 June 1930.[37]

King Alexander justified the introduction of the dictatorship, by blaming inter- party struggles. 'There were no other means to prevent the collapse of our beautiful country' adding that, 'one couldn't observe brothers fighting one another without intervening'. He stated that the measures were only temporary.[38] In fact King Alexander was never a true democrat. From the very beginning his aim was to destroy Croatian and Montenegrin statehood, strengthen Serbs in disputed areas, and weaken the Croatians and Slovenes economically and culturally so that they would become an insignificant part of the

---

As mentioned earlier, Pavelich's main base of operations was Mussolini's Italy, where he established an Ustasha para-military training camp in which up to 300 members were trained (Mario Jareb, *U-dp*, 68–75. Franjo Tudjman *HuMJ*, Volume 2, 29–33.).

The Ustasha conducted a number of assassinations of people connected to the brutal Karagorgevich regime. Its high point was the assassination of King Alexander and the French Foreign Minister, Louis Barthou, in Marseilles at the beginning of the King's state visit to France on October 9, 1934. The act was carried out in conjunction with the Ustasha by Vlado Chrnozemski (Črnozemski) who belonged to the Macedonian revolutionary organization VMRO. As a result of this assassination and the world outcry, Admiral Horti's government in Hungary closed the Janko Pusti training facility and Mussolini's government closed all Ustasha facilities in Italy. Most of these Ustasha volunteers were sent into virtual exile on the island of Lipari, while Pavelich and Eugene Dido Kvaternik, the mastermind behind the assassination, were imprisoned for up to 18 months. Upon his release, Pavelich was under strict police surveillance (. . . Franjo Tudjman, *HuMJ*, Volume 2, 126–128. Mario Jareb, *U-dp*, 303–315. Trpimir Macan, *PHN*, 400). This was a period through which all Ustasha activity in Italy was virtually frozen, and their work from April 1937 to the end of 1939 was very restricted (Mario Jareb, *U-dp*, 415–432).

37. Domenik Mandić, *HiS*, 261–262. Franjo Tudjman, *HuMJ*, Volume 2, 30–31.
38. Franjo Tudjman, *HuMJ*, Volume 2, 20–21

new State. He only accepted the name Serbs, Croats and Slovenes out of expediency.[39]

It was under these circumstances that the Serbian Orthodox Church had the freedom to propagate the Serbian national ethos. In his Easter message of 1931, Patriarch Varnava spoke of the Serbian Orthodox Church coming to its glory after five centuries of Golgotha 'together with the Resurrection and celebrating its national liberation and unity'. As 'Head of the Serbian Orthodox Church', Varnava called for upholding the pledge of Saint Sava and all traditions of Holy Orthodoxy 'for that has preserved our faith, national consciousness and provided the main help in the whole National resurrection.'[40]

The regime also interfered in purely religious and spiritual areas. The police interrogated and ill-treated people for spurious reasons, prisons were overflowing and people were treated in the most inhumane way. The Croatian scholar Dr Milan Shufflay (Šufflay) was killed by the police and Dr Vlatko Machek, the successor to Stjepan Radich, was sent to prison. The brutality was so intense that the world-renowned physicist, Albert Einstein, together with the German novelist, Heinrich Mann, the brother of Thomas Mann, submitted an appeal in 1931 to the League of Nations Secretariat for Human Rights, seeking that the Croatian people be protected from the 'horror and terror, which the government of the Kingdom of Serbia imposes on the Croatian people.' The appeal ended with: 'All countries in which there exists branches of the League of Nations for Human Rights, especially France, Germany, Poland and Austria,

---

39. Domenik Mandić, *HiS*, 262–263. In the name of the Croatian Peasant Party, Dr August Kosutich (Kosutić) and Dr Juraj Krnjevich (Krnjević) presented a memorandum to the League of Nations in Geneva on January 25, 1930, which stated amongst other things:

> . . . use of the Croatian name is prevented, which is recognised in international agreements. On the whole of the Croatian State an absolute regime of the Serbian King has been imposed. In this way the Croatian coat of arms and Croatian flag are forbidden, Croatian cultural and scientific societies have been banned. The Croatian language is being discouraged in schools and in the public service.

The memorandum highlighted the fact that Dr Vladko Machek, who was validly elected as a representative of the Croatian people, had been imprisoned using false accusations (Franjo Tudjman, *HuMJ*, Volume 2, 31–33. Trpimir Macan, *PHN*, 460).

40. Franjo Tudjman, *HuMJ*, Volume 2, 21–22.

have a duty to present themselves as protectors of this small, peace loving, enlightened people.'[41] Dr Machek commented on the appeal saying: 'Sadly, this protest did not wake the consciences of the western democracies.'[42]

The world economic depression of the early 1930s greatly affected Yugoslavia. According to the index of the National Bank, in 1932 the price of industrial exports production was thirty per cent lower than in 1924 and forty per cent lower than in 1929. As interest rates remained the same, and in some cases rose, it brought about catastrophic debts, especially to village farmers. The debt of villagers rose from three billion dinars in 1926 to seven billion in 1932. The life of the villagers, whose livelihoods depended on the land, was extremely hard.[43] In 1933, the unemployment of workers in factories reached its peak of 310,000, which was thirty-five per cent of the total work force. It increased the supply of cheap labor, and created abject poverty in towns and villages.[44]

The oppressive measures of the government and the economic crisis led to growing discontent amongst the people, with strikes becoming more numerous. In 1932 there were thirty strikes with some 10,000 participants, and forty strikes in 1933, culminated in sixty-five strikes in 1934. The most significant were the strikes of metal workers in Slovenia, the railway and textile workers in Croatia and timber workers in Bosnia, and some of these strikes turned into political demonstrations against the government.[45]

---

41. Franjo Tudjman, *HuMJ*, Volume 2, 121. Marko Sinčević, 'NDH u Svjetlu Dokumenata', 86. Mario Jareb, *U-dp*, 218. Albert Einstein and the writer Heinrich Mann, the brother of the more noted German writer Thomas Mann, were prompted to protest the slaying of Dr Milan Sufflay, a professor at the University of Zagreb and a world-renowned specialist on the ethnic origins of the Albanian people (Franjo Tudjman, *HuMJ*, Volume 2, 31-33. Trpimir Macan, *PHN*, 460). Dr Sufflay was beaten to death with iron bars. Albert Einstein's and Heinrich Mann's protest was carried by all the major newspapers of the world and was a huge moral blow to the brutal Karagorgevich regime (Mario Jareb, *U-dp*, 218. Franjo Tudjman, *HuMJ*, Volume 2, 54).
Einstein had a special interest in Croatian-Serbian relations because his first wife, Mileva Marich (Marić), a brilliant mathematician and physicist, and with whom he had three children, was a Serbian Orthodox Christian (Walter Isaacson. *Einstein His Life and Universe*. 42-47, 50-53, 55-59, 135-137, 234).
42. Dr Vlatko Macek, *Memoari*, 93
43. Franjo Tudjman, Volume 2, *HuMJ*, 100, 101.
44. Franjo Tudjman, Volume 2, *HuMJ*, 106, 107.
45. Franjo Tudjman, *HuMJ*, Volume 2, 112. Stjepan Matković, *HISiJ*, 210.

Within all this, the outlawed Communist Party began to organise itself. Hitler came to power in Germany in January 1933, and in April 1933 the Supreme Council of the Communist International called all workers of all lands to create a united proletarian front against Nazism, blaming the Social Democratic parties for what happened in Germany. Aware that spontaneous strikes and demonstrations were occurring, the Communists were to involve themselves

> with developing the daily struggle of the working class, the laboring peasants and the oppressed nationalities to help them achieve their demands and interests.' It saw itself as the supporter of oppressed people in their struggles for freedom. It called for a 'a seven hour working day, an increase of wages, assistance for the unemployed and freedom for workers to organise themselves, freedom of the press, the right to strike against rising prices and financial speculation, against fascism and the military dictatorship.[46]

---

46. Franjo Tudjman, *HuMJ*, Volume 2, 114–115. The Communist movement in Croatia and Yugoslavia were greatly affected by Stalin's purges. Its one-time Secretary, the Croat Milan Gorkich, was liquidated in Moscow in July 1937 and Josip Broz Tito became its head (Franjo Tudjman, *HuMJ*, Volume 2, 199–200. Jasper Ridley, *Tito*, 135). In 1928, the strongest section of the Communist Party was that of Zagreb. It had a membership of 134 members, and its organizing secretary was Josip Broz Tito, who was also then elected the Secretary of the Regional Committee of Zagreb (Jasper Ridley, *Tito*, 95–96). The Commintern in Moscow approved the Zagreb committee's stand for unity amongst the fractured Communist Parties of the country. At a meeting held in Samobor on the night of August 1–2, 1937, the Croatian Communist Party was reformed. This coincided with Tito's return from Russia as Secretary of the Yugoslav Communist Party, and he was to establish its central committee and reestablish the party's activities within the wider community.

Tito personally led the discussions and determined the formation of this meeting. The announcement of the establishment of the Communist Party of Croatia:

> . . . .*derives from the many year struggle of the Communist Party of Yugoslavia, which protects not only the interests of the working class . . . . . . .but the idea of freedom, equality and brotherhood amongst peoples. There can be no discrepancy between the interest of the workers and the interest of the Croatian people, for the workers are part of their people and they are very concerned that their people be free, that they have an opportunity to develop and that everything that is beautiful and progressive in its traditions and cultures be respected . . . . . .* (Trpimir Macan, *PHN*, 405–406).

As the internal and external political situation was changing, King Alexander was forced to relax his rule. Already during the first half of 1931 he began to give the appearance that he was 'leaving dictatorial methods and moving to the restoration of a constitutional and parliamentary government' but nothing came of it. Dr Machek, as head of the Croatian Peasant Party, could not come to an agreement with the Serbian opposition parties and all discussion by any opposition was under the strict police surveillance of King Alexander. There was student unrest, including co-ordinated demonstrations of university students from Ljubljana, Zagreb and Belgrade Universities which took place on the 19 February 1932, where the students called for an end of the dictatorial regime, a constitutional government and for the country to be arranged on a federal basis.[47]

With his position deteriorating, King Alexander, who conducted foreign affairs himself, attempted to find a modus vivendi with Italy and Germany. Firstly through secret contacts, and then quite openly, he announced that Yugoslavia was interested in working with all states. He also maintained his close relationship with France, which had already signed a treaty with Russia. The value Hitler gave to Yugoslavia was illustrated by the appointment of his deputy, Herman Goering, to oversee Germany's relationship with Yugoslavia.[48] To strengthen his position, King Alexander established the Balkan Pact, which was signed in Athens on 9 February 1934, and to which Yugoslavia, Turkey, Romania and Greece all joined.[49]

King Alexander took many public and secret steps, but they were more marginal than of any significance. In the second half of 1933, and the first half of 1934, there was much activity in trying to find a solution to the political crisis. The weeks before he set sail for France, the king had intended on his return to come to an agreement with Dr Machek, giving Croatia its autonomy, with its own parliament.[50]

Tensions were heightened when, on this official visit to France, King Alexander and the French foreign minister, Louis Barthou, were assassinated in Marseilles on 9 October 1934. The assassin was

---

47. Franjo Tudjman, Volume 2, *HuMJ*, 70.
48. Franjo Tudjman, Volume 2, *HuMJ*, 125.
49. Franjo Tudjman, Volume 2, *HuMJ*, 125.
50. Ivan Mestrović, *UnPLiD*, 235–237.

Vlado Chernozemski (Černozemski), a member of the Macedonian terrorist group VMRO, and Ustasha collaborators.[51]

The King had arranged that, in the case of his death, Prince Paul Karagorgevich would act as regent until Alexander's son, Peter, was old enough to assume the throne.

Although Prince Paul was a highly cultured, kindly and humane man, the assassination of King Alexander prompted the government in Belgrade to increase its oppression of the Croatians. Prince Paul did not relish his new role, as he was very aware of the crisis facing the country. He gathered around himself responsible and clear sighted people to help administer the country.

The Croatian sculptor, Ivan Mestrovich (Mestrović), informed the regent that time was running out and it was essential for the survival of the state that he come to an agreement with the Croats. Prince Paul, while agreeing, expressed the fear that the Serbs would oppose a basic change in the state. He thought it was important that he work slowly. Mestrovich further informed the regent that a group of Croatian intellectuals intended to meet with some Serbian intellectuals to prepare a memorandum for him with regard to the internal conditions of the country. Prince Paul told Mestrovich that he would welcome the memorandum, but asked him to keep the matter confidential.[52]

Returning to Zagreb, Mestrovich gathered a number of men together and they worked on a memorandum. It asserted that most Croatian people were supporters of the state but opposed certain features, such as the current widespread lawlessness. It agreed that all people should be equal before the law, and spoke against censorship and the prohibition of citizens organizing themselves into political parties. It sought the release of Dr Vlatko Machek and an amnesty for all political prisoners, and asked that elections be held with a secret vote.

---

51. Domenik Mandić, *HiS*, 263. Franjo Tudjman, *HuMJ*, Volume 2, 126. Ivan Mestrović, *UnPLiD*, 237. Mario Jareb, *U-dp*, 310–311. At the funeral of King Alexander in Belgrade, Germany was represented by Herman Goring, who stated on that day: 'King Alexander with one blow ended political parties and ended the decaying democratic regime. In his country he played the role of Hitler and enabled Yugoslavia to be a factor of order and peace, enabling her to play an important role in the development of Europe' (Franjo Tudjman, *HuMJ*, Volume 2, 127).

52. Aleksa Benigar, *A Stepinac*, *HK*, 181–183. Franjo Tudjman, *HuMJ*, Volume 2, 143–144.

When completed in November 1934, the memorandum was circulated among a wider circle. Among the thirty-eight people who signed it were Archbishop Bauer and his assistant Aloysius Stepinac. Mestrovich and Dr Milan Churchin (Čurčin) took the memorandum to Belgrade to seek the signatures of some Serb intellectuals, but they were only able to obtain the signatures of those who belonged to the Serbian club. Dr Albert Bazala and the President of the Academy of Arts and Science and Dr lvo Tartaglia from the Dalmatian region of Croatia were chosen to take the memorandum to Prince Paul. They waited in Belgrade for three days for an audience and on the fourth day, they were given time with Minister Antich (Antić), who received them very coldly, keeping them standing and lecturing them as children.[53]

The next day the Belgrade newspapers attacked the memorandum, with some writers calling for the arrest of the signatories. Prince Paul, who was accused of initiating the memorandum, took fright at the insults some high officials threw at him.

In Zagreb, students demonstrated against the memorandum, calling for the resignation of the rector, Dr Stipetica, one of its signatories.[54]

New elections were called for the Belgrade Parliament, which were to be held on 5 May 1935. The head of the Roman Catholic Church in Croatia, Archbishop Bauer, wanting to keep the clergy out of party politics, issued a circular on 12 February prohibiting any priest from nominating for any role. The government put great pressure on the electorate to vote for its candidates as opposed to those being led by Dr Vlatko Machek. Many candidates were unable to express their views and, in many districts, public servants were commonly forced to vote for the government party out of fear of being dismissed from their employment. Voting was not by secret ballot; voters were made to declare for whom they were voting.[55]

In the results published in newspapers the day after the election, results from the Zagreb region and Dalmatia were omitted, clearly because the opposition had won the majority of votes. The newspapers eventually produced the final result on May 7, indicating that the

---

53. Aleksa Benigar, *A Stepinac, HK,* 181-183. Ivan Mestrović, *UnPLiD,* 244-247.
54. Aleksa Benigar, *A Stepinac, HK,* 182-183. Franjo Tudjman, *HuMJ,* Volume 2, 143-144.
55. Aleksa Benigar, *A Stepinac, HK,* 183-184.

government party received 1,746,982 votes (60.6% of the vote) and the united opposition headed by Dr Machek received 1,076,345 votes (37.4% of the vote). Many were suspicious of the accuracy of the result, claiming there had been interference from government organizations.[56]

After the elections Archbishop Bauer was moved to intervene, having learned of violence and terror committed in many parts of Croatia against Croatian lay people and clergy. On May 24 he travelled to Belgrade with the Eastern Rite Bishop, Dionizij Njaradija, and Prince Paul received them. They submitted to the prince a strong protest against the brutality of the government agencies, and submitted a similar protest to the Minister of the Army, Petar Zivkovich. Returning to Zagreb on May 28, both bishops were thanked for their stand by Dr Torbar, a representative of Dr Vlatko Machek.[57]

The French political writer, Ernest Pezet, who visited Zagreb in 1935 while on a visit to Yugoslavia, spoke with Stepinac, the Archbishop's assistant, over a meal. He recorded details of their conversation which he subsequently published in Paris in 1959:

> The Monsignor showed me a whip which he kept in a small container which he called 'The Museum of Horrors'. The whip was made of plaited wire with iron pellets. Then he said to me the following:
>
> In a hundred years under Austro-Hungary there has not been so much blood spilt as has been spilt by the Serbian Zendars (Žendars) (Police) in Yugoslavia. The smallest incident is enough to cause horrific reprisals. During one of my latest visits through the Archdiocese two people were killed because of an argument which was provoked by the Zendars. Due to the memorandum of Archbishop Bauer which was presented to Stojadinovich's government, many threatening letters were sent to me and other priests. At Tabora four priests were killed. Oppression and provocation are beyond counting. The goodwill of Stojadinovich and Korosec is without question, but they are surrounded by the army and Zendars. The chief

---

56. Aleksa. Benigar, *A Stepinac, HK*, 183–184. Franjo Tudjman, *HuMJ*, Volume 2, 150. Vladko Maček, *Memoari*, 113–114.
57. Aleksa Benigar, *A Stepinac, HK*, 184.

of public security told me that he can do nothing with regard to the Zendars. The same was said by his deputy. Not one priest is sure of his life. Not a day passes that one of them doesn't ask to be placed under my care. They make complaints regarding the Croatian flag. Neither the bishops nor priests ask for this, but the Croatian people want it, they see in it the symbol of freedom. Austro-Hungary allowed it when, under the Croatian flag, it was sufficient to have just seven hundred Zendars to uphold public security in the country, while today there are six to seven thousand. It is said that this is because of communist infiltration, but this is impossible today in Croatia.

My pastoral visits are seen as political agitation, but what can I do? The Zagreb Archdiocese is very vast. Today it has one million seven hundred thousand people. It is my duty to go on pastoral visits. That offends them and they look on that as political activity. Concerning Dr Machek (Maček), I avoid meeting him in order to maintain my independence. On the day of the elections I left Zagreb. I informed Prince Paul but nothing came of it. He told me I was right but that he could do nothing.

One Zendar official wanted a woman to bring a wrapped parcel to the Archbishop's palace. It was a bomb. He said to her she would be rich if she delivered it. This was written up in a later report which was included in discussions with the said person in the drama which, thank God, failed.

At the end of the conversation Stepinac showed Pezet a receipt showing that a Croatian family had to pay for a bullet with which the Serbian police had shot the father of the family, his sole crime being that he didn't properly affix a postage stamp on a letter.[58]

As a result of the election a new government was formed with Dr Milan Stojadinovich, an economist, as Prime Minister. Although Dr Stojadinovich stood for a greater Serbia, he was far more humane than the brutal General Zivkovich. Stojadinovich felt for people who were struggling in life and the oppression of the regime eased considerably with him as Prime Minister.

---

58. Aleksa Benigar, *A Stepinac*, HK, 184–186. Esther Gitman, *ASPoHR*, 44–45.

Stojadinovich established a limited coalition, which included the main Slovene party and the Muslim party of Bosnia. It brought about a significant democratization in the country, to such an extent that he was attacked by leaders of the Serb military.[59] Stojadinovich also worked to develop closer relations with Mussolini's Italy, signing an agreement in Belgrade on 25 March 1937, by which both countries would respect one another's interests. Through this agreement Italy also clamped down on the activities of the Ustasha movement and had its leader, Ante Pavelich, under police surveillance.[60]

Stojadinovich also developed warmer relations with Germany, which was looking to strengthen its economic interest in South East Europe at that time. It suited Germany to maintain good relations with Yugoslavia and for it to continue its existence. When Stojadinovich became Prime Minister, the German government avoided anything 'which would weaken Stojadinovich (Stojadinović). This dictated the position of Berlin towards any opposition within Yugoslavia.'[61]

Throughout 1935 and 1936 there was an increase in strikes by workers. In 1936 alone there were up to 400 strikes, as well as a growth in communist membership from workers and intellectuals and increasing involvement in the trade unions. Of real importance was the decision made in June 1936 by the leadership of the Communist Party of Yugoslavia, headed by Tito, to leave Moscow and return to Yugoslavia.[62] This resulted in the creation of the Communist Party of Slovenia in April 1937, and the Communist Party of Croatia was then established at its congress in August 1937. Both these parties made the announcement to their respective peoples that their creation was witness to the fact the Communist Party of Yugoslavia worked for freedom of all nationalities and for equality and brotherhood amongst them.[63]

Although Stojadinovich introduced more freedoms, his government was oppressive. The police force reacted violently towards people who were demonstrating on behalf of national groups or involved in revolutionary activity, and also towards the general public, especially in Croatia. There were demonstrations in

---

59. Franjo Tudjman, *HuMJ*, Volume 2, 154–156, 165.
60. Franjo Tudjman, *HuMJ*, Volume 2, 171–173.
61. Josip Jurčević, *Bleiburg JpznH*, 24–25.
62. Franjo Tudjman, *HuMJ*, Volume 2, 189–191.
63. Franjo Tudjman, *HuMJ*, Volume 2, 197–199.

Zagreb in March 1936, where up to nineteen people and eleven police were wounded. A leading figure in the Croatian Peasant Party, Karl Bridjachich (Bridjačič), was shot in the Lika region on 9 April 1936. A week later on 16 April there was bloodshed in Serestinac, near Samobor, and later in August there were general strikes at Belgrade, Zagreb and Ljubljana Universities. The Croatian media expressed real disgust when, on 9 May 1937, police in Senj shot at youths who had attended a concert and were returning home. Up to eleven young people were killed. Dr Machek wrote in protest to Dr Stojadinovich: 'The Croatian people are not seeking any satisfaction from him, for they know very well - being taught by recent experiences, especially with the crime in Senj - that they can't receive it but in the future every ordinary criminal attack will be destroyed by its own aggression.'[64]

At its foundations, the political struggle between the Croats and Serbs was between the desire for a greater Serbia and Orthodoxy: it pitted the spiritual soul of the Serbian people against the majority of the Croatian people. The Croatian people wanted more autonomy for themselves and that basic human rights be respected.

There was more evidence that the Orthodox Church in the Kingdom of Yugoslavia had a privileged position. The state encouraged the spread of Orthodoxy by building Orthodox churches in areas of Croatia and Slovenia where few Orthodox Serbs lived. According to the 1931 census, there were over five million Catholics in Yugoslavia, but there was no final agreement between the Church and the Yugoslav government. In contrast, the state had defined its relationship with the Serbian Orthodox Church, the Jewish communities, the Islamic faith and the Protestant churches. The late King Alexander himself was instrumental in a Concordant being achieved, moving towards settling Croatian grievances and adding to the stability of the government.

After much discussion, reviews and stoppages, a Concordant was eventually signed in the Vatican on 25 July 1935. It was signed on behalf of Pope Pius X1 by his Secretary of State Cardinal, Eugene Pacelli, later Pope Pius XII, and on behalf of King Peter II by the Minister of Justice, Dr Ljudevit Auer.[65]

---

64. Franjo Tudjman, *HuMJ*, Volume 2, 193–197.
65. Aleksa Benigar, *A Stepinac HK*, 186–187.

The Concordant required ratification by the Parliament in Belgrade. The Serbian Orthodox Church opposed its ratification on the grounds that, as Orthodoxy was the official religion in Serbia and Montenegro, there was no reason to rescind its position. It informed the government on 13 September 1935, that the Concordant in its present form, could not be ratified.[66] The Serbian Patriarch Varnava accused the government officials of 'making a pact with the black international so that they attacked and betrayed the Holy Orthodox Church, the last bastion of Serbianism.'[67]

The Orthodox church organised demonstrations against the Concordant in a number of cities, including some 400 Communist demonstrators under the leadership of Milovan Djilas.[68] On 8 August 1937, a letter from the Orthodox hierarchy was read in all Orthodox Churches against the Concordant, stating that any Orthodox Member of Parliament who voted for it would be denied participation in Orthodox services and the Orthodox faithful were not to receive them into their homes.[69] Pamphlets were circulated among the people, outlining the sanctions imposed on parliamentarians who voted for the Concordant and urging Serbian people to have nothing to do with them.[70] Among those opposing the Concordant were extreme elements in the Serb military who were threatening a military coup.[71]

All this caused the ratification of the Concordant to be shelved when it was rejected by the senate on 19 October 1937.[72]

German policy at that time was not in favour of the creation of smaller states, rather it aimed to create large economic regions and bring existing states into a larger union. For this reason Germany aimed to maintain Yugoslavia, which it needed as a source of grain and raw materials. Both Berlin and Belgrade totally opposed the restoration of the Hapsburgs in Vienna, though there remained a certain nostalgia in Croatia for them. Belgrade also feared co-operation between Rome and Vienna; which then explains why Belgrade was not opposed to Germany's annexing or Anschluss of Austria in March 1938.[73]

---

66. Aleksa Benigar, *A Stepinac HK,* 187. Stella Alexander, *TTM,* 31–35.
67. Jure Batelia, *PGP 1934–1940,* XIX, 19.
68. Jure Batelia, *PGP* XIX, 19.
69. Aleksa Benigar, *A Stepinac HK,* 189.
70. Ivan Muzić, *KCSiP,* 236.
71. Ivan Muzić, *KCSiP,* 240–241. Franjo Tudjman, *HuMJ,* Volume 2, 174–176.
72. Aleksa Benigar, *A Stepinac, HK,* 190. Ivan Muzić, *KC SiP,* 25.
73. Franjo Tudjman, *HuJM,* Volume 2, 180–181.

Commenting on Hitler's occupation of Austria, Lieutenant Colonel Ivan Babich (Babić), who was an officer in the Royal Yugoslav Army at the time, wrote years later:

> It would not be right to blame Yugoslavia of passivity on the occasion of Hitler's occupation of Austria. More powerful and more interested states were passive too. Yet, it is worthwhile stressing that this act, though aggravating Yugoslavia's strategic situation, was greeted with no hidden pleasure in Serbian military and political circles. Serbian immediate interests, they reasoned, were not in danger; on the contrary Serbian hegemony might be reinforced because there was no danger of the restoration of the Hapsburgs; thus there was nothing left for the Croatians and Slovenes but to accept Yugoslavia and Serbia's dominance in it.[74]

Dr Sojadinovich called a second election for 21 December 1938. Nearly seventy-five per cent of 4,080,286 registered voters actually voted. The government party, headed by Stojadinovich, received fifty-seven per cent of the vote, which meant according to the regulations at the time that it received 82 percent of the seats (i.e. 306 seats out of 373). The united opposition headed by Vlatko Machek, received 44.9 % of the vote and therefore held eighteen per cent of seats (i.e. 67 seats). The pro-Fascist party, headed by the Serb Dimitrija Ljotich (Ljotić), received 1.01 % of the vote (i.e. 30,734 votes). The other parties that contested did not receive enough to be represented in the Belgrade parliament.[75]

Stojadinovich developed good relations with Italy and Germany, and in order to weaken the Croatian Peasant Party, he attempted to gain support amongst the Ustasha. Its main base was in Italy, and Stojadinovich allowed a considerable number of Ustasha to return to Croatia, including the writer Mile Budak. With the never-ending discussions between Dr Machek and the Croatian Peasant Party, and the openness of Stojadinovich towards the Ustasha, Prince Paul became suspicious. He suspected that Dr Stojadinovich did not intend to come to an agreement with the Croatian democratic movement

---

74. Lt Col Ivan Babić, *Yugoslavia In Western Strategy*, 330. From: *The Croatian Nation in its Struggle for Freedom and Independence*.
75. Franjo Tudjman., *HuMJ*, Volume 2, 183.

such as the Croatian Peasant Party, but with Pavelich's movement under the umbrella of Italy and largely for his own totalitarian aims.[76] As in the election, Stojadinovich didn't receive the overwhelming support he expected in parliament, in fact he lost the support of Anton Korosec, the leader of the main Slovene party, and Mehined Spaho, the leader of the Bosnian Muslims. Both had wanted an agreement with the Croatian Peasant Party to achieve national stability within an increasingly unstable Europe.[77]

Due to his dissatisfaction with Dr Stojadinovich's policies, Prince Paul, to Stojadinovich's shock, withdrew his mandate on 5 February1939, and asked Dr Dragisha Chvetkovich to form a government.[78]

In his declaration before the Belgrade parliament on 16 February 1939, Chvetkovich announced that the chief priority of the new government was the settlement of the so-called Croatian Question. This was the first time Yugoslavia recognised the uniqueness of nationalities and the unacceptability of one nationality dominating others, thereby moving the country to an autonomous, federal system. As Europe was moving closer towards war, it became extremely urgent to solve the inner tensions of the country. Prince Paul was in an extremely difficult position, with extreme groups even calling for the breakup of the country and suggesting the path to save the monarchy was to accept the demands of the various nationalities. He had to contend with those in the Serbian leadership who intended to maintain a centralist government with Serbian dominance, supported by the Serbian Orthodox Church and the military, over whom Prince Paul had never managed to impose his authority.

Dr Sekula Drljevich (Drljević) of Montenegro said in parliament that solving the Croatian Question would place on the table Slovenia, Bosnia-Herzegovina, Montenegro 'and other countries of the South Slavs' which would include Macedonia, the Albanians in Kosovo and the Hungarians and Germans in the Vojvodina region.[79]

---

76. Franjo Tudjman, *HuMJ*, Volume 2, 232.
77. Franjo Tudjman, *HuMJ*, Volume 2, 234–235. In his book, *Croatia in Monarchical Yugoslavia*, Dr Tudjman quotes Churchill's article in which he wrote that the discontent of the Croatians was of such urgency that it called into question the existence of Yugoslavia, if the Serbs who direct the future of the country did not accept a federal arrangement (Franjo Tudjman, *HuMJ*, Volume 2, 261. Quote from Daily Telegraph 10 February 1939).
78. Franjo Tudjman, *HuMJ*, Volume 2, 239.
79. Franjo Tudjman, *HuMJ*, Volume 2, 243–244.

Three changes in just a few weeks sent the international scene into chaos: the collapse of the Czech republic, which reduced it to becoming a German protectorate; the independence of Slovakia on 15 March 1939; plus the Italian invasion of Albania on Good Friday 7 April 1939. On his visit to Britain in July that year, Prince Paul was encouraged by Prime Minister Neville Chamberlain and his government to settle the Croatian Question by coming to an agreement with Dr Machek, stabilising the country.[80]

The pressure within Yugoslavia was building. The Ustasha movement accused Dr Machek and the leadership of the Croatian Peasant Party of betraying the Croatian people in failing to proclaim Croatian independence. It called on Machek and the leadership of the Croatian Peasant party to resign stating: 'so as not to shame the Croatian people any more' *for* 'someone who recognises and protects the borders of Yugoslavia cannot represent Croatia.'[81] Machek held discussions with the Serbian democratic opposition including Milan Grol, which resulted in a fruitful dialogue with only Prince Paul and Dragisha Chvetkovich.[82] With the war approaching, Machek reached a '*Sporazum*', or agreement, with the Prime Minister of the Kingdom of Yugoslavia, Dr Chvetkovich. It was signed on August 26, 1939, giving Croatia a certain amount of administrative autonomy within the Kingdom, including its own police force, civil defense and Sabor.[83]

August Koshutich (Košutić), a high official in the Croatian Peasant Party, described the new recognition of a Croatian state as:

> ... a field which has been flooded over; an orchard which has been destroyed by hail; a village which has been made uninhabitable by fire; a city which has been destroyed by an earthquake. When we now begin to organise the development of Croatia everyone knows and easily understands that we are not coming here with bayonets and cannon but with wounded hands. It is important that we share this work and organise it and that we all work at it. In these circumstances the Croatians are the last to think of war. It is not therefore the politics of this agreement that we would prepare to attack any

---

80. Franjo Tudjman, *HuMJ*, Volume 2, 247–249. Franjo Dujmović, *HnpkO*, 331. Ivo Rojnica, *Susreti .i Dozivlaji*, Volume 1, 22.
81. Franjo Tudjman, *HuMJ*, Volume 2, 260.
82. Franjo Tudjman, *HuMJ*, Volume 2, 262. Ivan Gabelica, *HISiJ*, 236–239.
83. ... Dominik Mandić, *HiS*, 264–265. Franjo Tudjman, *HuMJ*, Volume 2, 265–270. Jozo Tomasevich, *uDSR*, 34–37.

peoples of Europe or that we ally ourselves to any aggressive side. We wish with all our heart and a pure soul: so that we can freely give ourselves to the work at hand, and to arrange and organise our homeland to be a place of justice and peace.[84]

Dr Machek entered the new government in Belgrade as Vice President, with another four Croatians in the cabinet. This agreement brought a sense of freedom and democracy never experienced before in the Kingdom of Yugoslavia and a certain sense of relief. It was also the onset of reform for Yugoslavia on a federal basis, providing recognition to all the nationalities of Yugoslavia. With the agreement, there was a noticeable easing of tensions. People in all areas of the country, especially in Croatia, felt free, with no fear of police reprisals, but unfortunately it was too late. This transformation should have been implemented in the early 1920s when it could have prevented the blood bath which was World War II.

As soon as the agreement was signed critics undermined it, such as the Ustasha movement, claiming the agreement did not go far enough.[85] The Serbian Democratic parties, headed by Milan Grol, resented the fact they were not involved in formulating the agreement, nor was Dr Stojadinovich happy with the agreement, describing it as a *government coup*.[86] The leader of the Bosnian Muslims at the time, Dr Dzafer Kulenovich (Kulenović), expressed the wish for Bosnia-Herzegovina to become an autonomous entity.[87] Some Muslims saw the agreement as a Croat-Serb division of Bosnia, which excluded them.[88] The Serbian ultra nationalists, sections of the army, and the Orthodox Church, perceived the agreement as dangerous to Serbianism.[89] The Communist party, which initially welcomed the agreement, came to see it as the conceited middle class in Croatia prioritizing its own agenda and the Serbian Centralist maintaining control over Montenegro and Macedonia.[90]

---

84. Aleksa Benigar, *A Stepinac, HK*, 230–231.
85. Franjo Tudjman, *HuMJ*, Volume 2, 273.
86. Franjo Tudjman, *HuMJ*, Volume 2, 275–276.
87. Franjo Tudjman, *HuMJ*, Volume 2, 280.
88. Nada Kisic-Kolanović, *MiHN 1941–1945*, 29. Ivan Gabelic, *HISiJ*, 244. Kresimir Regan, *HISiJ*, 254–268. From: *Hrvatska Izmedu Slobode .i Jugoslavenstva*.
89. Franjo Tudjman, *HuMJ*, Volume 2, 277–280.
90. Franjo Tudjman, *HuMJ*, Volume 2, 282.

When the government of Chvetkovich-Machek opened diplomatic and trade relations with the Soviet Union, the Communists organised nationwide demonstrations against the war. Some of them ended violently, especially in Belgrade where, on September 8, 1940, the police killed ten youths and wounded many others. The Communists concentrated their energy in the trade union movement among the working classes, which grew significantly at that time.[91]

Of great significance for the Communist movement was its fifth congress, in spite of its illegality and police terror. It was held in Zagreb from 19–23 October 1940, with 105 delegates representing 6,500 members. It appointed a new central committee with Josip Broz, who took the name Tito, as its General Secretary, and affirmed its commitment to fight for democratic rights and *to struggle for national equality of oppressed peoples and national minorities*. It also committed itself to struggle for the demands of the poor peasants in the villages by dividing up land belonging to large landholders and the Church, and providing interest-free credit. Under the leadership of Tito, the party did not tie itself to some Stalinist policies. With their vision, ideas and activities, the Communists skillfully exploited the political situation of the time. They gathered around the Communist Party of Yugoslavia all the anti-fascist elements in the country. Together they created a revolutionary movement for the democratization of the country, which they believed would ultimately solve the national and social problems.[92]

The war escalated. By June 1940, Hitler's Germany occupied much of France, and Italy entered the war as a Germany ally. The Soviet Union occupied Bessarabia from Romania, but was forced to concede northern Erdelje to Hungary and southern Dobruja to Bulgaria, with both countries tying themselves more with Germany. Added to this was the coming to power of the dictator Antonescu in Romania, and Italy's invasion of Greece on 28 October 1940. With the international scene deteriorating, Yugoslavia found itself in a very unenviable position. It opened diplomatic relations with the Soviet Union on 24 June 1940, two days after France's surrender.[93]

Prince Paul and the government of Chvetkovich- Machek worked very hard to keep Yugoslavia out of the European conflict. Prince Paul met Hitler in Berchtesgarten on 4 March 1941, in an attempt to

---

91. Franjo Tudjman, *HuMJ*, Volume 2, 282.
92. Franjo Tudjman, *HuMJ*, Volume 2, 304–307, 310.
93. Franjo Tudjman, *HuMJ*, Volume 2, 316–318. Franjo Dujmović, *HnpkO*, 351–352.

convince him of the importance of Yugoslav neutrality. On returning to Belgrade, Prince Paul held a meeting with the Royal Vjece (or Royal Council), which came to the conclusion that joining the Axis pact was the only way of saving the country. In signing the Axis pact, Yugoslavia was guaranteed three provisions: its sovereignty and territorial integrity would be respected; there would be no request made of her to allow the transport of soldiers through her territory; and Italy and Germany would not ask for any military assistance. Germany valued Yugoslavia's neutrality, for it enabled her to receive its support and moral solidarity as it prepared its attack on the Soviet Union, for which the Royal Yugoslav Government was naturally inclined, as the Serbian royal family supported Tsarist Russia and the White Armies during the revolution. The pact was signed in the Belverdere palace in Vienna, in the presence of Hitler on 25 March 1941. It must be remembered that Sweden, which was in a better geographical and political position, signed a trade agreement with Germany and allowed German troops to pass through its territory, a fact which didn't prevent the Swedish government from maintaining good relations with the western powers.[94]

All this caused the upper echelons of the military, which was Serbian dominated, to look dimly on the internal and foreign policies of Prince Paul and the Chvetkovich-Machek government. Prince Paul, who was a highly cultured and humane man, very much inclined to the arts and literature, had no standing within the military. He also naively believed in the British, giving strict orders that neither the British Legation nor any of its officials or official communications were at any time to be monitored or in any way interfered with.[95]

The military elite belonged to the group that had eliminated King Alexander Obrenovich and Queen Draga in 1903, and brought the Karagorgevich's (Karadordgevićs) to the throne. The military provided the main support to King Alexander in the imposition of his dictatorship and maintenance of a centralist government. The military was very unhappy with the agreement, which gave a certain amount of autonomy to the Croatians. A coup was planned by Air Force generals Dushan Shimovich (Dušan Šimović), Bora Mirkovich (Mirković) and the former strong man general, Petar

---

94. Franjo Tudjman, *HuMJ,* Volume 2, 329, 331–333. Esther Gitman, *ASPoHR,* 40. Franjo Dujmović, *HnpkO,* 358–367. Jozo Tomasevich, *CuDSR,* 46.
95. Neil Balfour & Sally Mackay, *Paul Of Yugoslavia,* 258.

Zivkovich. Preparations began at the end of 1939, supported by sections of the Serb opposition, the Serbian Club, which supported Serb dominance in the country, the Serbian Defense Force and the Serbian Orthodox Church.[96]

Already in 1940 the British 'Special Operations Executive' was present in Belgrade preparing the ground work for a coup. If Yugoslavia joined the Axis pact, it 'was to use all means to bring about a revolt'. Winston Churchill and his Foreign Secretary, Anthony Eden, instructed their Ambassador, Ronald Campbell, in Belgrade, to take the necessary measures. In fact the British secret service sent George Taylor, to organise the coup, and he in turn paid Dushan Shimovich 100,000 British pounds for the task. One of the leading figures of the Serbian Club, Dragisha Vasich (Dragiša Vasić), had close contact with the Soviet Ambassador in Belgrade, VA Plotnjikov, and sought Soviet support in its aim to remove Prince Paul because of his anti-Soviet stand. At the time of the coup, Plotnjikov unexpectedly left for Moscow to avoid any suspicion that the Russians were behind the plot.[97]

The coup began on 26 March 1941, at 11:30 pm and concluded just hours later on March 27 at 3:30 am. It was conducted by some small army units, and only one policeman was killed. The leaders arrested some members of the government and some leading figures who opposed the coup. At six pm the new government was announced over the radio and a special newspaper announcement from King Peter II added that 'in these difficult times for the people he was heading the government', that the regent had resigned and the 'army is at the service of the king' with him giving the mandate to General Shimovich to create a new government. Prince Paul, who at the time was on his way to Zagreb, was caught by surprise, learning of the coup on the morning of March 27. He had a meeting with Machek and other leading figures of the Croatian Peasant Party in Zagreb, during which Machek advised Prince Paul to call on loyal members of the army based in Croatia and Slovenia to put down the coup. Prince Paul rejected such advice as it would place him against the King and his family, who were in Belgrade, which was controlled by the coup leaders. Prince Paul decided to leave the country, seeking permission

---

96. Franjo Tudjman, *HuMJ*, 334-337. Franjo Dujmović, *HnpkO*, 368-369.
97. Franjo Tudjman, *HuJM*, Volume 2, 338-339. Franjo Dujmović, *HnpkO*, 356-357, 368-369. Jovan Marjanović, *DMiBiN*, 24-26, 31, 36. Jozo Tomasevich, ČuDSR 47-48, 52. Also from *Serbian Voice Newspaper*, 12 January 2018, Edition 24. Ivo Omrčanin, *Hrvatska 1941*, 88

for himself and his family from the British council in Zagreb to enter Britain or one of her dominions. He advised Machek to enter the Shimovich government.[98]

One of the first people the coup leaders turned to for support was Patriarch Gavrilo Dozich (Dožić). He praised the coup over Belgrade radio as the solemn mission of the Serbian people and the Orthodox church, which created the state and should be the only one protecting and defending it. The chauvinism of this attitude filled the people who were concerned with the fate of the country with disgust. Ivan Mestrovich (Mestrović), who happened to be in Split visiting family, hearing the speech over the radio described it thus: 'This is a speech, which epitomises chauvinistic Serbianism and Orthodoxy, which only upholds its 'vowed mission', which created the state and which is the only one which will defend it. Listening to this speech, we all looked at one another without a word.' The speech caused everyone in the room to be shocked.

Mestrovich was the first to speak in the room: 'This is the beginning of a catastrophe, it's the first step. This speech is more deadly than all German arms, artillery and tanks. What will follow is the destruction of Yugoslavia and a tragedy for her people.'[99]

That morning there were celebrations in the British Legation in Belgrade and some sections of its population who supported the coup.[100] The Communists placed themselves at the head of the demonstrations with their acclamations and calls for a revolution. Together with national and allied flags there were also Communist proletariat red flags, with patriotic calls 'Long live the army', 'Down with the pact', 'We will protect the country', 'Better death than slavery', 'War is better than a pact'. There were also calls of 'Long live freedom', 'Down with fascism', 'Belgrade-Moscow - an alliance with Russia', 'For democratic freedom and a peoples government', and 'For peace and a pact with the Soviet Union'.[101]

News of the coup reverberated around the world. Britain and the USA welcomed it and gave moral support to Shimovich's government, although the Soviet Union was reserved. Churchill announced on the same day 'Yugoslavia has found her soul' while USA President

---

98. Domenik Mandić, *HiS*, 266–267. Franjo Tudjman, *HuMJ*, Volume 2, 341. Ivo Omrčanin, *Hrvatska 1941*, 78–81.
99. Franjo Tudjman, *HuMJ*, Volume 2, 340. Ivan Mestrović, *UnPLiD*, 267.
100. Neil Balfour & Sally Mackay, *Paul Of Yugoslavia*, 252.
101. Franjo Tudjman, *HuMJ*, Volume 2, 342.

Roosevelt sent a letter of support to King Peter II. The British and United States media described the coup as historically significant, and praised the bravery of a people of a small country surrounded by Hitler's armored divisions, who would prefer war rather than negotiate with him.[102]

After much planning of the successful coup, the leaders found themselves in a bewildering situation, not knowing what to do, for they had not planned beyond the overthrow of the government. In many ways the coup was an adventurous undertaking, but the critical situation required the coup leaders to act responsibly. Shimovich invited Machek to enter his government. Machek demanded a number of conditions such as the establishment of the *Krunsko Vjece* (Royal Council) with Serb, Croatian and Slovene representation as well as the Patriarch of the Serbian Orthodox Church and the Catholic Archbishop of Zagreb, without whose agreement, the King could not make decisions. Machek also demanded the depoliticising of the Serbian Orthodox Church and the military, recognizing the Croatian-Serbian agreement of 26 August 1939, and making more concessions for Croatia. Realising that it was critical for him to have Machek on his side, General Shimovich accepted these conditions and Machek entered the new government.[103]

Joining the Pact was just an excuse for the coup, for the Shimovich government accepted the Pact with Germany. The main trigger for the coup was the agreement for the autonomy of Croatia, which ended the centralised arrangement for the country and reduced the dominance of the Serbs.[104]

Machek wrote in his memoirs:

> Although I and all the Croats were convinced that the revolt of the 27 March against Prince Paul was due to this agreement, for it 'gave in too much to the Croatians', entering the Axis pact was a convenient excuse. In spite of this, there was no other way out for us. Not joining the Shimovich government would mean automatically joining with Hitler. Even if we were not to consider our democratic and anti- Nazi view of the world, we were convinced that Hitler would lose the war in the end and we Croats must, at the end of the war, be on

---

102. Franjo Tudjman, *HuMJ*, Volume 2, 342.
103. Franjo Tudjman, *HuMJ*, Volume 2, 345–346, Jozo Tomasovich, ČuDSR, 56.
104. Domenik Mandić, *HiS*, 266.

the side of the western democracies. I could not at that time foresee that the war would be won neither by Hitler or the western *democracies but by the communist Soviet Union. Had I foreseen what would be the outcome, my decision and possibly that of my colleagues may have been different.*[105]

Shimovich's government agreed that Machek was to be one of its Vice Presidents; it included representatives of Serbian democratic parties, the Agrarian, Radical Party and Serbian Independents, plus Slovene representatives and Dr Dzafer Kulenovich from the Yugoslav Muslim organization.[106] The Shimovich Government immediately began sending messages, assuring Hitler and Mussolini of the loyalty of the new regime and its readiness to adhere to the Axis pact; however, demonstrations of people against the pact, particularly in Serbia and Montenegro, were not encouraging. On March 28 the German Ambassador Viktor von Heeran was attacked as he returned from church where a Te Deum was sung for King Peter, resulting in von Heeran leaving the country.[107] Regardless of the government's efforts, Hitler had made his decision to invade Yugoslavia on March 27. The invasion began on Palm Sunday, April 6, and Belgrade was bombed that same day. The Serbian leadership, including Alexsander Cincar-Markovich (Marković), a former foreign minister, and General Radivoj Jankovich (Janković), initially tried to come to an agreement with Germany and Italy. They asked for the whole of Yugoslavia to be spared from occupation but to be allowed to exist in part in the form of Vichy France. This was rejected by the Germans. Yugoslavia signed its unconditional surrender on 17 April 1941 in Belgrade, thus enabling the complete collapse of Yugoslavia without a single battle.[108]

---

105. Vladko Maček, *Memoari*, 153.
106. Franjo Tudjman, *HuMJ*, Volume 2, 343–346. Jozo Tomasovich, *ČuDSR*, 57.
107. Franjo Tudjman, *HuMJ*, Volume 2, 346–348. Franjo Dujmović, *HnpkO*, 375.
108. Franjo Tudjman, *HuMJ*, Volume 2, 356–360. Jozo Tomasovich, *ČuDSR*, 58–60. Commenting on the collapse of Yugoslavia, Jozo Tomasovich wrote the simple truth:

> *The natural collapse of Yugoslavia must be explained not only by Germany's military strength but by the fact that for twenty years Yugoslavia was a divided country where the greater Serb politicians ignored the rights and needs of other nationalities in the country. It was a government of the elites, for the elites and nobody else. Just an insignificant minority of people had an interest in preserving Yugoslavia as it was before 1941 and even they thought that it wasn't worth fighting or dying for* (Jozo Tomasovich. Č.u.D.S.R. Volume 1. p. 88).

Chapter 3
The Independent State of Croatia 1941–1945

Hitler had initially intended to divide Croatia between Hungary, Italy and Germany but, with the German invasion of Yugoslavia, most Croatians saw this crisis as Croatia's opportunity to free itself from Serbian hegemony. It is a sad but true fact: countries use situations of war to gain freedom for themselves. When Napoleon invaded Spain in 1808 many Spanish settlers in South America saw in this event an opportunity to sever ties with Spain. Simon Bolivar in fact visited London in 1810 seeking British support. This was also true for Burma or as it is now known, Myanmar, which used the Japanese invasion to gain its independence from Britain after the war. The Indonesians led by Sukarno, also used the Japanese invasion to free themselves from the Dutch; and even the Kurds gained more freedoms for themselves when the United States invaded Iraq in 2003.[A/B]

When one reflects on it, it was natural that the Croatians used this German invasion as a way of freeing themselves from the oppression they had lived through during the previous twenty-three years. This was also true of the Slovaks, Lithuanians, the people of Finland, Latvians, Estonians, the Ukrainians, the Crimea Tartars, the peoples of the Caucasus as well as the Macedonians who allied themselves with Germany as a way of telling the world that they wanted their freedom and would take any opportunity to achieve it. In time of oppression people turn to those who are able to help, whoever they may be.

With the spontaneous rejoicing of the Croatian people, and a sense of unity never seen before, Colonel Slavko Kvaternik proclaimed Croatia's independence over Zagreb radio on the afternoon of 10 April 1941.[1/C]

---

1. Aleksa Benigar, '*Stepinac*', 332–333. Ante Pavelić, *Putem Hrvatskom Drzavnom Prava*, 59–61. Mario Jareb, *U-dp*, 576–580.

The German government was not favourably inclined towards the Ustasha and Pavelich's close ties with Mussolini. It also did not consider Pavelich had the same support among the people as Dr Machek, who was the head of the Croatian Peasant Party and also Deputy President of Yugoslavia. Although the German government favoured Dr Machek to head the new Croatian state, Machek refused, because he did not believe in the ultimate victory of the Axis. Furthermore, although he firmly supported the establishment of the independent state, accepting the position would have compromised his position. As a result, the functioning of the Croatian Peasant Party was frozen at a time that most demanded and needed its political activity and leadership.[2/D]

Germany and Italy were therefore confronted by a favourable and unforeseen event. Knowing the desire of Croatians for independence, they used the situation to their advantage.

On the same day as Croatia's burgeoning independence, the first German motorised units appeared in Zagreb. The village and civil defence disarmed the Yugoslav Army, which handed in its weapons without resistance. Slavko Kvaternik, through the German High Command in Zagreb, requested the Independent State of Croatia be recognised.

Berlin requested notification about the new head of state, given Kvaternik had declined. He assured the German Government that Dr Pavelich, as Head of State, would not be dependent on Italy for its foreign policy. Pacified, Hitler then decided to recognise the new state with Pavelich as its head.[3]

Pavelich arrived in Zagreb on the evening of April 14, and the next day he spoke over Zagreb radio informing the people that he was heading the new state. The Communists regarded him as a traitor; this is a not uncommon portrayal of patriotic leaders. This could also be said of Simon Bolivar in South America, Eamon de Valera in Ireland, Mahatma Gandhi in India and Sukarno in Indonesia.

---

1. Ivo Omrčanin, 'DaPHoC', 176–177 Franjo Dujmović, HnpkO, 113-114. Ivo Omrčanin. *Hrvatska 1941*, 292–293.
2. Vlatko Maček, *Memoari*, 158.
3. Aleksa Benigar. *Stepinac*, 333–334.

On Wednesday April 16, the new Croatian Government was sworn in with Dr Pavelich heading the Presidency and Ministry of Foreign Affairs.[4]

The Independent State of Croatia was recognised by Slovakia, Hungary, Bulgaria, Romania, Spain, Denmark, Finland and Japan, and later also by Thailand, Burma and Vichy France. Although Switzerland did not recognise the state, it maintained its consul in Zagreb and signed a number of trade agreements with Croatia. Argentina maintained its consulate in Zagreb until 1943.

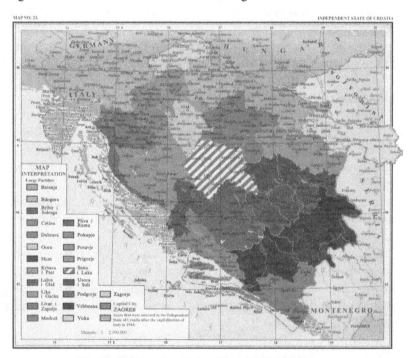

The Independent State of Croatia 1941-1945
(From Dr Stjepan Srkulj & Dr Josip Lučić *Croatian History in Twenty Five Maps.* page 106)

Hitler indicated that politically he was not interested in Croatia, but strategically he was most interested. For this reason he named General Glaise von Hostenau, an Austrian and a Catholic who was ill disposed towards Italy, to assist in the formation of the Croatian Army. This was to enable Germany and Italy to withdraw their forces and concentrate on other theatres of war.

---
4. Aleksa Benigar, Stepinac, 334. Franjo Dujmović, *HnpkO,* 123-124.

Although a vast majority of Croatian people supported the Croatian State, their mood sank greatly when Italy, under Mussolini, demanded for itself almost the whole of the Dalmatian coast with its largely Croatian population. ᴱ In fact, the Dalmatian coast was the most culturally advanced region of Croatia. Glaise von Hostenau strongly criticised Italy's demands. However, Hitler directed Siegfried Kasche, the German Ambassador to Croatia, to maintain good relations with the Italians, because where the Croatian question was concerned, Germany would have only an insignificant role to play.[5]

The government of the newly independent Croatia tried to correct much of the mismanagement of the previous twenty years. In the first two months it poured huge amounts of money into public works such as the dredging of swamps, the regulating of rivers and the building of public housing. All sections of the community threw themselves into national reconstruction.

The government also adopted measures to improve public morality. On Mothers' Day 1941, the Minister of Culture, Dr Mile Budak, spoke over the radio as to the importance of maintaining family life, the support of large families and the importance of removing bad language from ordinary everyday conversation. Pornography, which had been common in newspapers during the previous regime, was abolished. It forbade the display of indecent pictures and statues in shop windows, it stipulated that shops selling alcohol were to close at 9:00 pm and there was to be no gambling on premises where alcohol was sold. A law passed on December 4 made begging, loitering and sexual soliciting illegal. Strict laws prohibiting abortion were introduced, and swearing, foul language and fortune telling were also made illegal.[6]

Measures were also taken to ensure employment and job security. Education was arranged to prepare the young for the work force and to integrate them into society.

Out of respect for Sundays and religious feast days, government officials in various counties were asked not to hold meetings or other functions on those days.

The government began work on the publication of a Croatian encyclopaedia, and it also allowed the establishment of religious

---

5. Aleksa Benigar, Stepinac, 334–336. Franjo Dujmović, *HnpKO*, 126.
6. Aleksa Benigar, *Stepinac*, 336–337. Stella Alexander, *The Triple Myth*, 68–67.

schools. A mosque was opened in Zagreb and a Franciscan faculty of theology was established in Sarajevo.[7]

On 25 February 1942, the Minister of Justice, Dr Mirko Puk, announced: 'That the Croatian state at this time recognises three faiths in the Croatian people, that is, the Catholic faith of both Western and Eastern rites, the Muslim faith and the Protestant faith of the Augsburg and Helvelci confessions.' On 23 July 1942, a law was promulgated respecting the holy days of Catholics, Orthodox, Protestant and Muslim believers.[8]

Nikola Rushinovich (Rušinović), who was born in the United States but grew up in Croatia and graduated there as a medical doctor, relates a conversation he had with his father-in-law Marko Kozul two days after the proclamation of Croatian independence. When the two were alone together, Kozul said to him:

> My dear Nikola, all this is beautiful. Croatians always had as their aim a free and sovereign state. That was also my dream from the earliest days. I am rejoicing with everyone today over the Independent State of Croatia. But my joy isn't complete. I am afraid for the future of our country. Firstly you know well that the Germans didn't want it. They accepted it at the last moment as the lesser of two evils. They aren't really our allies . . . . and the Italians? They always had an appetite for Dalmatia. Italy is in a difficult position. She is losing on all fronts. If she wasn't helped by Hitler she would be in a bigger mess. Mussolini was given an opportunity to show his hungry and discontented people some sort of victory and he is able to do this by joining Dalmatia to Italy. How our own people will react to that, especially the Dalmatians, it's easy to imagine. It will be determined by the Dalmatian Serbs who would prefer to go with the devil than to be under us Croats. Ante Pavelić will need to be as wise as Solomon to overcome the difficulties which he will soon encounter. That he has good will – and I have no doubts that he is a patriot – is not enough. He won't achieve it with those who followed him outside the country and the small number of people who supported him within the country. As soon as he arrives in Zagreb he will have to ask all parties and eminent political

---

7. Aleksa Benigar, Stepinac, 337–338.
8. Nada Kisić-Kolanović, *Muslimani .i Hrvatski Nacionalizam*, 289.

people to co-operate and extend the hand of friendship to the Croatian Serbs. It would be senseless to blame them for the exploitation and political persecution of Croatians under Belgrade rule in the former Yugoslavia. Peace and order in the country and equality of all citizens before the law are the basic conditions for the development of the state. Oppression and crimes committed through the authority of the previous state on our people must be investigated and those guilty be brought before the courts. There is to be no vengeance or reprisals. Croatia must hold onto the just traditions and practices which were in place with us when we were part of the Austro-Hungarian monarchy. Croatia must be a just state. If this is not the case she will collapse dismally. The war is still going on. No one can tell for certain how it will end. It's true that Germany has shown exceptional military might, she has achieved significant gains, but to achieve victory is still a long road. In the past the Germans achieved great victories and in the end lost the war. I think a similar thing will happen this time. You can freely say this to Pavelić when you find yourself alone with him. He would have to have that always before his eyes. It is going to be sad for the small nations if Germany wins the war. With regards to us being their allies everyone knows that the Croatians did not choose it. It came about through necessity. The Croatians like all peoples under the sun have a right to their national sovereignty. They have fought for it through the centuries and this is known to the world. Not to proclaim national independence at the opportune time means being a traitor to ones self and ones past. It is really incomprehensible that this couldn't be seen by poor Machek. In spite of everything he should have accepted the leadership which the Germans offered him and devoted himself to the destiny of Croatia. For, the way we will be looked on when the war comes to an end will depend on the work and the stand of those who were leading us during this time. We should never lose sight of this.[9]

The Croatian State had difficulties, some of which could be understood in the circumstances of the time, but which Croatia's enemies later greatly exaggerated.

---

9. Dr Nikola Rusinović, *Moje Secanje Na Hrvatsku*, 97–98.

The oath which the members of the Ustasha movement took was appalling and not in keeping with Christian principles. The oath was taken before a table with two candles and a crucifix in the centre, and placed on the table were a pistol and knife.

The law protecting the purity of Aryan blood and the honour of the Croatian people was similar to the Nazi anti Jewish race laws passed in Nuremberg. This law had important consequences, placing Jews and Gypsies outside the law, and was detrimental to Orthodox Serbs.

Directions issued concerning changing ones religion were not in keeping with Christian moral principles and placed church leaders in a very difficult position.

Orthodox church-schools were closed as well as their cultural institutions. These laws enabled persecution of Jews and Serbs, especially in those areas near forests and mountains which allowed a closer association with the Partisans.[10]

Ernest Bauer, an official in the Croatian government at the time, wrote in his memoirs:

> ... I came across one day – it must have been some ten days after the Poglavnik's arrival to Zagreb – a very unpleasant surprise. I discovered a whole heap of placards newly printed which needed to be distributed on the same day. The placards began with the call: 'Serbs and Jews' – and it continued as an instruction that all citizens of Serbian nationality and Jewish faith must leave their present accommodation and move to the southern side of the city and await further instructions ... I wasn't prepared for this, but a special and naïve voice told me even then, that the political developments would not end well if they proceeded along this path ... [11/F]

When the Croatian sculptor Ivan Mestrovich openly asked Pavelich:

> How can Croatia exist without Dalmatia and with one-third of its population which regards itself as Serb being expelled?

---

10. Aleksa Benigar, Stepinac, 338. Stella Alexander, *The Triple Myth*, 69–70. Ante Pavelić, *Putem Hrvatskon Drzavnom Prava*, 180–186.
11. Ernest Bauer, '*Život Je Kratak San*', 91.

Pavelich answered him:

> I am not planning on the expulsion of those so-called Serbs, only of the Serb fifth column. With their help Serbia thought to hold us in eternal submission as one of their colonies. Many of these have lost their lives . . . others become afraid and flee across the Drina. Let them calm themselves down and become loyal citizens. There is no need to force them to become Catholic as some think. As if I care for the Catholic Church. Let them just recognise themselves as Croats and I will receive Orthodoxy. We will create a Croatian Orthodox church and lessen the misunderstanding.[12]

Dr Pavelich exerted enormous pressure on the Serbs in Croatia, even being accused of trying to convert them to Roman Catholicism. In a speech in the Croatian Sabor on 28 February 1942, he stated that it was not true that the Croatian State attempted to convert the Orthodox to the Catholic Church, but it left them to do as they wished.[13]

Much later after the war, while living in relative security in Argentina, Pavelich wrote:

> . . . in the Independent State of Croatia the Orthodox were not persecuted, but our struggle was focused against Serbianism, which under various guises, used every means, employed all force to hinder the development and stability of the Independent State of Croatia.
>
> We were not against Orthodoxy, but only against the Serbian Orthodox Church in Croatia. As I mentioned previously, Orthodox churches were national churches and according to this the Orthodox churches in Croatia could only be the Croatian Orthodox Church.[14]

Leading Croat-Bosnian politician, Dr Nikola Mandich, who later became President, related how in August 1941 he gathered a number of prominent Bosnian Serbs, including Nikola Stojanovich, Kojo Tosich, Vojo Ilich and Jovo Nalich, and with some Croatians and Muslims he proposed they directly approach Pavelich. Mandich left

---

12. Aleksa Benigar, Stepinac, 339. Ivan Mestrović, *UnPLiD,* 322–323.
13. Ivan Musić, *Katolicka Crkva Stepinac .i Pavelic,* 383-384.
14. Ivan Musić, *Katolicka Crkva Stepinac .i Pavelić,* 385.

for Zagreb to inform him of 'the evils committed against the Serbs and Jews' in Sarajevo. He gained the impression 'Pavelich didn't truly listen to him, but stated that panic and fear is necessary and it must be that way'. Mandich '. . . wasn't successful in his attempts and was just dismissed'. Mandich then returned to Sarajevo to further intervene for the persecuted people. During April 1943, while Mandich was staying in Sarajevo, he received up to 1,500 requests for help from 'various sections of the community and almost all were successful'.[15]

In early May 1943, the artist Jozo Kljakovich brought some of the misfortune happening in Croatia to Pavelich's attention. Pavelich answered him:

> You know Professor, we are being blamed for this but it is not our fault. We would not have even touched the Serbs had they not begun with slaughter and revolution. Now the revolution is continuing. . . I heard that you spoke with minister Budak that the Serbs are not to be persecuted, that those who want to be loyal to the Croatian state should be equal with Croatians, and for those who want to propagate their Serbianism, their properties are to be sold and for them to be sent to Serbia. Remember Professor, the Serbs don't want one or the other. Serbs want to destroy the Croatian state. We don't want to be battling with them. We tried all along to establish agreement with the Četniks, but they were never sincere with us. Now they have gone to the Partisans, to communism and through communism they are trying to destroy and annihilate us biologically.[16]

Pavelich went to great lengths to win the support of the Muslim populations of Bosnia and Herzegovina, affirming that they were an integral part of the Croatian State. The leading Bosnian Muslim, Dzafer-beg Kulenovich, became Vice President and his brother, Osman, a minister in the government. The capable Mehmed Alajbegovich became Minister for Underdeveloped Regions and later, Foreign Minister. Of 132 members of the Croatian Sabor, twelve were Muslims. There were Muslims in the diplomatic service and, of the officers in the army, up to sixty-four were of the Muslim faith.[17]

---

15. Nada Kisic-Kolanović, *MiHN*, 48.
16. Jozo Kljaković, *U Suvremenu Kaosu*, 210.
17. Nada Kisić-Kolanović, *Muslimani .i Hrvatski Nacionalizam*, 50–53. *Who Is What In The Independant State Of Croatia*, 4–5, 216–217, 219.

The major Muslim feast days were public holidays. Filip Lukas, the President of the Croatian Cultural Institute, *Matica Hrvatska*, encouraged dialogue between Christians and Muslims to develop mutual understanding: 'Till now, more or less, Catholics and Muslims have lived with one another with mutual respect, but still somehow maintained independence but now the time has come to find their common spiritual principles so that on that spiritual foundation, guarding the specifics of every faith community, we can build a large and many structured national culture.'[18] An important step in this direction was the building of a Mosque in Zagreb, including Ismet Muftich as its Mufti and a well-publicised opening in August 1944.[19 / H]

When Pavelich became Head of State, he mainly surrounded himself with men who had been with him in exile. Most of the former Croat politicians who had remained within Yugoslavia didn't recognise him and Dr Machek, the leader of the Croatian Peasant Party was, for a while, imprisoned and then placed under house arrest. Following the German invasion, Pavelich disbanded the Village Defence units; these played a big part in disarming the Royal Yugoslav Army and enabled a peaceful transition of government.[I] He also imprisoned the sculptor Ivan Mestrovich, the artist Jozo Kljakovich and others who did not agree with him. When Pavelich arrived in Croatia and Kvaternik explained to him that all assisting roles in government were arranged, Pavelich informed him all Croatian organisations would be absorbed into the Ustasha movement.[20 J]

In the difficult circumstances in which the new State found itself, Dr Pavelich thought that he alone was able to lead, pushing aside anyone who threatened or challenged his authority. He soon abolished the Ministry of Justice and when Minister Dr Milovan Zanich approached him concerning certain matters of law, Pavelich said to him: 'How am I able to govern when you will tie my hands with these laws?'[21]

The same fate awaited the Croatian Sabor (Parliament) which opened on 23 February 1942. When a number of its members criticised Pavelich about the state to which the country had

---

18. Nada Kisić-Kolanović, *Muslimani .i Hrvatski Nacionalizam*, 290.
19. Nada Kisić-Kolanović, *Muslimani .i Hrvatski Nacionalizam*, 291–292.
20. Aleksa Benigar, *Stepinac*, 339–340. Ivo Omrčanin, *Hrvatska, 1942.* 83.
21. Aleksa Benigar, *Stepinac*, 339– 340. Franjo Dujmović, *HnpkO*, 126.

degenerated, the President of the Sabor prepared a memorandum. Pavelich was also questioned as to why Dr Machek was under house arrest, and Pavelich's response was to dissolve the *Sabor* on another pretext. In the cauldron of war and with the general instability in the country, Pavelich thought it best that he Rely on himself rather than seek counsel from the Sabor. In essence, he did all he could to consolidate power into his own hands.[22/]

Pavelich firmly believed in the rights of the Croatian people for an independent state. Pavelich sent Dr Nikola Rusinovich to Rome to negotiate recognition for Croatia from the Holy See, and when Rusinovich returned, he informed Pavelich of the rumoured arrest of Archbishop Stepinac. Rusinovich advised that the Holy See would look dimly upon this act by Pavelich, and the West would be equally critical. Pavelich replied:

> How could that news reach Rome? What the Archbishop gives out to the Germans in his sermons is known by the swallows on the roof tops. They are furious with him and because of this I have difficulties. When he speaks of ungodly ideologies it's easy to work out at whom he is aiming. For him ungodly ideolog ies are of the same perniciousness, whether it's called Nazism or Communism. And even if there is truth in this, there is a clear difference in the stand of the Germans towards the Croatians to those from Moscow. Berlin recognised the Independent State of Croatia and now the Germans are our allies. Moscow supports Yugoslavia. The Archbishop just can't accept our alliance with Germany. If the Americans and the English can co-operate with Stalin and his Bolsheviks, why is there resentment at our co-operation with Hitler? Just as Roosevelt and Churchill aren't Communists, so we aren't Nazis. We went with the might of the Axis so that we could achieve our statehood and now our aim is to preserve it.[23]

Did Pavelich have a point?

Unfortunately Pavelich's tendency to become more isolated and suspicious had fateful consequences for Croatia and its people.

---

22. Aleksa Benigar, *Stepinac*, 340.
23. Dr Nikola Rusinović, '*Moje Sjecanje Na Hrvatsku*', 122.

In May 1941 the Serbs had already begun to organise themselves into the Chetnik movement under Draze Mihaljovich. The movement was centred in the Serbian region of Ravna Gora and soon controlled the whole of Montenegro. From there, they conducted a guerrilla war, attacking Croatian regions, especially in Herzegovina, expelling and slaughtering Croats and Muslims.

According to the respected Croatian historian Krunoslav Draganovich: In the four eastern Bosnian districts of Foca, Rogatica, Visegrad and Cajnice the Chetniks of General Draze Mihajlovich alone slaughtered 29,000 Muslims in the winter of 1941-1942, about one third of the population in these districts.[24]

The Croatians ruthlessly returned this cruelty, believing they could frighten the Serb population. This ruthlessness was countered by the Catholic Church, headed by Archbishop Stepinac, who interceded on many occasions on behalf of the Orthodox Serbs. For example, on 13 May 1941, he heard of the killing of some Orthodox Serbs in the vicinity of Glina and immediately wrote to Pavelich:

> I have just received news that the Ustasha shot without trial or investigation 260 Serbs. I know that the Serbs have committed great crimes in our homeland during the twenty years of their rule. But I think it is my duty as Bishop to raise my voice and say that according to Catholic morals this isn't allowed, and I ask you to take emergency measures in the whole Independent State of Croatia that no Serb be killed if it can't be proved that he was at fault for something deserving death. Otherwise we can't count on blessings from heaven, without which all will collapse. I hope you will not resent these frank words. With sincere respect. Stepinac, Archbishop. Zagreb 14 V 1941.[25]

Nikola Rusinovich, whom Pavelich sent to Herzegovina to settle the situation there, relates how the Ustasha Army, led by Colonel Ivo Herenchich, inflicted vengeance on the local Serb population without any trial or adherence to the rule of law.[26] Rusinovich also related cases where wounded Partisan guerrillas were given equal medical care in hospital together with the Ustasha and Domobrani soldiers.[27]

---

24. Prof Antun F Bonifačić & Prof Clement S Mihanović, *The Croatian Nation*. Rev Prof Krunoslav Draganović, 295.
25. Aleksa Benigar Stepinac, 373. Jure Kristo, *SS*, 134–135.
26. Dr Nikola Rusinović, '*Moje Sjecanje Na Hrvatsku*', 155.
27. Dr Nikola Rusinović, '*Moje Sjecanje Na Hrvatsku*', 100.

Archbishops Stepinac's reply in his trial in Zagreb on 6 October 1946.
'The Croatian people unanimously declared themselves in favour of the Croatian state and it would have been remiss of me to ignore the desire of the Croatian people who were enslaved by the former Yugoslavia.'

Orthodox Churches were burnt or destroyed during the establishment of the Independent State of Croatia. The Catholic bishops, in their session in November 1941, demanded of Pavelich that such vandalism cease.[28]

In May 1942, news spread that the Orthodox would be expelled from the Kordun region. Stepinac, unable to prevent their expulsion, wrote to Pavelich:

> The news has spread amongst the population of the expulsion of the population from Kordun, without regard to whether they converted to Catholicism or not. Some very good people have asked me to intercede with you regarding this to ensure that at least the handling of children will be humane, for the children are not at fault for being alive. I hope that you will do all to ensure that the law of God is not transgressed and that the children will be fully protected.[29]

---

28. Aleksa Benigar, *Stepinac*, 377.
29. Aleksa Benigar, *Stepinac*, 374.

It was Stepinac's opinion that Pavelich was behind the persecution of the Serbs, for when he was under house arrest after the war in his native village of Krasich, he said to Josip Vranekovich, the priest he was living with: ' . . . It seems to me that the persecution of the Serbs was the action of Pavelich. When I accused him of this he simply answered me that his conscience was clear before history.'[30]/K/L

All through the war, the great Croatian youth worker of the late 1920s and 30s, Ivo Protulipac, would often say to close friends: 'No people shed foreign blood that they didn't pay in blood. And we will pay with blood. Blood provokes blood; this blood will fall on us. There must be justice, the courts must function and not slaughter without law . . . all this will take its vengeance on us.'

Towards the end of the war, when he was in Southern Austria and aware of the approaching tragedy of Bleiburg, Protulipac said to a friend: 'what we sowed, that's what we are now reaping.'[31]/M

Many Serbs fled into the forest and joined the Partisans or the Chetniks and avenged themselves on the Croatian population wherever they were able to do so.

A bitter war broke out in Croatia. German, Italian, Hungarian, Croatian, Serbian Chetnik and Tito's Partisan armies clashed. The war was virulent, and it divided many families whose members were either Ustasha or Partisans. [N]

The Croatian Army was divided into the Domobrani, who were conscripts in a regular army, and the Ustasha, whose volunteers and elite units were given better clothing, equipment and food. The Ustasha had their own command and their strategy was mainly in guerrilla form. The Domobrani were under German command and among them were officers who had belonged to the previous Yugoslav Army and were lukewarm in their support of the new state. On occasions they would deliver entire units to the Partisans so that the ordinary soldier was unaware of what was happening.[32]

In a refugee camp in Italy after the war, Vinko Nikolich was told by a friend and fellow refugee: 'We had excellent soldiers, both Ustasha and Domobrani, they were equal. Our problem was the officers, they committed all the evil. Through deceit they led many units to the Partisans. Our whole collapse is a result of betrayal. Just betrayal.'[33]

---

30. Josip Vraneković, *Dnevnik* (Diary), 236.
31. Vinko Nikolić, *Tragedija Se Dogodila u.Svibnju*, Volume 2, 297–298.
32. Aleksa Benigar, *Stepinac*, 340–341.
33. Vinko Nikolić, *Tragedija Se Dogodila u Svibnu*, Volume 1, 354.

Betrayal and discord bred further atrocities. The Germans, with their SS troops and the Werhmacht, would swiftly capture and shoot hostages in reprisal whenever a German soldier was killed. The Italians had their Fascist and Regular Army and would often collaborate with the Serbian Chetniks. The Chetniks were regarded by the exiled Royal Yugoslav leadership in London as their army, and were therefore supported by the British.

The German Ambassador to Croatia, Siegfried Kasche, informed Ribbentrop that the Italians were arming the Serb forces and protecting them. Hitler remained firm in the dispute between the Italians and the Croats, maintaining favouritism must be shown to the Italians. The Italians began giving the Chetniks food, clothing and equipment and the Chetniks in turn took massive vengeance on the Croat and Muslim population.[34/O]

The Communist Partisan forces under the leadership of Tito, began conducting a guerrilla campaign against the Croatian State. [P] Tito's guerrilla forces worked to destroy the newly established state, portraying themselves to the people as the 'Yugoslav Movement of national liberation against the occupier'. They were careful to appear as a truly democratic, peace- inspired movement which would respect the national, religious and cultural heritage of the various peoples of Yugoslavia.[35]

Tito's guerrillas eventually found support from the British and slowly the Serbian Chetniks were attracted to the movement. Tito met Draze Mihaljovich on 19 September and 25 October 1942. They came to a verbal agreement for co-operation, although Tito's methods and aims were substantially different. Tito came to Mihaljovich's Command Centre disguised as a Russian Officer and Mihaljovich, believing him to be a Russian colonel, showed him the operation plan for how the Croats were to be exterminated. Tito had very different plans.[36]

The German High Command in Belgrade knew of this contact between the Partisans and Chetniks and, fearing a general uprising, issued a strong command that any contact with the Partisans was to

---

34. Aleksa Benigar, *Stepinac*, 341. Ivo Omrčanin, *Hrvatska 1941*, 420–423.
35. Aleksa Benigar, *Stepinac*, 341. Josip Jurčević, *BJpznH*, 89–90.
36. Aleksa Benigar, *Stepinac*, 342. Josip Vraneković, *Dnevnik* (Diary), 63, 612–613. Nora Beloff, in *TFLYatW, 1939-84*. 69, 71. Has Tito meeting Draze Mihaljević on 17 September 1941 & 19 October 1941.

cease. The Italian Army continued to collaborate with the Chetniks and co-operate with the Communist Partisans, whose numbers were depleted down to 18,000 fighters. The Germans almost captured Tito but he managed to escape.[37 Q/R]

All this was inflicted on the small Croatian state. Military operations took place according to the interest of the various warring factions. The people would frequently experience a change of masters, even in the one day, and did not know to whom to give their allegiance. Every unit that came to a district had its own agenda, aiming to defeat its enemies and impose its rule. The population was in turmoil and reduced to poverty. The regions of Bosnia, Lika, Herzegovina and Dalmatia were cauldrons of fire, and the populations fled to the cities and towns to save their lives.

With Italy's surrender on 8 September 1943, the Partisans obtained much- needed weapons. At Teheran in November 1943, the big three (Britain, USA and Russia) accepted Tito as an ally and on 22 November 1943, Tito officially declared the People's Republic of Yugoslavia under the control of the Communist party.[38 S]

The Croatian people found themselves in these murky and difficult circumstances at a time when they had hoped to live in a free and independent state. Many Croatian politicians hoped that Croatia would be a haven of peace in the midst of war, similar to Denmark, but it was not to be.[39]

Although the Vatican did not recognise the Independent State of Croatia, in order to provide moral support to the Catholic bishops and people, the Holy See sent two representatives to the Catholic Bishops of Croatia. One was its Papal Delegate, Giuseppe Marcone, Abbott of the Benedictine monastery of Montevergine near Avellino, who at one time was lecturer in the history of philosophy at the Anselmianum University in Rome. His secretary was Don Giuseppe Masucci from the same monastery who spent a year studying in England and spoke fluent English. These papal delegates found themselves in a Croatia that had begun with so much hope, but was being transformed into a battle field and a blood bath. They began their work by making

---

37. Aleksa Benigar, *Stepinac*, 342.
38. Aleksa Benigar, *Stepinac*, 342. Ante Beljo, *'Genocide'*, 80. *Who Is What In The Independent State Of Croatia*, 50.
39. John Prcela & Stanko Guldescu, *'Operation Slaughterhouse'* Slavko Kvaternik, 541.

immediate contact with high officials of government, while also continuing their charitable and spiritual work.

Don Masucci, who learnt to speak Croatian, was often very open and blunt with Croat officials.

The police chief, Dido Kvaternik, who was ruthless at times, asked Don Masucci: 'If you have come as a friend I ask you to tell me everything that you have heard about me – what you know of me'.

Don Masucci openly told him the evils that he was accused of, adding:

> ... And is it possible that you can live in peace after so many terrible, evil things have been done, things which you have on your conscience which cry out to Heaven? They have a name for you also in Italy, which is clearly regretful for they received you with open arms like other refugees; they call you bloodthirsty; if everything that is said of you is true, then if you haven't surpassed certainly you are completely equal with that monster Nero.

At which Kvaternik said to him:

> Before everything else I must tell you sincerely, that you are, as I imagined you to be, when for the first time I had the opportunity to listen to you at an Italian civic occasion: without hesitation and fear you have told me everything that they are accusing me of. I am grateful to you for this reminder. I must tell you that I will greatly value your true friendship. Some of the things that they accuse me of are true but others are exaggerated.

Kvaternik admitted that some Ustasha had committed atrocities and for this reason they were shot. He then proceeded to speak negatively of the Jews, despite his own mother's Jewish background.[40]

By the end of 1943 it was obvious that Germany was losing the war and a number of Croatian politicians were attempting to save the State by pressuring the Croatian leadership to switch allegiance to the allied side. This attempt was spearheaded by the Croatian Foreign Minister, Mladen Lorkovich, and the Minister of the Army, Ante

---

40. Giuseppe Masucci, *Misija U Hrvatskoj*, 52–53. Ivo Omrčanin, *Hrvatska 1941*, 420–423. Also *Who Is What In The Independant State of Croatia*, 254–255, 258–259.

Vokich. Pavelich blocked their efforts by having them arrested and eventually shot, together with forty of their co-conspirators.

From this moment onwards, Pavelich had absolute control over Croatian affairs.[41] There were cases of high German military officers suggesting to Croatian officials that Croatia was to switch sides so that the state could be saved.[42] As a result of the failure of the Lorkovich-Vokich coup, which Pavelich knew about and apparently initially supported, the Independent State of Croatia remained the last European ally of Germany. T

By November 1944 Tito's government was well established in Belgrade, controlling the whole of Serbia and Macedonia. Tito led the Partisan forces with the intention to establish control over the whole of pre-World War II Yugoslavia and set up a Communist Government.[43]

As the war was coming to an end, Don Masucci was very blunt with Pavelich. In March 1945, during a meal attended by church dignitaries, among them Abbot Marcone and Guisseppe Masucci, Pavelich called out to Masucci:

'Don Guiseppe, will you do something for me and be of good humour, for like all the others you are always angry with me and protesting.

'How can it be any different,' answered Masucci, 'when you, as the man who is most responsible, lead me to be angry and protest?'[44]

Don Masucci's diaries written during his mission to Croatia are evidence of his high regard for the Croatian people. Deeply touched by their nobility and religious devotion, he attempted to objectively judge the facts and circumstances. His diary also shows that the Croatian authorities took notice of his interventions on behalf of those who were held in suspicion by the State.[45]

In April 1945 the scene in Zagreb was one of desperation, with refugees flooding into the city from all parts of Croatia. Vinko Nikolich, who was living in Zagreb at the time, wrote about these refugees in his diary:

---

41. Josip Jurčević, 'Bleiburg', 65–67. AnteBeljo *Genocid,* 82–85. Ivo Omrčanin, *Hrvatska 1944,* 349–358, 378–392.
42. Ivan Stir colonel, *IrioubzHD,* 36–37.
43. Milan Basta, *Rat Je Završijo Sedan Dana Kasnije,* 508.
44. Giuseppe Masucci, *Misija U Hrvatsko,* 192.
45. Aleksa Benigar, *Stepinac,* 347.

> ... many of whom had left their homes even before the Partisans arrived ...... This appearance of the refugees ... in the month of April reached a level of flood proportions. A real picture of confusion existed ... Now frantic masses were pouring into Zagreb, filling all the streets and squares ... and our capital city in those terrible days was trebled, possibly even more so ... Many of these refugees found lodging on their carts ... always ready to move on.[46]

Nikolich further reflected on the sad mood around the celebrations of the fourth anniversary of the state:

> No, it's announced, it has to be admitted, there is no doubt. More pain. Bleeding pain. We were aware, but our awareness wasn't enough; our will, our strength isn't enough. Our readiness even to die. There is a power external to us which will decide the destiny of our freedom. We wanted our state; we showed the ability to have it, the strength to maintain it, to defend it and feed it, but even that was not enough. In a time when in the name of justice injustice is woven, in which a lack of principles is proclaimed in the name of principle, and one way is spoken but another way is acted our state could not survive.
>
> For this reason our celebration of the fourth anniversary was and will be sombre. Dignified, but we can say also sad. We gathered around the State like relatives gathered around the bed of one who is dying, whose life they love, patiently standing around him to see whether he will overcome the last crisis. Will the heart hold out, or possibly the thread of another life be broken? And how many celebrations were being conducted loudly through the last few days, especially amongst the young; it seemed to be the screams of the desperate with their echoing call for salvation that the nation could be saved. One people suspended between life and death, dying in their wounds and praying for mercy. Save us! The Croatian youth were afraid for the inheritance they had received from their forefathers and looked at the homeless, who like slaves are longing for scraps of bread and freedom. For this reason a whole people, united in love for the State and

---

46. Vinko Nikolic, *Tragedija se Dogodila. u Svibnju*, Volume 1, 29–30.

the national leader, fused in pain and suffering, expressed its national will for freedom. But who listens to a small nation? Who pays attention to an ant which in the middle of a road carries its little bit to the ant heap? It remains on the road, like a small nation, trampled. Where is justice for the ant so that it can exist next to a big man? Nature celebrates her glory and the power of the Creator who created all, the large and the small. For this reason that celebration was very subdued.[47]

On 30 April 1945, at its last sitting, the government of the Independent State of Croatia discussed the matter of the future direction of the State. It decided that the Croatian Army was to withdraw from Croatia through Slovenia into Austria, where it would surrender to the British army. All were hoping that the British would respect the international protections of the Geneva Convention and The Hague for prisoners of war. All members were in agreement that under no condition would they surrender to the Russians or Tito's Partisans.

The Croatian Government decided to send a memorandum to the Allied Supreme Command for the Mediterranean, based in the Italian city of Caserta. The memorandum was signed by the president Dr Nikola Mandich and eighteen ministers of his government. It was carried by Vjekoslav Vranchich, a minister of government, and Andrija Vrkljan, a naval captain who spoke fluent English. They left Zagreb by plane on 5 May, landing at Klagenfurt, southern Austria, then proceeded by car to Caserta, the headquarters of the British VIII Army. Their mission failed as they approached Venice[48] and they were interned by the British on 8 May.ᵘ

To prepare the Allies for the coming memorandum, on 4 May the Croatian government had sent two captured American aviators in a plane to notify the allied command of the impending arrival of the memorandum. Nothing came from all this, because on 5 May, Harold MacMillan sent a telegram to the British Ambassador in Belgrade, Ralph Stevenson, to inform Tito: ' . . . of the arrival of the Ustashaplane and the message of the government of the Independent

---

47. Vinko Nikolić, *Tragedija se Dogodila u Svibnju*, Volume 1, 23.
48. Franjo Dujmović, *Hrvatska na putu k Oslobodjenju*, 169–173. John Prcela, MA and Stanko Guldescu, PhD, *Operation Slaughterhouse*, 64–65. Nikolai Tolstoy, *The Minister and the Massacres*, 162, 384.

State of Croatia instructing Stevenson to inform Tito there would be no discussion with these parliamentarians.'[49] [V]

On 6 May, Pavelich informed the army's supreme command of the Croatian government's decision. All generals present accepted the news with great difficulty, but calmly and with resignation, knowing it would be the end of their professional life in the army. Their main concern was saving the lives of 200,000 soldiers.

The only general who objected was Luburich, who asked, 'What if the English do not receive us as prisoners of war but hand us over to the partisans?' According to Luburich, Pavelich answered: 'Then the English are responsible.'[50]

According to Colonel Ivan Stir, the fighting spirit of the Croatian Army was very high. He wrote:

> Amongst the old fighters the spirit of resolve to continue the fighting was equally firm. We were ready to burn the 'Ustasha regime' and our medals and insignia which were so highly valued, so that the state might be saved. We were prepared to fight for her whatever Croatian government was hers. We were all awaiting a change in the government as the last attempt to save the state, but it didn't come to this. There was similar thinking among the latest Croatian Partisans, who at our withdrawal from Slavonia, surrendered to us and joined us.[51]

A few days before the Croatian Army was ordered to withdraw north to Austria, Pavelich invited Archbishop Stepinac to be the head of the authority who would hand Zagreb to the Partisan authorities. Stepinac rejected the invitation: 'To whom you hand over authority is a matter for your concern. I am not mixing in politics, but am remaining here no matter what happens.'

> Pavelich then gave the authority of the city to Dr Djuro Kumichich.[52]

---

49. Martina Grahek Ravančić, *Bleiburg .i Krizni Put 1945*, 47–48. Vjekoslav Vrančić, *BZPA*, 48–55. Vjekoslav Vrančić, *Branili Smo Drzavu*, Volume 2, 448–452.
50. John Prcela & Stanko Guldescu, '*Operation Slaughterhouse*,' 54–58.
51. Ivan Stir colonel. '*IrioubzHD*', 31.
52. A Benigar. *Stepinac*, 455. Masucci Giuseppe, *Misija U. Hrvatskoj*, 198–199.

As the Croatian Army was withdrawing from Zagreb, Archbishop Stepinac and Dr Giuseppi Masucci, the Secretary to the Papal representative, convinced the Germans, and later with great difficulty General Luburich, to withdraw peacefully from Zagreb.[53]

The order for the Croatian Army to withdraw from Croatia was issued on Sunday 6 May, and the army began moving northwards accompanied by the Croatian government and thousands of civilians. Although it is uncertain, Pavelich seems to have left Zagreb in the early morning of 7 May, while the last units of the Croatian Army, with civilians, had left by the morning of 8 May.[54]

Josip Jurkovich explained the decision of the Independent State of Croatia to withdraw in the following way:

> The political leadership of the Independent State of Croatia . . . at its meeting on the 1st of May discussed the possibility of the withdrawal of the Croatian armed forces and the Croatian population . . . towards Istria and further into north Italy. This plan was rejected due to the aggressive progress of the Yugoslav fourth army . . . The government of the Independent State of Croatia at its night sitting of 3rd – 4th May decided to send a memorandum to the Western Allies with the request that the Allied Forces enter Croatia . . . The government of the Independent State of Croatia with Pavelich present came to the decision to withdraw the Croatian armed forces and Croatian population towards Slovenia and further into southern Austria. They thought that there they would be received by the western allies and that . . . the leadership of the Independent State of Croatia and the fleeing population would soon be able to return to their homeland as allies of the Western Alliance (against Communism) and as liberators of Croatia from Yugo-communism.[55]

General Fedor Dragoljov wrote after the war:

> The basic situation which existed was the Croatian army, under the presidency of the Poglavnik, decided on 5 May to withdraw towards the west, when the head of state left on the

---

53. Giuseppe Masucci. 'Misija u. Hrvatskoj', 197–198..
54. Josip Jurčević, Bleiburg, 319. Josip Jurčević, TBBoCiC, 60. Martina Grahek Ravancic, BiKP 1945, 37–53. Franjo Dujmović, HnpkO, 434–436.
55. Josip Jurčević, Bleiburg, 215. Josip Jurčević, TBBoCiC, 46–47.

afternoon of 7 May. This decision was made as it wasn't seen as worthwhile 'shedding the last drop of blood' and in this manner place the people in a more difficult position. This plan was decided on in order to save the lives of the young Croatian Army of two hundred thousand fighters, who saw in the Independent State of Croatia their ideals.[56]

Jurcevich continued:

> On 8 May the main Ustasha command at its meeting at Rogaskoj Slatini decided that all formations of the Croatian armed forces were to withdraw, at the discretion of their commanders, towards Slovenia and from there to southern Austria. They were to surrender only to allied units.[57]

> Ivo Rojnica, who was in Zagreb at that time with his wife and two small children, relates meeting Dr Milovan Zanich, who was preparing to leave with his family. Dr Zanich told him with tears in his eyes: Just hurry otherwise it will be too late. We couldn't have expected anything better with such a leadership and head of state.' Weeping they said goodbye to one another.[58]

The tragedy of May 1945 was described by Vinko Nikolich as:

> Worse than Dante's Hell...such a catastrophe for the Croatian people in such a way as to destroy and humiliate the Croatian army – undefeated in war – it's something which the exuberant writer can't conjure up ... It seems to me that in the Croatian language there aren't enough suitable words. Everything that till now had been expressed like this was just a pale picture of one ghastly reality.[59]

Ivo Rojnica described it as:

> A terrible scene. It is known that in such a tragedy there can't be any order, but it was seen here as a general movement without head or tail. Automobiles, trucks, village carts, elderly women

---

56. Martina Grahek Ravančić, *Bleiburg .i Krizni Put 1945*, 50.
57. Josip Jurčević, *Bleiburg*, 217.
58. Ivo Rojnica, *Susreti .i Doživljai*, Volume 1, 231.
59. Vinko Nikolić, *TsDuS*, Volume 1, 76.

and men, women, children, the wounded, soldiers, everyone is carrying their essentials and going forward without word. Exhausted through hunger, thirst, sleeplessness, with pain in their hearts for they were leaving what was theirs or their fathers' home, their most dearest, they are all patiently bearing it and asking: where to?[60]

Pavelich and the leadership of the Independent State of Croatia fled, many of them seeking refuge in Argentina. As the communist forces of Marshall Tito began taking control of more territory which had been under Croatian Military control, it took vengeance on the Croatian population, destroying homes and killing the civil population and the clergy. In those difficult times, the only source of comfort and consolation for many people was their religious faith. The Catholic Church was the only institution which was not under the control of the Communist party and, due to the high moral quality of its leadership, particularly Archbishop Stepinac, the Church was a source of spiritual nourishment and a beacon of hope in those dark days.[61] W

Vinko Nikolich wrote in his diary, as he headed north, seeing the Croatian peasants in their fields as if they were saying:

> We are staying! And whoever comes, they are only passing through. We are slaves and masters of this earth. We are its guardians ... The government and parties change, we remain. We will remain even now. You, unfortunate ones, must go to a foreign country. May it be for your comfort that we remain, we the only true masters of Croatia. We will look after her.[62]

The Partisans began to enter Zagreb in the early afternoon of 8 May 1945. Awaiting them in front of the Bishop's residence was Dr Djuro Kumichich and the Secretary to the Papal Delegate, Don Giuseppe Masucci. From a distance sirens could be heard as well as the blowing of car horns.

Don Masucci wrote in his diary: 'Kumichich became completely white as if dead when I asked him how he felt. He threw himself on his knees, wept bitterly and I barely heard him say, "I want to confess and

---

60. Ivo Rojnica, *Susreti .i Doživlaji*, Volume 1, 233.
61. Vinko Nikolić, *BTHN*, 195–196.
62. Vinko Nikolic, *TsDuS*, Volume 1, 76.

receive absolution for the last time because when these gentlemen see me they will skin me alive.'"

Don Masucci blessed and comforted him saying: The devil isn't as black as they paint him.

Two commissars arrived in an army vehicle at exactly 1:30 pm Don Masucci approached them saying that, as they could observe, it was as quiet as a cemetery. Not one shot could be heard, no dogs barked, the windows and balconies were all shut and empty. Don Masucci asked them to be big hearted towards those who surrendered, and he introduced Dr Kumichich, who by this time was composed. The two commissars embraced Dr Kumichich as if they were brothers, and both were kind towards Dr Kumichich and Don Masucci.[63]

After entering Zagreb during the afternoon of 8 May, Alexander Rankovich, one of Tito's deputies, replaced the Chief of the OZNA, the Partisan security service for Zagreb two days after the end of the war because so few people had been shot. 'Because,' he said, 'you went against our orders. We told you to work quickly and energetically to complete everything in the first few days.'[64]

The fate of the Croatian Army and the fleeing civilians was something that very few could foresee. As the allies made their way from Northern Italy into Austria, the flight before Tito's Partisans was described as follows:

> General Richard McCreedy's Eighth Army had the job of clearing the way to Southern Austria . . . At their head was General Kneightley's V Corps made up of veterans of the western desert, Sicily and Monte Casino. What they discovered on the other side of the mountain chain were not the empty meadows of the Alps but frightened crowds the size of cities which had raced in from Yugoslavia.[65]

Harold MacMillan, who was British Minister for the Mediterranean, based in Rome, flew to Klagenfurt in Austria on Sunday 13 May 1945. He was in the vicinity when the fateful decision was made and he must have played a key part in the decision; he virtually admitted it himself. In his diary he wrote:

---

63. Aleksa Benigar, *Stepinac*, 457–458. Giuseppe Masucci, *Misija u. Hrvatskoj*, 198–199.
64. Josip Jurčević, *The Black Book of Communism in Croatia*, 60.
65. Gregor Dallas, *Poisoned Peace 1945, The War that Never Ended*, 444.

Sunday 13 May flew to Klagenfurt in Austria. Ustasha or Chetniks mostly with wives and children fleeing in panic into the area in front of Tito's advancing troops. Those fleeing included Slovenes and Croats and Serbs who fought Tito, armed and maintained by the Germans, and people who, either because they were Roman Catholics or conservatives in politics or for whatever reason, were out of sympathy with revolutionary communism . . . It was heart-breaking but we could do nothing to mitigate the suffering of these people.[66]

It was a pity Harold MacMillan lacked the courage to reveal the whole truth and his certain involvement in the decision to hand these unarmed soldiers and fleeing civilians to Tito's Partisan army.

One of the reasons that may have prompted the British to hand over the Croatians (although Nikolai Tolstoy doubted this reason), was the dispute between the British and the Yugoslavs regarding the borders between Italy and Tito's Yugoslavia, and between Austria and Yugoslavia. British military experts assessed on 12 May that if Tito refused the demand to withdraw from Austria, a very difficult situation would arise for General Alexander, because he had only one division in Austria at the time. In mid-May 1945, Churchill decided to firmly block Yugoslav demands regarding its border with Italy and Austria. This was exacerbated by Tito sending new proposals to leave Yugoslav formations in British occupied zones in Southern Austria. President Truman resolved not to get involved in another war unless Tito's forces attacked. All these considerations possibly influenced the British in their decision, and so handing back the soldiers and civilians was a way of placating the Tito regime.[67]

The Croatian Army surrendered to the British on 15 May, in the southern Austrian town of Bleiburg. Fleeing north through Slovenia, the Croatian population and army were under the illusion that the British would protect them and keep to the Geneva conventions.

Daniel Crljen, who was a radio journalist in Croatia during the war and who had the rank of a colonel, arrived at the Bleiburg field on 14 May and wrote:

---

66. Harold MacMillan, *Tides of Fortune*, 18.
67. Nikolai Tolstoy, *The Minister and the Massacres*, 162.

The night was approaching; we descended through the clearing into the valley, which spread out before us. The head of our column reached some English units. We all stopped, awaiting instructions. General Herenchich with some other officers hurried ahead to come in contact with some English. The column spread out along the fields, trees and any spaces on either side of our road.

I reached the meandering stream which was flowing to our right. In the circle of the generals and high officers there was an unusually high optimism, in fact a feeling of celebration.

General Herenchich announces: 'As soon as we were informed from the advanced units that they had reached the first English units, a message was sent to the English command in the company of our interpreter Lieutenant Deutsch-Maceljski.'

He quickly returned in an English jeep to bring our representatives to the English. Through the decision of our military command, Generals Herenchich and Gregorich went. They were immediately received by the English major and commander of the unit very warmly.

Our generals informed the major that they came to surrender the army to English units and to place the civilian population under their care. The Major answered that he had been informed of our arrival and that we were to cease further progress for behind his units there were partisans. As evening was approaching there could be incidents which under all circumstances he wanted to avoid. On the morrow without any hindrance we would be able to proceed further. We may hold onto our weapons and if we had any wounded we could transport them with our vehicles to Klagenfurt. The stream at the head of our column was seen as the border of our progress, so that no confusion would develop.

Turning to me General Herenchich asked me to go through the column and inform the people of the news so as to lift their spirits. Some were filled with optimism thinking that it was the end of our Calvary. No one suspected that it was the beginning of the most difficult part of our Way of the Cross, the beginning of our crucifixion and death.

The following morning Crljen wrote what happened:

> From the English side there is the arrival of a vehicle. In it is our officer for communication, Deutsch-Maceljeski, who last night during the first meeting remained in the English command. He was serious and in low spirits.
>
> It seems to me that the attitude of the English has changed from last night and it doesn't look good. While yesterday they received me warmly, this morning all is serious and they avoid any conversation with me. This morning some new officers of theirs arrived from Klagenfurt and I met some Partisan officers in the English staff office. I was told that an English general is arriving from Klagenfurt and that he will receive our representatives at 1:00 pm.
>
> At the head of the column everything was alive. General Herenchich called a meeting of all commanders of all units; there were some sixty to seventy officers. Among them was the elderly General Stancer, a supervisor of the Croatian armed forces. A very lively discussion ensured.

As midday passed Crljen, related that he, with Generals Herenchich and Servatzi, had been appointed to negotiate with the British. He wrote:

> We went to the meeting with sombre forebodings weighing heavily upon us. The British headquarters were located in an ancient castle. To reach it we passed through lines of British combat-ready tanks.
>
> Surrounded by a large number of officers the British general awaited us in the castle. An American sergeant of Croatian descent served as interpreter. He informed the British commander that General Herenchich was chief of our delegation. Hearing this the Englishman offered Herenchich a seat in front of him. The rest of us remained standing, the British officers at one side of the table and we on the other.
>
> Herenchich told the interpreter in Croatian that we came in the name of the Chief of the Independent State of Croatia to offer to the Western Allies the surrender of the Croatian Army and to ask the right of political asylum for the mass of civilian refugees.

There were moments of disturbing silence following the interpreter's translation of this statement to the British commander ... I asked the interpreter to tell the Englishman that I wanted to add something to Herenchich's remarks.

The General nodded to me and indicated with a wave of his hand that I might take a seat beside General Herenchich. I spoke bluntly and pointedly. The problem concerning us could not be judged from only the military stand point. From the moment we left our country, without undertaking the offensive actions of which we were still capable, we exchanged our role as warriors for one of political exiles. It is the custom of all civilised nations to receive and protect political exiles. We expect from the United Kingdom, the United States of America and France this kind of protection.

Crljen related how the British General, as a soldier, could not deal with political problems but had to take his orders from Field Marshal Alexander, Commander-in-Chief of Allied Forces in the Mediterranean. When Herenchich asked they be given an opportunity to send a delegation to General Alexander, it was refused. General Alexander had issued his orders to cover the situation and he had certainly received instruction from the Prime Minister Winston Churchill. Conscious of this Crljen raised the plight of the thousands of civilians who had been fleeing in fear. The General stated that the civilians had nothing to fear, because the Yugoslavs were allies of the British, whose respect for human rights and international law meant the civilians were safe from illegal persecution.

Crljan then desperately tried to enlighten the British General:

> I am extremely sorry to have to express a contrary opinion. The flight of hundreds of thousands of civilians from Croatian territory is a consequence of the crimes perpetrated by the Communists upon this territory and against the Croatian people. Since the great migrations of the peoples of 1,500 years ago that attended the break up of the Roman Empire, there has been, right to the present day, no mass movement of similar proportions to the Croatian exodus that is taking place now before your eyes. There has been no such instance of a people abandoning their own country as the Croatians are doing today in the face of the Serbian and Soviet Communist

advance. Not only had we (the military element) no desire to have the civilians flee the land and so hamper our withdrawal (I was referring here to an allegation that he had made a few moments previously to 'propaganda' that we military men were supposed to have employed to scare the civilians), but we also had no way of preventing such an exodus. In the course of the apocalyptic journey that they undertook, many people committed suicide because of despair or nervous or physical exhaustion. But there was not one individual who decided to return to take his chances with the Communists. This was proof that our people prefer death to the prospect of returning to their Communist controlled country. Today these suffering political refugees of Croatian nationality are addressing their pleas to England, which is in a position to decide their fate. On her, therefore, falls the moral responsibility of deciding whether our defenceless people are to be turned over to the Communists to be slaughtered or allowed their freedom.[68]

Herenchich and Crljen were asked to wait in an adjoining room as the British talked with representatives of the Partisan army.

The chief Partisan representatives at these talks were Colonel Milan Basta, a Serb from the Lika region of Croatia, and Ivan Kovachich Efenko. In his book, Basta wrote:

At the door we were received by a tall slender general, commander of the V English Expeditionary Corps Charles Kneightley, who was completely grey, carefully shaven and with a firm military manner. We shook hands warmly, and he informed us that he was especially glad that he had come in contact with Tito's army and its higher officers. He told us he had heard a lot about us during the time of the campaign in Italy and was inspired by our efforts and heroism.

After inviting them to sit, the General informed them of the arrival of the Croatian Generals and then went on:

Before you there are three hundred thousand enemy soldiers. That army for understandable reasons does not want to surrender to you. What's more, it is ready in case these talks fail to continue fighting. In the meantime the war has ended

---

68. John Prcela & Stanko Guldescu. *Operation Slaughterhouse*, 150–152.

and there is no sense in shedding any more blood. They want to surrender to us and since we are allies we will later settle the matter.[69]

After some discussion, Basta stated:

> I have a clear order to take over the enemy army and with the forces that I have at my disposal, force them to surrender. As a soldier I have a duty to respect this order and do all to fulfil it, no matter what the circumstances. I came here due to an agreement that this is to be fulfilled in the smoothest possible way[70]

The British General left these two Yugoslav officers on their own. Basta himself admits he grew suspicious of the British. During this time of prolonged and uncertain waiting they noticed, as they looked out of the window, more Slovene Partisans had arrived, which greatly reassured them[71], after which Basta and Kovachich Efenko were called to sit at table with Crljen and Herenchich.

The Communists demanded the immediate surrender of the Croatian Army. Basta recalled it, saying:

> The remains of your Ustasha – Home Guard army finds itself in a situation it can't get out of. It is surrounded on all sides by strong forces of the Yugoslav army. I think you have been informed that four armies of the liberation forces of Yugoslavia, with some 100,000 men, from all sides have created an encirclement around you. I am correctly informed through prisoners that you do not possess serious and organised battle forces which are capable of breaking through. Time works for us. Now we are able to force you to an unconditional surrender or destroy you. More fresh forces are arriving. It is in your interest to accept surrender without resistance.[72]

Basta also promised that the civilian population would return to their homes and all soldiers would be sent to camps where they would be treated according to international law.

---

69. Milan Basta, *RJZSDK*, 420.
70. Milan Basta, *RJZSDK*, 421.
71. Milan Basta, *RJZSDK*, 423–424.
72. Milan Basta, *RJZSDK*, 425.

As Crljen was pleading with the British General, Basta recalled he became nervous. The British general then turned to Basta saying: 'Commander, my tanks are at your disposal.'

Basta was surprised at the firm and clear words of this British General, and he realised then that the general had placed himself on the Partisan side.[73]

Crljen asked for twenty-four hours in which to inform the scattered army units, which Basta refused. He even refused the two hours suggested by the British Commander. Eventually one hour was negotiated.

Crljen's comment on all this was:

> The action of the British general seemed to us to be a calculated and cheap attempt at intimidation. It shattered effectively any illusion that we had cherished up to this time about the proverbial British spirit of fair play. This official British spokesman had offered the aid of British arms to delegates of the Communist Yugoslav Army to coerce us into a premature and unconditional surrender. He also proposed that a British commission assist the Communists in carrying out the details of the surrender process. General Herenchich at once said that we would be pleased to have the British supervise the surrender process. To this the British general replied flatly that we were in no position to solicit anything; he had offered the help of an English commission just in case his allies needed such aid.
>
> This was the end of the negotiations. All doors were closed to us. There was no hope for our Army or for the refugees. The only alternative was to decide whether to surrender, fight or flee. And we had just sixty minutes to decide.[74]

The British General was Brigadier General T Patrick D Scott of the Irish Infantry brigade, who realised that the Croatians wanted to surrender to the British. He wrote much later: 'On referring this nice little problem of the Croats to higher authority, I was told that on no account could we allow them to surrender to us; they had fought

---

73. Milan Basta, *RJZSDK*, 427.
74. John Prcela & Stanko Guldescu *Operation Slaughterhouse*, 154.

against the Yugoslavs in aid of Germany, and Yugoslav prisoners they must become.'[75]

The day before, Ivan Kovachich Efenka, the Commander of the Yugoslav Assault Division, and Major DC Owen, the Chief of the Anglo American Army Command for the 1V operative zone, had reached an agreement for the repatriation of the Croatian forces.[76]

As the negotiations were coming to an end, an aeroplane happened to fly over. Brigadier Scott later recalled: 'By the luck of God an aeroplane happened to come over and I said: 'You see this aeroplane? I have just called that up on my wireless set. That's just a reconnaissance aircraft, but the next lot will have bombs . . . '"[77]

When they saw there was no further hope, Crljan and Herenchich hurried back and informed the high-ranking Croatian officers and unit commanders the result of the discussion. Although some refused to surrender and went into the mountains, a vast majority laid down their arms.[78]

An elderly General Slavko Stancer, who had lost an arm during the war, under the impression the Partisans would respect a disabled old man, volunteered to meet the Partisans but nothing came of his attempt.[79][X]

Crljan, on his own admission, informed the waiting officers and the political functionaries about the result of the negotiations with the British. He and Herenchich joined a group of officers who refused to surrender and went with them to nearby mountains. They both eventually found sanctuary in Argentina. Herenchich lived long after the war, but said or wrote nothing of his wartime experiences or his part in negotiating the Bleiburg surrender.

Instead of accepting them as prisoners of war, the British handed between 120,000 and 140,000 unarmed soldiers plus many thousands of civilian men, women and children to the Partisan forces of Josip Broz Tito. These forces massacred the vast majority of them.[80][Y][Z]

---

75. Martina Grahek Ravančić, *Bleiburg .i Krizni Put 1945*, 100.
76. Martina Grahek Ravančić, *Bleiburg .i Krizni Put*, 100.
77. Borivoje M. Karapandzich, *TBYS 1945 TKaG*, 66. Vinko Nikolić, *BTHN*, 87. Nicholas Bethel. *The Last Secret*, 119.
78. John Prcela & Stanko Guldescu. *Operation Slaughterhouse*, 154–155.
79. Milan Basta, *RJZSDK*, 429–430. John Prcela & Stanko Guldescu. *Operation Slaughterhouse*, 155.
80. Vinko Nikolić, *BTHN*, 157.

A. The English writer Evelyn Waugh, who spent some time in Tito's headquarters as a British intelligence officer, wrote of Yugoslavia:

> Yugoslavia was the creation of the Liberal peacemakers of the First World War, who light-heartedly placed the old Hapsburg dominions under the Karageorge dynasty. From the first years of the peace disruptive forces were apparent. Croats and Slovenes almost unanimously sought independence from the Serbs. Moreover outside the country three neighbours at least – Italy, Russia, and Hungary – were training agents to exploit these disruptive forces at the first opportunity. This opportunity was provided by the English and French declaration of war on Germany. At the first pressure the country fell to pieces. Croats and Slovenes received their independence, at first gladly, then with growing resentment when they discovered that its price was the ceding of territory to Italy and an Italian king. Serbia dissolved into bands whose leaders made their own policy from stubborn resistance to open collaboration with the enemy.[81]

B. Winston Churchill was himself the soul of pragmatism. He declared to his assistant private secretary John Colville in 1941: 'If Hitler invaded Hell, I would make at least a favourable reference to the devil in the House of Commons.'[82]

C. Croatian independence was first proclaimed on 8 April 1941 in the town of Bjelovar by Petar Cvek, a Croatian officer in the Royal Yugoslav Army. Unfortunately he didn't have the advantage of a radio transmitter to announce it to the whole nation. No one knows what happened to Petar Cvek or to Captain Mraka and Senator Wagner from Bjelovar, who co-operated with Cvek in the proclamation. At the time, Bjelovar and its surrounds held up to 20,000 soldiers who became the nucleus of the Croatian army.[83]

D. While living in the United States after the war, Dr Machek greatly regretted his decision not to become head of state, saying: 'That was the greatest mistake in my life! I was afraid that I couldn't satisfy

---

81. Christie Lawrence, *Irregular Adventure*, 12–13.
82. Lynne Olson & Stanley Cloud, *For Your Freedom and Ours*, 218.
83. Vinko Nikolić, *Bleiburg Usroci .i Posljedice*, 15–16. Damir Jug, *OSNDHSU*, 13. Nada Kisic Kolanovic, Arg, 39–40.

the Germans. And added to that Pavelich with his Ustasha would blackmail me. He would give the Germans and Italians more than I would be prepared to give. And that would have been enough for me not to be able to prevent the slaughter of the Serbs'.[84]

Dr Machek also thought that the coup d'état of 27 March was a tragedy, saying: 'I am certain that the date 27 March was catastrophic. I am convinced that if it had not been for the 27 March there would not have been Hitler's or Mussolini's occupation nor the terrible inter-ethnic slaughter. What is most important is that all the peoples of Yugoslavia would not be groaning under the Communist yoke'.[85]

The author spoke with Zvonimir Kulundzich, who specialised on the life of Stjepan Radich and the Croatian Peasant Party, and stated it was a tragedy and mistake that Dr Machek did not assume the leadership of the Independent State of Croatia., it being his biggest political mistake. Kulundzich, pointed to him saying: 'Dr Franjo Tudjman was sitting where you are sitting for three hours saying the same thing'.[86]

E. Pavelich signed the Roman protocols on 18 May 1941.[87] Pavelich developed the habit of deciding important matters of state on his own, without having his closest collaborators present. Eugene Dido Kvaternik wrote:

> The practice from the beginning which Dr Pavelich introduced in diplomatic discussions and they preceded the Roman agreements, was that he acted independently of his advisers and of his closest collaborators. Neither on the 29 March in the Vila Torlonia, nor on 11 April in Palazzo Venezia, nor on 14 April in Karlovac during his talks with Alfuso, nor with the first phase of talks with Count Ciano in Ljubljana on 25 April, nor with his talks with the Italian ambassador Rafael Casertano, nor at Monfalcono on 6 May in his meeting with Mussolini. There wasn't present one Croatian, nor did Dr Pavelich show any thing written or a record of these talks. During these talks there was created an Italian mortgage on Croatia the formulation of the Roman agreement, a mortgage

---

84. Bogdan Radica, Živjeti .i Nedoživljeti, Volume 2, 420.
85. Bogdan Radica, Živjeti .i Nedoživljeti, Volume2, 504–505.
86. Conversations with Zvonimir Kulundžić, Zagreb, Sunday 5 April 1992.
87. Bogdan Krizman, Pavelić izmedju Hitlera .i Mussolinia, 37.

which enabled the presence of the Second Italian army in Croatia with its well-known fatal results, which brought the Croatian state to its May catastrophe.[88]

F. Franjo Dujmovich later wrote on Pavelich's manner of acting during the formulation of this Roman agreement:

> He is an example how a foreign policy for a nation, which just achieved its independence, is not to be conducted. If Pavelich was convinced of the truth of his external political position and the taking on of the responsibility before history and the nation, he should have shared that responsibility with as wide a body as possible of participants such as an advisory council or a state committee. He consciously avoided this, for he did not want to have any supervision above him, for he was afraid that he would not find anybody who would accept responsibility before the Croatian people for such a catastrophic national failure which the Roman agreement was.[89]

G. Pavelich would not recognise a Serbian Orthodox Church in Croatia for he saw it as a catalyst for expanding Serbian nationalism. For him it had to be a Croatian Orthodox Church. On 3 April 1942, he signed into law the establishment of the Croatian Orthodox Church and on 7 June 1942, Archbishop Maksimov Ivanovich Germogen was installed as its Archbishop in the Orthodox Church in Zagreb. It had four dioceses with Archbishop Germogen as its head. Maksimov Germogen was already a Bishop in pre-revolutionary Russia who sought refuge in the kingdom of the Serbs, Croats and Slovenes in the early 1920s. Almost all of the sixty clergy belonging to the Croatian Orthodox Church came from this Orthodox Russian or Ukrainian background. Together with Archbishop Germogen, they were almost all shot by the Partisans after the war.[90]

H. Although Pavelich's Government made great efforts to integrate the Muslims into the Croatian State, from the very beginning there were efforts to create an autonomous Bosnian state within Croatia. Led by Uzeir-aga Hadzihasanovich, in 1942 the Muslim leadership sent

---

88. Bogdan Krizman, *PiHiM*, 57.
89. Franjo Dujmović, *HnpkO*, 126.
90. Jure Krišto, *Sukob Simbola*, 245-259. Ivo Omrčanin, *Hrvatska 1942*, 94–95. *Who Is What In The Independant State Of Croatia*, 129.

a memorandum to 'His Excellency Adolf Hitler' The movement also received the support from the Grand Mufti of Jerusalem, Muhamed Emin El-Huseini, who before the war was one of the leading figures in the struggle of the Arabs against British rule in the Middle East.

The German Government put pressure on the Croatian Government to welcome El-Huseini, who arrived in Zagreb on 31 March 1943. He visited Banja Luka and Sarajevo, where Uzeir-aga Hadzihasanovich tried to convince him that Muslims were equally oppressed by Serbian and Croatian nationalism in the Independent State of Croatia.[91] Although Pavelich tried hard to integrate Muslims in the Croatian State, and leading Muslim intellectuals were a part of its government and public life, Kisich Kolanovich concludes her study with:

> Although from 1941-1945 the Muslim political elite attempted to find a modus vivendi with the government of the Independent State of Croatia, the religious leaders and large sections of the Muslims did not share a common identity with the Croatians but thought that they possessed their own historical rights, their own territory and their right to autonomy in Bosnia and Herzegovina.[92]

It is interesting to note that the first volunteer unit to be decorated on the Eastern Front was led by the Muslim Lieutenant Asima Nozich from Mostar.[93]

In the composition of the elite *Crna Legia*, Black Legion, named for its black uniforms, eighty per cent of its members were of the Muslim faith.[94]

Although in the beginning there was strong support on the part of the Muslims for the Independent State of Croatia, the historian Jure Kristo wrote:

> After another unsuccessful German- Croatian military operation to destroy the Partisan movement in Bosnia-Herzegovina, known as operation "Shwarz or in Partisan

---

91. Nada Kišić Kolanović, *Muslimani .i Hrvatski Nacionalizam,* 329-330, 367. *Who Is What In The Independant State Of Croatia,* 162.
92. Nada Kišić Kolanović, *Muslimani .i Hrvatski Nacionalizam,* 408.
93. Nada Kišić Kolanović, *Muslimani .i Hrvatski Nacionalizam,* 371.
94. Related to the author by Pavo Gagro.

terms the "Fifth Enemy Offensive" from 15 May to the middle of June 1943, the Muslims began in massive numbers to side with the Partisans so that large numbers of them saw the end of the war on the victor's side.[95] This trend of the Bosnian Muslims joining the Partisans, reminds one of a quote by Count Galeazzo Ciano, the Italian foreign minister: *Victory has a hundred Fathers, but defeat is an orphan.*

The Mufti of the Zagreb Mosque, DrIsmet ef. Muftich (1876-1945), was hanged by the Partisans near the main door of the mosque soon after they entered Zagreb.

I. The Croatian cultural worker and one time manager of the Zagreb Opera, Dushan Zanko remembers when at the end of 1941 Filip Lukas, the president of the Croatian cultural institute *Matica Hrvatska* said to him: 'Professor, in this new revolutionary Croatia there are people in power who are inclined to kill a person.'

Zanko also recalls how, towards the end of 1942, Professor Vinko Krishovich, said to him before leaving for Switzerland:

> My dear friend, I did what I could in the Sabor to protect the human person and human rights for the citizens in this state, but sadly I can't see any possibility that the end of the war will bring the Croatian people freedom and democracy whoever wins the war. I am old and I am going to Switzerland so that I don't again live through what I lived through in 1918 and you young stay and save what is able to be saved.[96]

J. From 1935 Dr Machek worked towards the formation of Village Defence and City Defence Units, their main purpose being security for villagers and towns. It was more of a civil body, helping in flood mitigation, protecting forests, combating forest fires, ensuring the wellbeing of people, and later it carried light arms. At a march past held in Zagreb on 24 July1939, the British Consul T. C. Rapp was very impressed at the discipline of these units, informing his government that they numbered up to 150,000 members in the whole of Croatia.[97]

---

95. Jure Krsto, *Sukob Simbola*, 335.
96. Dušan Žanko, *Svjedoci*, 33.
97. Želko Karaula, *MV*, 387.

In October 1940 the command of the Italian second army was informed that the units of the Croatian Peasant Party numbed one hundred and eighty thousand.[98] According to Milan Pribanich, who was an officer in these units, it numbered two hundred thousand members by the beginning of 1941.[99]

An officers school was established in Zagreb where in 1940 up to one hundred and one cadets graduated.[100] With the German invasion on 6 April 1941, the Village and City Defense did much to disarm the Royal Yugoslav army and establish law and order. In Zagreb, it was ably led by Zvonimir Kovachevich, who later transferred to Sarajevo to supervise a peaceful transfer. This civil defence established order in Vareždin, Požega and Osjek and played a crucial part in stabilising the country during those uncertain times.[101]

Colonel Ivan Babich, who was close to the Croatian Peasant Party, wrote after the war that the Ustasha regime showed neither the ability nor the will to unite the Croatian people:

> It was shocking, the disarming of the Croatian Village and City Defense; these armed formations played a very critical role during the war and in the first few days of the Independent State of Croatia. Through their spiritual cohesion they were better able than the improvised Ustasha units to uphold order and respond to those who revolted.[102]

K. The artist Jozo Kljakovich, who lived through the establishment of the Croatian State wrote in his memoirs:

> Never in my whole life have I ever had such a feeling of uneasiness towards people, as during the time of the formation and organization of this state. Some strange people emerged, both known and unknown, those who were called and those who were not called. Rectors and professors from universities would be dismissed as simply as a servant during normal times. An Ustasha official would control the administration of the university as was the case with me at the Faculty of Arts.

---

98. Želko Karaula, *MV*, 389.
99. Želko Karaula, *MV*, Milan Pribanić, 187.
100. Želko Karaula, *MV*, 267–268.
101. Želko Karaula, *MV*, 441–456. Ivo Omrčanin, *Hrvatska 1941*, 927–935.
102. Želko Karaula, *MV*, 466.

> There was an order that the Aryan origin of all government officials was to be investigated . . .
>
> . . . On the streets of Zagreb I met men, women and even small children in prams with yellow flags on their chest and back with the sign Z. These were our Jews, who on the bases of Hitler's catechism were excluded from 'human society'. To humiliate and insult an old and cultured people is a moral defect. I had the inclination to grab these signs and place them on myself as I walked the streets of Zagreb. Fortunately I didn't do this, for today I would not have been writing this book.[103]

L. Stepinac interceded almost daily on behalf of people, and so Pavelich issued an order on 26 June 1941 regarding the spread of false information. It concluded: 'Everyone is to cease any intervention with whatever State or similar authority with regard to people or material subjects, for every intervention will be regarded as sabotage and it will be handled by the courts.' This was directed at Stepinac to prevent further intervention.[104]

This did not silence Stepinac. On 21 July 1941, he wrote to Pavelich asking that people who were being deported to camps be treated humanely:

> I hear from many quarters that during the deportation the non Aryans are treated inhumanly and cruelly; what's more, from such behaviour the children, the old and the sick are not spared. I know that amongst those who are deported are recent Catholic converts, and it is all the more for me to be concerned . . . . . .
>
> I am free to mention some specific things are necessary: (a) that deportation to camps be conducted in such a manner, that people are able to collect their most important items as well settle their most urgent duties to their family and their various services in the community; (b) That the deportation be not conducted in cramped, sealed wagons, especially to distant places; (c) That those who are interned be given adequate food; (d) That the sick be given medical assistance;

---

103. Jozo Kljaković, *U Suvremenom Kaosu*, 176, 178.
104. Aleksa Benigar, *Stepinac*, 374–375.

(e) That they are able to receive the necessary food and allowed to write letters to their family.[105]

Stepinac was also a great protector and defender of the Jewish people of Croatia. As soon as the racial laws were passed in Croatia, he wrote to Dr Andrija Artukovich, the Minister of Justice, on 23 April 1941, asking he take into consideration Jewish people who converted to Christianity, adding:

> .. . . ..with all this we see that every day there are arriving stricter and stricter orders without regard whether one is guilty or innocent. Today's newspapers brought the order that all Jews must wear the Jewish sign. There are so many of these measures now, that people who know the situation say, that even in Germany itself these racial laws were not passed with such severity and such haste . . . ..
>
> I ask you, dear Minister, that you command that Jewish and other similar laws (measures against the Serbs and others) be implemented in such a way that every human being is respected as an individual. The rule on the carrying of Jewish signs could be implemented in such a way that it not be carried out.

He then appealed to the minister for those Jews who had converted to Catholicism:

> Many of these were converted long before the persecution of the Jews, that is when becoming Christian for them meant a loss in material status. Many of them are already assimilated and no one knows they are Jews. There are those who are eminent in the national and Ustasha movement. I myself know personally some of them who are contented and practical Catholics . . . . .[106]

Stepinac's concern that the dignity of the human person be respected can be seen in the speech he gave at the opening of the Croatian Sabor, reminding Dr Pavelich of its obligation:

---

105. Aleksa Benigar, *Stepinac*, 375–376.
106. Jure Kristo, *Sukob Simbola*, 273–274. Esther Gitman, *ASPoHR*, 148–151, 246.

> May it pass just laws, which will not transgress the law of God, so that it brings down the Blessing of God the Creator. For Scripture says: 'There is one lawgiver and judge who is able to save and to destroy.' (James 4, 12). May the Sabor pass good laws: where everyone is treated equally and where there is the same law for all."
>
> Poglavnik! The renewal of the Sabor is proof of your deep and living conscious responsibility, whose burden you wish to share with your colleagues. This renewal is also accompanied with the prayer of the Church and our hearts: may the Eternal Judge, who cares for the destiny of the people, engrave into the foundations of the Croatian Sabor His mighty right hand and place into the heart of all your co-workers that same conscientious responsibility, in helping you, the head of the Independent State of Croatia, in successfully renewing and developing our beloved homeland on the eternal values of Christ![107]

Before he left for Italy in 1941, Ivan Mestrovich visited Stepinac to say goodbye. Mestrovich writes:

> Stepinac was sitting at his typewriter table and he had in front of him a pile of letters with a stone the size of a fist on top of them, Stepinac said:
>
> This greeting I received a few days ago on the shoulder from our fascists, as I was being driven in the car and these letters are threats from the Germans and Ustasha. They are in German and Croatian and their contents are the same: 'We know that you are our greatest enemy, and we are letting you know that if you continue to speak against us as you have been doing until now, despite that Roman red belt, we will kill you in the middle of the street like a dog. – They will not frighten me, these criminals.

We moved to the sitting room and he began to bewail and revile the Ustasha and especially Pavelich and the young Kvaternik.

---

107. Juraj Batelja & C Tomić, *Alojzije Kardinal Stepinac, Propovjedi, Govori, Poruke 1941-1946*, 98–99.

Mestrovich asked Stepinac: 'Do you think that all this cruelty against the Serbs is happening with Pavelich's knowledge?'

He replied:

> It is not that I think, I am certain that nothing is happening without his knowledge and orders. They are criminals and maniacs, just like Hitler. And this traitor calls himself the greatest of Croats, he who sold the cradle of Croatia, our beautiful Dalmatia and shamed us all by his bad actions. During the darkest days of our history we didn't have one Croatian who signed over a part of Croatia to a foreigner.

Stepinac gritted his teeth, tears flowing down his cheeks. He suddenly stood up, opened the door, and cried out to an eaves dropper.
Shame on you. Is that dignified of you?
See I am not secure even in my own house from spies. He replied: By the afternoon Pavelich will know what we were talking about. – He told me the name of him who was listening through the key hole.[108]

Already on 29 December 1941, Hans Helm, the German police attache in Zagreb, informed the office of the Security Service in Berlin, about the troublesome archbishop.

> 'We are informed all along about the political meddling of the cleric (Stepinac) in the internal affairs of the country. He has connections in every department; most churches in Croatia have contacts with London and the government in exile. This approach undertaken by the Church could be viewed contrary to the interests of the Third Reich and the NDH. Our objective is to eliminate the influence of the cleric.'[109]

Hans Helm sent another dispatch to Berlin dated 25 August 1942, detailing why the Gestapo finds the Church working against it. Another dispatch dated 25 March 1943 states: 'This dispatch has not been confirmed but considering the fact that it is known Archbishop Stepinac is a great friend of the Jews, it can be assumed he is getting involved in their interests'. On 11 October 1943 Helm let his superiors in Belin know that there was an open rift between the Ustasha regime

---

108. Ivan Mestrović, *UnPLiD*, 325.
109. Dr Esther Gitman, *ASPoHR*, 127.

and Archbishop Stepinac. A dispatch of 10 December 1943 refers to the 'sharp attack by Dr Stepinac against the regime in his sermon on 31 October 1943.'[110]

It is significant that on 23 November 1943, the U.S. consulate in Berne, Switzerland, sent a telegram to the Secretary of State quoting a Zagreb headline of 20 November: 'Controversy between the Roman Catholic Primate and the State Authorities.' The same consulate also sent Washington a summary of an editorial in the daily *Hrvatski Narod* (Croatian People), in which Dr Julija Makanec, minister of education, mounted an attack on Stepinac based on sermons in which he stated: 'The Catholic Church only knows races and peoples as God's creatures and values the one with the noblest heart more than the one with the strongest fist; all men are alike in God's eyes whether European or coloured men from Central Africa.'[111]

Dr Esther Gitman described Stepinac as a 'Pillar of Human Rights'. In her thorough study on Stepinac during the Second World War, Dr Gitman came to the following conclusion with these words:

> My objective in presenting Dr Alojzije Stepinac, in his role as head of the Archdiocese of Zagreb, is to demonstrate his unenviable position of being between a rock and a hard place, between the Ustasha and the Communists. Under such circumstances, he acted to the best of his abilities as a loyal servant of the Roman Catholic Church, while never forgetting his belief in the moral law as a guiding principle. His role and position encouraged him to denounce, at every opportunity, the inhumanity of the Ustasha laws and actions.
>
> Throughout the war years, Stepinac followed but one maxim: only one race exists, and that is the human race created by God.[112]

The Catholic Church has been greatly criticised for not opposing the Ustasha regime more forcefully and protecting the oppressed. It was interesting that Cardinal Seper, who worked closely with Stepinac,

---

110. Gordan Akrap, *KSuDGiO*, 33 & 29. Dr Esther Gitman, *ASPoHR*, 130 & 207 & 327. Also see 326–328.
111. Dr Esther Gitman. *When Courage Prevailed*, 98. Dr Esther Gitman, *ASPoHR*, 129–130.
112. Dr Esther Gitman ... *ASPoHR*, 121.

told Jozo Tomasevich in 1967: 'If the Catholic Church in Croatia were again faced with the same problems as during the Second World War, it would again act in the same way.'[113]

It is true there were some cases of Ustasha officials forcibly converting Serbian Orthodox believers into the Catholic Church. According to Stjepan Hojt this was a triviality as a vast majority of Serbs in Croatia remained Serbian Orthodox. These forced conversions were greatly exaggerated after the war to accuse Archbishop Stepinac of encouraging them in order to have something to accuse him of in his trial after the war.[114]

M. Ivan Protulipac was born and grew up in Karlovac before qualifying as a lawyer. Before the war he was a leading figure in the Croatian Youth Movement, and it was said there wasn't a parish in Croatia or the Catholic parts of Bosnia-Hezegovina where his foot didn't step. 'He was described as a rare person amongst the Croats, one of the rarest; honest, crystal clear, of firm purpose, insightful and zealous'. The Ustasha Government imprisoned Protulipac for a short time, and he was sidelined from any public role upon release. He was killed by the Yugoslav Secret Service on 31 January 1946, while helping refugees in Trieste[115]

N. Politically, the Communist Partisans acted very differently from Dr Pavelich. During November 1942 they established a 'war Parliament' in the Bosnian town of Bihac. They called it the Anti-Fascist Council of National Liberation Movement of Yugoslavia, and it was the provisional civilian arm of the Partisan movement, with the acronym AVNOJ (*Antifasisticko Vijece Narodnog Oslobodjenja Jugoslavije*)[116]

O. According to Mirko Zivkovich, an Ustasha police official all through the war, the Independent State of Croatia effectively saved the Croatian people. The German Army had a policy of killing 100 civilians for every German soldier killed. This is why Serbia was relatively peaceful during the war. The Partisans would have continued fighting the Germans in Croatia and there would have been German

---

113. Jozo Tomasovich, *War and Revolution in Yugoslavia 1941-1945*, 565.
114. Conversation with Stjepan Hojt, 2 November 2003.
115. Vinko Nikolić, *Tragedija Se Dogodila U Svibnju*, Volume 2, 296-298. *Who Is What In The Independent State Of Croatia*, 332.
116. William Deakin, *TEM*, 98.

reprisals on the Croatian population as a consequence. But because the Independent State of Croatia was allied with Germany, the Germans could not take reprisals against the Croatian population. This lack of opposition to the Germans in Serbia is confirmed by Basil Davidson who wrote: *Only in Serbia was the situation blank.*[117]

Mirko Zivkovich also stated that half the Croatian leadership had wives who were Jewish or partly Jewish. He was Police Chief in Dubrovnik for some time, and eleven of the thirteen Jewish families in Dubrovnik there were saved. He had badges made for them which were quite discreet. He also mentioned that in the Adolf Eichmann trial, held in Israel from 1961-1962; it was mentioned Croatia was a region where Jews could seek refuge.[118]

P. With the German invasion of Yugoslavia on 6 April 1941, Tito had several meetings with the Soviet military attaché. Tito used the meetings with the attaché as an opportunity to send reports to the Comintern and for an exchange of opinions.[119]

Tito proved himself a very able politician. Willian Deakin, the first British representative to Tito's headquarters, described him as: 'a deceptively quiet personality, used to imposing his authority with few words or gestures, commanding an instinctive and total respect from those around him, sure in judgement and deeply self controlled, always sharp.'[120]

Deakin was impressed by the way Tito organised the Partisans, with each division being self-contained.[121] Basil Davidson, who parachuted into Bosnia on 16 August 1943, and met Tito a few days later in Petrovo Polje wrote of his impression of him:

> It seemed to me that under any dispensation Tito would have made his mark.[122] It is likely that his greatest strength was the unerring judgement of character and the capacity that he had for others; and the success of the movement was due in large part to his unfailing ability to pick the right man for the right job, and then delegate responsibility . . . Davidson did add

---

117. Basil Davison, *PP,* 14.
118. Interview with Mirko Živkovic in Buenos Aires, Argentina, 24 June 1992.
119. Milovan Djilas, *Memoires of a Revolutionary,* 376.
120. William Deakin, *TEM,* 79, 117.
121. William Deakin, *TEM,* 100–102.
122. Basil Davidson, *PP,* 13.

after describing Tito's facial appearance: these were the marks of a face that could be pitiless, hardbitten, and then added, he was supremely confident of himself.[123]

Lindsay Rogers expressed his impressions of Tito: 'I couldn't help wondering at the breadth of his information in these very troublesome and darkened days.'[124] The Partisans collaborated closely with the Serbian Chetniks right to the end of 1941, based on an agreement between Tito and Mihaljevich on 20 September 1941 to not attack one another. This agreement eventually collapsed.[125] Tito met Draze Mihaljevich in the middle of September 1941 and again a month later.[126] Tito also began dialogue with the Germans, led by Vladimir Velebit, in which some German military personnel held by the Partisans were exchanged for the leading Croatian Communist, Andria Hebrang, at Posuse on 4 September 1942.[127] There was a second exchange, once again headed by Vladimir Velebit, but included Tito's deputy, Milovan Djilas, and his leading military commander, Kocha Popovich. These meetings took place in Zagreb where Velebit met Glaise von Horstenau and Siegfried Kasche. Involved in this exchange were not only important military personnel, but, Tito's former wife Herta Hass.[128] When the question was raised:

'What will the Russians say?' Tito replied almost angrily:

'Well, they also think first of their own people and their own army! Our first duty is to look after our own army and our own people.'[129]

After breaking with Tito and a five year prison sentence, while on a visit to the United States Milovan Djilas said of Tito: 'Without Tito nothing would have been achieved. He was always, especially in action, the most ready and experienced to take hold of difficult situations. He was the strongest of all of them . . . his strength was his instinct.'[130]

---

123. Basil Davidson, *PP*, 17–18.
124. Lindsay Rogers, *GS*, 85.
125. Mira Šuvar, *Vladimir Velebit Svjedok Historije*, 262.
126. Mira Šuvar, *Vladimir Velebit Svjedok Historije*, 279-282. Milovan Djilas, *Wartime*, 88. WilliamDeakin, *TEM*, 75–76, 136. Basil Davidson, *PP*, 86.
127. Mira Šuvar, *Vladimir Velebit Svjedok Historije*, 279-282.
128. Mira Šuvar, *Vladimir Velebit Svjedok Historije*, 283-287. Milovan Djilas, *Wartime*, 229-245.
129. Milovan Djilas, *Wartime*, 231. Jasper Ridley, *Tito*, 205-208.
130. Bogdan Radica, *Živjeti Nedoživjeti*, Volume 2, 573.

Tito's skill as a politician can be seen in a speech he gave to the Anti-Fascist Council of National Liberation of Yugoslavia with its acronym *AVNOJ* on 29 November 1943 at Jajce. He stated that the aims of the Partisans' struggle was 'to realize the national aspirations of the Yugoslav people for a free, genuinely democratic, fraternal and federal Yugoslavia.'[131]

Tito also met with Winston Churchill in Naples on 12 August 1944 as well as Field MarshalAlexander in the course of this visit.[132] Field Marshal Alexander again met Tito in Belgrade from 21 to 24 February 1945, arriving in Belgrade at the head of a large United States and British military delegation.[133]

Q . . . Tito's ruthlessness can be seen when he was nominated by the Croatian Communist Andrija Hebrang to be the secretary of the of the Zagreb regions Communist party branch, in February 1928. This was a big step in boosting Tito's career in the Communist party. At an important meeting of the leadership of the Communist movement in October 1943 Hebrang affirmed that the Croatian Partisans were fighting for a 'democratic republic of Yugoslavia which would be constituted on a federal basis which would ensure all peoples national rights, national freedom and autonomy.' As Hebrang was defending Croatian interests at important party and state functions after the war, Tito eliminated him.[134]

R. Some members of the Croatian Peasant Party joined the Partisans believing it was the best way to help the Croatian cause. Its leading figure was the journalist Bozidar Magovac, who joined the Partisans on 4 December 1942, in the hope that through them they would create a national, social and democratic freedom for Croatia and build a bridge between the Croatian and Serbs who were involved in an inter-ethnic slaughter. In July 1943, under the auspices of the

---

131. Basil Davidson, 326–328. Jasper Ridley, *Tito,* 221.
132. Milovan Djilas, *Wartime,* 400–401. Pero Simić. *Tito,* 190–191. Jasper Ridley, *Tito,* 241–242
133. Mira Šuvar, *Vladimir Velebit Svjedok Historije,* 147–148. Milan Basta, *Rat Je Zvrsijo Sedan Dana Kasnije,* 512. Japer Ridley, *Tito,* 251. Nora Beloff, *TFLatW, 1939-1984,* 85.
134. *Tko Je Tko U Nezavisnoj Drzavi Hrvatskoj,* (Who Is What In The Independent State Of Croatia 41–51 & 151–153.) (*Who Is What In The Independent State Of Croatia,* 49–51 & 151–153.)

Partisans, he established a weekly newspaper, *Slobodni Dom* (Free Homeland).[135]

When Dinko Shuljak met Magovac amongst the Partisans in November 1943 and expressed his disgust at the brutality of the Ustasha, Magovac answered him: If you only knew in what brutal way these slaughter . . . We want. . .humanity, justice and freedom. It is for this reason that I write to affirm this to the annoyance of the comrades and I don't know how long they will put up with me. They are merciless . . . " It was a emotional goodbye between Shuljak and Magovac for they knew they would not see one another again.[136]

S. According to the Croatian physicist Ivan Supek, who was in the Partisans but never a member of the Communist Party, the bulk of the fighting against the Germans and Italians was conducted by Croatian Partisans, led by Andria Hebrang and including Bozidar Magovac. After the first sitting of the National Antifascist Council for the Liberation of the People of Croatia, known by its acronym, ZAVNOH, by the 'summer of 1943 Croatian Partisans had become the strongest military and political force resisting the occupier.'[137] According to Supek, by including some elements of the Croatian Peasant Party, the Anti Fascist Council became a coalition of parties in the struggle for national liberation.[138] 'The Croatian Political leadership, that is, the Communist, with Andija Hebrang as its head, saw itself not only as the creation of Radich's republicanism but also as a renewal of Yugoslavia on a democratic and confederal basis.'[139] Supek blames Tito's deputy Milovan Djilas for the weakening of the Croatian Communist leadership.[140] as well as accusing Djilas of not being fair towards Croatians. Djilas does not want to acknowledge that the people's liberation struggle was brought about in Croatia, based on a people's front with political pluralism.[141] This seems to be reflected in William Deakin's experience of the Croatian Partisan movement when he writes: The optimism of Major Jones seems to

---

135. Jozo Tomasovich, *War and Revelution in Yugoslavia*, 362–364. *Who Is What In The Independent State Of Croatia*, 250–251.
136. Dinko Suljak, *Trazijo San Radičovsku Hrvatsku*, 143–144.
137. Ivan Supek, *PM*, 133.
138. Ivan Supek, *PM*, 135–136, 167.
139. Ivan Supek, *PM*, 148.
140. Ivan Supek, *PM*, 145.
141. Ivan Supek, *PM*, 164.

reflect in some degree the excitement, and ambitions of the Croat Partisan leadership. Tito, on learning the substance of Jones' requests, sent to the General Head Quarters Croatia, on the 23 May, a signal which indicated a lurking anxiety at the independence being shown by a subordinate headquarters.[142]

T . . . . . . Dr Mladen Lorkovich and the minister of the army Ante Vokich together with Dr Ivanko Farolfi, the politician Ljudevit Tomashich and a group of officers who collaborated with them as well as the Ustasha university official Milivoj Karamarko, In total some forty Croatians, were shot in Lepoglava prison on 24 or 25 April 1945. It is almost certain that Pavelich gave the order that these Croatian men, who gave so much for Croatia, the first two of whom had worked very closely with him, be shot.[143]

U . . . . . Ante Beljo in his book 'Genocide' gives more details of this Memorandum, which was signed by the President of the Croatian government, Dr Nikola Mandich and eighteen ministers who were present in Zagreb at that time. Ivo Omrčanin, in his book *Hrvatska 1945* gives further details of the memorandum. The memorandum was sent with a minister of the government, Dr Vjekoslav Vranchich, and Captain Andre Vrkljan, who were to bring it to the headquarters of Field Marshal Alexander at Caserta, Italy. Although Vranchich and Vrkljan were prevented from meeting Field Marshal Alexander, we do know both he and Harold MacMillan were familiar with the memorandum. It was the last official document of the Independent State of Croatia.[144]

V . . . . . . Dr Vranchich told Ivo Rojnica later in Buenos Aires, that when they arrived in Venice they contacted the English who received them kindly and accommodated them in a hotel, telling them they would inform the Supreme Allied Command for the Mediterranean in Caserta and when a reply arrived they would be flown to Caserta. This was on 7 May. The following morning they noticed a change of

---

142. William Deakin, *TEM*, 221.
143. Jozo Tomasovich, *War and Revolution in Yugoslavia 1941-1945*, 768. Bogdan Krizman, *Ustaši .i Treći Reich*, 362–363. Bogdan Krizman, *Pavelić u Bjekstvu*, 9. Ante Belo, *Genocide*, 82–83. *Who Is What In The Independent State Of Croatia*, 112, 182, 237–239, 417–418, 399–400. Bilić-Erić Mirko, *Sluga Domovine*, 521–530.
144. Ante Belo, *Genocide*, 82–87. Ivo Omrčanin, *Hrvatska 1945*, 322–335. Hrvoje Matković, *Povijest Nezavisne Države Hrvatske*, 296–304.

mood in the English; there was no longer the kindness of the previous day. Instead of taking them to Caserta they were taken to prison. That was 8 May, the same day the war ended in Europe.[145]

W. Tito's Partisan forces followed the Communist ideology, and some officers were Communists and former fighters in the Spanish Civil War. During the Spanish Civil War, thousands of Catholics had been killed, including up to thirteen Catholic bishops, 4,184 priests and student priests, 283 nuns and thousands more religious believers. The Partisans also took on an anti-religious stand, especially against the Catholic Church, in Croatia.[146]

Rev. Ante Bakovich concluded his study: by the end of the war, the Partisans had killed 314 Croatian Catholic priests. After 9 May 1945, up to 118 were killed, plus sixty-four priests and Divinity students were handed over by the British. During the war Serbian Chetniks killed fifty-two priests, the German army killed eleven, and six others were killed by the Italian army, the Ustasha two and the Croatian Home Guard one. The youngest victim of the Communists was Ivan Skender, a twelve-year-old seminarian. In total, 568 Croatian Clergy, male religious and Divinity students were killed in Croatia alone during and immediately after the war.[147]

The Partisans also shot the Protestant Bishop of Croatia, Dr Filip Popp (1893–1945) on 29 June 1945. Dr Popp had the pastoral responsibility for the scattered Protestant Lutheran communities in Croatia, and had no political involvement.[148]

X. Slavko Stancer was a major in the Austro-Hungarian Army in 1914, as was Ivan Tomasovich, but an officer of lower rank at the time. Serving under both of them was the young Josip Broz who was a corporal and later took the name Tito. In his biography of Tito in the English language, Vladimir Dedijer mentions Ivan Tomasovich but there is no mention of Slavko Stancer. Tito showed no mercy to his former commanders from the First World War.[149]

---

145. Ivo Rojnica, *Susreti .i Doživlavi*, Volume 1, 227.
146. Juraj Batelja, *Crna Knjiga*. XX111. Taken from V Ortić, Buio sull'altare 1931–1939: la persecuzione della Chiesa in Spagna, Edited Citta Nouva, Roma, 1999.
147. Rev Ante Bekovac, 259–260. Also see Catholic Bishops of Croatia and Bosnia-Herzegovina as well as *HMiŽiVKV*, 153.
148. Martina Grahek Ravancic, *Represia .i Zloćin. Komunistickog Rezima u Hrvatskoj*, 100. *Who Is What In The Indepenent State Of Croatia*, 328.
149. Vladimir Dedija, *Tito Speaks*, 28. Milan Basta, *Rate Je Zavrsijo Sedam Dana Kasnije*, 117. Jasper Ridley, *Tito*, 63–64. *Who Is What In The Independent State Of Croatia*, 389–390, 399.

The Croatian Armed Forces

Y. Opinions vary about the number in the Croatian armed forces. In his book Damir Jug wrote about the Domobrani or Home Guard, who were the regular conscripted soldiers: 'It is a fact that in the armed forces in general as well as the Home Guard the trend was of continuous growth right up to 1943 and this number remained somewhere between 150,000 and 200,000 and with small variation was maintained to the end of the war, that is to May 1945.'[150] This does not include the Ustashi units who were the elite fighters. He concludes that, by the end of 1944, the Croatian land-based army did not number more than 200,000.[151]

According to Vinko Nikolich and Nevjestich, there were 269,000 soldiers, or 279,000 after the fifth recruitment. However, Jug concludes that these figures were to be taken with caution.[152]

Jozo Tomasovich wrote that by September 1943 the Croatian armed forces numbered 262,326 personnel.[153] and it is reasonable to conclude that by the end of the war the number had grown. This seems to agree with the assessment of Mladen Schwartz:

By the end of 1944 the Croatian Armed Forces numbered two hundred and sixty thousand personnel and that number, with the later mobilization, grew to three hundred thousand.[154]

Dr Krunoslav Draganovich, who was a very objective Croatian historian and gathered many eye witness accounts of the Communist massacres of Croatians after the war, wrote that there were two hundred and fifty thousand in the Croatian armed forces by the time the war ended.[155] Vjekoslav Vranchich, who was a minister in Pavelich's Government and who drew on the knowledge of General Fedor Draglonjev, put the total number in the Croatian army as two hundred and fifty-eight thousand.[156] Ivo Omrchanin, concludes that in total the Croatian Armed Forces numbered 270,000.[157] Milan

---

150. Damir Jug, *OSNDHSU*, 139.
151. Damir Jug, *OSNDHSU*, 141. Ivo Omrčanin, *Hrvatska 1941*, Volume 2, 925–927.
152. Damir Jug, *OSNDHSU*, 141.
153. Jozo Tomasovich, *Četnici*, 107 also Jozo Tomasovich, *WaRiY 1941-1945*, 423.
154. Mladen Swartz, *Bleiburg .i Haag*, 29.
155. Vinko Nikolić, *BUiP*, 82.
156. Vjekoslav Vranšić, *Postrojenje .i Brojcano Stanje Hrvatskih Oruzni Snaga*. (The Units and Numerical Number of the Croatian Armed Forces.), 324–325.
157. Ivo Omrčanin, *Hrvatska 1945*, 184–200.

Basta, who was a high ranking Partisan officer, wrote that in the Srem region alone, in the eastern part of Croatia by the end of 1944 with the Russian advance where the Croatian army was fighting the Russians, there were up to two hundred and thirty thousand Croatian soldiers.[158]

Led by General Vladimir Kren, the Croatian Airforce had its permanent aerodromes in Zagreb, Mostar, Sarajevo, Zemun and Banja Luka, and a pilot training facility at Borovo. The airforce had up to 6,000 personnel and up to 250 aircraft of various types, although this figure is to be taken with caution.[159]

Croatia also had a small navy, which mainly patrolled the rivers. Although Croatia is a maritime country, the development of its navy was greatly hindered due to Italy's occupation of much of Croatia's coastal region and almost all of its islands. Its navy numbered up to 1,000 personnel with Admiral Nikola Steinfl its last commander.[160]

Lord Nicholas Bethel drew from General T. Patrick Scott, the British General who repatriated the Croats from Bleiburg, the statement:

On 14 May I received news, that two groups of the Croatian army, which in total numbered 200,000 are approaching British lines at Bleiburg . . . They are accompanied by 500,000 civilians, wishing to reach the British area, to surrender and place themselves under British protection.[161]

In Tito's first biography in the English language, Vladimir Dedijer wrote: 'The liberation of the whole territory of Yugoslavia was completed during the period from March 20 to May 15, when the Yugoslav army inflicted losses of 99,907 dead and 209,639 captured, including many commanders . . . '

The ones who were captured were mainly in southern Austria, and he wrote nothing of the slaughter which followed.[162]

---

158. Milan Basta, *Rat Je Zavrsijo Sedam Dana Kasnije*, 508.
159. Damir Jug, *OSNDHSU*, 148-154, Vjekoslav Vrančić, *Postrojenje .i Brojčano. Who Is What In The Independant State Of Croatia*, 207-208.
160. Damir Jug, *OSNDHSU*, 157-161. Vjekoslav Vrančić, *Postrojenje .i Brojčano Stanje Hrvatski Oruzni Snaga*, 331-332. *Who Is What In The Independant State Of Croatia*, 367.
161. Nicholas Bethel, *The Last Secret*, 118.
162. Vladimir Dedija, *Tito Speaks*, 244.

Z The Handza Division

This division was formed at the beginning of 1943, through the instigation of Heinrich Himmler, because Muslims wanted more autonomy for themselves and were dissatisfied with the Croatian government.[163] It was given the name Handza, the Turkish word for knife or dagger,[164] and its 21,000 members included almost 3,000 Croatian Catholics.[165] The Christian churches made efforts to appoint chaplains to the German army and the SS, although the German government refused this, but Himmler made sure Imams were appointed to Handza to care for the spiritual welfare of the Muslims. They led Friday prayers, cared for the sick and wounded, conducted funerals and played a liaison role between German commanders and the local district mayors in Bosnia. Its supreme commander was the able Karl-Gustav Sauberzweig, who saw relations with the local population as crucial[166] directing his soldiers to see: *Not how many enemies have I killed but how many friends have I made.*[167] Although all Handza members wore the Croatian coat of arms on their left uniform sleeve, many of the Bosnian Muslims felt little affinity with the Croatian state and some disliked the state.[168]

One former Imam to the division sums up the feeling of all the Muslims of the division:

> I was young then, religious and raised as an anti Communist. And in the division, I must honestly say, we saw a bulwark against Bolshevism. Moreover we had witnessed what the Chetniks had done and we determined to aid our countrymen. This stirred us to join the division. Who else was in a position to help us? The Germans were willing to provide us with weapons and military leadership. We weren't politicians – in my eyes, our decision was a purely military one. We sought to end the Serbian attacks and to save what was left of the

---

163. George Lepre, *HBDtWSSHD 1943-1945*, 15. Ivo Omrčanin, *Hrvatska 1943*, 120-121.
164. George Lepre, *HBDtWSSHD 1943-1945*, 47.
165. George Lepre, *HBDtWSSHD 1943-1945*, 35. Ivo Omrčanin, *Hrvatska 1943*, 194-195.
166. George Lepre, *HBDtWSSHD 1943-1945*, 178.
167. George Lepre, *HBDtWSSHD 1943-1945*, 179.
168. George Lepre, *HBDtWSS 1943-1945*, 347.

Muslim settlements in Bosnia after the massacres at Gorazde, Foce, Zenica and near the Drina.[169]

As the Russians were penetrating into Hungary on 14 November 1944 the division was transferred to the Eastern front.[170] Some Muslims members returned to Bosnia against the advice of their German commanding officers, who knew what awaited them at home, and the rest became refugees in ravaged Germany and Italy.[171]

According to Stjepan Hojt, Germany had no more than six divisions in whole of the former Yugoslavia and with the Handza and Prince Eugen divisions there were no more than eight. This is confirmed by Jasper Ridley.[172]

---

169. George Lepre, *HBDtWSS 1943-1945*, 316-317.
170. George Lepre, *HBDtWSS 1943-1945*, 278.
171. George Lepre, *HBDtWSS 1943-1945*, 302-308.
172. Stjepan Hojt, *Conversation* 2 November 2003, Jasper Ridley, *Tito*, 220.

Captured Croatian forces near the town of Celj, Slovenia, May 1945 from Glas Koncila

Chapter 4
Death Marches Part 1

Witnessess Give their Accounts

Now that we have covered the analysis and background of what happened during 1941 to 1945, it is important to hear the real life accounts of people who lived through the time, and continued to suffer repercussions for years to come.

There have been countless accounts of these Death Marches written, such as that of Joseph Hecimovich in his book, 'In Tito's Death Marches and Extermination Camps', as noted in the Bibliography.

I have chosen what I consider some of the most significant accounts from other sources.

The following account was given in Rome, Italy on 7 April 1955. Because of the fear of repercussions against themselves and their families, especially in Communist Yugoslavia, some of the accounts are anonymous.

> It was perhaps 3:45 pm. when the first tidings of the coming disaster reached us. We were told that our leaders had signed a treaty of surrender to the British. The terms were onerous indeed. The entire Croatian army had to give up all of its arms and ammunition to the Englishmen. Then the leaders would turn our soldiers over to Tito's army. The Communists had promised the British that no reprisals would be taken. All Croatians would be allowed to return to their homes without hindrance or molestation.
>
> Promptly at 4:00 pm the order came to lower the Croatian flags and raise white ones in their place as a sign of surrender. This was a bad omen of things to come. Everyone was beginning

to feel that the situation was taking the worst possible turn. Soon after receiving this order we saw several British officers, accompanied by a number of Yugoslav Communist officials, passing along the vehicle line that had been drawn up behind us. They eyed us with visible satisfaction as the surrender began.

Not far from my position, there was a Croatian Army officer who was acquainted with a friend of mine. I sent my friend to ask this man about the details of the surrender. My friend soon returned from his talk with the officer. Even from a distance it was obvious that he had depressing news. The officer had told him that everything was lost. The British would turn us over to Tito's people who would do with us as they pleased. Since the officer had his wife and son with him he was especially upset. However, many of our officers had decided not to surrender. My friend told me that he was going to hide in the woods and fight to the end.[1]

This witness goes on to relate that it began to rain, but the British had not completed the circle they had tried to draw around them. He, together with a friend, had decided to go to the wood and pick up some wood for tent poles. He encountered several Montenegrin National units watching the happenings on the Bleiburg field. He goes on.

My friend flatly refused to surrender to the British because they were turning us over to the Partisans. Encouraged by his example, I decided to follow him into the woods. We took a few of our belongings that we had brought with us from our bags and turned the pack horses loose. Before making our last break, we crept up a hill which afforded a view of what was going on in the field below us. It was a terrible and dramatic scene of the final separation of families, husbands, wives, sons and fathers. Many soldiers were determined not to surrender and were only waiting for night to fall before they tried to get away into the mountains. Partisan soldiers and officers were pushing amongst the crowds, trying to separate the officers and soldiers from the civilians. Whenever they could isolate military personnel from their families, they marched them off

---

1. Prcela John & Guldescu Stanko, *OS*, 156.

to an unknown destination. A huge mountain of arms and ammunition was lying on the field as our men laid down their arms".[2]

When the witness awoke the next morning, his little party descended to the field below, where by that stage, there were few people. He goes on:

> As we were descending the little hill, we ran into some men who told us that during the night many of our officers had gone around advising everyone not to surrender. We regretted that we had not encountered these officers. Had we done so, we would have taken their advice to lose ourselves in the mountains.
>
> After a long discussion of the predicament in which we found ourselves, we decided that the best thing we could do now would be to surrender to the British. I accompanied a friend to the lower part of the slope, where we found a few small groups who were angry with themselves because they had not joined those who had fled to the mountains during the night. Many Yugoslav Communists wearing red arm bands were standing or walking around, but the big piles of guns and munitions were gone.
>
> We remained on the lower slope for about twenty minutes. Some seventy other individuals joined us there. They too had seen that it was too late to get away to the mountains and had decided to give themselves up. After a time we moved off in the direction indicated to us by the British the night before. We had gone hardly a mile when a Yugoslav Communist patrol came up and took us prisoners. Some of them remained with us while others in the patrol went on to pick up more prisoners at the designated place of surrender.
>
> About 10 am on 17 May, all civilian refugees and soldiers were told to line up in columns of four. We moved off escorted by heavily armed communist soldiers who lined up on either side of us. As we marched we saw British soldiers here and there. We were marching along the right bank of the river Drava, the historic northern border of our country.

---

2. Prcela John & Guldescu Stanko, OS, 157.

After an hour's march we came to a wooden bridge that spanned the river. An English military detachment was guarding the crossing. Since the bridge was in poor condition we had to cross in small groups rather than in column. On the far bank of the Drava, armed Communists mounted on horses, met us and took over escort duties.

From that moment we saw no more English soldiers. Now we began to realise how desperate our situation really was. We understood clearly, although unfortunately much too late, what lay before us. The emergency measures we might have tried a few days earlier were useless.

As long as the Communist units were in sight of the British troops, they refrained from maltreating us. But the moment the Englishmen were no longer in evidence, the Communists began to behave as though we were wild beasts and they were the same, but bigger and stronger. The first thing they did was to start us on a run. Whenever someone could not keep up, the Communist guards fell upon him and beat him mercilessly.[3]

With this fast paced march, we arrived in the vicinity of Dravograd about 5 pm. This was a short stop, since Tito's Partisans quickly took over from our former escorts. These Communists were wild beasts, too. They took all our valuables, and in robbing us, let us know that we would have no further use of material possessions. On the other side of the line there was a young soldier of the regular Croatian Army. This boy wore a ring with his father's picture set into it. The father had given it to his son when the boy was sixteen, and now, a few years later the ring was very tight. Several of the Communist soldiers tried to remove this ring, twisting his hand so that he screamed with pain. When they saw that the ring would not come off, they gave up and left him alone. This little act was repeated several times. Finally, a Serb Partisan came up. He took one look at the ring and told the boy that he wanted it right away. The lad replied that he would be glad to give it to him, but it fitted too tightly to be removed from his finger.

---

3. Prcela John & Guldescu Stanko, OS, 158–159.

'Well, you bandit' said the Serb, 'come here. I'll show you how to take it off.'

The boy went off with him into the surrounding woods. He never came back; we knew that his life had ended and the Serb had cut off his finger somewhere in that leafy expanse.[4]

A few hundred yards from the scene of this tragedy stood a store house. As we approached it, two husky Partisan soldiers grabbed me. They held a pistol at my head and took everything that my previous escorts had not discovered on my person. They threw me out of the store house just as our column began to move off again.

This witness goes on to describe how, when they reached another bridge that crossed the Drava, their guards separated them into two columns, one which followed the left bank and the other the right bank. As they approached a railway station at a fork in the road, two soldiers began directing the sick, elderly and very young to the railway station while the others were directed to continue along the main road to Celje.

The witness continues:

> I suggested to my friend that we pretend to be sick. It was our only hope of escaping the massacre in store for all prisoners who were sufficiently healthy to be possible opponents of Tito's state, and supported by Soviet Russia, Britain and America.
>
> At first, my friend refused to agree to my suggestion. At last, however, he agreed that we might try this subterfuge in lieu of any better course of action. But as soon as the Communists saw us mingle with the old and sick, they yelled at us: 'Where are you going, bandits?' My friend replied that I was dying and that he did not know what to do with me. The Partisans swore and shouted at us but, at least, they did let us go on to the railway station.
>
> Several hundred refugees were milling around there. Among them were other young people who probably had the same

---

4. Prcela John & Guldescu Stanko, OS, 159.

idea and employed the same kind of trick that we had to get to the station. The rest of our column was driven by the Partisan guards along the main highway towards Celje.⁵

Another witness, who gave his testimony in Fermo, Italy in October 1945 also wished to be anonymous. He was an officer during the war. He gave his account of his arrival at Bleiburg.:

> Shortly before noon on 6 May 1945 I received an oral command to evacuate the school during the night from Captain George Markovich, who had arrived at Kerestinac from Zagreb. He directed me to take all of the students and as much of the equipment as possible to Celje. Here our group would join the staff and student bodies of the several officers' schools. We would receive further orders and instructions once we had reached this Slovenian locality.
>
> I set about immediately to organise the retreat. Besides our own students, I brought with us part of the Fourth and Seventh Lieutenants' Corps as well as the Female Work Service group employed on state properties at Keresinec.

He goes on to relate how, with a group of 300 civilians and 220 well-equipped military cadets and officers, he reached Dravograd on 13 May. They found 80,000 people, soldiers and civilians in and around the town with many more military and civilian columns continuing to arrive. He described the vicinity as being unbelievably crowded.

After conferring with a number of Croatian Generals and officers, he received orders to set out for Bleiburg on the evening of 13 May because Partisan forces were opening fire, despite the truce arrangements that were to last until the following day. He continues:

> At once, Generals Boban and Herenchich (Herenčić) and Colonal Sudar led forward units which swept the Partisans aside and opened the way to Bleiburg for our columns. Sporadic battles continued throughout the night, during which Colonel Sudar's men brought in more than 100 captives. On the following morning the Partisans attacked again. They were now supported by the Bulgarian artillery, whose fire was

---

5. Prcela John & Guldescu Stanko, OS, 159–160 Signed JU, Rome 7 April 1955.

very effective against our closely packed columns. Although we lost several hundred men in this canon fire, we broke through the Partisans again, and established a rear defense line to protect the withdrawal of our troops and civilians from Dravograd to Bleiburg.

My division took a side road which ran westward out of Dravograd, and reached the outskirts of Bleiburg without much trouble that same evening, on 14 May. We found a great number of civilians and members of the Croatian Armed Forces assembled there. We found the English as well as Partisan troops were blocking the entrance into Bleiburg through which we intended to pass in order to get to Klagenfurt in Carinthia. These troops were awaiting orders concerning us from their respective commands.

A number of our higher generals arrived in our midst. On 15 May, Generals Herenchich, Servatzi, Metikos and Colonel Crljen went to negotiate with the British commander. I do not know how the negotiations were conducted, but I do remember that on this same afternoon these officers ordered us to hoist white flags as signs of surrender.

Great emotional confusion prevailed amongst our officers and soldiers following the receipt of this order. Many officers, myself included, wanted to take their units into the adjoining woods and wage a last ditch resistance. However, General Metzger and Lieutenant Colonel Bobinac thought we should obey the order our superior officers had given us. Metzger said that the British and Partisans were capable of firing deliberately on the women and children we had with us if we offered any resistance. I talked with a number of officers who also foresaw the worst from the British. Some of them disregarded the surrender order and led their men into the nearby forests. I also heard that General Boban and Colonel Sudar were already returning to Croatia to organise fighting groups. Their intention was to take shelter with their bands in the great beech and oak forests of the Homeland, and which they would now defend to the bitter end. This is what all of us should have done when our lines were still intact and our soldiers still confident. At that time, despite the German collapse, the Croats were still confident that they could hold out almost indefinitely against Tito's Communists and their Anglo-American, Russian and Bulgarian allies.

After considerable hesitation, I got rid of my weapons and joined the column which was going to surrender at Bleiburg. From then I understood that we were to be returned ultimately to Croatia.

To our great astonishment we had to surrender to the Communists rather than to the British. At first it seemed they were going to treat us decently and conduct us safely back to Croatia. As soon as the columns of prisoners had left the British lines behind, the Reds started looting our belongings. Then they commenced to disband groups of officers and shoot or otherwise dispose of them. As soon as I saw what was going on, I made up my mind to escape before my turn came to experience the lethal attentions of our captors.

'*Kaj Bog dade I sreca junačka*' (What God may give and a heroic heart). The motto given to our Army by Ban Jelachich in 1848 when it crossed the Drava into Hungary held good for me now, almost a century later. I got away into the woods and after eight days of wandering and deprivations arrived at Villach in Carinthia. Here I enjoyed Austrian hospitality for three months before I sought final safety in Italy.[6]

A Statement from the Commander of an Armed Unit of the Croatian Army.

Note that this statement of Kazimir Kovachich, who was born in Pula in 1914 has been slightly changed from the original Croatian in order to be more easily understood by English-speaking readers. No changes in meaning have been made.

I was a soldier all through the war. In 1944 I was the Commander of the tanks and armed vehicles in Markusevac. The Commander of the reserved armored command was Captain Marijan Subotich from Vinkovaca. The other captains in the unit were permanent Captains Zlatko Orsevich and Marinovich. I was the only temporary Captain. Also in the unit were permanent Captains Dragutin Ribich, Zlatko Sokola, and temporary Captain Ivica Bushich, Lieutenants

---

6. Prcela John & Guldescu Stanko, OS, 160–163 Signed: BJ Fermo, 22 October 1945.

Hrastich, Cvjetkovich, Dimsa Oreskovich, temporary Captains Lesich and Savich (active), colour bearer Filkovich, permanent Captain Fabris and Captain Ivica Schmidt.

Our unit never received the order to withdraw. We left Markusevac this way: Captain Subotich went to Zagreb on the Sunday, to look into the situation, for we had not received any information from the Ministry of Defense. When he returned we held a meeting of officers to decide what we would do. We resolved to leave Markusevac, to disband the newly enrolled recruits, most of whom came from the vicinity of Zagreb, and to destroy the ammunition which we had left over. On Monday we made our way towards Zagreb and at around mid-day at Medvescak we stopped for new information. Captain Subotich couldn't decide whether to leave Zagreb, while the other officers wanted to go towards the western side of the city. On arriving at Crnomerac we held another officers' meeting in the evening. At this meeting Captains Oreskovich and Marinovich were not present, for they had already left the unit. At this meeting Subotich again asked that during this time of lawlessness the unit perform guard duty in the area of Zagreb. When no one agreed to this, he asked that at least it stay on Croatian territory and wait for the unfolding of events. We, Captains Ivica Schmidt and Hrastich asked that the unit leave the country. We decided to ask the soldiers their opinion. At that time the unit amounted to 120 to 140 soldiers who voted unanimously for the withdrawal from the country. The general consensus was that we would return to the country in the near future and fight the Yugoslav communists. With this, Captain Subotich passed on the command of the unit to me, while other captains who were not in agreement remained.

Later I learned of the fate of individual Captains. The Commander of the Partisan army was General Jovanovich, who was an officer in the prewar Yugoslav army. He was killed in 1948 when Tito broke with Stalin, as Jovanovich supported Stalin. This same Jovanovich informed the former officers of the Yugoslav army, amongst whom were Subotich, Zlatko Oreskovich and Marinovich, that he would spare them.

Captain Subotich was accepted in the Yugoslav communist army but sometime in autumn 1945 was found in Ogulin with his throat cut. Zlatko Oreskovich was imprisoned by the

Partisans in Nova Vesa, disappearing one night without trace, as happened to Marinovich. Lieutenant Savich was hanged at Sveta Ana. Sokola wasn't involved in the withdrawal but was betrayed and shot.

Lieutenant Obelich, whom I didn't mention earlier, was held for a long time in a Partisan camp. Captains Fabris and Ribich were sentenced to many years imprisonment and, after five years, released. Lieutenant Cindrich, whom I also didn't mention, was for some time in prison before being released. Captain Dimša Oreskovich and Lieutenant Franjo Hrastich were shot by the Partisans in Tezna after they had been handed over, while Lieutenant Ivica Schmidt was seriously wounded in fighting near Dravograd. Later I learnt his leg was amputated and he later lived in Zagreb.

On 6 May, under my command, the unit took the Podšušed, Zaprešić, Krapina direction. Our unit was fully motorised. We had twenty motor cycles of Zindap make, two trucks, three assault armored Fiat vehicles of one ton, three armored cars of various makes, weighing five tons each and two civilian cars. The tanks had thirty-five-millimeter canon and the assault vehicles had machine guns. The rest of the men had repeat and automatic weapons. The ammunition and food were in sufficient supply and the discipline and morale was excellent. The leaving of the city was made difficult due to the large column of civilians and the movement of the German army, but the unit kept moving. We came to the crossing before Zaprešći, when we turned east towards Krapina.

We arrived in Krapina at 7 am on 7 May, where the men rested, refreshing themselves and cleaning the vehicles. In Krapina I found one German unit guarding the food storage facility which enabled me to gather more food for my men. The police general of Nikolić informed me that the Russians were in Maria Bistrica and advised me to go to Rogask Slatina, for they could cut the road during the night; I discovered later this had not happened. While in Krapina, General Rafael Boban arrived to tell me that he wanted to go back to Zagreb to prevent the Partisans from entering the city.

At around midnight we arrived at Rogaska Slatina where we met a section of Ustasha units under the command of Colonel

Oreskovich. He directed us towards Maribor, for the Croatian Government were headed that way together with sections of the Croatian Army. Without delay we set off towards Maribor, but some two kilometers from Rogaska Slatina, two trucks of German soldiers came to our assistance and in frightened panic informed us that the Russians were already in Maribor and that we couldn't pass; all troops who went in that direction fell into their hands. With this information I resolved to head towards Celje through Potplata (Unterplatt), where we stayed the night.

Although in Potplat I learnt that Germany had surrendered and that Celje was in Partisan hands, I decided to go in the same direction and we travelled without any difficulty. We arrived just before Celje at around eleven in the morning. Sometime before this, we came across an abandoned German train, which the local villagers were pillaging. Dispersing the villagers, I secured the unit with further supplies.

Before entering Celje, I sent Lieutenant Dimis Oreskovich with three soldiers to investigate the situation there. Oreskovich was away for some three hours. In the meantime General Servatzi arrived with a number of Generals, an artillery unit and other larger military units. When Oreskovich returned, he informed us that Celje was already in Partisan hands, they were not allowing any one to pass through, and he added the Germans in Celje had already surrendered. We consulted one another; Servatzi was in favour of dialogue with the Partisans to request that we be allowed to pass through peacefully. Relying on our ammunition and the fighting spirit of my unit, I decided any dialogue was unnecessary and as I was at the head of that column, I moved forward.

In Celje I found the following situation: the city decorated with flowers and bunting, the whole population in the streets, mainly women and no unfriendly feeling towards us. The traffic was under the control of the Partisan police. One of these was close to my vehicle and when I asked him the situation in the city, he told me not to be afraid of the Partisans for they were too weak to attack us and when the last units passed through the city he would go with them for he, himself, was a Croatian, who just happened to join up with the Partisans. At that time, there were various groups entering the square, including Ustasha units, Montenegrin patriots under the command of Dr Krivokapich and Chetniks who were collaborating with the Croatian Army. I thought they were under the leadership of Koste Pecanac.

We lost almost the whole afternoon in Celje. I noticed some activity in the building of the local district council, in which Partisan couriers were entering, driving Ustasha vehicles. This could have been a contact between the Ustasha command in Celje and the Partisan command in Sempeter. In the square there was general disorganization amongst the soldiers, for the Ustasha units were under their own command, my unit was independent, the artillery unit without its command and the Chetniks and Montenegrins each with their own command.

Before evening, Professor Daniel Crljen spoke to the gathered units in the square ordering them to the border. This was well received by the units which then began to leave the city. The column was some two kilometers long and could have numbered up to 15,000 people. My unit remained at the rear. After we left, a good number of Ustasha units, under the command of Maks Luburich and Rafael Boban, remained in Celje.

Some six kilometers from the city, the column stopped overnight, following the instructions of General Herenchich, who had taken over command. When the column stopped, I returned to Celje with two soldiers to look for an Air Force Lieutenant, who had joined us earlier with the intention of coming with us. On the journey I was stopped at two places by groups of Partisans and to their question of where we were going I answered '*To Celje*' and they allowed me to pass. I concluded they were afraid of Luburich's threat, that he would take vengeance for every Croatian soldier who was killed during the withdrawal through Slovenia. I was able to return to my unit without hindrance.

When in the morning the column began to move, I left the rear, moving to the front of the column with my motorised unit. At one bend I came across a Cossack division under the command of a German officer, whose staff member was busy burning the archives and destroying all vehicles. When we attempted to extract out of the rubble an undamaged truck, a squabble developed between my unit and the Cossack unit which had already taken up positions. The German officers did not want it to fall into enemy hands. In my discussions with their command I explained that behind my unit there was a column of exhausted civilians on foot and it was for this reason we needed the truck. If we did not take the truck it would fall into enemy hands. The night of 9–10 May we spent on the road before Windischgraetz. There was a panicked race developing among the motorised units to reach the Austrian border, for there was, we thought, a 48-hour time of grace to cross the Austrian border. Before Windischgraetz, we met a Croatian column made up of civilians, students, police and people from all walks of life. Parallel to us, Cossack cavalry units were also withdrawing.

On 11 May we were the first units to reached Dravograd. We began to organise the civilian groups and units who came with us, arranging where they were to be placed, their commands and organising hospital facilities which were run mainly by students. We did this with the realisation that we were involved in the last phases of our withdrawal.

Just before Dravograd a joint military command was formed arranging defensive positions. I was named Commander of the scouting unit and was given a Ustasha armored company, under the command of Sub Captain Kovachevich. Our defensive lines were some two kilometers from the road that led to Dravograd, at a place where there was a stream with a mill. It was some 100 to 200 metres from a forest, in which there was a small force of Partisans from Dravograd. There was no trouble for the first few days and one could go to and from Dravograd without any difficulty. At the command there were Generals Herenchich, Metikos, Servazi, Boban and Perichich, who came with his mountain units from Kutina telling us that he, Perichich, felt he was deceived. He did not receive any order to withdraw and on top of that he had to act as a security to a German unit, which moved in front of him.

On 12 May there came a Bulgarian captain by the name of Orlov, who announced that his visit was of a private nature, for he wanted to do something for the women and children. It was Professor Crljen who spoke to him, telling him that the

Croatian army had no desire to fight against the Bulgarians; it wanted to surrender unconditionally to the allied forces and not to the Partisans. Crljen asked for some bread and milk for the children, which this man promised but did not deliver.

On 13 May there came from Dravograd a Partisan captain accompanied by a soldier on a motor bike, seeking to be taken to the Central Command with a message from a division of the Third Army. I personally took him to the Command; although I was not present at the discussion, I later heard the following: They sought an unconditional and immediate surrender; if it were rejected we would be placed outside the law. These talks were conducted with Generals Servatzi, Perichich, Metikos, Herenchich, Professor Crljen and some others whose names I do not remember. It included Dr Krivokapich in the name of the Montenegrins and supporters of Dr Sekula Drljevich who were with our column. Through the demands of the Partisan representative, the surrender was to take place at 2 pm. The answer was negative, that is, there was to be no question of surrender. Instead, the request was for a free pass through to Austria with the intention of surrendering to the Allies. From our side, it was guaranteed that there would be no fighting; we only sought a free, unhindered passage but if we were prevented from passing we had enough armaments to use force.

At that time the arrangement of the units in case of action was as follows: In the center was my unit, strengthened through the already mentioned Ustasha armament unit and another section of police from Banja Luka. To my right was the mountain unit of General Perichich and on my left the Black Legion under the command of General Boban. In the vicinity of the guest house, there was an organised rest area, a field hospital and other support services.

Exactly at 2 pm, mortar firing started from Partisan units and from positions that had been strengthened on higher ground before Dravograd. As a result of this, we suffered a considerable number of losses, especially in the area of our command where the largest number of people were concentrated. After the understandable shock, we began a counter action, turning our forces towards Dravograd, intending to cross the bridge to reach Austria. In the meantime, we received the unexpected news to turn left towards the direction of Bleiburg, because all the bridges had been mined. The action of my unit was as follows: After the Partisans opened fire using mortars, I ordered our armored vehicles in the direction of the forest, which was along the road, some 250 to 300 meters in length. We also received a reasonable amount of machine gun support. The action succeeded in spite of our loss of an armored Fiat vehicle, in which the driver was killed and Captain Ivica Schmidt seriously wounded (who I learnt later had his leg amputated). Penetrating into the forest, I came across the abandoned knapsacks and ammunition left by the Partisans. The movement of the column continued all night before Bleiburg. After some time, I joined my unit in the column at 8 pm and we continued in the same direction.

At seven in the morning of 14 May, I heard continuous gunfire at the head of the column, after which a courier arrived from General Herenchich with the order that my armored unit was to move to the head of the column and smash the attack. The attack came from two well-fortified positions, completely preventing passage towards Bleiburg. The place was at the crossroads between Ljubljana and Bleiburg. At this spot, the Partisans had destroyed a German motorised unit the day before. It was still burning at our arrival.

My unit took a position on a hill opposite the Partisans and we began firing at eight o'clock in the morning. Other units began at the same time, clearing Partisan positions from the mentioned areas. That operation was completed successfully by 5 pm. Considering the difficult situation, there were some 100 casualties on our side, some of whom were killed while others were wounded.

Immediately after this, a small column was formed which accompanied Servatzi, Professor Crljan and Herenchich to the border, where I stopped to organise my unit. My unit gave security to the delegation hoping to make contact with the Allied Forces with the intention of surrendering. After an hour and a half, the delegation returned to inform us the English and Americans would accept us as prisoners of war. We continued the reorganisation of the units with the aim of writing up the names of the units, their commanders, and the number of civilians included, which information was requested by the Allied Command in Bleiburg.

All this brought about a happy disposition to the mass of people on the Bleiburg field, which in my estimation numbered some 80,000 to 100,000 people. In contrast to this there also developed a feeling of uncertainty and doubt which proved to be warranted the following day, when, at around noon, Spitfires appeared overhead, flying back and forth at low levels over the field. They and American Sherman tanks prevented any further progress to Bleiburg. A short time after that, news spread of demands for an unconditional surrender within the hour. If we did not comply, we would be attacked by air and ground forces, without regard to the civilian population. Partisans began appearing on the same field. In addition, we received news from the Allied Command that we were to fly white flags.

The surrender played out in the following way: after the announcement of the unconditional surrender within the one hour, a general consternation developed. One section of the organised soldiers, under the command of their officers, destroyed their weapons and vehicles so that they would not come into the hands of the Partisans. Others organised themselves into smaller groups, arming themselves with lighter weapons, intending to trek over the Karavank Mountains into Austria escaping capture. There were those who, in the same manner, decided to return to Croatia.

I saw General Boban with a group of soldiers going into the forest to begin guerrilla activity. There were also those who accepted the disintegration of their units and joined with the civilian population intending to return to their homes. I chose this course of action with my unit. I gathered them together and dissolved any military duty that was theirs. Of those who accepted the call to surrender I remember Generals Stancer, Servatzija and Metikos, Colonel Girickca and some fifteen others, some Generals and higher officers. While I didn't see General Perichich amongst them, I later learned that he safely crossed the border. I mention him, for he was my last commander.

Before I speak any further of the captivity, I would like to note some of my observations and experiences of the disaster. I have no intention of blaming anyone or holding anyone responsible.

a. The plan for an organised guerrilla campaign, planned before the withdrawal, and in which my unit and I were partially involved, was completely destroyed through the order to withdraw.

b. The propagation of the idea that the Allied Command would accept us, reorganise us and use us in its fight against Communism had no basis in reality. This contributed to the complete withdrawal of the army out of the homeland.

c. The lack of notification to the military leadership of the morale and material state of the fighting units and the lack of communication and co-operation between the commanders on the field and the tactical command caused problems.

d. The abandonment of the army by its supreme command without any concrete order during the whole of the withdrawal was disastrous.

e. The spread of optimism caused problems and the uncertainty sapped morale. This uncertainty lead to a complete spiritual unpreparedness of the people to face up to the negative result of the surrender.

The Same Witness Continues to Relate the Surrender and the Death Marches

As I had arranged delegates to be at the mentioned places, I stayed there, where I completed the reorganisation of my unit waiting for the order to come for the surrender. Upon receiving the order I absolved the soldiers of any duty and with Lieutenants Dimis Oreskovich and Franjo Hrastich I went forward, when they called the officers to identify themselves. The place of gathering was at Bleiburg itself, in a building meant for agricultural services. The building seemed stables. There appeared to be approximately 300 to 400 men, officers and under officers. The Partisans paid little attention to the ordinary soldier unless they were Ustasha.

The attitude of the Partisans in the presence of the English was correct, but when we distanced ourselves from the English as evening approached, we noticed rougher actions from the Partisans. We heard shooting, shouting, beatings and there began a general stealing of our belongings. At this point they took the watch from my hand.

Before daylight on 16 May, we left Bleiburg, crossing the Drava to Rudan. We left Bleiburg while it was still dark, and we passed a row of Partisans who systematically confiscated our belongings. We continued to Dravograd, and with only one exception, there weren't any organised guards accompanying us, although strategic points along the road were occupied by Partisans. The left side of the road was occupied by the Partisans and on the right was the Drava river, so escape was impossible. Before Dravograd, at the place where the Drava bends creating a peninsula, we were stopped by a Partisan formation, armed with machine guns. Its commander was a Dalmatian Serb, but he could have been called Drakula or something similar.

The actions of the Partisans were sudden and nervous and we expected trouble. It was here that they organised a selection process, moving the officers to the peninsula, ordering us to sit and later cursing and swearing, ordering us to lie down. Taking into consideration the confined place where we were, we expected annihilation. After about three quarters of an hour, we were ordered to line up on the road in rows of four, after which we set off for Dravograd.

On the way we came across both men and women Partisans, who hurled insults and attacked us. I had the impression that it was an organised attempt to frighten us, so that we would enter Dravograd as a cowardly, frightened mob. It is a fact that there was not one case of cowardice, in fact the stance was noble and defiant. This was also the case during the whole period of withdrawal from Dravograd to Kovin; many acts of heroism and bravery occurred.

We arrived at two in the afternoon at Dravograd, where we formed columns of officers, sub officers, Ustasha and Domobrani. A few hours later this column began moving towards Maribor. It was now that, for the first time, we noticed we were fully under the control of the Partisans, who were armed to the teeth. We stood on the left side of the Drava River. Partisans accompanied us on the left side of our column, while at specific points other Partisans were stationed with machine guns. There began drastic repressive measures such as the killing of individuals. At one place they broke the column and began shooting the front and rear, causing many casualties. For the first time many asked: what was the intention of the Partisans and what will they do with us?

There was a general feeling that, at least, we officers would be liquidated. As a result, prisoners jumped into the Drava River while the Partisans opened fire on them, killing them. At some point I saw the length of the column and estimated the number of people: our column could have numbered 10,000 people. Behind our column, I could see another column, but I was not able to estimate its numbers. The march was inhumane and after every one and a half hours we had ten minutes for rest and were not allowed to move from the spot. The men sat and lay down in the rain and mud. The men in the column were physically exhausted, having been without food for two days. Under these conditions we moved on towards Maribor.

Just before Maribor the Partisans forced us, completely exhausted, to run through the city for about two kilometers to the place of gathering. Those who accompanied us were Serbs from the inner parts of Dalmatia. I think at Lawamund, but certainly on the road from Ruden to Dravograd, we came across Bulgarian units stationed there. They were completely uninterested. I, for example, asked an officer for a piece of bread but he refused.

We arrived at Maribor in the morning between nine and ten o'clock. We were taken to a certain gathering place, where Partisans divided the Ustasha from the Domobrani. They took from us all sharp implements but acted quite gently with us, although, as yet, we hadn't received any food.

The Partisans formed the fifty or so Domobrani officers into a circle and, what I thought was a Partisan commissar, gave instructions in an attempt to establish contact. He promised us a strict but fair judgment. Those who the people's court did not find guilty would be received, if he so wished, into the ranks of the People's Army. The Ustasha Unit was to be arranged under the command of Ustasha officers and sub-officers and, under Croatian command, was taken to a place of confinement, which was also reserved for us.

Maribor gave us the impression of being a city that showed no sympathy towards the Partisans. A few observers followed us with sorrow and compassion, and I saw one woman secretly give some bread to the prisoners. We stayed the night in a railway building, we Domobrani at the bottom, while the Ustasha were on the first floor. I heard they were treated cruelly on the first floor.

The next day, we were taken to another building, which was cleaner, where we were able to take a bath and were given our first piece of food. In this second building, we were frequently visited by Partisan officers and I had the impression that the purpose of those visits was to gain inside information.

In this building with me were Major Zlomislich, who had been on the eastern front, Major Stencer, adjutant to General Markulja, who was hanged in Mostar, Captain Zvonko Lukachevich, and the artillery Sub Colonel Mladich, who was of Slovene origin. All together there were around 100 of us. The next day, just before evening, they moved us to a two-story school building and gave us lectures on the aims of the People's Liberation Army. They spoke of its big heartedness and its intention to include the selected officers into its ranks with the same rank they had in the Croatian army, if the people's court did not find them guilty of activities against the people.

At the invitation of the Partisan officers, the commissioned officers were asked to step forward from the reserves. My two area officers, Oreskovich and Hrastich, who were commissioned officers, asked my advice. Doubting the sincerity of the Partisan offer, I couldn't advise them. They decided to acknowledge their role as commissioned officers and stepped forward. All commissioned officers were taken that same night and never returned. I never heard from them again.

Later I learnt that at Tezna, near Maribor, the Croatian officers were liquidated on 25 May, Tito's birthday, which was celebrated with massive shootings of his opponents.

The Partisans took us out of the building in an unknown direction. They announced they were taking us for a 'walk'. We were convinced that they were taking us to be shot. I remember that at the head of a particular column was Professor Dr Maksimilian Petanjek. After we walked for two to three kilometres in a southerly direction, a messenger arrived on a motor cycle. He gave a dressing down to the commander of the column, after which the column returned to the school. As I was in the front of the column, I followed everything closely and I got the impression that the initial order was being changed. After our return to the school, where we stayed the night, they loaded us in the afternoon onto train wagons that were designed for cattle; they told us they were taking us to Zagreb for trial.

The wagons were meant for forty soldiers, but there were more than 100 of us in each. The wagons were closed until we arrived at Zagreb. In spite of the difficult circumstances of the journey, the morale was so high that as we crossed the Slovene-Croatian border we spontaneously sang *Jos Hrvatska Ni Propala* (Croatia Has Not Yet Fallen). In Zaprešću, through an opening in the wagon door, I recognised an acquaintance, who brought me two pieces of salami. We reached Zagreb at 10 am, where at a side platform the Partisans took our belongings, making us undress, leaving us almost naked. They even took our wedding rings.

On the same day, at around 10 pm in the evening, they took us to the camp at Prečko. We stayed at this camp till 27 or 28 of May. Prečko was a collection camp, where there were already several thousand members of the Croatian Armed Forces. Here we were militarily divided into barracks of up to 100 people each. An identification of individuals took place in preparation for trial in Bjelovar.

Every evening in this camp there was theft of property from the prisoners. During the stay in Prečko, the identification of individuals was done by using a questionnaire. It consisted of some fifty questions, which had to be filled in briefly and truthfully, under threat of death. I saw one incident where a young man, when he recognised his mother, he came closer to the fence and was killed. Although the people were friendly to us, for we were in Croatia, the Partisans would place people among us as spies and some people fell prey to this tactic.

In this camp General Jerkovich delivered a speech in which he promised that all who had not committed a crime would be forgiven and if they wished they would be received into the People's Liberation Army, being treated equally. Continuously before Jerkovich's talk, there was the questioning and release of those reserved and commissioned Domobrani officers, who collaborated with him.

Immediately after this speech, many vicious looking Partisans came into the camp, they surrounded us, lined us in columns and began tying us with wire. Sometime later, they took the wire off us Domobrani officers, leaving the Ustasha tied up. After an hour, they started to march us through Zagreb's Maksimir Park in the Lepoglava direction. Along this road the column was accompanied by well-armed Partisans with machine guns who, based on their appearance, could have been gypsies from Baranja or Serbs from the Kordun region. At the end of the column, there were four to six Partisans who had the task of shooting anyone who lagged behind.

As we walked, a young Croatian Air Force Officer fainted and his comrades helped him. The Partisan guards said to leave him on the side of the road, for a vehicle was coming from behind which would collect him. When the Partisans who were at the rear reached this young man on the side of the road, they immediately shot him. This served as an example to the others, so from then on the men, with great effort and sacrifice, carried their sick and exhausted comrades.

Walking all night, the column finally reached Lepoglava on 29 May at noon. We stayed there, cramped up in the sun, surrounded by wire, without food or drink until five in the afternoon. It was now completely clear that everything that had happened to us from Lepoglava to Časma, was organised with the intention of killing all of us. I think that our group could have numbered up to 2,000 men. On the road from Lepoglava towards Časma, we entered the Časma forest which was covered in fog. It was already dark and the rows quite cramped. The way was very slippery due to the heavy rain, which made further progress of the column difficult. The Partisans forced us to squeeze close to one another. The accompanying Partisans would, from time to time, distance themselves from the column and shoot at it. Some time about three in the night, I had the impression that the Partisans were completely distant from the group, which moved through short forest tracks. The intention was to encourage a panic and attempted escape towards Časma. When panic did ensue, a indiscriminate shooting at the column occurred, especially at the rear where the Ustasha were tied. Between 300 to 500 people lost their lives.

When we emerged from the Časma forest in the morning, we saw that behind every tree and shrub there lay Partisan units. If we attempted to save ourselves by escaping, they would shoot. A Muslim Domobran officer walked exhausted in front of me and threw himself into a pool of water for a drink. At that moment a Partisan named Tonkovich shot him with his automatic weapon. This same Tonkovich later boasted that on this night he had killed a good number of Domobrani and Ustasha.

On 30 May we reached the Časma-Bjelovar road and walked another forty kilometers. As we approached Časma the Partisan guard was changed, again not Croatian. We walked with very few stops and, just before Bjelovar, they ordered us to run. All this time we were without any food or drink. It was some time in the afternoon that they ordered us to lower our heads to show our remorse. As none of us obeyed the order, a number of shots were fired into the column and a number of hand grenades were thrown.

In Bjelovar we were lined up in the square, where the Partisans and their women attacked us with filthy language and insults. In the square a child recognised his father who ran to him and, as the father moved to his child, a Partisan shot the father.

We stayed in Bjelovar for three days. That same evening the Partisans took us into a camp building, where we saw about 150 young people aged seventeen to eighteen, who were novices in the Ustasha army. We saw how they were lying on the cement, unprotected from the sun, without food or water, exhausted and with the Partisan guards around them, batons in hand. For us, as soldiers, that was a most painful picture; for they were village children, who hadn't even begun to shave, who'd never even touched any arms.

In this confined space, there were up to 100 German soldiers. On 2 June, we were loaded onto a train with about fifteen wagons, which took us through Virovitica to Podravska Slatina. We traveled all day in completely closed wagons, with windows boarded up, so that there was a danger of suffocation. After loud protests the boards were removed.

At Podravska Slatina we stayed all night in a field under the clear sky, under the control of these same vengeful Partisan units. There was also talk of massive retribution. In the meantime the situation changed suddenly and the Partisan guards were replaced by Partisans from the Croatian region of Slavonia. Their attitude was milder, although those who remained behind were still liquidated. It was 3 June and we proceeded to walk towards Doljnjem Miholjcu. The unit which accompanied us was made up mainly of Partisan women. We stayed the night at Doljnjem Miholjcu and the next day went towards Osjek. Now we were not accompanied by fighting units bent on vengeance, but by combined units of mobilised Partisans. I remember one Muslim Partisan sergeant, who offered us cigarettes.

Reaching Osjek that night we stayed at the showground. The next day we were moved to a green field near the abattoir. At this point the Partisan units were replaced by the police. As we moved from the showground to the green fields, we were surprised by the courage of the people, who gave us food and clothing. For the whole three days of our stay on the green field, women would come with baskets of food and clothing. I mention that from Zagreb, all the way to Osjek, Croatian villagers gave us food; when they learned a column was coming, they would prepare food and share it amongst the people. When the Partisans hindered that, they would do it secretly or throw a loaf of bread from their homes into the column.

At the same time, the postal service functioned excellently. We threw out of the wagons or the column our correspondence to the women, who would often gather as we were passing. Those papers, letters and precious items wrapped up with addresses would arrive at their destination. I do not know of one instance where someone kept something for themselves. I myself in this way sent my wife my wedding ring and a gold medal on a chain.

On 8 June we went by train from Osjek to Srjemsku Mitrovicu where we stayed the night in prison. Nothing noteworthy happened to us, except one Partisan woman, in a moment of Partisan madness, with a pistol in her hand attempted to attack us. Four men were needed to stop her. On 10 June we marched to Rume, where we stayed the night at the showground, and the next day in the morning we went through Iriga, Fruške Gore and Kamenice to Petrovaradin.

In Iriga the population was unfriendly to us. We weren't attacked, for at the time of our passing Tito was speaking in Belgrade and most of the people were listening to him over the radio. In Iriga most of the population were of Orthodox faith, which was different to Kamenice, where the Croatian population gave the column food. On 11 June, we entered the fortress of Petrovadina and stayed until about 2 July 1945. Our column at that time numbered about 600 men, and some eight days later a column of Germans, mainly navy officers from Trieste, was brought to join us. A very vicious Partisan for no reason whatsoever, opened fire at them, and a considerable number of exhausted and hungry Germans fell. During these three weeks we were tortured by hunger, lack of hygiene and episodes of beatings. On around 2 July 1945 we boarded a train at Titula, for we were incapable of walking due to exhaustion.

On the way to Vrscu I saw the German villages whose inhabitants had fled or been sent to the camps. In these villages I saw one or two houses inhabited, but the people did not leave their homes. In Vrscu we were placed in a very large area encircled by wire. There were a number of large hangars that the Germans had built. We stayed here for about three weeks, until around 25 July 1945. In Vrscu the OZNA took responsibility for us for the first time. Again they divided us according to units; we had to fill in forms giving details of ourselves.

As happened in Petrovaradin, some professors who were among us sought to send a petition to Tito, expressing loyalty and asking for kinder treatment. The initiator of this attempt was an elderly Austrian major. Neither of these suggestions was agreed to; in fact, nearly all the younger officers firmly rejected such attempts. This stand was not without danger for them. Lectures were held on the doctrines of Marxism for the inmates of the camp. There were possibly several thousand men in this camp, including Croatian officers, German officers, Italians and even one Turk. From my close circle, a student of philosophy from Dubrovnik, named Matovich, who was also a Ustasha color bearer, was taken away and never heard of again.

From Vršcu on 25 July, a selected number of men were taken to Kovin where we were placed in a silk factory, in an area close to the home of the commissar and his family. The Commissar's name was Prpich and he came from the Lika region of Croatia. Our group came to Kovin, as did the previous one, in which the OZNA (Odeljene Zastita Naroda – Department of National Security) conducted a selection process which was carried out in a milder manner.

The OZNA took people away each day. On our arrival, we had to fill in forms giving our name, place of birth, rank in the army and place of capture. On the basis of this form, I was questioned by the OZNA, I think it was 27 August 1945 at midnight. The next day I was among three hundred officers taken to Pančevo.

At the station at Kovin there was a Russian artillery transport nearby and we came into contact with its officers. The attitude of the Russians towards us was very friendly. We walked from Pančevo to Zemun, accompanied by Commissar Prpich and two or three soldiers. In Zemun we boarded a train, and were ordered to return to our place of residence and report to the local authorities. Naturally I didn't do this, but after some time hiding, and with documents that a friend obtained for me, I crossed over to Italy.

The Partisan term 'zarobljenik' (prisoner) was a misnomer because the majority of the Croatian army was never defeated in its battles with the Partisans. The treachery of the Allied armies meant that the Croatian army was handed to the Partisans when they crossed over the Austrian border. For this reason, I never regarded myself as a prisoner.[7]

Kočevski Rog

Another witness IGI, who because of fear of Communist reprisals did not want to give his full name relates his account of the events.

> After completing four years of secondary school at Vela Luka, I lived at home with my parents until 10 September 1943. On that day I was forcibly drafted by the Yugoslav Communists. They had appeared in Vela Luka after the surrender of Italy to the Western Powers earlier that month, and after the Italian troops serving in Dalmatia had either surrendered or gone over to the Partisans.
>
> I was assigned to the Twenty-Sixth Dalmatian Division, but since I was under age, I was detailed to work in the British hospital on the island of Vis. After the fall of Gospić to the Communists in March 1945, I was transferred to the Eleventh Dalmatian Brigade, which was based in Gospić. I participated in battles fought by this unit in the vicinity of Trieste. We advanced through the valley of the Soca River all the way to the village of Kranjska Gora. We arrived there either on May 15 or May 16, and I remained with my unit there until the German and White Russian troops under the command of General Vlasov had surrendered in the nearby mountains, which extended into Austrian Carinthia.
>
> We crossed the frontier line into Austrian Carinthia and I was stationed near Klagenfurt for six days. Here I witnessed the surrender of the Croatian troops to the English, who extradited them into the hands of the Yugoslav Communists.

---

7. Nikolić Vinko *Bleiburgska Tragedia Hrvatskog Naroda*, 314–327. Statement of Kazimir Kovačić, who after the war moved to live in Buenos Aires, Argentina. Witnessed by: Dr Milan Blazeković, vr.
    Dr Franjo Nevestić, vr, Buenos Aires, 10 May 1963.

After the disarmed Croatian soldiers had been turned over to Tito's people, the Western Allies did not allow us to stay in Carinthia. We were sent back to Yugoslavia via the Jesenice tunnel. After a one-day stop at the border, we went by foot to Kranj on about May 24 or 25. We remained for another day at Primskov near Kranj. Here, orders were received by the Brigade Command that the most trustworthy Communists, whether officers or privates, should be selected from all four battalions of the Brigade. These reliable elements had to carry out a 'confidential task.'

A special company was to be formed from the men picked out. Second Lieutenant Jokovich, who came from my village, let me know right away that these men had been selected from Croatian, Slovene and German war prisoners. The third company of the Third Battalion, to which I belonged, was assigned to escort and protect the newly formed company of executioners, which numbered between sixty to seventy men. Its commander was Nikola Marshich, who was a native of the Makarska coastal district. Formerly, he had been Vice Commander of the Second Battalion. The company Commissar was Ivan Bokez, nicknamed 'The Montenegrin'. The supreme command of this detail was Major Sima Dubajic of the War Operations Section of the Headquarters of the Fourth Army.[8]

It must have been May 26 when the 'extermination company', escorted by my own Third Company of the Third Battalion, set off for Ljubljana. We arrived at the Slovenian capital

---

8. This same Sima Dubajac was living in Croatia at the time of the breakup of the former Yugoslavia in 1991, and stated publicly that he regretted not killing more Croatians in Kočevski Rog. He gave an interview that was published by the Croatian magazine *Globus* on 3 February 1995, in which he stated:

> For the 30,000 Ustasha that I buried at Kocevski Rog I have no regrets. I am only sorry if among them there were Chetniks! I only regret there were not 100,000 Ustasha there! I brought 30,000 Ustasha to Kočovski Rog and there is also a document in the English language about this. Tito made the decision that they were to be eliminated and I completed the task (Mio Ivek. *Život i Djelo Krunoslava Draganovića*, P, 136).

Sima Dubajac also stated that Milka Planic had chosen the executioners. Planic later became Prime Minister of Croatia, within the communist Yugoslavia, but denied Sima Dubajac's statement.

at about 5 pm. The trucks carrying us stopped at the front of a concentration camp. This detention centre contained many wooden barracks, which housed great masses of war prisoners, as well as civilians, including women and children. Entire families were incarcerated there. I learnt that this was St Vid concentration camp and that the gymnasium of the Ljubljana Church Diocese was located there.

The camp was entirely surrounded by barbed wire. All of us, with the exception of the 'extermination company', were forbidden to approach the prisoners or to communicate with them in any way. However, the exterminators were allowed to enter the enclosure in order to loot the prisoners of their watches, fountain pens, rings, gold jewelry and other valuables.

We spent the night of our arrival in barracks. At six the following morning, four truckloads of prisoners and a truck loaded with the 'exterminators' left the camp. The nickname 'Crna Marica' (Black Maria) was given to the prisoner trucks. All of us knew that the prisoners had been taken off to be killed. At 10 am our third company was loaded into two trucks to gather up and load the clothes of the slain prisoners. We went about one mile towards Ljubljana, and then turned to the right and proceeded for two miles along a rather wide country road, until we came to a peasant house that stood in an orchard. Behind this house was a forest with a big field adjacent to it. A big hole had been dug some 300 feet from the house.

Our trucks stopped at the house, where I saw a prisoner group, about fifty strong. They had been stripped of their clothes, their arms were bound with wire and they were tired together in pairs. It was evident that they had been beaten by the guards. They all looked quite depressed; indeed they had good reason to feel that way. Some had collapsed with exhaustion, and had been placed between stronger pairs so that the latter could carry them to the death pit that had been prepared. All the victims were ordered to chant in unison 'Sjeno slama kuca jama' (Hay straw house pit). As they reached the pit the 'exterminators' shot them down and they fell into the great yawning cavern that had been excavated for them.

We remained here throughout the day. New groups of trucks arrived every hour. In all, about forty truckloads of victims were brought to that place before sundown. These death wagons were escorted by Slovene courier troops, who were commanded by a blonde-haired Slovenian captain. He looked like an Austrian or German.

That evening the 'exterminators' had boasted that they had killed between 800 to 1,000 men. They accomplished this massacre with British-made light machine guns to which silencers had been attached to muffle the sounds of the firing. Usually, the victims were shot in the back of the head, but some of them jumped alive into the hole, even though it was a good fifty yards deep. At frequent intervals the 'exterminators' tossed hand grenades that the British had given them on top of the masses of bodies in the pit. Most of the people murdered here were anti-Communist Slovenes, but there were also Croatian soldiers among them.

At about 11 am. I approached the hole and looked into it. Before I could note any details other than a mass of bodies covered with blood, Bokez and Captain Marshich ran up and began to beat me furiously with the butts and barrels of their service revolvers. I fell to the ground bleeding quite profusely. After this incident, our escorting company was moved some distance away from the death pit and none of us was allowed to go anywhere near it or to watch the massacres that continued throughout the day.

When evening came we were put to work packing the greenish uniforms that the massacred men had worn, along with their other belongings. About 8 pm., we returned to St Vid and the concentration camp. That same evening, Major Dubajic ordered that future killing be carried out further from the city. He was afraid the civilian population would find out what was going on, because the scene of the executions was barely four miles from the town. I overheard other Communists discussing the advisability of dynamiting the hole and the corpses in it to obliterate all traces of the massacre. Actually, a peasant had brought quicklime to the place during the massacres; the lime was poured over the bodies to keep flies from being attracted by the blood and to eliminate the stench that would emanate from the decaying corpses.

On the day following the mass slaughters, we were sent by train to Kočevje. This town was fairly well shot up during the war so that the best place that could be found to house us was a partially destroyed military building, half a mile outside the community. German troops had previously been stationed there. The 'extermination' company had preceded us to Kočevje, but we did not see them there. I heard that they were encamped in a forest two hours away. During the war the Slovene Communists had posts in the centre of this great wood, named Kočevski Rog.

My company had been assigned the duty of standing by while Slovene Communists escorted new batches of prisoners into the military building where we were being accommodated. Once they had the prisoners inside, the Slovene Reds would strip them of their clothes and valuables; they collected some twelve pounds of gold in all. The Commissar of the Third Company, Ljubo Barbich, a Croat from the island of Hvar, was made responsible for the custody of all valuables. We were told clothes taken from the prisoners were to be exchanged for military uniforms.

Our job was to guard the prisoners until trucks arrived to take them away from this place, and we then loaded them into trucks. During the eight days we remained at Kočevje, ten or more trains came in every twenty-four hours. Each of these trains was composed of ten to twenty boxcars, all nailed up and sealed, loaded with prisoners. The captives came from Ljubljana and other places. Most were men but there were some women amongst them. These unfortunate women were subject to mass rape as soon as they were brought to the building we were guarding.

There were more Croats than Slovenes amongst the prisoners with whom I came in contact. Also there were some Serbian Chetniks brought there. I do not know to what units they belonged. We heard that during our eight-day stay, 30,000 to 40,000 prisoners were slaughtered in two nearby mountain ravines. The commander of our company was Ivo Frankovich, from Hodilje on the Peljesac Peninsula. I do not know how he felt about the murders that were being carried out at the expense of his countrymen.[9] Another witness to these massacres mentions Djuro Marich of Vareždin who, during the war, was in the Croatian Army but defected to the Communists at the end of the war, as did Ivo Frankovich. This same witness mentions a Second Lieutenant Daniel Jokovich, from Vela Luka on the island of Korcula. These were all Croatian.[10]

On the eighth day of our stay at Kočevje, a dance was arranged to honor and amuse the 'execution company.' Women were brought in for them and the men swaggered around boasting that they had 'liquidated' 30,000 to 40,000 people during the past eight days. I judge from the number of prisoners we saw guarding the building that there must have been more than 30,000 victims. Since we shipped more than twenty railway carloads of clothes from that place, it would appear that this estimate was not far off the mark. I saw only about ten or fifteen women amongst the captives, but there were certainly more who were murdered there. Naturally I didn't see every arrival since I was not always on duty. I know that the women were not stripped of their clothes near the building where we were stationed, but were conducted fully garbed to the place of execution. They were dishonored again in the ravines close to their final destination.

There was another Croatian Communist Bozo Kachich, from Hvar who bragged about what he had done to the women prisoners. Those that I saw all looked miserable and wept constantly. They were the widows of Croatian officers who were massacred at Kočevje. I saw no children, these evidently

---

9. Prcela John & Guldescu Stanko, OS, 370–374.
Another witness of the Kočevski Rog massacre corroborates the testimony of Ivan Gugica. The witness, known as ML, was from the town of Blato on the island of Korcula. ML relates how he and fourteen others from his town were forcibly mobilised by the Partisans in September 1943. He related how one of his townspeople protested against his mobilisation and was shot in the Blato cemetery. This man was Nikola Cetinich Krnjan, the sacristan of the Blato church, whose actions suggest he was a martyr of conscience. His murderer was Ivan Jurjevich, nicknamed 'Crnogorac', or Montenegrin', but he was actually a Croat from Lumbarda on the island of Korcula (John Prcela & Stanko Guldescu, *Operation Slaughterhouse*, 379).
10. Prcela John & Guldescu Stanko, OS, 382.

having been separated from them. Most of these officers' widows were dressed in civilian attire, but some wore military slacks and boots; I assume they found such garb more practical rather than conventional feminine wear during the retreat from Croatia. We of the escort company were not allowed to approach the women at all; evidently the exterminators were keeping them for themselves.

There were about 200 boys between fourteen and sixteen years old who wore the uniform of the Ustasha youth. I knew that the blonde-haired Slovene captain saved one of these boys from being shot, probably because he knew him or his family. They were all saying they were innocent of any wrongdoing. Many of them cried like the women.

The condition of the railway box cars in which the prisoners were brought to Kočevje was terrible. Since their guards did not allow them to leave the cars, even to relieve themselves, the filth in them was indescribable. During the days that they were locked in these wagons, the captives received neither food nor water. I do not know if they were fed after they reached the concentration camp. Some men lost consciousness or went mad while they were locked in the cars. Others collapsed from the heat and exhaustion after they were pulled from the railway wagons. Such victims would be beaten by their escorts, who then would load them onto stronger fellow prisoners. All the prisoners were well aware that they were being led away to their deaths. Some of them looked like they would make a fight for their lives, but most were tired, exhausted from lack of food and drink. They did not seem to care greatly what happened to them, but only hoped that it would happen quickly. Many men warned the 'exterminators' that a day of reckoning would arrive. Others said that they had committed no crime and had even saved Communists from execution at the hands of the Ustasha during the war. They asked that their lives be saved but they might as well have saved their breath. No one was spared except the boy previously mentioned. There was no questioning of the prisoners, nor did any of them receive any kind of trial. Everyone who was brought to Kočevje was doomed to die. Ustasha, Serbian Chetniks, General Rupnik's soldiers, most of them officers and a variety of other anti-Communists were all killed together. Some

German soldiers, most of them officers, were brought to Kočevje too. Two or three Ustasha colonels were amongst the victims but I do not recall their names.

I heard that quite a few of the captives made attempts to escape just before they were to be shot. Some of these men timed their escape so well that they actually got away into the woods and mountains. Others were shot down by the guards as they fled. I am glad to be able to say that I risked my own life to allow some prisoners to escape from the building we guarded.

This company of slaughterers was only active in Kočevje for eight days. The day on which the final massacre took place was a Saturday; five or six high-ranking Communist military officers visited the military building in which the prisoners were housed before execution on that day. Among them was a Serb from Kordun, Colonel Dule Korac, whom I knew. Two or three well-dressed civilians accompanied the officers. The whole party was welcomed by Major Dubajic and Commissar Bokez. These high-ranking officers had come to check on how we had packed the uniforms and valuables of the victims, and they devoted great attention to the gold that had been gathered from the victims. Commissar Bokez handed everything over to them without keeping anything for himself, and they offered him no reward. However I learnt that after this episode, Bokez had no difficulty with the Communist authorities to whom he had handed over the valuables.

The inspecting committee spent not even half an hour in our building. From there they went into the forest to inspect the mass graves in the ravines. I was told that they had come to Kočevje to see how the mass killings had been carried out and to make sure that all visible signs of the massacres, that is the ravines into which the bodies had been thrown, were covered up. Before they left Kočevje, we heard several loud explosions in the forest. We assumed that the bombs and dynamite had been used to topple masses of rocks onto thousands of corpses choking the ravines. The commission did not return to Kočevje after its inspection of the places of slaughter.

On Sunday at 7 am, the 'extermination company' left by train for a vacation at Lake Bled. I didn't know this at the time, but learned it much later. They told us that as a reward for the massacres they had committed at Kočevje, they had received twelve days' vacation on the island of Bled, where they were lodged in a former luxury hotel. They received good food, entertainment, went swimming, had sail boats at their disposal and had plays performed for their benefit every evening. In addition all of the 'exterminators' received two or three decorations from the Tito government, along with gold watches, cameras and other gifts of value.

Among these much decorated 'exterminators' was a 22-year-old courier from Brigade Headquarters, Ante Chepich, unfortunately another Croatian like myself. He was also a youth leader and came from Makarska, like Captain Marsich. From then on, the 'exterminators' remained the most trustworthy of all Yugoslav communists. I heard however that some of them became epileptic later on, developing what was called 'Partisan Bolest' (Partisan sickness), a form of nervous breakdown which developed with time as they realised the crimes they were involved in.

The Third Company remained at Kočevje until the evening of the same Sunday on which the 'exterminators' had left. We boarded a train to Kranj, where we stayed for ten days. From there we were sent to Tetovo in Macedonia, which we reached on 7 July.

I do not know whether the Communists carried out any massacres at Kočevje before or after the eight days of slaughter I referred to above. But I do know what happened during those terrible eight days of murder, rape and pillage. I am willing to testify to the truth of what I have stated. Also, I am ready to testify to these facts before any authorised international commission and to risk my life, if by doing so, I can bring to justice any of the 'exterminators' and the people who charged them with their inhumane duties.[11]

---

11. Prcela John & Guldescu Stanko, OS, 374–377. Signed August 14, 1953. Also in part Nikolai Tolstoy, *TMatM*, 169–170
Borivoje M Karpandzich's book *The Bloodiest Yugoslav Spring 1945 – Tito's Katyns ans Gulags*, corroborates what happened at Kočevski Rog in pages 42–48. (Borivoje M Karpandzich, *The Bloodiest Yugoslav Spring 1945- Tito's Katyns and Gulags,* 42–48)

Milan Zajec, a Slovene, was one of the prisoners waiting to be killed at Kočevje but through the grace of providence survived; He wrote an account of the massacres, under the title *The Facts about Tito* which appeared in a religious journal *The Saint Clair and Superior News*. It detailed his experiences and the way he survived this horrific event. The Serb author, Borivoje M Karapandzich, mentions that up to 1,200 Serbian volunteers and Slovene Home guards were killed at Kocevje.

Testimony of Ilija Perushina

A Croatian mariner, Ilija Perushina, relates his experiences during those dreadful times of May 1945. Perushina was a celebrity in the United States and decorated with a gold medal by President Coolidge in 1926 after the Yugoslav steamship Izabran rescued the crew of the American schooner Albert W Robinson.

Perushina, who was a mariner at the time, begins his account:

> My first conversation with the British took place in the Alps, which their advanced units had reached in the course of their march from Italy into Austria. The initial contact I had with them was most unfavourable. While I was trying to explain our reasons for abandoning our homeland and was expressing our doubts about the equity of 'justice' likely to be meted out by Tito's communist courts, they informed me that, in spite of everything I was saying, we Croatians would have to make our peace with Tito as best we could because sooner or later we would be placed under his jurisdiction.
>
> After this interview, I went on into Austria and arrived at Wolfsberg on 12 May. This place was occupied by various formations of the British Army and their numbers were increasing steadily. Here we also encountered some compatriots who told us that a large group of Croatian fugitives would arrive from Judenburg near nightfall. In fact it was just about dusk when the first of a column of some 150 vehicles pulled into the town square. Between 2,500 and 3,000 refugees were loaded into the various automobiles and trucks which made up this column.
>
> We attached ourselves to this caravan as it left Wolfsberg. The caravan proceeded in a southerly direction towards Sankt

Stefan, about 2.5 miles distant. Here, our column halted and we camped out in the open meadows that met the road on both sides.

On the morning of the following day, General Tomislav Rolf called me. He informed me that during the previous night the British had captured our Minister of Defence and Naval Affairs, Admiral Steinfl. Rolf asked me to go back to Wolfsberg in order to ascertain Steinfl's fate and to do something on his behalf if possible.

In accordance with this request, I made the round of the British units asking everywhere about the Admiral. Finally, I met a junior officer of Irish descent who cautiously conducted me to the building in which Steinfl was confined. I introduced myself to the guards stationed at this structure and asked them to take me to the officer in charge. After hesitating briefly they offered to do so. The officer in charge of the guard then brought me to the British Major.

In moving words, I explained to this officer who the Croatians were and how we had struggled to obtain our freedom from the Serbian dictatorship. I also told him about the persecutions and sufferings that our people had endured at the hands of the Communists, as well as the Serbians. In particular I endeavored to impress upon him the situation of the Croatian people vis-à-vis the Communists and their leader Tito. I bluntly said that if Admiral Steinfl were extradited to Yugoslavia, he would be murdered. I also asked this officer to do everything he could to prevent the general extradition of our people.

Apparently the information I gave him made some impression upon him for he went off to consult with superior officers by telephone. When he rejoined me, he said, 'Your Admiral is in this unit. He is not a prisoner but, unfortunately he cannot leave here right now. His situation is considerably different from that of your group. Keep your group where it is now but have them dispose themselves so as not to block the traffic on the road.'

He spoke to me in a resolute but friendly tone and my further pleas on behalf of Admiral Steinfl had no effect upon him. It was evident to me what the fate of the Admiral would be. Our own probably grave destiny preoccupied me too. I told the Englishman that we had no food at all and he at once said that we should send two trucks to pick up supplies of food every second morning. The English would give us enough for two days on every such trip.

When I returned to our roadside camp, I informed General Rolf of Admiral Steinfl's plight and expressed my apprehension about the fate that awaited all of us.

On the evening of 16 May, a British First Lieutenant came to where our cars were parked and told us, 'Tomorrow, at 8:00 am, your group must be ready to move. Before you set out all soldiers will be disarmed. Do you have a sufficient number of vehicles to carry your whole group?'

When asked for information about our destination, he flatly replied that he did not know where we were being sent. The harsh manner in which he delivered his orders increased my fears about what was in store for us at the hands of the English and their allies. From this moment the size of our group began to decrease steadily. A number of people shared my forebodings and slipped off by themselves to seek their safety as best they could.

General Rolf, however, continued to believe quite firmly in the military honor of the British. He simply refused to entertain the idea that they might hand us over to the Communists. Nonetheless he did accept the advice that I gave him concerning hiding some of the small arms. He also put Major Hodko's unit, a tough fighting force, at the head of our column. It was agreed that Hodko and his men would halt at the junction of the highway leading to Wolfsberg, Klagenfurt and Lawamuend. If we were directed to proceed towards the latter, that is, in the direction of Yugoslavia, then they would be ready for trouble.

At the appointed hour on 17 May a detachment of the British Army, commanded by a captain of Irish descent, arrived at our camp site. The captain commanded us to surrender our arms; we did this in accordance with the plan we had worked out amongst ourselves the previous night. No individual registration or general inventory of weapons was taken by the British. Their soldiers made a rapid inspection of all the handed over arms and then either loaded them into lorries or destroyed them.

I questioned the captain about our destination. He replied that he had no idea where we were being sent. When I replied that I could believe the statement made to this effect by the officer who had visited us the night before, but could hardly believe he had orders to take us somewhere without knowing where, he remained silent.

According to our pre-arranged plan, Major Hodko's fighters started off at the head of our column. After we had gone about two miles, a halt was made near Sankt Andrea at the Klagenfurt-Lawamuend road crossing. We understood at once that we were going to be sent to Yugoslavia. Hodko and his men were ready to fight, but it appeared useless because the Klagenfurt road was blocked by a powerful British tank formation. With only pistols and other light weapons they had concealed, what could our men accomplish against these iron monsters that were well equipped with machine gun and cannon?

We then asked the English point blank to shoot us down where we stood rather then send us back alive to that Communist hell, Yugoslavia. I myself approached one British officer and explained to him as briefly as I could the history of our nation, the struggle for freedom from Serbian tyranny that we had waged since 1918 and our anti-Marxist sentiments. Since he and most of the British soldiers who had charge of us seemed to be Irishmen, I stressed our firm Catholicism, the common religion of our forebears as well as his. I believe that he himself was convinced that I was telling him the truth. He seemed to be torn between his sense of military duty, which required the execution of orders he had received from his military superiors, and his Christian feeling and the dictates of his conscience. Finally he asked us to be considerate of the position in which he found himself and to continue to march without forcing him to resort to armed violence. He assured us that at least this day, 17 May, we would not be extradited into the hands of our enemies. He pointed out that the road to Lawamuend passed through forest country, that there were several villages along the way and that neither he nor his soldiers could have their eyes everywhere. In this way he invited us to leave the column if we wished to seek safety in the woods or among the Austrian villagers who were anti-Communist Catholics like ourselves. Before 1918, they were also our fellow citisens, at least in a sense.

So we decided to continue our journey without putting up a fight. As we went along, I could see how the seats in our vehicle gradually emptied. As the Irishman promised, his soldiers saw nothing of what was going on. At about 4:00 pm. we came to a forest half a mile from Lawamuend. The remainder of our column stopped here. The British soldiers remained with us while their commanding officer went on into town. Soon he returned, accompanied by a British First Lieutenant who was attached to their Intelligence Service. They had me accompany them to Lawamuend, where they brought me before an English Colonel who was charged with the job of extraditing us into the hands of our enemies. I repeated to him what I had said to the other English military men concerning our status as Croatian patriots, and I appealed to his conscience, asking him to do what he could to prevent our extradition. I urged that the British Army take us under its official protection. Finally he promised to do what he could for us. After this talk I returned to the remains of our group with the officer in command of our guards.

The British colonel visited us several times during the evening to acquaint himself with our situation. It was about 9:00 pm when he called our leaders together and said, 'Tomorrow at ten in the morning all of you military men will be extradited. Let the civilians who do not want to return to Yugoslavia remain under my protection.'

I told him bluntly that I doubted the veracity of the statement that he had just made. Obviously much displeased he said sharply, 'Who are you that you do not believe the words of a Colonel of the British army?'

I replied that I had no intention of offending him and that I knew he was a soldier and obliged to carry the orders that his superiors gave him.

'That is true,' he replied, 'but I assure you that your civilians will not be forcibly extradited tomorrow. They will remain under my protection. What will happen to them later on depends upon the resolution of His Majesty's Government.'

His words convinced me that at least the civilian members of our group would not be delivered against their will into the hands of the Communist butchers, who I knew were preparing a holocaust for every Croatian who came under their control. While I was reflecting on the significance of his speech, Ivo Bogdan asked me to introduce him to the Colonel. When I had done so, Bogdan handed the colonel a telegram which he wanted to send to the Holy Father. The proposed telegram contained information concerning the extradition proceedings to which we were exposed and requested the intervention of His Holiness on our behalf. I explained all this to the colonel who accepted the text of the wire and promised to forward it.

An hour or so later, the Irish officer who had charge of our escort came up to me and said goodbye. He seemed to be deeply affected but he assured us that the Colonel had told us the truth. He added that he and his men were being sent back to Wolfsberg and that another officer had taken over our custody. He also said that he had spoken to the Colonel on our behalf, as far as his military rank had allowed him, and that the officer who was replacing him was a man of good feelings and would look out for us in the same way that he himself had tried to do. He wished us good luck and took his leave, obviously quite moved by the circumstances in which we found ourselves. I certainly believe that he fulfilled his promise to do all he could to prevent our extradition.

As soon as he left us, tanks belonging to another English unit surrounded us. Their commander called me to him and said quite frankly:

You can believe the words of the Colonel in their entirety. That is, only your army personnel will be extradited tomorrow. As far as I am concerned, I am letting you know right now that you should not consider the tanks I have placed around you as enemies. This means that those of you who consider your lives endangered by the extradition proceedings have a whole night at your disposal. There (pointing with his hand) is the forest (and covering his eyes with his hands) my soldiers don't see anything they don't want to see.

He invited me to have tea and biscuits with him. This refreshment did a good deal to cheer me up, for I had eaten nothing all day long. Of course we were not slow to follow the advice that he had given us and by morning our group counted barely 600 people, around one-fifth of our initial figure.

I slept for a while that night, but was awakened early in the morning by the announcement that Tito's Communist Army had taken up positions around us, but that the British troops were still between us and our mortal enemies. I was also informed that General Rolf and his wife had taken poison, and General Dragojlov had tried to take his own life by slashing his wrists. I advised the British captain in command of our escort about what had happened to Rolf and Dragojlov and he immediately asked the intelligence officer to arrange the transfer of Dragojlov to the hospital at Wolfsberg. He said quite forcefully that people who were dying should not be extradited before they received medical assistance, whether they were military men or not. Because of his intervention, all three who attempted to take their own lives were taken to the hospital. The Partisans protested this action, but the British paid no heed to their arguments.

General Rolf died en route to the hospital, but his wife and General Dragojlov were hospitalised, and so were saved from being extradited. After they left in an ambulance, Dr Gomez told me that General Rolf had poisoned himself and his wife in a fit of despair because he felt responsible for leading all of us into a death trap from which there was no escape. I was so angered by this comment that I seized Dr Gomez by the shoulders, shook him roughly and asked if he had taken leave of his senses. I told him I had received permission from the intelligence lieutenant himself for General Rolf and others to go and fetch water from a nearby spring. The General who still had his revolver could therefore have put himself out of reach of the Partisans easily enough.

While all this was happening, the Partisans surrounded us and glared at us with undisguised ferocity. But whenever any of them approached us, the British soldiers turned them back. Shortly after ten o'clock that morning, 18 May, the British Colonel came to us in the company of a Montenegrin lieutenant by the name of Tomich. The Colonel called me over and declared, 'As I informed you last night, the military personnel will be extradited now, while the civilians who do not want to return to Yugoslavia will stay here under my protection.'

I asked him who is a soldier after the war is over. He answered: 'Whoever considers himself as such,' and then added, 'Let those who do not wish to go back to Yugoslavia separate themselves from those who are going to be extradited.'

As soon as the Communists saw that most of the soldiers were joining the group who did not want to go back to Yugoslavia, they began to protest that these soldiers were officers who had to be extradited because of agreements concluded previously between the British and Yugoslav governments. The English Colonel called me to him and asked if what the Communists were saying was true. This was no time to stick to the letter of the truth, so I told him that the men wearing military uniforms were returning from German work camps and they had exchanged their ragged civilian clothes for discarded uniforms of the Croatian Army. This improvised explanation could hardly have sounded convincing to anyone, let alone to an astute observer like the English Colonel, but he appeared to accept it at face value. He interrupted the yelling and screaming of the Partisans to tell them that all of the people who were not going to Yugoslavia were civilians and were under his personal protection and that of the British Army. At the same time he gave orders that about 400 people, most of them women and children, who had sufficient faith in Communist justice to accept extradition, should begin their journey back to the homeland.

The British now encircled the group that was remaining on Austrian soil, for the purpose of extraditing us, and in order to protect us against the Partisans. There was a noticeable change of countenance among the British soldiers. Up to this time they had worn very glum expressions, knowing that military discipline had required them to perform a very unpleasant duty. Now they openly rejoiced at being converted from our gaolers into our defenders. Undoubtedly the savage-looking Serbian and Montenegrin Partisans had impressed them unfavorably.[12]

Account of Pero Martich

Pero Martich, who was a member of the Ustasha Army, gives the following account:

> From the fall of 1944 until the great retreat in May 1945, I served as an enlisted man in the Ustasha Railway Battalions. About the middle of April, my unit was ordered to withdraw from Dubocac because our High Command in Zagreb had ordered us to evacuate Bosnia and to retire northward. We withdrew to Zagreb by way of Bosanska Kostajnica, Sunja, Sisak and Petrinja. From the capital we retreated northwards towards Celje early in May. We had a couple of fierce battles at Bosanska Kostajnica and near Petrinja. I was wounded in an action between Sisak and Petrinja and still boast a scar on my leg to remind me of the encounter.
>
> When we were close to Celje, about 3,000 Ustasha, Domobrana and civilians left the main highway and went across a hill in order to avoid having the same trick played upon them that the Partisans had used to capture the German troops who had preceded us into this area. When they saw that we were not going to allow ourselves to be disarmed as the Germans had, the Communists concluded a truce with us. This agreement provided for a mutual ceasefire and allowed us to go past the disarmed Germans without meeting resistance.
>
> A day later, the Communists broke the truce and began to fire upon us. They quickly found out that they could not stop our march and disappeared when we pursued them. A little later we came to a railway bridge near the village of Kamnik and discovered that British troops were holding the far end of

---

12. Prcela John & Guldescu Stanko, OS, 163–169. Signed Ilija Perusina. At Ramos Mejia, Buenos Aires, 10 June 1961.

the bridge. The leader of our column, a Domobran Colonel, negotiated with the commander of the British troops. The Englishmen demanded that we lay down our arms, and then we could cross over to the other side. The Domobran Colonel flatly refused to surrender to the British or anyone else. He knew that Yugoslav Communist forces were concealed in the woods at the back of the Englishmen, and that Croatian troops who had come through there previously had been turned over to the Reds.

The author then relates how they refused to surrender, eventually deciding to break up into small groups and make their way to Croatia, come what may. He was eventually captured in the vicinity, together with his friend; both were questioned by the Partisans. He goes on:

After this exchange, the Communists told us to go up the hill that overlooked the house they were using for headquarters. Another Communist began to question us there. He wore no insignia of rank and looked like a private, but I suspect he was a commissar. He asked us all kinds of questions about our column. When we left, a group of twenty-five to thirty Ustasha and Domobrans were brought to where we were sitting. There were three women and an Ustasha first lieutenant among them. These people were guarded by Partisans, who kept their guns leveled at them all the time.

The Ustasha lieutenant was taken off to be questioned while the rest of us remained together. After a while he returned, telling the men in his group that they had an obligation to aid in the reconstruction of their war- devastated country. He lined up his people and invited my friend and me to join them. The Communist commander asked seven men from the group to volunteer to remain with him. All of them were willing and anxious to do so, but he arbitrarily picked out my friend, me and five others from the lieutenants' group. The rest were taken towards a nearby lake where, the civilians told us afterwards, the Communists tortured them, cut the letter 'U' for Ustasha on their foreheads and chests, and finally killed them.

While this was going on, two higher German officers were brought to brigade headquarters. These men were promised safe conduct back to Germany. After they were questioned, guards led them off towards the lake, which was in a different direction from the road that would have taken them to Germany. The Germans stopped and refused to go any further along the path that was pointed out to them. Their guards cried out loudly, 'Comrade Commander, they don't want to go where they are ordered. They want to go to Germany.'

The commander bellowed blasphemous oaths and told the guards to bring the officers back to headquarters so that he could show them where Germany is located on a map. But the Germans threw their knapsacks down and bolted into the woods. The guards fired a hail of bullets after them and both of them were fatally wounded. The Communist officer then remarked, 'There! They arrived in Germany.'

Half an hour later, the Communists brought in four German privates. The Communists questioned them, made a lot of false promises and took them off towards the lake where I presume they killed them.

After a time, two Croatian Domobrans and a Ustasha were also brought to headquarters. The Ustasha man had been discovered hiding in the house of a peasant, and he was forced to don a Communist uniform. As dusk came on, I was sitting with other Croatian captives in front of a stable, being guarded by armed Partisans. There was also a large group of other Communists in the vicinity, who sang derisive songs about Croatia and Germany.

Since the Communists were afraid that we would take advantage of the night to escape, they made us go into the stable. There were horses and cows on one side of this building and pigs on the other. Between them ran a small corridor. About half an hour after we had been incarcerated, two Communists armed with light machine guns came into the building. They told us to give them our watches, fountain pens and rings. We had already been relieved of any money we had. I hid my watch and fountain pen in the straw. The Communists yelled at one man because he did not have a watch to give to those who wanted one.

The Communists left with all our valuables but returned soon and ordered us to undress right down to our underwear. The Ustasha said to me that he was not afraid to die, but that he didn't like to die a slave's death and one that, without doubt, would be accompanied by atrocious torture. I tried to persuade him that nothing so tragic was going to befall him, but I had hardly spoken when two more armed Partisans came in and shone their flashlight on us. 'Bosnian, go out for the examination!' they said to the Ustasha man. He resisted them, but they succeeded in tying his hands with wire and took him off. For the next twenty minutes, I could hear nothing but the Communist singing and amusing themselves. Then the guards came back and told us, 'Now let's have a Dalmatian to be examined!' They took another of our group for 'examination.' At the end of another twenty minutes they led out another Dalmatian. I heard this man ask them something, but they told him to keep quiet.

At similar intervals, the Reds brought a fourth and fifth victim from the stable. It occurred to me if I should be killed trying to escape, at least I would avoid being tortured. I examined the stable windows, all save one had bars outside. This one unbarred window was nailed shut, too, but while the Partisans were disposing of the sixth man, I pulled out the nails, opened the window and jumped out. The remaining Croatian soldiers followed me, just as the Communists returned to get their seventh victim.

The soldiers yelled: 'Pobjegli, pobjegli'. (They fled).

A hail of bullets came after us and two of our number fell. I came to a little stream, ducked into it and pulled branches over my body. The Reds thrashed all around through the woods and fired haphazardly into the dark, but they never found me. When everything quietened, I crawled further into the forest, but was close enough to the stable to hear Communists officers cursing their men because they had allowed us to escape. I think they may have shot some of the guards to punish them. Later, I heard sounds indicating that they were digging graves for the victims of this macabre night.

Martich related how he made his way into Austria where he worked for villagers. By the time the English discovered him, they were convinced that their Communist allies were massacring all Croatian soldiers and civilians. They therefore allowed him to continue working in Austria.[13]

Captured Croatian soldiers in a camp in Maksimir, Zagrab, May 1945. From Glas Koncila

---

13. Prcela John & Guldescu Stanko, OS, 172–177. Signed: Pero Martic, Cleveland, Ohio, 4 December 1960.

A collumn of captured Croatian soldiers passing through Koprivnica, May 1945.
From Glas Koncila

Chapter 5
Death Marches Part 2

Pavo Gagro was born in the village of Veliki Ogranak, Herzegovina on 18 September 1927. At sixteen years of age he joined the Ustasha forces and was present at the surrender at Bleiburg. After migrating to Australia in 1950, he was very active in Sydney's Croatian community. He was a family and personal friend of the author.

Pavo zealously supported Dr Franjo Tudjman and the Croatian Democratic Union as it sought and achieved independence for Croatia. He died in Sydney, Australia on 17 June 2014.

This is a recounting of Pavo Gagro's story:

> Sometime during September 1943, I joined the Ustasha Obrana (Ustasha Defense) units, and began five months of training at Stara Gradiška, some forty kilometres from Zagreb.
>
> When Banja Luka was surrounded by the Partisans at the end of June 1944, my company, which numbered up to 200 men, went to their help as did many other units of soldiers. I was wounded at Topola and hospitalised for two weeks, after which I rejoined my unit at Safski Maraf.
>
> In October 1944, just thirty of us from my company joined the First Croatian Assault Division: its First Commander was General Solz and then later General Ante Moshkov. I remember that early in May 1945 we were in the Podravina region near the town of Bjelovar and it was apparent that the Croatian Army was retreating. This was very obvious by 6 May. I remember clearly when on the night of 7 May, around 11:00 in the evening, some 3000 of us walked along Ilica

Road, one of the main roads of Zagreb. The city was in total darkness, although occasionally we noticed a lamp alight in windows. There was not a soul anywhere and we were ordered to walk on both sides of the road and not to turn into any side streets. When daylight came we had already reached Safski Maraf. That day, 8 May, we marched to Predgrade near the Slovenian border where we stayed till the afternoon when we received orders to march further; we marched all night and arrived near Celje by the morning of 9 May.

On the morning of 10 May, Colonel Mamich gave the order that we were to pass through Celje and we were told firmly and clearly that we were to refrain from shooting. As we entered Celje, we saw that the town was massively overcrowded with Croatian soldiers and civilians, whole families with children. There were goats and cattle tied to carts as families took what they could. For two hours we couldn't move even two kilometers.

On 13 May we arrived at Dravograd at noon, with the Bulgarians and Partisans blocking our passage. Up to five companies consisting of 1,000 men went into action until a breakthrough was achieved. As the bridge over the river was destroyed, I joined with three companies that went to the left of the river into the mountains. High in the mountains we found an Austrian house and stayed there the night. All in all there were about 10,000 soldiers around the house; added to that were civilians, including women and children.

Among the women I remember with us was Dara Ostojich, the wife of Colonel Ostojich. She had a two-year-old daughter called Kriza Ostojich and a four-year-old daughter whose name I can't remember. As we charged to break through the Bulgarians and Partisans, finding herself in a desperate situation, Dara left little Kriza there because she couldn't cope. She didn't see that Zarko Ostojich, the brother of her husband, took the child.

I would say that up to 75,000 Ustasha and Domobrani soldiers, many wounded, and civilians, stayed in Dravograd. Some fought the Bulgarians and Partisans, while others just remained there hoping for clemency when the Communists eventually overran the town.

Another woman, Lausa Odak, was a neighbour of mine. She had four children including a two-year-old son whom she left behind there because she could not manage with all the children. The boy was found by a Montenegrin Partisan Colonel who took the boy and looked after him. Lausa later found the boy in 1946 through the Red Cross.

There were about 10,000 of us as we left our mountain lodging, and I remember walking along a road which followed a narrow river. We saw a Croatian Army truck in the river with four dead Croatian soldiers in blue uniform in it. We just looked and moved on.

I thought it was 15 May when we reached the slopes to the Bleiburg valley at midday, but I asked an officer and he told me it was 17 of May. It was only much later that I learnt it actually was the 15 May. I saw the whole valley covered with Croatian soldiers and civilians–it was like a sea of soldiers and civilians where everyone had stopped. I believe we were the last group to arrive at the valley, and we just stopped there on the slope looking down at the sea of people. Behind us were the forest and the mountains from which we had emerged. When some of the women who were with us saw where we were, they were very angry at Pavelich. One of them cursed Pavelich, using unrepeatable language saying: 'Where did . . . Pavelich bring us?'

Although we were all tired and hungry, I was unsettled and I said to the sergeant, Kine Glamuzin: 'Kine, let's go and see what this is all about. Why are those tanks lined up and why has the army stopped?'

We went right to the edge of the mass of people, and thirty metres further on was a row of British tanks. There was a group of around twenty Domobrani and Ustasha officers standing between the tanks and ten meters from the edge of the crowd. I then saw General Herenchich and another person come from the direction of the tanks in a Skoda car. I knew Herenchich from Mostar; it was later that I learnt the second person was Daniel Crjen. I saw them stop to talk to the high officers for about fifteen minutes. Herenchich then came to the edge of where the army was waiting; I was only two meteres from him and I heard him say:

'Rat je završen, podignite bjele fane, I nek nitko puca, svatko nek ide svojin kučama.'

('The war is finished, raise the white fane; let no one shoot; may everyone go to their homes.')

He used the word 'fane' for flag. I remember the sentence clearly, for I had never heard that word 'fane' before. It was only later that I learnt it was the German word for flag. In a split second people were taking off their white shirts and hanging them on their rifles. Kine and I returned immediately to our unit and as we were passing through the masses of people, we saw all sorts of weaponry thrown onto the ground, including parabella and automatic rifles. When we reached our units we all put the weapons we had on the ground, although some of our soldiers went into the forest behind the trees to see what would happen.

Within an hour the Partisans appeared and gathered all the weapons that were lying on the ground. It was easy to recognise them as they were all dressed in British uniforms. I remember one Partisan carrying up to ten rifles at the one time.

I remember two young captains, both students and handsome men, one's name was Ico Ostojica. His wife Andja cried when the Partisans took him away. She didn't have time to say goodbye to him and she never knew what happened to him. The other man's name was Brzica; I can't remember his given name.

We hid some of the automatic weapons and then Captain Mandich, Kriza Ostojich and some fifteen others went into the mountains. I wanted to go with them but they said to me: 'You are young; they might not do anything to you.' So I stayed.

Dara Ostojica, whom I knew from Čitluk, also stayed, as well as Andja Ostojica.

We were lined up in rows of 16 and I was forced to take off my shoes and new army jacket. A Partisan said to me: 'You don't need that', and I said to him: 'Doesn't the U bother you?' It was the U on the lapel of the jacket and it stood for Ustasha. He hit me with his rifle butt in my ribs. Andrija Bojich who was next to me said: 'Keep quiet or they will kill you.'

We stayed there until the following morning, when the Partisans lined us up in five rows and forced us to march. I remained close to Kine Glamozina, Andria Bojchich and Maria Luburich as we marched in a thirty-kilometre long column. Just before we reached Celje, the road came to a pass that was about five meters wide, with cliffs on either side. Suddenly two tanks and an armed car ploughed into us, crushing the bodies and heads of a mass of people. Andria Bojchich, Kine Glamozina and I stood next to the cliff and so I was spared. Sadly I never saw Andria Bojchich and Kine Glamozina again; they never came home.

We kept marching and reached the outskirts of Celje by nightfall. We were then lined up into twenty columns. The Partisans started asking if there were any Herzegovians amongst us. I and Medich remained quiet while Ante Chavar and four others acknowledged they were. They took Milko's watch and shot him while they took Ante Chavar's ring, then shot him and the two others.

We continued our walk through the night. By the next day we passed Safski Maraf and reached Gorica. I believe at this time we numbered about 40,000. While there we saw a lady fetching water from a well and four of our number jumped out from our forced column to quench their thirst. Two of them were shot while the other two jumped back into the rows. As we left Gorica there was a small bridge over a stream. Two Partisans stood at the ready on either side, hitting us with hard blows using clubs as we were shoveled through. Although I went past quickly, I was nevertheless struck on the shoulder as I passed.

We were put into a camp when we reached Sisak. All I had eaten on the journey was a few blocks of sugar that I had in my pocket from Bleiburg. While camping there we saw people being taken away to the Sava River where they were shot. Among the victims was Gabro Sivirich, who was a captain in the Ustasha and whom I had known for ten years.

On the second day they divided us, ordering all who were Domobrani to move to one side. Vrane Lesko, my cousin Nikola Gagro, and I were all Ustasha, but we moved into this group.

The next day they then ordered the young to one side. There were some older people amongst us and all together we were about 7,000. After this they moved us to a glass factory in Sisak where we stayed overnight. There we found up to 2,000 Croatian gendarmerie and some 2,500 Croatian police. They put us there together, some 11,500 men, all hungry and thirsty with not a blade of grass to eat.

The next day we young ones, some 7,000 of us, were marched from Sisak towards Popovaca. The Partisans would occasionally kill someone at random as we walked. One of the young guards in front of me killed up to twenty-one of the prisoners. One unfortunate young man, just in front of me, a tall, blond handsome young man, was shot just there and then by this same young Partisan. I just walked over him. I have never forgotten him, feeling very sorry for him. Jozo Nakich, who came from my own village, could not walk any further and Velko Santac helped carry him. When Jozo could not walk any further, this young Partisan just shot him as well.

We halted and sat down in a field when we arrived in Popovaca. We were so ravaged with thirst and hunger that within ten minutes there wasn't a blade of grass left, so desperate were we to put something into our mouth.

People from the surrounding district approached us weeping at our plight, throwing loaves of bread to us until the guards dispersed them. Later in the afternoon as we sat in the field, Commissars came asking us who belonged to Max Luburich's or Rafael Boban's units. We all remained silent. There I found Bozo Cavar.

After two hours we were marched back to the glass factory in Sisak. When Ante Bulich and Pavao Bojich, who were both policemen, saw me, they were distraught at how emaciated I looked. All of us stayed there all night.

We were lined up at around ten in the morning the next day, and I asked Pavao Bojich and Ante Bulich to stay together. I estimated there were between 50,000 to 60,000 prisoners at this point. We proceeded towards Popovac and when we reached the intersection to Zagreb or Časma, we took the Časma turn. As we were marched towards Časma up to fifty to sixty former Croatian Zendars, who were older and lagged behind, were all killed.

At Časma the column was marched towards Bjelovar. We were in rows of four or five, and a Partisan guard marched every five or six meters. It was a very long column, several kilometers, and at one point we heard shooting at the rear as the straggling elderly members were shot. I changed rows so that I could be next to Stipe Medich. It was a starry night and we could hear killings farther down the column. When the column turned a bend, the guard on our side moved two yards forward, and I grabbed Stipe's hand and jumped down into the bushes down the gully towards the creek. The guards started shooting at us but fortunately they missed us. We stayed there in the creek, behind the rocks in the dark. Eventually we pulled ourselves out and came to a wheat field where we ate grains of wheat. While in the field we heard someone coming in our direction and we lay down and hid. Three people walked past us in the dark, and it was only later when I reflected on it, that I realised they must have been others who had escaped from our column.

There was a stream there where we drank water. We were dying of thirst; we were so thirsty that our lips were white and splitting and we just quenched our thirst. We also came to a patch of onions which we ate. The next morning we came to a church, and a priest opened up after we knocked on the door. He gave us some bread and milk, which strengthened us on our way. Eventually we made our way to Herzegovina and after other hair-raising experiences we reached Italy and freedom.

It was an extremely terrible experience as I think of the thousands of young people, the fleeing families with children, who were handed over to a very vengeful and heartless enemy, like lambs for the slaughter. The column from which I fled numbered 50,000 to 60,000 soldiers and when it eventually reached the Rumanian border, only 4,000 were left. All this is a painful memory that I have and will always carry for the rest of my life. It is my conviction that Dr Ante Pavelich must take much of the blame, for he, as Head of State, had the responsibility to foresee all possible eventualities when he ordered the withdrawal of the Croatian Army to southern Austria and their ultimate surrender to the British[1]

Statement of Branislav Todorovich on the Slaughter and Theft

Branislav Todorovich was a Serb, born in Belgrade. He was thirty-three years old, of Orthodox Christian tradition, unmarried. He had been a student of technology before the war, and then became a captain in the Partisan army. In 1945, Todorovich fled Yugoslavia and his unit of the People's Liberation Army. He arrived in Italy and gave a very significant statement on 25 June 1945.

This is Branislav Todorovich's statement:

> I served in the third army, sixteen Assault Division, in the first Vojvodanski Brigade, first battalion and third company of which I was the commander. The last place where I served was at Rosenbach, in the role of Liaison Officer between the People's Liberation Army and the Allied Forces.
>
> Before arriving in Rosenbach, I served in Jesenicama. There, on 24 May 1945, I received orders to move on. The order came from the commander of the brigade whose name I don't know. The order came verbally at six in the evening. I was told to prepare for a journey to Rosenbach where I would meet the English, who would hand some prisoners over to us. Two of us travelled together to Jesenice to the headquarters of the twenty-sixth Dalmatian Division. In the meantime my battalion was ordered towards Kransko Mountain to take up positions on the border, with the utmost secrecy, so that the Allies would be unaware, and we, forewarned, could prepare for attack.

---

1. Interview given in Sydney, Australia 27 July 2009, 7 December 2009 and 10 May 2010.

In the headquarters at Jesenica, I was present at conversations between the commander of the brigade and Captain Slavka Savich, the commander of the battalion. Also present were the commissar of the battalion and the deputy commander. Captain Savich asked the commander of the brigade who were we to attack, and he was told: 'Ah, everyone knows this: who else but our dear allies?' Before this, the political commissars had told the troops we would attack the British if they would not hand over Istra, Carinthia and Trieste. We were told if they weren't handed over to us peacefully, then we would take them by force.

While I was in Jesenica, I learnt that over the past few days in Rosenbach, representatives of the Peoples' Liberation Army had received 800 prisoners of war from the British. The prisoners included Yugoslav citizens, Domobrani, Ustasha or Slovenian 'White Guards', as they were known by the Partisans, plus civilian refugees, who were family of the aforementioned soldiers.

On the same day that we heard this, 24 May, I travelled to Rosenbach in a special train with the commander of the brigade and another officer. We met Captain Domeniko, from Makarska, the deputy to the Commander of the twenty-sixth Division, an interpreter, two officers and a Partisan woman who was nursing while awaiting demobilization. Her name was Anica Popovich, also known as Luka, and she came from Vukovar.

At around ten or eleven in the evening, Captain Domeniko introduced us to a British Lieutenant, called Lockheed, an officer in the 'Sixth Specialized Unit' who was responsible for communication. Lockheed told us that we would need to prepare a train by ten in the morning on the following day. It was to pick up 1,500 prisoners and take them to Maria Elend. That same evening, Captain Domeniko told us about an Ustasha minister who was sent back to the country in a previous transport, and he showed us a gold watch that he had taken from the Ustasha. Comrade Popovich also showed us a larger and smaller bag full of watches, necklaces and other jewelry which she had taken from the prisoners. She told us that we could do so without any fear.

A train arrived a little late the next day, and was boarded by half of the Third Battalion. The train was stationed on the other side of the tunnel in the village of Hruscica, on the Yugoslav side. The soldiers entered the wagons unobserved, so that the prisoners did not realise they were being taken to Yugoslavia. The British had previously told the prisoners they were being transported to Italy.

When we arrived at St Maria Elend, our soldiers hid themselves in the railway station and remained there right up to the time the prisoners boarded the wagons and the doors were locked. The prisoners boarded the train under English supervision. Panic broke out when our soldiers appeared: the prisoners were terrified and astonished. Some began shouting: 'Long live the English. Don't hand us over. These people will kill us.' The train moved off and fifteen minutes later arrived in Rosenbach, where it was surrounded by our soldiers and English guards. A number of people then boarded the train: The Commander of the brigade, Captain Rasa, that was his Partisan nickname, the Commissar of the battalion, I can't remember his name, two Slovene officers of the fourteenth Division and officers of the already mentioned units.

We then moved on to Hrusciva, at which point a whole battalion encircled the train. The Commandant of the third battalion said to me: 'Commander (here he used a word which I am unable to repeat) now even you will have work to do'. I did not know what I was supposed to do, but there had been talk in the train about decapitating those who were to be slaughtered. Fearing this, I didn't give any reply so that later I could appear dumb, as if I knew nothing.

The Partisan officers went into the two wagons that held the officers of the prisoners. They selected fifty-four officers and soldiers, and told them to go with the Partisan officers. The Partisan officers had already agreed amongst themselves that these men were to be liquidated.

The Partisans first took them to the command of the battalion, where they were searched, and their belongings stolen. I am a witness to this. They began to beat the prisoners with wood, so viciously that they fell to the floor. The officers waited until it was dark and took them about 100 meters away to a clump of trees behind the command post. They started arguing amongst themselves about who was to do the killing. I don't know who did it, because I disappeared as I did not have to do it. I think they all lined themselves up for the killing. I went to the kitchen for a meal, although I could hear cries and some shooting from revolvers. The cooks who brought the food to me said nothing, but one could see from their facial expressions just how much they hated all that was happening.

All the officers who were involved in the killing returned later singing. Amongst them was one by the name of Mile, a Serb, and captain of the machine gun company of the third battalion. He did most of the butchery. So that I could confirm what I had heard, I went to the spot and found fifty-four bodies. Soldiers were already burying some of the bodies, but I could see pools of blood, and one stabbed body. I would say others had also been stabbed with knives, because even though I heard only two or three shots from a revolver, there were fifty-four dead.

The prisoners who remained on the train were mercilessly robbed by our soldiers. Fourteen Chetnik's committed suicide, in the presence of the English, on the way from St Maria Elend to Rosenbach. The English took their bodies and buried them near the railway station, although I can't remember exactly where, for the train moved on soon after.

The train travelled from Hruscic towards Jesenica. A company of youths belonging to the First Vojvodinski Brigade boarded the train at Hruscic. They were mainly children between ten and sixteen, and were scattered throughout the wagons. I heard gun fire and even automatic weapons all through the journey, as if there was a battle taking place. When we reached the bridge over the river Sava, I saw Partisans throwing bodies out of the moving train. Some fell into the river while others landed on the bank.

The prisoners were taken out of the train at Jesenica, and forced to march to a camp some three kilometres away despite being in a terrible state. Some forty per cent of the prisoners had been separated from the rest when we arrived at the camp. I asked the guard the reason for this and he told me that they would first liquidate the larger number of prisoners.

I left the camp when it was already dark. I heard automatic firing and the camp guard who was in my company said to me: 'Ah, they are killing them.' He was angry they were doing it without him, for I had deceived him. When I told him that he was not to talk like that to an officer, he said: 'Prokljestvo (Curse you), If it wasn't for you, I would be also sharing out the loot. Now I will get nothing since I am with you.'

That same night I returned to Rosenbach in a special train made up of a locomotive and one wagon. I resolved I would not accompany any more trains and I would try to get myself out of the situation at all costs. In fact, on two more occasions I accompanied the train to Hruscevo, but after this I did not travel any further than Rosenbach. I told Lockheed what was done with the prisoners, so he arranged with my command that I remain with him. The excuse was that a Liaison Officer for Communication mustn't be far from his central command.

During each transport–and there were sixteen of them–there were bodies of people who had committed suicide. Due to a request from the English, they were removed from the train at Rosenbach and buried. I had sought this outcome from the English so they would see the truth of what had happened and become convinced about how badly the prisoners were treated. I was not present at any further slaughter or killings, but I heard of them from my soldiers and from the soldiers of the units who were given the task of participating in these activities. I know the events that happened with the first transport were repeated with all the others. The only difference was the numbers: sometimes there would be more and other times less. Those who weren't killed were sentenced to forced labour without adequate food, so I believe they would not have survived for long.

On 3 June I prepared an evening meal for the English, and I thought I was the only Partisan who would be present. There was a large transport prepared for the following day and the officers who were present at the killings also came, except the commander of the brigade. There were several English officers at the meal: Captain Brown, two captains of the regiment at St Jacobs, Lieutenant Lockheed and Lieutenant Galbraith. Later in the evening a special train brought more officers to the meal:

the assistant Commissar, and the Commissar of the third battalion, a Montenegrin whose name I do not remember. I came in close contact with the English that evening and that is why the Partisans became suspicious of me. The following day they contacted me by phone and ordered me to come immediately to staff headquarters. I knew what that meant and, for that reason, I fled to Italy.[2]

A Civilian's Account of the Death Marches from Bleiburg to Zagreb

I, Marko Bozidar, born on 8 November 1915 at Bjelom Polju near Mostar, finding myself in Italy, express and sign with the greatest sense of moral and human responsibility the following:

When the Independent State of Croatia was established, I was employed as a treasurer in Višegrad. In the summer of 1941, the Chetniks from Serbia penetrated into Višegrad. The small Croatian unit, due to pressure from the Italians who supported the Chetniks, handed this town to Draze Mihaljevich's Chetniks, who committed a terrible slaughter of the Muslim population. After this I moved to Zagreb, where I worked for the Ministry of Internal Affairs right up to the end, that is May 1945.

I was with my family in the Croatian region of Slavonia during the second half of April 1945 when the Croatian army was withdrawing. There was talk of a planned escape. It wasn't just a withdrawal of the army but a spontaneous exodus of large numbers of people in front of the advancing Partisans. Women, men, young and old, were all on the move in trains and along roads. Villagers left their homes and whole families carried their belongings on carts, all headed towards Zagreb. The army was not successful in discouraging the people from leaving their homes, though they tried to convince them they would soon return. Anyone who had come to know the Partisans over the last four years fled in fear.

---

2. Branislav Todorović as quoted in Vinko Nikolić's, *BTHN*, 406–409. Borivoje Karapandzich, *TBYS. 1945–TiKaG'* 78–83. Nikolai Tolstoy, *TMatM,* 163–167.

> All means of transport and roads were so over-crowded that progress was very slow. On passenger and cargo trains people clung like swarms of bees on branches of trees. We travelled for two days from Slavonski Brod to Zagreb, which was overcrowded with refugees. Croatians, Serbians, Chetniks and Montenegrin patriots were all fleeing. There was a welcoming attitude towards everyone, although the Chetniks had done much evil towards the Croatians during the war.
>
> On the afternoon of 6 May 1945, we set off with some colleagues in a truck heading from Slovenia to Austria. The roads were overcrowded, especially with village carts.
>
> On 14 May 1945, in the afternoon, we reached a valley which was several kilometers wide and long. Along the edge of this valley, under the mountain, there was a road which led to Austria. Some several hundred thousand people gathered here. I had never in my life seen so many people.
>
> We received more news at daylight on 15 May, but no one moved as midday approached. No one was able to explain why. In the afternoon we received news that was like a thunderbolt from a blue sky: the army was to lay down its arms.

Bozidar continued to describe the dramatic surrender of the army, the reorganisation of the refugees and the lining up of the columns for the purpose of their handover.

He went on:

> There was no brutality or killing in the first few kilometers. Slowly there was a strengthening of the Partisan guards, dressed in Serbian national costume. We went along a poor path, along the edge of the Austrian border, to the north of Dravorgrad. As we approached Dravograd, the terror began. A number of times there was machine gun fire from the nearby forests, killing those who were cut off or lagging behind. The Partisans began stealing our belongings. They took shoes and clothes, money, watches, rings and all valuables from people who were tortured, hungry and exhausted. The Partisans took everything from them, bangles, chains, necklaces, earrings, rings and so on. It is impossible for me to describe all the forms of theft. I saw at least 150 of these incidents, and it looked as if this theft was normal.

We were also afraid of beatings with batons.

Just before Dravograd, we crossed a bridge where we were beaten with batons. A number of Partisans pushed the prisoners onto the bridge with batons and beat them. It was then I saw the first of those who had been killed: two dead soldiers were lying next to the road near the bridge. The road was very poor and the bridge was made of wood, but strong. The bridge swayed from side to side as we ran to escape the beatings. There was a woman ahead of me with a child in her hand. A Partisan hit her so hard on the back that the poor lady fell. He shouted at her: 'Where were you fleeing, you Croatian prostitute?' When a man attempted to lift her, he was shot. I was running with lowered head receiving such a blow on the shin bone that I barely stayed on my feet. When we crossed the bridge, I noticed the lines of Partisans became thicker. It was obvious that they were preparing to confiscate things from us. Firstly they approached those of us who were better dressed. They took a ring and watch from me. Yesterday, the column had been well dressed, but it was now in rags and bare-footed. There were only a few soldiers who were completely clothed. When they were asked about their uniforms, they were not allowed to answer, for that meant condemning the Peoples' Liberation Army. I didn't want to look behind, or notice the terrible things that were happening around me.

In the evening of this same day, we passed through Dravograd. In less than a single day thousands of prisoners were killed in the surrounding forests, mostly Croatian officers.

The Slaughter and Defiling of Women

The evening after we passed Dravograd, they lined us up in smaller columns and strengthened the guard with machine guns. What awaited us was a grim night that brought death to many. They brought in more guards, and we could see from their appearance that they were thirsting for blood. That evening the river Drava swallowed many. Often we heard the firing of machine guns, people crying aloud for help, the cry of women and girls. Some were raped and then killed, some put to shame and returned to the column. The following day a girl by the name of Maria related to me terrible things which they had done to her.

New Scenes of Terror and Cruelty

Instead of subsiding, the terror increased the following day. It was warm and the sun was burning. No one was allowed to have a drink of water, and people collapsed from thirst, hunger, and most of all exhaustion. Those who couldn't follow were battered. I saw that many carried their friends on their backs, while the guards shouted:

'Leave them. We will heal them.'

There were piles of bodies close to every stream or pool. It was there that the Partisans were usually waiting and killing. For this reason I didn't try to get close to the water.

At one place on the right side of the road, I saw something that not even animals would do. There were troughs close to the road, and water dropped through a pipe from a wall. I was dying of thirst, and I focused my eyes on this water dropping from the tank pipe. But my thirst immediately left me when I saw five or six bodies and the mutilated body of a woman. They were lying around a well in a pool of blood and water. A few meters away was a Partisan with a pistol and bombs, shouting:

'Anyone who is thirsty may drink fresh water.'

He eagerly awaited the next sacrifice to come closer.

I also saw Partisan officers riding on horses, and they were the originators and authors of this slaughter. I remember two cars that sped from Maribor to Dravograd with higher officers. One was very fat, richly decorated with medals and regalia on his shoulders.

That day we passed through the town of Marenberg. I saw there Russian soldiers with Partisan officers on horses. On leaving the town, the Partisans took away the younger soldiers, and they took another three from my group. On the road there were Russian soldiers who took soldiers from the column. There were also Partisan officers in this 'commission', as we in the column called them.

I was tired and hungry. Anyone with a block of sugar or biscuit was regarded as wealthy. I had half a kilo of sugar; and it was my only nourishment till we reached Croatia.

New Thefts, Killings and Unimagined Cruelty

When we distanced ourselves from Marenberg, we met a Partisan on the right side of the road, and he called me out of the column. Close to him lay a dead soldier on his back and one civilian lying face down. Altogether six of us were taken. The Partisan looked us over and took our money and some other things. When he searched the third person, he found a watch under his armpit, tied with a string around his shoulder. He took everything and then killed him, claiming that he wanted to deceive the People's Liberation Army, although the victim had pleaded to be spared.

All vehicles, including village carts, were confiscated by the Partisans. Parents carried their infant children, and they endured a marvel of parental love. I was young and unmarried and barely lived through it. We helped many by carrying their children in our arms. I also offered to help many parents from our group. Many women wept bitter tears when their husbands were taken away to be shot, and many mothers lost their children. We extended the hand of help in this way on the on this Way of the Cross to the little ones who couldn't endure the pace, and who were not with their parents. It was hardest for the parents, when the children asked for water and they had to be told there was no water. Many lost their lives because there was not one drop of water.

In the Trench Being Shot

In the afternoon of that day I met a young man, barefoot, wearing tight trousers, a shirt and no hat. He told me that the previous day he was taken out of the column with some others and taken into a forest. There he found a large number of prisoners. The Partisans forced them to undress and they were shot in groups of ten to fifteen in front of many Partisans and two officers. All of them were armed with machine guns and anyone who attempted to escape was immediately shot.

He told me that the Partisans would bring new groups, ordering them to take off their clothes, which were placed in a heap. This operation involved mainly officers and lower ranks of the Croatian army, but there were a considerable number of German officers and soldiers. The young man told me that by the time he arrived, there were about a 100 men ready to be shot and a lot more already dead. When his turn came to be shot, seeing the heavy machine gun handled by a Partisan, he decided to throw himself into the hole the moment the Partisan started firing. He carefully watched for the right moment to jump into the hole. The shot soldiers fell onto him and he remained buried under their bodies. Drenched with blood, he stayed still. The Partisans left at dark after finishing their executions, so he pulled himself out and wandered through the forest searching for water to wash himself. He found a stream and a little afterwards quietly came to a house of a Slovene villager and asked for clothing. They gave him the trousers that he wore. Later, he very carefully joined the column. I am certain that he spoke the absolute truth. He was a lieutenant of the Workers' Service. I remember that he came from Zagreb. His name was Zlatko, but I have forgotten his surname.

New Tortures and Horrors

The night passed without any great dramas for me and those next to me. When night fell we turned into the forest where we stayed: there were up to 2,000 of us. The next day was 17 May 1945, and they took Andrija Zovka, who came from the same region as me, and who was a government official in Sarajevo. I am certain that they killed him. We continued towards Maribor, and suffered from thirst because they did not allow us to drink water. I always walked along the middle of the road, for I felt more secure from the beastly attacks of our guards. But in spite of this, one guard took me to the side and stole my suit, giving me his torn trousers. I still had my summer coat, which I intentionally dirtied and crumpled up. He also took my shoes but returned them because they were too tight. I could work out from their speech that our guards were Serbs.

At about 11:00 am that same day, we reached the source of a spring on the right side of the road. There were a number of dead there and one Partisan was waiting for more victims. When the last group arrived, one Partisan told us to turn around. We were ordered to move backwards and forwards repeatedly between the spring and its source until it got dark This torture had so weakened the poor people who were dying from thirst that many collapsed on the road or the side ditches. The Partisans then rested, although one on the horse was looking to inflict more suffering. Some hundred meters from me was a man who could not hold out any longer; he ran towards the water. We heard a shot and afterwards I saw his body lying in the water. One boy, about eight to ten years old, asked for permission to drink some water. Cruelly this was refused him. When he reached Maribor an acquaintance told me that the man who ran to have a drink purposely did that to end his sufferings. He had lost his reason and wouldn't desist when those closest to him tried to discourage him.

Those who fell from exhaustion, the Partisans beat and tortured and made them continue their journey. When in the end that sadist who forced us to circle around the forbidden water was satisfied with our suffering he ordered us to proceed to Maribor. It was easier for us.

Before we reached Maribor we came across three youths who were decorated with communist stars and who spoke Slovenian. They separated those from the column who still had some belongings and they took those. Our guards didn't even say a word.

From Maribor to Croatia

We reached Maribor late in the night. Our guards left us alone. We lay along the road, the squares and pavements, exhausted. In the morning they again separated the youths from those dressed in army uniforms or the remainder of uniforms. Fortunately they didn't touch me for I had a thick beard and I looked older, dressed in a ragged civilian suit. Only a few from our group remained. We were no longer walking in a column but in groups of fifty people. Most of them were held up in Maribor. Just as we were to get on our way, I was stopped by a Partisan who demanded my shoes. In exchange he gave me his worn out and tight fitting ones. My feet were sore and I had a wound on the base of my foot. I was afraid that I would lag behind and be killed. I threw the shoes away, bandaged my feet and continued on. The confiscations and tortures resumed but to a less extent, and they did allow us to ask for water from private houses.

Soon we reached Croatia and in Krapina, they placed us in a small area, crowded with prisoners and refugees. The peoples' 'authority' appeared and they separated the youths from those who were in their fifties. They separated the elderly and the women. They lined us up in rows in an army building, searching us and taking what they could find. They didn't have anything to take from me. One wanted to take my summer coat but it was too big for him.

From there they took us in the direction of Zagreb. After some walking we reached a village, on the side of a hill and near the village an area surrounded with wire. It was full of people; there was fire and smoke and we concluded that it was a camp for prisoners. I resolved to escape and in the village of Sveti Kriz I lost myself amongst the houses and hid in a pigsty with a friend. When the column passed we were found by the lady of the house. We were afraid she would reveal who we were, but she gave us bread and asked us to flee. She was in danger, as were we.

We walked over fields towards Zagreb and on the outskirts of the city we joined a group of old men, women and children. In a forest on the outskirts of the city were some tables where some officials were sitting. We learnt later they belonged to the 'military section'. They were all from Zagreb and willing to help us. They didn't ask many questions, giving us papers to return to our homes. They gave me some documentation so I could return to my home at Vučevca, near Djakovo, in the Croatian region of Slavonia, where my parents sheltered me during the war from the evils of the Chetniks. Since the railways were functioning poorly, I set off on foot, avoiding the Partisan control. This document was of great value to me on many occasions.

Nine Thousand Killed out of a Column of Twelve Thousand Prisoners

I saw another column of Croatian refugees and prisoners under heavy guard going in the same direction. I came across an acquaintance who had escaped from the column of death. He told me that there had been 12,000 of them, but when they reached Novi Sad, only 3,000 remained. He knew this exactly for his role involved dividing bread for the column: 150 grams for every member. He knew up to 9,000 people lost their lives, often killed by the civilian population as they walked through Serbia.

When we were asked on the way who we were, we answered that we were Serbs, returning from forced labour in Germany to our homes in Serbia. Because of this we heard the most terrible, most chauvinistic tales against the Croats. The Serbs with the help of the Russians, would expel the Croats in the years ahead. Along the way we saw trucks and trains full of furniture and other belongings being transferred from Zagreb to Belgrade.

I arrived in Vučevac on 27 May 1945. During the war a number of families from Herzegovina came to live there, and all wept for their dead brothers and sons. Afterwards I settled in Osjek, working in a factory where I got to know Antu Runju, who was a tailor by trade and Croatian by origin. As he withdrew through Slovenia, he linked up with the Partisans who put him in the platoon for shooting. He had to shoot at the prisoners, killing them in their hundreds. His nerves were completely shattered because of what he saw and lived through.

The Partisan Sickness

I had to leave Vučevca, because after Croatia was overrun, Serbs started to settle there, persecuting the Croats. There were those who suffered from the so-called 'Partisan Sickness', including Djuro Vujnovich and Bosiljka Durich. Bosiljka, a Serbian Partisan, admitted to me that she had killed up to 100 German prisoners in the Krndija camp. Later she suffered from this Partisan sickness. When she suffered an attack, she would roll on the floor and in delirium search for more people to kill.

The Communists organised agents who would call young Croats to join the Krizari (Crusaders) in the forests. They destroyed a good number of people whom I had known, but luckily I was saved from this as I wasn't at home.

At that time we received sad news from Bijelog Polja in Herzegovina. The Partisans, who were former Chetniks, killed many people, amongst whom were the elderly and the sick. They were killed without question or any trial. It was enough that someone was reported to have a link with the so-called 'Crusaders'.

Later, the repression became milder, but we continued to live in oppression and in danger. The police would select certain prisoners and force them to denounce others. Many innocent people were denounced.

I consider myself fortunate to have survived; this was not the case for so many of those whom I had known. At times I did wish to die to end my physical and spiritual suffering. After so many terrible tortures I retained my life thanks to my strong constitution and because there was no accusation against me other than that I was a Croatian patriot.

I have written about something that the Croatian people have called the Way of the Cross.

I conclude this, my account, signed in the St. Antonio Refugee Camp on the 25 March 1961 before the following witnesses: Count Horvat–Badinsky, of Hungarian nationality; Kajtazi Nik, Albanian, student; Andria Simchin, Russian, secretary; Ivan Sarich worker, Croatian; Stjepan Markotich, worker, Croatian and Andjelko Barichević, farmer, Croatian.[3]

---

3. Marko Bozidar as quoted in Vinko Nikolić's *BTHN*, 356–363.

Chapter 6
Suffering of the Slovenes

Some of the darkest days in the history of the Slovene people were a result of the Second World War, when Slovenia was torn between Italy, Germany and Hungary. Under occupation from the Third Reich, Slovenians faced particular difficulties and suffering.

However, the crippling damage inflicted by those three occupiers was as nothing compared to the terror inflicted by both local and foreign Communists. The Communist Party in Slovenia wasn't especially strong.[1] The people had no other option but to organise themselves in defence against the main and most dangerous enemy, the Communist Partisans, who remained small in number until the war's end.[2]

Taking into account the geopolitical situation of the country and the strict occupying forces in the country, it can be seen why it was impossible for the majority of people to organise themselves. With the Western Allies giving the Communists support, the Communists managed to save themselves and organise themselves in the border regions. They conducted decisive activities, including a brutal guerrilla war, which in turn provoked the occupying units to commit reprisals against the population. The Communist Partisans followed Clausewitz's words concerning such reprisals: "from the worst and darkest misery emerges a fighting flame".

The revolutionary war conducted by the Communists wrought criminal and bloody terror amongst an oppressed and helpless population. A vast majority of the Slovenes-villagers, workers, farm

---

1. Mira Suvar, *Vladimir Velebit Svjedok Historije*, 259.
2. Milovan Djilas, *Wartime*, 339

labourers, mostly firm Catholics–foresaw a Communist victory would eliminate free peasant societies, ending their democratic inheritance, leading to the gradual death of the Slovene nation.[3]

For these reasons the Slovenes moved to defend themselves wherever it was possible. Such acts of self-defence were in accordance with international law during times of war.

Units were formed of *Vaske straze* (Village Defence) in Dolenjsko and Notranjsko in the Italian occupied zone, and in the Brambovci in Stajerska, which was under German occupation.

These units were poorly equipped and had minimal training and weapons. During the day they worked in the fields, and at night they guarded the villages. The occupiers restricted free movement, only allowing it to protect one's life. In spite of the difficulties, the number of volunteers grew to 13,000, 6,000 in the Italian zone and 7,000 in the German zone. This was a considerable number when compared with the Communists who, in August 1943, numbered only 3,000 plus a handful of veterans from the Spanish Civil War. But as the occupation continued, the Communists emphasised their national aspirations, thereby attracting people to them. They also reorganised their fighters into the Slovene XIV and XV Divisions of the 'National Liberation Army of Yugoslavia', thus ending forever a Slovene Communist army. This had a significant bearing for Slovenia's future.

Almost the whole of the Village Defence in Gornjoj Kranjskoj, Bela Krajina, Suha Krajina and parts of Notranjskom and Dolenjskom was destroyed and their citizens slaughtered by the Communist Partisans. Imprisoned Slovene patriots at Krimskoj Jami and Jelen Dol were also killed after their tragic defeat at Grčaricama and Turjaku.

---

3. The New Zealand surgeon, Lindsay Rogers, worked among the Slovene Partisans in 1944. Later, Dr Rogers wrote about Dr Boris Kidrich, a Slovene Communist who became a important minister in Tito's post war government. Kidrich was present at a Partisan dance. Rogers writes:
It was hard to realise that here was a man who had eliminated the collaborator, Dr Ehrlich of Ljubljana. Kidrich had shot him outside the Church of St Cyril just after Mass, and had pinned on his cassock a card 'With the compliments of Comrade Kidrich.' Again it was Kidrich who organized the assassination of Dr Natlachen, the last governor of Slovenia. His revolutionary path knew no road block, his ends justified the means and his power was feared in all the land (Lindsay Rogers, *Guerrilla Surgeon,* 89).

This brutality convinced the majority of people, who were all of the Roman Catholic faith and democratically orientated, that the Communists aimed to impose a dictatorship rather than free people from foreign domination.

With the surrender of the Italian army in 1943, a large amount of heavy weaponry passed into Communists hands. This weaponry, and increasing Communist numbers as they mobilised villagers, enabled the Communists to organise up to 26,000 men into twenty different brigades, some of whom were of Italian nationality. By the end of 1943, the Partisans controlled a small area of Slovenia.

On the back of Western Allied indifference, the collapse of the Italian army and the continued German oppression and occupation, an opportunity for hope and order was found. This came with a Slovene officer of the highest rank, experience and ability. Leon Rupnik was able to organise the Slovenes and advanced their ardent democratic aspirations.

Leon Rupnik was without doubt the most eminent Slovene soldier, a veteran of the old Austro-Hungarian army and, as Mayor of Ljubljana, he was held in high esteem by the population.[4] Although he wasn't given the command of the *brambovaca*, he was able to take steps and give direction to certain professional officers, in this way preventing the collapse of the civilian defence.

Despite considerable autonomy given by the Germans, and with a culture of circumventing German collaboration unthinkable, Rupnik organised the Slovene army, giving it the name *Slovensko domobranstvo* (Slovene home guard). It was able to contain Communist activity in accordance with international law. This army was made up of volunteers, eventually numbering 15,000 soldiers.[5]

---

4. Vinko Nikolić, *Bleiburgska Tragedija Hrvatskog Naroda*, 217–222.
   Vinko Nikolich recorded a conversation he had with General Leon Rupnik, in which Rupnik said:

   > 'I did everything, firstly as mayor and then as commander of the Slovene Home Guard, to save the Slovenes from a total national tragedy . . . and now I have to flee . . . hide . . . shave off my beard in order to save myself . . . what I did with all my strength so that some hundred thousand Slovenes would survive . . . and now I am a war criminal. But I am consoled that there are many good and wise Slovenes who are also good patriots, who realize what was threatening the Slovenes if someone wasn't prepared to sacrifice in their interests' (Vinko Nikolić, TSDuS, Volume 1, 418).

5. Vinko Nikolić, *Bleiburgska Tragedija Hrvatskog Naroda*, 217–222.

Lindsay Rogers, a New Zealand surgeon, based in Slovenia in 1944, writes that the Slovene villagers called them: 'Our Ones'.[6] He writes of the Slovene Partisan patients he was treating in hospital: 'Most of them loathed the Communist principles, and though few would have the courage openly to show their disapproval, many were completely indifferent to the new faith.'[7]

Slovensko domobranstvo participated in a critical battle on the shores of the river Krk, near the village of Mrseca Vas, on 12 September 1943. They barred the advance of the Communist forces, securing territory the German authorities recognised as being under Slovenian control. Over the five weeks until 21 October 1943, the Slovene Home Guard freed the regions of Rakek, Rakitna, Ljubljana, Litija, Krmelj, Trzisce, Skojan and Kostanjevica. This operation halted the advancing Communist forces, which had been asserting control on the whole of Slovenia by cutting communication, destroying public buildings, terrorising villagers, sowing chaos and death, and establishing bases for future activities.

It would be a full study all on its own to describe the way in which General Rupnik led the Slovene army to secure the territory of Slovenia during 1943 to 1945. Suffice to say, the Slovene Home Guard, under his capable leadership, was a crucial factor in securing Slovene autonomy in the lower and central parts of Krajnska. By extending its political influence and military organisation over other regions, it gathered together a united defence against the Communist forces. It was this influence that brought about the formation of a people's defence on the Adriatic coast. The defenders of Stajerske almost destroyed the XIV Communist Division in the IV zone of operations as well.

Proof of the Slovene Army's victory, despite its lack of resources, was illustrated by the reinstatement of the Slovene flag, a civil Slovene administration, Slovene military command, postage stamps, local currency, and the almost complete disappearance of foreign signs. Slovene schools, which in previously Italian occupied areas were closed after the First World War, reopened.

As the war neared its end, by mid April 1945, the Partisan forces were numerically larger than the Croatian and German forces

---

6. Lindsay Rogers, *Guerrilla Surgeon*, 173.
7. Lindsay Rogers, *Guerrilla Surgeon*, 176.

and General Vlasov's Russian army. The Partisans were also better equipped in all forms of weaponry due to the aid they received from the Russians and Anglo-Americans. The Partisan command of the air over the Adriatic was absolute.

On the night of 3 May 1945, the freely elected National Parliament in Slovenia met in a secret assembly. It comprised forty-one representatives of Slovenia's Ljudska Party, twenty-eight representatives of the Liberal Party and one representative from the Socialist Party.

In Ljubljana, protected by Slovenian national troops and by three regiments of the Serbian Volunteer Corps, the National Committee of Slovenia, headed by Dr Joze Basaj, recognised this parliament as the provisional government of free Slovenia. The parliament hoped the victorious powers, especially the West, would recognise Slovenia as a free state, within a federal Kingdom of Yugoslavia.[8]

As all this took place, the Partisan armies moved north in a three pincer formation. The first came from the west along the Adriatic coast, taking control of the Soce river valley heading towards *Korusku*, which was of great significance for the Slovenes. This army was under the command of Petra Drapshina. The second arm, under the command of Peke Dapchevich, followed the Sava river valley, aiming for Zagreb and Ljubljana. The third, which headed north along the Drava river valley, was commanded by Kosta Nadj.[9]

These three numerically large armies slowly progressed towards the Slovene border, just as the Russian army had advanced in Hungary and the Allies in Italy. The Croatian and German armies found themselves almost surrounded with the Russians on one side and the Anglo-Americans on the other. Tito's army aimed to crush the Croatian and German armies, and this was achieved through the surrender of Germany at 1:00 am on 9 May 1945.

The Slovenes used the surrender of Germany to their advantage, managing to destroy the Partisan stronghold in the region of Bele Krajine. They prepared for the defence of Slovene territory together with Croatian, German, Serbian and some Greek and Russian units belonging to General Vlasov. Considering the enormous difficulties the Slovenes were under, they performed well under the command of General Leon Rupnik.

---

8. Borivoje M Karapandich, *TBYS 1945-TKaG*, 23–24, 49–50..
9. Vinko Nikolić, *Bleiburgska Tragedija Hrvatskog Naroda*, 220–221.

On 28 April 1945 the *Narodni Odbor* (Slovene People's Committee) met in Ljubljana. After much effort, General Rupnik managed to convince the German General Rosener that it was the right moment to pass authority to the Slovene People's Committee, which in truth, was the Government of the Slovene National State. On 5 May 1945 Rupnik was removed and dismissed from all duties including command of the army. With Rupnik's removal, all hope was lost for an eventual intervention by the Western Allies into Slovenia and the independence of Slovenia.[10]

The Slovene army withdrew north on 8 May 1945. The Slovene People's Committee was unsuccessful in their attempts to have the Allies recognise the Slovene army as an Allied army. The army therefore crossed the Austrian border and laid down its arms to the British, as friends. They were interned in a camp at Vetrinje near Klagenfurt, together with many civilians who had crossed the border with them. Some believe that some 30,000 Slovenes were included in this mass of refugees.

While at Vetrinje the Slovenes were visited by some eminent British personalities such as Lady Louis Mountbatten and the Commander of the British Seventh Army, General McCreery.[11]

The Slovene People's Committee and the supreme command of the Slovene army tried on a number of occasions, without success, to establish contact with responsible British figures in the civil administration or army. They were always received by figures of lower rank. The Slovene leadership was at pains to explain to the English they had never fought against the Allies, even though the Partisans often killed innocent people, burning their houses and occasionally their villages. Their only concern was peace and order in Slovenia. The activities of the Home Guardsmen were justified by international law in that they had protected themselves and their people from internal enemies.

Although they had no guarantees of the truth in the English dialogue, the Slovene People's Committee repeated and confirmed that the army and the civilian refugees would be taken to Italy and help serve the English.[12]

---

10. Vinko Nikolić, *Bleiburgska Tragedija Hrvatskog Naroda*, 222–223.
11. Borivoj M Karapandich, *TBYS*, 51. Vinko Nikolić, *BTHN*, 224.
12. Vinko Nikolić, *Bleiburgska Tragedija Hrvatskog Naroda*, 224–225.

The British military authorities had already decided to return the Slovene army and civilians, a fact kept hidden from the Slovene representatives, so that their return to the Partisans would be without resistance. The handover of the flower of Slovene youth to certain death was made gently. It betrayed the overwhelming trust the Slovene People's officials had in the English as allies.

It was only after the escape of Lieutenant Colonel Tatalovich, leader of the Serbian Chetniks, and Vladimir Ljotich, who had been transported by the English on 24 May 1945 that the Slovenes received news they were being handed over to the Partisans. The Serb author Borivoje Karapandzich records a section from the diary of the Slovene Lieutenant Colonel Ivan Drcar:

> 27 May 1945, Sunday. About seven in the morning, Vul Rupnik entered my room. Usually approachable, this time he was sullen and confused. He asked if Krener was up. I suggested he be awakened. Soon I learnt the reason for this visit. The night before, Ljotich's son came to see Vule (Major Vuk Rupnik) and brought frightening and incomprehensible news that Serbian volunteers with Lieutenant Colonel Tatalovich had been turned over to the Partisans near Podroscica. Ljotich's son jumped from the train right before entering the tunnel, then after hiding for a while he returned to the camp. This news was a shock to me and to others, too.[13]

Doubt swept amongst the Slovenes, even as more transports were sent, with those aboard still believing they were travelling to Italy. However, more escaped and notified people in the Viktring camp of the actual facts. The leaders of committee and the commander of the Slovene army, General Krener, sought to speak to Major-General Murray, the commander of the sixth British armoured division. The British commander did not receive them and, through a lesser officer, ordered the Slovenes to move peacefully to the waiting trains.

One British officer, John M Parry, accompanied the Serbs and Croats on one of these transports, and recalls: 'The men, when they had been informed by the Slav speaking engine driver of their destination, fought to get hold of our weapons and pleaded on their

---

13. Borivoj M Karapandich, *TBYS1945-TKaG*, 54–56.

knees for us to shoot them! This wasn't a military action, soldier to soldier; it was beyond our belief and comprehension!'[14]

Nigel Nicolson, who was a British officer at the time, also kept a diary of the events, and wrote:

> The only point on which they were unanimous was in their fear that we should return them to Tito, and this was unfortunately exactly what we had intended to do. They were not told of our intentions till they saw for themselves Tito's guards boarding their train. We allowed them to remain at Viktring in blissful ignorance under only nominal guard, for the huge size of the camp ruled out any attempt to wire them in or keep them under constant supervision of our patrols.[15]

Over three days between 29 May and 31 May 1945, up to 10,000 innocent young men, the flower of Slovene youth, were handed over to the Partisans to be slaughtered.[16]

There is one exception that must be mentioned. On 31 May 1945 the English administrator of the Slovene army camp ordered the 6,000 civilians to be transported. The next day up to 1,500 were transported to the Pliberk railway station and another 1,200 to the Maria Elend station. Dr Valentin Mersol, was the Chief Medical Officer of Ljubljana Hospital, and a former chairman of the Slovenian Medical Association. He had studied for one year as a postgraduate student at John Hopkins University in the United States and spoke fluent English. Dr Mersol cared about the Slovene refugees and interceded with two Canadians, Major Barre and Major William Johnson, who put him in contact with Field Marshal Harold Alexander, the commander of the Mediterranean theatre of war. In doing so, Dr Valentin Mersol saved many thousands of people in the English zone of occupation, and it was the first glimmer of light in the darkness of those days.[17]

Field Marshall Alexander actually visited the camp on 4 June, when Dr Mersol informed him of the genuine plight and fate of those

---

14. Nicholas Tolstoy, *The Minister and the Massacres*, 135.
15. Nicholas Tolstoy, *The Minister and the Massacres*, 147.
16. The Serbian author, Borivoje M Karapandich, in his book *The Bloodiest Yugoslav Spring 1945–Tito's Katyns and Gulags,* from pages 52–59, corroborated Vinko Nikolich's account (Borivoje M Karapandzich, *TBYS 1945-TKaG,* 52–59).
17. Martina Grahek Ravančić, *BiKP,* 190–191. John Corsellis. *Symposium 1995,* 226–227. Nikolai Tolstoy, *TMatM,* 293–294.

repatriated. The Field Marshall expressed regret for his ignorance, saying: 'Since you speak English, I will tell you in English: it is unfortunate that I did not know this before. I am sorry nothing can be done now. As far as I am concerned, you can remain here. Please rest assured that we will help you and your people.'

As far as the surviving civilians were concerned, Alexander provided a firm assurance of their safety. That evening he issued the directive that no Yugoslav would be returned to Yugoslavia or handed over to Yugoslav troops against their will. Dr Mersol and the Canadian officers Majors Barre and William Johnson, officers who were concerned for the fate of the six thousand displaced persons in Viktring, worked together until the others, scattered across British occupied Austria were safe and felt secure.[18]

Vinko Nikolich, who met Leon Rupnik in an Italian camp, related what Rupnik told him:

Some 7,000 Slovene home guards were taken to Skofju Loku and there in the monastery of the Ursuline sisters they were tortured during the day and then at night taken in groups of a hundred to be shot. That's how some 5,000 Slovene home guards were killed. Some did manage to escape . . . . .

Something similar happened to 3,500 Serbs belonging to Ljotichev's units. They were all herded and locked on the bridge where the Partisans shot at them from the higher ground, after which they were thrown into the river. That was on the bridge over the Sava, near Radovljica.[19]

Father Valerian Jenko was the chaplain for many years to the Slovene community in Sydney, Australia. He was a high school student during the war, and then became a member of the Franciscan order. He was reunited with his brother Franchek at the Viktring camp.

Father Valerian related:

> I was with a group of some ten Franciscan students and I met my brother Franchek at this camp. Assured by the British, he was waiting with others to be transferred to camps in Italy.

---

18. Nicholas Tolstoy, *The Minister and the Massacres*, 302–303. Vinko Nikolić, BTHN, 225–228.
19. Vinko Nikolić, *Tragedija Se Dogodila u Svibnju*, Volume1, 377.

> Late that afternoon with my Franciscan fellow students I returned to the Capuchin monastery in Klagenfurt. The next morning I returned to see my brother, only to be told that they had all left in trucks for camps in Italy.
>
> After a few days we learnt from people who had escaped that they were handed over to the Partisans and killed. I felt terrible and sad that I had not stayed with my brother and shared their fate.[20]

The number of Slovenes eliminated totalled 11,751, although this does not take into account the people massacred near and around Trieste, nor those killed in the year 1946.

The defence of the Slovene people against the Communist armies of Tito brought them untold suffering. Statistics show a loss of 221,000 people between 1940 and 1945: this equates to losing a little more than one in seven of a total pre-war population of 1,650,000.[21]

The Slaughter and Expulsion of the German Minority in Yugoslavia

Although the expulsion of millions of Germans from Poland and the Czech Republic is well known, what is not so well known is the expulsion of the German minority from the former Yugoslavia after the Second World War.

Before the war they numbered over half a million, mostly living in the Banat region, a part of Croatia, Bosnia Herzegovina and also Slovenia. They had settled there in the seventeenth, eighteenth and nineteenth centuries, and numbered 50,000 in the census of 1948. Before the war there had been national discrimination in favour of the Serbs and, where religion was concerned, in favour of the Orthodox. But these Germans, who were mainly Roman Catholics or Protestant, lived in peace and harmony, integrating well with the various nationalities. Difficulties began to arise upon the creation of Yugoslavia, which was not concerned with integrating and harmonising the various nationalities among its citizens. The country

---

20. Conversation with Rev Valerian Jenko OFM in the presence of Rev Darko Žnidaršič OFM, 15 January 2014 also a letter from Rev Valerian dated 21 Februaryy 2016.
21. Vinko Nikolić, *Bleiburgsa Tragedija Hrvatskog Naroda*, 229. Jozo Tomasovich, *WaRiY*, 771–775.

was ruled in the interests of the Serbs, who were just a quarter of the combined population of the country, and although the main tension was between the Serbs and the Croats, this tension had an effect on the other minorities in the country.

During the inter-war period from 1918-1941, the German minority in the Vojvodina region accepted the new state, working to preserve its rights. In Croatia and Bosnia Herzegovina they tended to orientate themselves with Croatians and vote for Croatian candidates in elections. Tensions were heightened during the dictatorship of King Alexander, who took unfriendly steps towards the German minority, viewing them as an obstacle to the Serbianisation of the Vojvodina region. Under the dictatorship of King Alexander Karagorgevich in 1929, all political parties belonging to national minorities were banned, and the leader of the German minority, Dr Stefan Kraft, was attacked and seriously wounded.

The military coup of March 1941 caused great tensions. The German minority was faced with a difficult choice: loyalty to the German people, or to a Yugoslavia that persecuted them. The coup brought about demonstrations against Germans, which were exploited by the propaganda of the Third Reich.

The Yugoslavs, especially the Communists, accused the German minority of acting as a fifth column, something which was greatly exaggerated. To avoid further conflict, some of the German minority fled to Hungary, Austria or Rumania. Those who were mobilised had no inclination to fight.

With the surrender of Yugoslavia, Vojvodina, which had the largest concentration of Germans, was annexed to Hungary. Another section of it came under the control of the German occupying regime; this meant a significant number of Germans were harboured within the Croatian state. On the basis of an agreement between the Croatian state and Germany, the SS Division Prinz Eugen was formed. Its primary tasks were policing, guard duty along railway lines and protecting certain districts from Partisan attacks. Their losses were relatively high, due mainly to later massacres. When the war ended, the German minority was expelled, deported, transferred or killed.

Many Germans in Croatia, and some in Slovenia around the area of Kocevlje, were transported. On the basis of an agreement between Croatia and the Third Reich, German communities began leaving at the beginning of 1944, and this movement took on massive proportions as the war continued. The German groups in Kocevlje had begun to leave in 1941 as Kocevlje was joined to Italy.

The departure from Croatia began at the start of 1944, and by the end of the war it was an uncontrollable massive flight.

The movement from Baranje and Bačka occurred later and consisted of a disorganised flight before the advance of the Soviet forces at the end of 1944. A majority succeeded in reaching Austria and Germany, though the majority of Germans from Banat were overrun by the Russian advance. Close to 200,000 stayed in Yugoslavia, primarily north of the Danube and Drava, under Soviet occupation. The Soviet treatment of them was similar to that in other areas under their control: theft, rape of women, the confiscation of vehicles and food and forced labour. When the Partisans, ninety per cent of whom were Serbs, took control of these areas, the repression continued. The first wave of arrests and killings consisted of those who were eminent in public life, the leaders in state and public institutions and some women. In some places the shootings numbered into the hundreds. Special companies of people were created to go from place to place fulfilling the directions of the local Communist authorities.

After this, almost all Germans, male and female, old and young, were rounded up. It began in larger areas, such as Pančevo, now a suburb of Belgrade, in Vrsac and Veliki Beckerek, and then in smaller places. Those who survived the mass slaughter, deportation to Russia or expulsion, spent a number of years in selected camps.

The Communist government immediately prevented the Germans from moving from one residence to another, from buying and selling goods and services, as well as movable and fixed belongings. Before long all the belongings that these people had in the camps were confiscated. This was decided at a gathering of the supreme council of the Partisan movement (AVNOJ) on 11 November 1944, in which the Germans lost all civil rights and the right to ownership of property. This decision of AVNOJ is the only case in the civilized world where a whole people lost all civil rights. On 21 November 1944, AVNOJ passed a resolution that: '... all property of German nationals, except Germans who fought in the ranks of the People's Liberation Army, will be confiscated'.[22]

---

22. Josip Jurčević, *Bleiburg*, 354

To replace the deprived Germans, new settlers were brought in, primarily from Montenegro, Bosnia and the Lika region of Croatia. Most were of Serbian nationality and lacked the skills and ability to farm the land like the advanced German farmers of the Danube basin. To prevent the Germans from returning to their properties, the head of the OZNA for Croatia devised a plan of action: 'Firstly put them in camps; do not allow them to return to their villages and later take them across the Drava. In this way we will give security to the villagers who are colonizing there.'[23] The removal of the German farmers caused a dramatic drop in agricultural production; this had to be made up through American assistance to Tito's regime.

The Vojvodina and Slavonia region, a region in Croatia, housed camps for the ethnic Germans. They were forced to undertake heavy labour, with many dying of hunger and disease.

With the Soviet occupation of Vojvodina came a massive deportation of Germans to Russia, especially between 25–31 December 1944. The deportation was mainly of males aged seventeen to forty-five, but because there weren't many men left in this age group, the Russians began deporting women aged eighteen to forty years. In some convoys there were seven to nine times more women than men.

The hunt for males and females for deportation began around Christmas, when more people would be found at home. Between 27,000–30,000 were deported, although some researchers claim there were more. The deportees were placed in rail wagons with thirty to forty people in each. The journey lasted between fifteen to twenty days under terrible conditions, and with little food and no hygiene. Up to sixteen per cent died enroute, and many others became seriously sick. The regime in Russia was very strict, and when a large number of survivors were later transferred to East Germany, many of them were sick and incapable of working.

An extremely sad fact was the fate of children whose mothers were deported to Russia and whose fathers were killed in the war. Thousands of these children died in the camps without any medical care. Later, through the intervention of the Red Cross, a group of these children was transferred to Germany, while previously a group of sick and elderly people were transferred to Hungary and Austria.

---

23. Josip Jurčević, *Bleiburg*, 356.

Ivan Borasa, a former officer in the Croatian army, who was captured near Derventa in May 1945, witnessed the fate of up to 5,000 German children aged from four to fourteen, whose parents had been killed or had fled to Austria or Germany. He and the other prisoners took these children from the trucks to be gassed, and afterwards took the bodies to a place called Lukovac on the banks of the river Bosne. After covering the bodies with petrol, they set them alight, and the remaining bodies were either run over with road levelling machines or thrown into the water. This atrocity was committed under the direction of Momchila Popovicha, who later worked for the Yugoslav embassy in Bonn.

The same Croatian officer, Ivan Borasa, was an eyewitness to the slaughter of 300 German and Croatian prisoners in Usori, Bosna. This crime was committed by the Partisans under the command of Kocha Popovich, later Minister for Foreign Affairs in Tito's government.

Some years later the camps in which Germans were imprisoned were disbanded. Former inmates were sent to work on various state projects or to factories as workers for the new authorities. Others were transferred to West Germany following Tito's break with Stalin in 1948 and through an agreement between the Soviet government and West Germany. The number of Germans leaving grew continuously, so that by the early 1970s there were practically no Germans left in Tito's Yugoslavia.

After the war, the population of this German minority group had been decimated and scattered around the world. In West Germany, there were 163,000 Germans from the former Yugoslavia, 150,000 settled in Austria, and 15,000 found their way to North and South America, Australia and New Zealand. During the war, and in captivity, up to 28,000 died while captured or via the shootings in Slovenia in May 1945.[24]

Let me quote what Vladimir Geiger wrote in his study of the subject:

> According to some estimates, to October 1944 when the National Liberation army and the Red Army occupied Vojvodina, up to 28,000 Yugoslav Germans had lost their lives, mainly soldiers but also civilians. After that massive retribution in camps up to 67,000 Yugoslav Germans lost

---

24. Vinko Nikolić, *BTHN*, 230–236. Also see Jozo Tomasovich, *War and Revolution in Yugoslavia*, 201–209.

their lives, in the main, civilians. According to some other estimates, up to 13,000 Yugoslav Germans lost their lives, mainly soldiers, during the Second World War. Up to 10,000, mainly civilians, were killed through a massive retribution by the end of 1944 and up to 60,000, mainly civilians, women, children and the elderly lost their lives in camps from the end of 1944 to the beginning on 1948 . . .

Taking into account the 10,000 Slovene Germans, with all the soldiers and civilians in total, it could be said that the number of the Yugoslav Germans who lost their lives was 95,000, possibly 100,000.[25]

According to Michael Portmann's study, 'During the period 1944 to 1945 up to one hundred and twenty thousand Yugoslav Germans and some thirty thousand Hungarians were imprisoned in concentration camps and death camps, mainly in the Vojvodina region. All their property was confiscated and they lost all civil rights.'[26]

Taking all evidence into consideration, it is reasonable to estimate that the Communists killed 98,000 of the German ethnic minority in Yugoslavia. This equates to 19.1 per cent of their population, or the murder of one in every five Germans who had lived peacefully for generations in Yugoslavia.

It was a dreadful fate for the progressive German colony in Communist Yugoslavia, a land where their forefathers had lived for a number of centuries, and where they had participated in the struggle for freedom and independence of their adopted homeland.

It must also be stressed that the Yugoslav Communists slaughtered the elderly, women and children in this German population, none of whom could be classified as war criminals.[27]

Account by Wendelin Gruber S.J.

Wendelin Gruber was born 13 February 1914, in the village of Filipovi, in the Vojvodina region. He completed high school in Travnik, Bosnia, and then entered the Society of Jesus in Zagreb in 1934. After studies in philosophy in Gallarate, Italy, and theology in Sarajevo and the

---

25. In Romana Horvat, RiZKRuH. Vladimir Geiger, BPoLGHuDSRiP, 80.
26. In Romana Horvat: Represija .i Zlocin Komunistickog rezima u Hrvatskoj, 156. Michael Portmann, NTIDiDKJ1944–1945.
27. Vinko Nikolić, BTHN, 236.

Gregorian University in Rome, he was ordained priest in Rome on 13 May 1942. After working in Zagreb and Dubrovnik and realising the plight of his fellow German nationals in the Vojvodina and Bačka regions, he decided to return and help them. He was eventually arrested by the Communist authorities in 1947, and sentenced to fourteen years imprisonment. Due to the intervention of the West German Chancellor, Konrad Adenauer, Father Gruber was released in 1956, along with other Germans. After some time in Germany, in 1962 the General of the Jesuit Order asked him to go to South America. He worked in Brazil for thirty years, in villages settled by German people from his homeland, and then moved to Paraguay. He returned to Croatia in 1999, dying in the care of the Sisters of Mercy at the age of eighty-nine. His grave is in the Jesuit section of Zagreb's main cemetery, Mirogoj.

Gruber kept a diary of his experiences, which he used to write the autobiography that was first published in Germany in 1989. A translation was published in Croatian in 2010, under the title *U Pandzama Crvenog Zmaja* (In the Claws of the Red Dragon). The following is based on extracts from his account.

After Tito's Partisans entered Zagreb on 8 May 1945, Gruber was one of many priests arrested. He found himself with other priests, including a Franciscan from Bosnia. The Franciscan was a military chaplain who had accompanied his men through Slovenia towards the West, but found the Partisans were already at the Austrian border. 'Our clean shaven soldiers put down their arms and thousands of them were killed in a barbaric way. Those who were able to penetrate further were returned by the English . . . ' When Gruber asked him how he happened to be saved he said: 'Don't ask me, it might have been better had I been with the corpses.'

Gruber relayed his sufferings while being questioned: 'Judas, a traitor from our Order gave himself that evil task. A former colleague, a Brother from the Order, was the interrogator of the priests. It is to such a Judas we have been handed.'

'Hasn't it always been like that? And was it any better for the Lord? Didn't even Stalin study theology?' He went on: 'It's about Nedo Milinovich. He organised the trials for the priests. That hypocrite didn't hesitate to greet me in the name of Jesus as well as quoting a number of biblical phrases.'[28]

---

28. Wendel Gruber, *U Pandzama Crvenog Zmaja*, 21–22.

This Nedo Milinovich eventually questioned Wedelin Gruber, who was imprisoned for months. Sometime in 1946 he was unexpectedly released. After working for a while in Zagreb he asked permission from his superiors to return to the Vojvodina region.[29]

When he arrived in Novi Sad, he met his friend Father Emerik, who told him of the concentration camp in Novi Sad:

> In two wooden barracks, built for 200 people, up to 1,000 are crammed in. In the women's section where there are also children, there isn't an opening for air. That's where they lie with tuberculosis germs, not to mention the lice and bugs, from which the children suffer.
>
> With the fourteen Catholic priests, now we have in prisons a Protestant pastor, more engineers, lawyers and high school teachers, who are under special observation. That is the remains of the leadership of a people who wanted to preserve its right to a homeland.
>
> This is what remains of those who were preserved from the punishment units as well as the mass killings during the first few days following the arrival of the new authorities. Great courage was shown by the former German representative in the Belgrade Parliament and the president of the higher court, Dr Wilhelm Neuner, with his protest letters to Tito's regime. The Dean and parish priest of Palanke, Father Weinert, was the first to lose his life.
>
> Our people in the camps are in torn clothes, very thin and wasting away. All must get up at 3:00 in the morning and they don't have any peace till 10:00 in the evening. For people who work hard and have little food, four to five hours of sleep is not enough.
>
> In the beginning they were beaten up, trampled on and abandoned. The guards shot some of them on the way to work, with the excuse that they were attempting to escape. The rest were lying on the side of the road or in the fields. They took our good shoes, so that many in the midst of winter had to go to work bare footed, around which they wrapped

---

29. Wendel Gruber, *U Pandzama Crvenog Zmaja*, 25–26.

rags or bags. These horrors are now milder but there still remain heavy handed measures. For trivialities people are thrown into bunkers where they are forced to stand in water twenty-five to thirty centimetres deep all night.[30]

Gruber later met his sister, who related her own hardships with the care of her two children and what her father had told her: 'In the First World War I was in a Russian prison camp. There we suffered greatly from hunger. I experienced the Communist revolution. But the days of that misery weren't even a shadow of these misfortunes.'[31]

Gruber visited the assistant priest at Gakovo, Matija Johler. After a warm greeting he said to Johler: 'Did we just have to meet after such a long separation?' His face was pale and his hands were shaking. His dark hair over a short period had turned grey. 'We have come to Christ's painful Way of the Cross. It seems to me that this camp for mass killings has become the Calvary for our whole Church in our homeland.'[32]

Later on Gruber visited some children's homes:

> Here the children are lying in a room on straw, some twenty to thirty of them, very poorly covered. Only skin and bones . . . sickness . . . full of wounds and abrasions. No one is caring for them . . . The little ones are calling and crying. It is hunger which is staring from their eyes. Some others are lying still. They just haven't the strength even to cry. They are exhausted. I go from one room to another: it's always the same scene. They are looking at me with large bright eyes. They haven't a clue who I am. One woman, who took over the job of nurturing the children, takes me to a horrifying room. Carefully she removes the covering from the children, who are lying in a heap. What have I got to see here?
>
> Shaken I ask 'Are they still alive?' I bent over to them. They were all naked those little ones, all lying on one rag. A ripped shirt, the only thing between each. Truly, they were just skin and bone. They were opening their mouths still able to breath in air, the last thing the world was able to offer them.

---

30. Wendel Gruber, *U Pandzama Crvenog Zmaja*, 34–35.
31. Wendel Gruber, *U Pandzama Crvenog Zmaja*, 47.
32. Wendel Gruber, *U Pandzama Crvenog Zmaja*, 49.

'These ones were separated, because they are unable to take in any more food, they are the first candidates for death.' Controlling the terror and the disgust, I once again bent over to them, making the sign of the cross on their foreheads individually, giving them my priestly blessing. I cried, sobbing: 'The innocent children must die of hunger, only because the world has become merciless.'[33]

Gruber resolved to visit the Hungarian, Croatian and Serbian villagers in the area to collect some food for the children, which with great difficulty he was able to provide.

Gruber was eventually arrested. In his book he gave details how a comrade, Masnich, a former Catholic priest, who went over to the Communists, questioned him. Gruber thought: 'God is able to write straight along crooked lines. I could possibly draw out of this failed character something beneficial for the innocent people.'[34]

In his book, he mentioned some heroic Serbs, who faced extreme suffering and did not want to betray their fellow inmates. One such person was Milovan Dordevich, a barber from Belgrade, who cut the hair of prisoners. The prison commandant pressured Dordevich to spy on the prisoners, but he rejected all promises of enticements. To avoid any further pressure, Dordevich hanged himself in the cellar of the second building.[35]

A Macedonian medical doctor by the name of Dr Cirila Topuzovski, whom the authorities tried to use for their own ends, would answer the authorities: 'Don't interfere in matters you do not understand. As a doctor I must perform my duty conscientiously without regard for what happens to me.' As a result Dr Topuzoveski worked in the brick works and was often heard saying: 'I will do everything that they order me, but I am not going back to the hospital, because there I sell my medical conscience. It is true that I suffer physically but spiritually I am at peace.'[36] One interesting incident Gruber recorded was when he was in prison in Sremska Mitrovica. Placed in a lower cell, he heard tapping on the wall. It was in Morse code: a former Croatian officer wanted to make contact. Gruber, who knew Morse code, answered him by telling him he was a Catholic priest.

---

33. Wendel Gruber, *U Pandzama Crvenog Zmaja*, 118.
34. Wendel Gruber, *U Pandzama Crvenog Zmaja*, 143–144.
35. Wendel Gruber, *U Pandzama Crvenog Zmaja*, 264.
36. Wendel Gruber, *U Pandzama Crvenog Zmaja*, 296–297.

The officer replied: *Is it possible for me to confess through the wall?*

'Yes, that is possible.' Gruber responded.

When is it possible to do this? The liquidation could possibly happen tonight.

'If you wish to, I am at your disposal.'

We will do that sometime later . . . At the moment there is too much noise . . . It could interfere.

'Agreed! Simply call when it is most suitable.'

Father, if you do achieve freedom, inform my wife!

'Gladly! But in my case the investigating judge is speaking of liquidation.'

Will we start? asked the candidate for death.

'Good! I am ready! was the reply.'

Thus began the celebration of the Sacrament of Forgiveness, through the tapping of Morse code through a Sremska Mitrovica prison cell. At the end of it all Gruber had bruised and bleeding fingers and knuckles.[37]

Prinz Eugen Division.

The Prince Eugen Division was created in 1942 mainly from Germans from Croatia and the Banat region. It was named after a prominent general and statesman of the house of Savoy, who lived during the late seventeenth and early eighteenth centuries.[38] The Division's overall commander was general Artur Phleps.

It was involved in conflicts with Partisans in Bosnia-Herzegovina, Montenegro and Serbia. Its last commander was General Otto Kumm. Kumm wrote that the Division's surgeons would also treat wounded Partisans.[39] The Division surrendered to the Partisans, together with

---

37. Wendel Gruber, *U Pandzama Crvenog Zmaja*, 226–228.
38. Otto Kumm, *Prince* Eugen, 274–281
39. Otto Kumm, *Prince* Eugen, 240.

other German units, near the southern Austrian town of Villach on seventeenth May 1945. Kumm wrote of the end of the division:

> The fate of the Division was sealed when it gave up its last weapons. Now the former cowardly enemy groups had no restraints and began to plunder and lead the remnants into captivity.
>
> They were blocked in by heavily armed Partisans. On the morning of 16 May they began searching the men and then they marched them off into captivity to Cilli. Some were also taken to St Veith near Laibach.
>
> This march of a hundred and fifty thousand disarmed German soldiers into captivity went down in Yugoslav history as a great victory in the 'pocket battle of Cilli.' That was because they told the history, not us.[40]
>
> At the request of Yugoslavia, the English and Americans repatriated all of the German soldiers in their possession, who were charged by the Yugoslavians with war crimes. In Yugoslavia they were put on show trials, convicted on trumped up charges and sentenced to death. This included almost all of the Division's commanders who served in Yugoslavia and several regimental and battalion commanders from the Division 'Prince Eugen.' I only escaped the same fate because the Americans wanted to keep me as a chief witness in the trial against the generals of the southeast.

Kumm then concluded on the Yugoslav trial of the officers of the Prince Eugen Division: 'If they had received fair trials, not one member of the Division would have been sentenced to death.'[41]

The Croatian Catholic Origin of the Montenegrin People

The Montenegrin people are a distinct ethnic group occupying a region north of Albania, south of the coastal region of Croatia and west of Serbia. Ethnically they originated in Croatia in the eighth and ninth centuries when the region was known as South Croatia or Red

---

40. Otto Kumm, *Prince Eugen*, 266.
41. Otto Kumm, *Prince Eugen*, 272–273.

Croatia. The colour red depicted south, it followed an ancient Iranian custom of delineating north as white and south as red.

The eminent Croatian historian Dominik Mandić, in his authoritative book *Crvena Hrvatska* (Red Croatia), showed that ancient Croatia extended to the river Valona in central Albania and incorporated the whole of modern day Montenegro. He used primary sources such as the *Ljetopis Popa* Dukljanin (The Annals of the Priest from Duklja), which was written sometime between 1149–1153.[42] The author wrote an account of the history of that region, basing it on a Croatian work known as *Knjizica o Gotima* (A Book of the Goths), which in Latin translated as 'Sclavorum regnum'. As this work was quite short he used other sources, especially those in monasteries and oral tradition. Dukljanin was the first writer to mention Red Croatia. In the seventh chapter of his work, which he wrote in Latin, he mentioned that the Croatian King Budimir called a state Sabor on the field at Duvno. There he divided the Croatian state into two parts, one coastal and the rest beyond the mountains. The determining factor for each region was the direction in which the rivers flowed. In the coastal areas the rivers flowed west and ended up in the Adriatic, while in the mountain areas they flowed east into the Danube. The King and the Sabor divided the coastal area into two parts: White Croatia from Duvno to Vinodol, in fact to Rasa in Istria, and Red Croatia, from Duvno to Valone in today's Albania, the southern part of Croatia.

Mandić placed great value on the witness of the Priest from Dukla with his reference to Red Croatia. He, as a native son, knew what the land of his birth was called and to what people he belonged. If he stated that Dukla belonged to Red Croatia, he may be believed.[43]

Another source which referred to Red Croatia was the ancient *Hrvatskoj kronici* (Croatian chronicle), which in many ways was word for word from the *Ljetopis* of the Priest of Duklja. Mandich concluded that the Croatian chronicle predated the *Ljetopis* and was used by the Priest from Duklja as he wrote his *Ljetopis*.[44]

---

42. Dominik Mandić, *Crvena Hrvatska*, 29.
43. Dominik Mandić, *Crvena Hrvatska*, 17. Also see NZ Bjelovučić, *Crvena Hrvatska i Dubrovnik*, 13–18 & 20–21. Dušan Žanko, *Svjedoci*, Essey on writing of Dominik Mandić, 304–305.
44. Dominik Mandić, *Crvena Hrvatska*, 19–20.

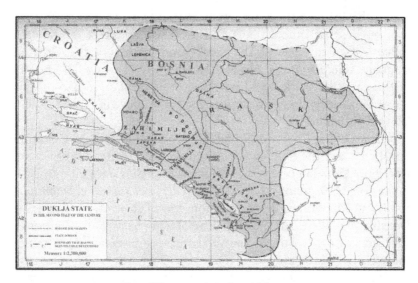

Map of Montenegria in the middle ages.

Mandich writes how the Priest of Duklja came to write his work. The priests in the Duklja Archdiocese and his fellow citizens in the town of Bari asked him: 'to translate from the Croatian language into Latin the book on the Goths, ... which contains all their past wars'. The author added: 'because of the fact of my old age, encouraged by brotherly love, I attempted to fulfil your requests' and completed the translation. The introduction to the Ljetopis is as follows:

> Requested by you, the loving brothers of Christ and holy priests of the Archdiocesan chair of the Dukljan church, and by many elderly and many of the youth of our city (Bara), ... that I translate from the Croatian language into Latin the Book of the Goths, which in the Latin is called Sclavorum regnum. I attempted to fulfil your request. But may no one of the readers think, that I wrote anything different, other than that which I read, and heard from the conversation of our fathers and our one time elders as the real truth.

The title *The Book of the Goths* (Libellus Gothorum), was the name given by the contemporary Romans, who were the Latin speakers of Duklja. The Latins called the Croatians 'Goths,' for it has a disparaging and insulting meaning to it. The true title the work was given and which the Priest from Duklja translated into Latin was: *Sclavorum regnum*. At that time Italians and the Latin speakers in Dalmatia called Croatians 'Sclavi'. The work must have had the Croatian language title: *Kraljvstvo Hrvata* (Kingdom of the Croats). The title of the Croatian work could not have been: *Kraljevsvo Slavena*, for the same writing did not recognize the name 'Slaveni,' nor 'Serb' only 'Hrvati' Croatians.[45]

Copies of the *Croatian chronicle*, discovered in 1500 by a Domine Papalich, carry the title *Kraljevstvo Hrvata* (The Kingdom of Croats) which the Croatian epic writer Marco Marulich translated into Latin in the year 1510, giving it the title: *Gesta Regum Croatiae et Dalmatiae*. In his introduction to this translation, Marulich wrote: 'Greetings to Dominik Papulich. The makeup of what you recently found amongst very old writings... I translated into Latin at your request. It contained the activities of the kings of Croatia and Dalmatia, which were truly very valuable, so that not only they, who know our national language, but also the Latins would understand it . . . With best wishes! In the year of the Lord 1510.'[46]

---

45. Dominik Mandić, *Crvena Hrvatska*, 42–43, 44–45. The word 'Got' meant Croatians in the Middle Ages and it was used disparagingly of them by the Latin speakers of the Dalamian coast. NZ Bjelovučić, *Crvena Hrvatska i. Dubrovnik,* 13–18

46. Dominik Mandić also used a French chronicle of the year 817 where it mentioned 'Dalmatorum . . . Slavorum', used by the Croatian historian Racki, Doc, 317. He also used a letter from Pope John V111, year 879, in which he wrote to the Croatian duke: 'Sedesclauo, glorioso comiti Sclauorum' (ib 7). On a stone inscription of Abbott Teodeberta from the 9 century at Nin, there is written: 'Temporibus domno Branimero dux Slcavorum (mistaken for Sclavorum) . . . Pope John X, year 925, often mentions Croatians and Croatia under the name 'Sclavi' and 'Sclavonia' (ib 189). The Venetian chronicler John the Deacon at around year 1000 often calls Croatians 'Sclavi' (ib 364, 366 and so on) or 'Croati Sclavi' (ib 424). In the Darovnici (. . .) Biograd, (A Croatian town on the Adriatic) year 1076, it is written: 'apud Sclavos Suinimiro regnante' (ib 109). Pope Gregory V11, year 1078, wrote to the Croatian King of Duklja, Michael: 'Michaheli Sclauorum regi'. (ib 211). A contemporary of the Priest of Duklja, Vilim Tirski, called Croatians: 'Sclavi' or 'Sclavi Dalmatae' (ib. 463) as did another contemporary of his, Rajmund de Agiles (ib 461–63).
(All this is taken from the footnotes of Dominik Mandić's: *Crvena Hrvatska*, 58.) Dominik Mandić, *Crvena Hrvatska*, 44. Domink Mandić, in his footnotes, had the quote from Marko Marulić in Latin: 'Marcus Marulus Dominico Papali salutem. Comentariolum a te in Craina nuper repertum, inter vetustissimas gentis illius scripturas, dalmatico idiomate compositum, tuo rogatu latinum feci, Croatiae Dalmatiaeque regum gesta continentum; res certe digna relatu, et quam

The *Ljetopis* of the Priest from Duklja came down to us as we knew it in two Latin forms of the seventeenth century and also in an Italian translation made by the Abbott of Mljet, named Mavra Orbinija in 1601.[47]

On the *Kraljevstvo Hrvata*, Mandich concluded that the work was written by a secular priest or Benedictine, for they were members of the literate minority of that time. The work was written in the Chakavski dialect, which the Croatians spoke when they came to these regions. The work is the oldest written piece of any of the Slavic peoples.[48] Dukla State as it was in the Second Half of the elevent Century.

Foreign writers also mention Red and White Croatia. The Venetian Doge and writer Andrija Dandolo (1300-1354) wrote of the Sabor held at Duvno:

> Svetopulk, king of Dalmatia . . . crowned at the field at Duvno, divided his kingdom of Dalmatia into four parts . . . From the plain at Duvno to Istria he called White Croatia; from that field to Drača, Red Croatia; the mountainous part from the river Drina to Macedonia he called Rasom, and from that river to here, he called Bosnia . . . The modern part, that is the

---

non solum nostrae vernaculae linguae gnari sed etiam Latini intelligent . . . Vale. Anno christianae salutis MDX'
(Taken from Dominik Mandić, *Crvena Hrvatska*, 58)

47. Dominik Mandić. *Crvena Hrvatska*, 44-45. Also Nikola Zvonimir Bjelovučić, *Crvena Hrvatska i Dubrovnik*, 20.

48. Dominik Mandić, *Crvena Hrvatska*, 46-53. Mandić concluded that the work *Kraljevstvo Hrvata* was written between the year 1074, after the death of Kresimir the Great, when King Mihajlo began to work towards a independent Kingdom of Red Croatia, and the year 1089, when Mihajlo the first king of Duklja died. In his footnotes Mandić had the following: King Mihaljo was alive in April 1081, when he married his son Bodin to the daughter of leading figure in Bar Arhirisa: '1081 . . . Et in mense Aprilis Archirici perexit ad Michalam regem Sclavorum, deditque eius filio suam filiam uxorum . . .'. Lupus Protospatharius, Chronicon, MGH SS, V 60, GL. Also the Priest of Dukljan, Ljetopis, pogl, 42, Sisic 360, Mosin 96. This was also confirmed by Ana Komnena, who wrote that King Mihaljo was alive, when George Monomachatos, the commander of Draca, fled to Duklja, after Aleksija Kommen was crowned as emperor on 3 April 1081. When in the summer of 1081 Robert Gviskard disembarked at Draca, Mihaljo was no longer mentioned among the living. GL. Anna Comnena, Alexias 1V 5 & 6 (1 204, 214); V1 (1 294); Vizant. Izvor (section . . .) 376-379.
(Taken from footnotes of Dominik Mandić. *Crvena Hrvatska*, 61.)

whole of the coastal part, he called Dalmatia, the mountainous part Croatia.[49]

Another Italian writer who mentioned the Sabor at Duvno was the well known Italian humanist Flavije Biondo or Flavius Blondus, 1388-1463. In his well known book *Historiarum ab inclinations Romani imperii decades*, he quoted Dandelo almost word for word concerning the Sabor as well as White and Red Croatia but added: 'Raska and Bosnia are regarded as parts of the kingdom of Croatia.' He thus confirmed that in the fifteenth century when Biondo wrote, Bosnia was regarded as a Croatian land.[50]

The writers of Dubrovnik also mentioned Red Croatia. These included Mavra Orbini, *Il regno degli Slavi;* Jakova Lukarevich, *Copioso ristretto degli annali di Rausa libri quarto,* published in Venice in 1605; and Junija Resti, *Chronica Ragusina*, published in Zagreb 1893.

The authors of Dubrovnik's history often mentioned Red Croatia and Croatians south of the Neretva River. All without exception were familiar with the Ljetopis of Priest of Duklja, some of them incorporated it completely or some part of it.

The evidence of the Dubrovnik writers is especially significant, as it dealt with their name in the more narrow Croatia, which was known as Red Croatia. They knew the mindset of their people, where they lived and their country's name. They had at their disposal older sources which are now lost. The writers provided evidence of Southern Dalmatia being called Red Croatia and that it was inhabited

---

49. Dominik Mandić. *Crvena Hrvatska*, 64. In his foot note Mandić quoted in Latin L '. . . *Svethopolis rex Dalmacie . . . in plano Dalme coronatus est regnum suum Dalmacie in 1111or partes divisit . . . A plano itaque Dalme usque Ystriam, Chroaciam Albam vocavit, et a dicto plano usque Duracium, Chroaciam Rubeam, et versus Montana, a flumine Drino usque Macedoniam, Rasiam; at a dicto flumine citra, Bosnam nominavit . . . Moderni autem maritimam totam vocant Dalmaciam, Montana autem Chroaciam*'. A Dandolo, Chronica (Muratori, Scrpitores rerum ital X11, Published E Pastorello), 156.
(Dominik Mandić, *Crvena Hrvatska*, Foot notes, 75.)
50. Dominik Mandić, *Crvena Hrvatska*, 65-66 in his foot note stated the following in Latin: 'Rassiaque et Bosna pro regni Chroatiae regionibus habentur'. Blondus Flavius, Historiarum ab inclinatione Romani imperi, December 11, lib 11 (Venetiae 1483, f 115r; ed Basilea 1559) 177;
(Dominik Mandić, *Crvena Hrvatska*, 75)

by Southern Croatians. Had this not been the case they would not have mentioned the sources which witnessed the existence of Red Croatia or they would have corrected the false claims.

Mandich also quoted the names and works of five other Croatian and foreign writers of the sixteenth to eighteenth century who wrote of Red Croatia and Croatians south of the Cetina River, in this way supporting his evidence.[51]

In his thorough study of the subject, Dominik Mandić mentioned seven Byzantine writers of the Middle Ages who mentioned Red Croatia or that Croatians lived in the region of Duklja.[52] He then mentioned four western writers of the Middle Ages who spoke of the Croatian population of what is today modern Montenegro.[53] Mandić also stated archaeological evidence bore witness to the Croatian culture and spiritual traditions of the peoples of these parts in the

---

51. In his footnote on Junia Resti and Jakov Lukarević, Mandic added in Latin: '*Dioclea metropolis Croatiae Rubeae, tempore Samuelis Bulgarorum imperatore . . .*'. *Metropolis ragusina* 1, the hand writing was in the Franciscan library in Dubrovnik navod quotation at Zv Bjelovucic, Crvena Hrvatsk I Dubrovnik (Red Croatia and Dubrovnik) (Zagreb 1929) 17. This quotation of S Crijevica of Crvena Hrvatska was really a translation and confirmation of Orbinijev's thinking: '*Dioclea Metropoli di Croazia Rubea . . .*' Orbini, Il regno degli Slavi 211, biljeska na rubu.
(Domenik Mandić, *Crvena Hrvatska*, 75. Following these footnotes on page 76 Domenik Mandić wrote the following:
Of all old writers of Dubrovnik, in so far as it is known today, there was one Benedictine of the seventeenth century whose name is unknown, from the Monastery of Peter and Paul near Dubrovnik. It questioned the value of the *Ljetopis of the Priest of Dukljan* and then, the claim in the ninth chapter of the unity of the Croatian state from Istra to Draca in Albania. In this he mainly relied on Lučić's work *De regno Dalmatiae et Croatiae*. He meniond Porfirogeneta and some other Byzantine and western writers, but his knowledge of older sources was inadequate when compared with our knowledge today. The written work of the unknown Benedictine is found today in the City of Padua Museum under the title: Antiquitatum Illyricarum 1. The third section of that work, under the title: 'Fabulae Diocleatis de divisione Dalmatiae' was published by Lj Thalloczy, in Archiv fur Slavische Philologie 20 (Berlin 1898), 209-212.
(Footnote of Domenik Mandices work, *Crvena Hrvatska*, 76.)
Also see NZ Bjelovušić. *Crvena Hrvatska i Dubrovnik,* 19-20, 30.
52. Mandić Domenik. *Crvena Hrvatska*, 166-193.
53. Mandić Domenik, *Crvena Hrvatska,* 210-213.

Middle Ages, but he himself admitted that a lot more archaeological work would be required to consolidate the evidence.[54]

Today's Montenegro was called Duklja in the Middle Ages, and after that, Zeta, but by the middle of the fifteenth century it received its present name of Montenegro. In the Middle Ages it was populated by people who regarded themselves as Croatian. During the time of Serbian rule from the end of the twelfth century to the middle of the fourteenth century, Croatian Duklja continually regarded itself as something separate from the Serbian state. As soon as Serbia began to lose its power with the death of Dušan the Great (+ 1355), leading families in Duklja led a revolt, freeing Duklja of Serbian rule, re-establishing their Croatian Catholic heritage. In old Duklja which was then known as Zeta, Catholic and the Croatian consciousness were very evident when Turkey occupied present Montenegro in 1496.[55]

During the seventeenth century, due to a shortage of Catholic clergy and the enmity of Turkey, Catholicism slowly disappeared from Montenegro. One part of the population turned to Islam but a majority to Orthodoxy; however a Croatian sentiment in the people did not end.[56] Dr Krunoslav Draganovich in his study concluded that Catholics broke away from Rome and turned to Orthodoxy because of the privileged position of the Orthodox church during Ottoman rule, the lack of Catholic clergy, taxes imposed on Catholics and the lack of Franciscan monasteries.[57]

---

54. Dominik Mandić, *Crvena Hrvatska*, 222–229. Dr Nikola Zvonimir Bjelovuchich in his book: *Red Croatia and Dubrovnik*, brings out the relationship between Montenegro and Dubrovnik. He also refers to archeological findings of the tenth century. (Nikola Zvonimir Bjelovučić. *Crvena Hrvatska i Dubrovnik*, 46, also photos of Ston, 46–66).
55. Dominik Mandić, *Crvena Hrvatska*, 302–304.
56. Dominik Mandić, *Crvena Hrvatska*, 305. Mandic used the letter of G Vuskovic, a missionary from Sestana near Bar, to the Sacred Congregation Kongr. De Propaganda the Holy See dated 16 June 1634: '... maggior parte di questi populi si sono fatti scismatici e Turchi per causa che non hanno delli buoni pastori ...' He also referred to Krunoslav Draganovic, *assenubertritte von Katholiken zu 'Orthodoxie'* (Rome 1937) 19, bilj, 2. A more detailed account of the conversion of Catholics in Montenegro to Orthodoxy and Islam was written by I Markovic, Dukljansko–barska metropolija. (Zagreb 1902), 128, 134 and the following. (Taken from Dominik Mandić, *Crvena Hrvatska*, 310)
57. Mijo Ivurek, *Zivot .i Djelo Krunoslava Draganovica*, 153.

On this theme Dominic Mandich wrote: 'The true apostle of Serbianism in Montenegro was bishop Petar Njegosh (1830–1851). Under strong influence of Serbian propaganda from Ilija Garasanina and Vuka Stefanovich Karadzich, Njegosh wrote his great epic 'Gorski vjenac' (Mountain Wreath) . This work, which praised Serbian Orthodoxy, played a major role in Serbianizing the Montenegrin intelligentsia'.[58] Through Orthodoxy, some Montenegrins regarded themselves as Serbs, being culturally orientated to Serbia. There was a sub-culture but the majority of them always regarded themselves as Montenegrins, and saw themselves as a distinct ethnic group, with a desire for an independent state.[59] Dr Krunoslav Draganovich also wrote of the massive conversion of the Montenegrins to Orthodoxy.[60]

The Croatian origins of the Montenegrins can be evidenced through their closeness with the Croatian Herzegovians. Their language and customs are similar, the difference being that the Croatian Herzegovians are Roman Catholics while the Montenegrins are Orthodox. The population of some of the Croatian islands, including the island of Korcula, speak a language similar to that of the Montenegrins.[61] Although the Montenegrins were orientated towards Serbia, there had always been a strong part of the population who regarded themselves as Montenegrins, desiring to live in an independent state. This was achieved when Montenegro achieved its independence from Serbia in 2008.

The Situation of the Montenegrin People

The Ottoman Turks were unable to subjugate the Montenegrins completely. They controlled two thirds of Montenegro; the rest fell under the control of the various Montenegrin chieftains and clans. It must also be remembered that before World War I, Montenegro was an independent state with its own monarchy.

During World War II Montenegro was annexed by Italy and the Montenegrins suffered terribly. Some supported the Serbian Chetniks under Draza Mihaljovich, their aim being the restoration of the pre-Second World War Yugoslavia under the Serbian Karagorgevich

---

58. Dominik Mandić, *Hrvati .i Srbi*, 131.
59. Oton Knezovic, *Povjest Hrvata*, 107
60. Mijo Ivurek, *Zivot, I Djelo Krunsolava Draganovica*, 153.
61. Don Bozo Baničević, conversation in Blato, Korcula, Croatia, 27 July 2016.

family. In the summer of 1941 the Italians began to co-operate with the Chetnik groups in a movement which became known as the *Milizia Voluntaria Anticomunista*.[62] Also part of the picture were Tito's Communist Partisans, and Montenegrin Royalists who fought for an independent Montenegro.

In fact, the last King of Italy, King Victor Emmanuel, was married to Jelena Petrovich Njegosh (1873-1952), one of the daughters of the last king of Montenegro, King Nikola Petkovich who was expelled from his throne by King Peter Karadgorgevich after World War1.[63] The movement for independence was led by Dr Sekula Drljevich who dedicated his life to the struggle against greater Serbian hegemony for the independence of Montenegro. He gave up his life for this ideal. He and his wife were killed by Serb Chetniks in the refugee camp Judenburg in Austria in the Autumn 1945. Dr Krivokapich also worked hard for Montenegrin independence as well as Sava M Stedimlija, who was a Montenegrin writer; all three were allied with the Croatians. Sava Stedimlija was captured by the Russians and sent to a prison camp for ten years and then handed over to Tito's government which killed him.[64] Of all the nationalities in the former Yugoslavia the Montenegrin people suffered the most, with up to 150,000 Montenegrins killed out of a population of 500,000. Much of the Montenegrin's suffering was due to the fact they fought one another. This became even more severe after the Italian withdrawal in 1943. The Italians were replaced by the Germans, who occupied only the strategic parts, leaving the Montenegrin factions to fight amongst themselves.[65]

---

62. Mira Suvar, *Vladimir Velebit*, 268-269.
63. Dragan R Zivojinovic, *AIatBoY*, 22-23. Mijo Ivurek, *ŽidKD*, 145. *Znameniti .i Zasluzni Hrvati*, LXXXV1, 86.
64. Oton Knezović, *Povjest Hrvata*, 108. Ante Belo, *Genocide*, 106. Stuparić Darko, *Who Is What In The Independent State Of Croatia*, 100.
65. Ivan Mestrovich records his conversation with Dr Petar Plamenac, who was president of the Montenegrin government during the First World War. The conversation took place in Mestrovich's home in Zagreb in 1933. Mestrovich writes:, Plamenac began talking of his own personal hardships, and the hardships of Montenegro. He criticized the Serbs and their actions during the war. He strongly condemned the slander against King Nikola and the expulsion of the Montenegrin dynasty. He was very bitter and spoke with real hate. I only listened to him, and when I tried to calm him, he became more exasperated and he insisted that he came to inform me as to the true situation there.' (Ivan Mestrović, *UnPLiD*, 221)

Some 10,000 of the Montenegrin fighters found themselves at Bleiburg in May 1945. Below is an account by Dimitrija Petrovich, who came from the village of Sokolski Oraha, county Cetinje, in Montenegro. He related his experiences from 12 to 20 May 1945:

> On 6 May we left Zagreb, where we were told that we were heading for Ljubljana, but when we reached Zidni Most we were told that we were going to Celje, for Ljubljana was in the hands of the Partisans. The Partisans stopped our first group in Celje, where the Croat General Luburich was also present.
>
> General Luburich, together with Colonel Janjic, the commander of the First Montenegrin Brigade, ordered their units to take up battle positions but the Partisans who were few in number quickly dispersed. From Celje we took the road towards Maribor. When we reached the cross roads at Maribor-Dravograd, we saw Cossack soldiers who were returning from Maribor and heading towards Dravograd. We joined them and some three kilometres before Dravograd we came across the Partisans and we stayed for two days trying to negotiate some agreement with them. They told us that they would decide on the third day at three whether they would allow us to pass or not. At 2:30 in the afternoon there began a fierce battle which lasted that day and into the night. General Luburich defeated the Partisans and the following morning we proceeded onwards. We reached the border before evening on the 14 May 1945. Our people in command told us that they had made contact with the English units and any fighting was forbidden. In the morning the Partisan unit which had prevented our progress passed by and they made out they were English. They told us that the English, Americans and Russians had decided that all Yugoslav soldiers who were not Partisans must gather in Maribor, where Tito would judge them.
>
> On top of this, they told us that everyone was to return to their homes, that a referendum would be held and the people would decide whether they wanted Tito or the Monarchy. The Croatians left that evening for Dravograd but we Montenegrins left the following day. We laid down our arms on the border, the same as the Croatians. We reached Dravograd before evening; there they ordered the women and anyone under

the age of seventeen to one side. They sent the women by train to Maribor and the under-aged children they put back with us. In the evening we went some seven kilometres from Dravograd where we stopped. In the morning we headed to Maribor. Along the way on both sides of the road we saw piles of Croatian bodies which I recognized from their uniforms; they had their shoes removed as well as their watches.

I saw an anti-aircraft shelter the Germans built, full of bodies. Protruding were the feet, hands and heads. There were many of these shelters, but I couldn't determine the exact number because the Partisans ordered us to run. We went in the direction of Maribor and when we were some thirteen kilometres from Maribor we caught up to a Croatian column which was walking in rows of four. We had to run to Maribor. We covered that distance in an hour and a half and we met there another group of Croatian soldiers. They placed us in some barracks on the edge of the town where we stayed for two days. We also found our wives there who had come on the train from Dravograd. Then they separated the women and the children, with the intention of sending them to their homes. They took them to the city. The next day at around eleven or twelve, they sent the women and the children to an unknown destination in a south easterly direction.

The Partisans would come to us, taking our watches, rings and clothes which were in better condition and beat, hit and tortured us. The Partisan women were worse than the men. They began to divide us according to the districts we came from, telling us that after seven kilometres we would embark on trains which would take us to our homes.

The first group they separated were those who came from the county of Berane. Before my county of Podgorice was selected they had taken away four counties. When they called for the county of Podgorica, up to fifty-four soldiers responded. One person went out of the premises accompanied by the Partisans. From there they took us into the city into a building where we saw a large pile of Montenegrin uniforms up to a meter and a half high. They then took us into a wide room of another building. There they ordered us to take off our uniforms. We remained half naked. They began beating us and ordering us to go out of the building. There they tied our hands with electric wire; hitting and kicking us they loaded us onto trucks. There were some twenty-four of us and we were accompanied by three well-armed Partisan guards. In the truck I managed to untie myself and five others. I asked the Partisans where they were taking us and they answered that we were to be shot as we had shot many of theirs. That moment I resolved to escape. With four of my companions we jumped on two of the Partisans and the driver and jumped from the truck. They shot at us without hitting us. The truck had to travel eight kilometres. At seven kilometres I saw holes being dug by German prisoners for the burial of slaughtered Croatians. I saw with my own eyes, how, out of these collective graves, there were protruding body parts. It is my estimation, and I am saying this under oath, at that place there could have been up to fifty thousand slaughtered Croats and about some seven thousand Montenegrins. I believe, judging from the unfortunate women and children whom they took and beat before my very eyes, even bayoneting some children before the very eyes of their mothers, that all were slaughtered.

After this I was wandering through the forests for ten days and I succeeded in reaching the English zone near a place close to Jesenica in Gorenjskom. I registered myself with the English and I related to them all that I had seen and lived through. They took me to their command at Velden, where one major and two captains questioned me, expressing disgust at the inhumanity of the Partisans.

In conclusion, I swear by my life that what I have said above is true. If a committee is formed to investigate, I would be prepared to reveal the places and affirm all I had seen.

I confirm what has been written and it has been read to me.

Dimitrije Petrovich, Villach, Austria, 20 June 1945.[66]

Another Montenegrin, Mihajlo Minich, also related his experience:

> On 6 May 1945 I left Zagreb in the direction of Trieste, but because the Partisans were blocking the way we went towards Klagenfurt, reaching Bleiberg. There we were stopped by the

---

66. Vinko Nikolić, *BTHN*, 309–311.

Partisans. My group was made up of up to eight thousand Montenegrins, at least five thousand of them being women and children. Some two kilometres before Bleiburg we sent to the Partisans as our representatives a member of our parliament and director of a high school, Velimir Jojich, and Captain Mirasa Sarich. Jojich returned while Sarich was held by the Partisans and we knew nothing of him. Jojich returned with a commander and political commissar of one Partisan brigade, who told us we were to disarm and return to our homes and our lives would be spared. He told us the English had announced that a commission would be formed in each place made up of one Englishman, one American and one Partisan which would investigate each individual case. Whoever was pronounced guilty would be handed to the People's Court; the rest would be able to return peacefully to their homes. On this basis the soldiers laid down their arms and the next day they led us to Maribor. The men had to run in two rows, forced by Partisans who were on horses. Those who could not endure it were immediately shot. No one was allowed to drink from the wells which we were passing, and anyone who attempted this was immediately shot. Along the road we found many bodies. On 18 May 1945, when we were near Maribor, they took from us our clothing, shoes, money, watches and rings. The same day, under heavy guard, we were placed in some barracks in Maribor. There they conducted a separation of children from ten years to seventeen years who were taken to an unknown destination. From the barracks they took men, with hands tied, to a building 250 meters away. They undressed them of everything except their shirts and trousers, and began beating them with rubber clubs and whips.

'Where is your King Peter and the English to help you?' The Partisans cursed the King and the English, who they said awaited a similar fate. After this the prisoners were loaded onto trucks, twenty two to twenty five people on each, taken to the forest at Pohorje and shot.

When they took me, I saw many guards and bodies of many whom I knew they previously had taken from the barracks. The truck stopped and I heard louder shooting than before and the cries of people. When we disembarked from the truck a commissar approached to see whether we were well tied.

They then took us some ten meters to the left into the forest, I managed to free myself from the telephone wires with which I was tied. I jumped over the bodies of those killed, losing myself in the bushes. They were shooting after me, but I made out that I was dead and in this way I saved myself. From there, following the river Drava, I crossed into Austria and then over the Alps, arriving at this camp for Slovenes where I am now.

I confirm that they were especially cruel to the priests, eliminating some fifteen of them. They slaughtered all adult males older than seventeen years, I don't know what happened to the children, women and the teenage girls; these were not separated but were together with their mothers and other women.

Having all this in view, I judge that some three thousand were massacred from our group alone.

I express this and sign it for the papal delegate for aid, Dr Krunoslav Draganovich, in the camp of Peggetz, Linz, Austria, 28 June 1945.

Mihaljo Minić[67]

Miljan Marsenich, aged 19, was born in Andrijevice, Montenegro, and gave his account:

The Partisans disarmed us Montenegrins in Celje and took us to Kamnik with the promise that they would allow us to go to our homes. On 13 May 1945, when we were in Kamnik, they gathered us in a large room. There were some six hundred of us and they ordered us to take everything off other than our shirts and trousers and tied us together in groups of four.

With us there were some thirty women and children whom they also robbed and tied up.

That same afternoon they led us into a forest, together with the women and children, placing us in formation of circles. Then they started shooting at us from all sides, with the result that two Partisans were shot and two injured by their own comrades.

---

67. Vinko Nikolić, *BTHN*, 311–312.

Three bullets hit me on the right side of the forehead and the four centimetre scar can be seen to this day. Becoming unconscious, I fell. When I regained consciousness I heard cries for help and I saw one Partisan who shone a lamp on me and then left me thinking I was dead. My three brothers were killed there. I heard the painful cries of the women and children and their pleas that the Partisans finish them off, which they did. In the morning I saw two or three people get up. I made a big effort, undid the wire and fled into the forest to reach Austria on 22 May 1945. All who were shot were Montenegrin and, in the near vicinity, four thousand Croatian soldiers were shot.

This statement was given to the assistant of the Papal Delegate, Father Krunoslav Draganovich, in the camp Peggetz, near Linz, Austria, 28 June 1945.

Miljan Marsenich[68]

---

68. Vinko Nikolić, *BTHN*, 312–313. Mijo Ivurek, *ŽiDKD*, 216–217.

Human remains were discovered in 2009 in Huda Pit, Slovenia. From Glas Koncila

Chapter 7
Graves and Burial Places

It is important, and our humanity calls us, to acknowledge the graves and places of burial, the final resting place of the dead. When crimes against innocent victims are committed, the perpetrators cover the places where their victims lie and it is left to future generations to discover them.

In Australia, a project has begun mapping First Australian's clan massacres during the colonial wars. The project has documented so far one hundred and fifty massacres resulting in at least six thousand deaths in the early years of the colony. This research is being conducted by Professor Lyndall Ryan of Newcastle University, together with author and academic, Henry Reynolds. In seven years, when the project is completed, Professor Ryan expects to find fifteen thousand people killed in massacres (defined as where six people or more died). Like massacres throughout the world, these massacres were conducted in secrecy and few perpetrators were brought to justice. 'They were not spontaneous events. They were well planned, designed to eradicate the opposition,' Professor Ryan said.

At the Myall Creek massacre on the Gwydir River on 10 June 1838, twenty-eight members of the Wererai clan were killed by settler John Henry Fleming and eleven stockmen. 'Aboriginal people tied up in daylight, driven to a stockyard and killed with swords, clubs and pistols, muskets.'

The most shocking incident for the two researchers was the Jack Smith massacre in Warrigal Creek in Victoria in 1843, where between one hundred to one hundred and seventy Brataualang people were killed over five days in retaliation for the killing of Ronald MacAlister, the nephew of a local squatter. Professor Ryan described it as a rampage 'The perpetrators went to huge lengths to keep quiet and hide the true horror.'[1]

In Australia these massacre places and burial sites of the First Australians are now being searched for, discovered and due reverence given to the dead. It is hoped that all the massacre sites in southern Austria, Slovenia, Croatia, Bosnia-Herzegovina and Serbia will all be discovered and respected. The following account is of the major known sites where people were massacred immediately after the Second World War in the former Yugoslavia. It will take decades for all the sites to be discovered and fully investigated.

Mass Graves

With the breakup of the former Yugoslavia and the democratisation of Slovenia and Croatia in the early 1990s and with similar processes later in Bosnia–Herzegovina and Serbia, people felt much freer, uninhibited from the fears of a police state, and began quite openly to recall where people were killed and buried after the end of the Second World War in Europe. In Slovenia, up to five hundred and ninety-one mass graves have been found, in Croatia there are up to eight hundred and thirty four, in Bosnia-Hercegovina up to ninety one.[2]

How many people were killed is still unknown. Milovan Djilas, one of Tito's deputies, wrote later concerning the end of the fighting:

> Along with the Germans, our enemies who collaborated with the invaders or bound their destiny with the fascist powers–the Chetniks, the Ustasha, the Home Guards and the Slovene Home Guards–also laid down their arms. Some of these groups got through to the British in Austria, who turned them over to us. All were killed except for women and young people who were under eighteen years of age; so we were told at the time in Montenegro, and so I later heard from those who had taken part in those senseless acts of wrathful retribution. These killings were sheer frenzy. How many victims were there? I believe that no one knows exactly, or will ever know. According to what I heard in passing from a few officials

---

1. Sydney Morning Herald, Thursday, 6 July 2017.
2. Martina Grahek Ravančić, *BiKP 1945*, 203. From *Delo* (Ljubljana) 10 March 2009. Also from Srećko Božičević, *Jame (koa) grobnice* (Zagreb 1991) latest number from Josip Jurčević, *PSiG*, 53.

involved in that settling of scores, the number exceeds twenty thousand though it must certainly be under thirty thousand, including all three of the groups just cited. They were killed separately, each group on the territory where they had been taken prisoner. A year or two later there was grumbling in the Slovenian Central Committee that they had trouble with the peasants from those areas because the underground rivers were casting up bodies. They also said that piles of bodies were heaving up as they rotted in shallow mass graves, so that the very earth seemed to breathe.[3]

Djilas knew quite well that far more than thirty thousand were killed, but he didn't want to admit the truth.

Slovenia

In the Republic of Slovenia until now up to six hundred grave sites have been discovered, the main ones being:

Areh Near Pohorj

In the vicinity of Areh, near Pohorj, mostly Montenegrin Chetniks were liquidated. This group was taken to a camp where they had been told they would be classified and then sent home. As the column arrived at the designated place, there was a large number of trucks accompanied by Partisans. The people were taken into the building in groups where they were searched. One victim relates the following:

> I remained in a shirt and in short home-made underwear. Partisans made us place our hands behind our backs. One Partisan came to me and tied my hands with telephone wire. In this way they called us two by two as we embarked onto the trucks. After we arrived at Pohorj the truck was surrounded by Partisans, who accompanied the prisoners to the graves. I saw at the place which was a number of meters deep, bodies one over the other, covered in blood without any head covering. Other victims witnessed the same event. They brought us to a clear hole, in which we saw naked, dead bodies of those who had been killed. They lined us along the edge of the hole and opened fire on us, firing at our backs.[4]

---

3. Milovan Djilas, Wartime, 446–447.
4. Martina Grahek Ravančić, *BiKP*, 227.

Some of the prisoners were able to save themselves by falling before a bullet could hit them.[5]

One person involved in the killings was Zdenko Zavadlav, a deputy to the head of the OZNA for the district of Maribor. In a book published in 1990 he wrote: 'At Pohorj at night we again shot them! We called the transport.'

A group of sixty prisoners (mainly Germans) was brought from the camp at Strnisce (Sterntal, today Kidričevo), and some from the prison in Maribor. '... the prisoners were taken from the trucks and from there to the dugout graves in groups of five and shot with light machine guns, so the victims fell into the trench ... The systematic shooting continued ... At the end, their clothing was taken to the trucks to dispose of.'[6]

Later Zavadlav told a Croatian Sunday newspaper: 'We were ordered to kill them and I, personally organised the killing at Areh near Pohorj. The order came to him from above and it was: "Kill the enemy without trial for the revolution is still continuing."'[7]

'It is an accepted fact that the civilian population and military authorities saw no difference between our (Yugoslav) forces and the occupying forces.'[8]

Bistrica OB Sotli

In May 1945 in Bistrica ob Sotli, it was whispered that several hundred members of the retreating Croatian army were shot and buried at several locations. One of the largest mass grave sites extends over a meadow southeast of the old fire station all the way to the new fire station, which lies south of the elementary school Maria Broz.[9]

Crngrob

There are five marked graves in the area of Crngrob, where a large number of Croatians were purportedly killed between 20 May and 25 May 1945. It is believed that among them were some members and

---

5. Martina Grahek Ravančić, *BiKP,* 227.
6. Martina Grahek Ravančic, *BiKP,* 228.
7. Martina Grahek Ravančic, *BiKP,* 228.
8. Martina Grahek Ravančić, *BiKP,* 229.
9. Bože Vukušić, *Hidden Croatian Mass Graves in the Republic of Sovenia,* 70–73.

officials of the government of the Independent State of Croatia as well as members of their families. They belonged to a group of sixty-nine individuals that the English occupying authorities in Austria had turned over to the Yugoslav authorities on 17 May 1945. Fifteen of the most important members of this group were taken to Zagreb on 21 May 1945, where they were court marshalled. A few minors were sent to Croatia, and the majority were killed.

Based on unofficial sources, mainly Burdych's list, plus eyewitness accounts and scattered photographs of victims of Crngrob, we can identify a few individuals who were shot on 25 May 1945 in Crnogrob and who are still at rest there. They were Baron Alpi Rauch, Dr Zvonimir Cihlar, Franjo Keller, Ivan Prpich, Lucijan Blazekovich, Ustasha lieutenant Dina Milinkovich, the physician of Pavelich's guardsmen Dr Schafer, the elderly mother of Ustasha lieutenant Juca Rukavina, the daughter of the Croatian Minister Mile Budak, Grozda Budak, her cousin Ana Budak, the daughter of Croatian Minister Frkovich, Mirna, Celina Blazekovich, Anka Blazekovich and editor of *Hrvatski List* Franjo Babich and Antun Vidnjevich.

In Crngrob, there may also be Croatians who were killed from the groups that had arrived at Skofja Loka between 15 May and 22 May, as well as a group of Slovene Home Guardsmen from the camp at Skofja Loka.[10]

Frajhajm

Near the village of Frajhajm it is estimated up to 8,000 people were liquidated and their bodies lie in the vicinity of this village.[11]

Huda Jama

Huda Jama has been recently discovered and is still being examined. According to those who remember, it is thought that the victims are mainly Slovene Home guards and Croatian soldiers who were brought from a camp at Teharje. The exact number is unknown as the area was covered for more than sixty years by 400 cubic meters of concrete and building material. Bodies were discovered in a row fifteen meters long and two and a half meters wide.

---

10. Bozo Vukušić, *Hidden Croatian Mass Graves in the Republic of Slovenia*, 86–89.
11. Roman Leljak, *MNSH*, 129–130, 132.

> At the beginning of the rows bodies were piled one on top of the other up to seven deep, while at the end up to five bodies one on top of the other. Observing the victims, in the main they were killed through being hit by blunt implements. One victim, and it is suggested she attempted to escape, was hit on the shoulders. Whether some of the victims thrown alive in the row, it has to as yet be established.[12]

It is believed that some of the victims were thrown into the rows alive:

> . . . some were holding their hands; most possibly they were conscious when they were covered with lime, which cracked up, which means they were moving. Some skeletons were protruding which means that they tried to crawl out. The movement in the mine is seen through the blood on the walls.

Dr Jozo Balazich from the Ljubljana Institute of Medicine stated: 'One cannot imagine how much these people suffered. It can be seen how they were supporting one another with their hands and climbing one over the other. Death didn't come quickly. I saw one holding on to a leg of another body.'[13]

On 25 October 2017, the Slovene government announced that the remains of up to 1,416 victims were exhumed from the site and reburied at the Dobrava Memorial Park near Maribor.[14]

The Slovene government has established a commission with the responsibility of extracting the remains and identifying all those who were killed, and placing them in a specially built building to be preserved and identified. It is estimated that there are up to 4,000 soldiers of various nationalities, including women and children. The former Barbara coal mine is in the vicinity, and at least 1,600 Croatians were killed here, according to Jakob Ugovshek, a former bus driver who was forced by the Partisans to transport prisoners.[15]

---

12. Martina Grahek Ravančić, *BiKP*, 241–242. From Zelimir Kužatko, *War and Post war evils: Hudina Jama near Lasko the hell of the Yugocommunist regime*. From *Hrvatsko Slovo*, Zagreb, 13 March 2009. Boris Oresic, *The Last Secrets out of Hudine Jame. A Crime hidden for 64 years*. Globus, Zagreb, 13 March 2009, 21.
13. Martina Grahek Ravančić, *BiKP*. From Brane Piano, Matjaz Albeht, *The uncovering of the hidden graves at Huda Jama near Laskem*. Delo (Ljubljana), 5 March 2009.
14. Wikipedia, last accessed 4 February 2019.
15. Roman Leljak, *HJsct*, 198–202. Josip Jurčević, *PSiG*, 188–189.

Kamnik

In the urban surroundings of Kamnik, in the Čuzakov field, about 500 prisoners were killed on 11 May 1945, at the edge of a pool (today it's a titanium plant). They were soldiers and civilians mainly of Croatian and Montenegrin nationality.

In mass graves in the area of Kamniska Bistrica, a large number of prisoners, mostly of Croatian nationality, were buried, brought there from the camp in Kamnik Dolski. It is now a large mound measuring five metres by 17.5 metres.

About five hundred metres from the bottom station of the cable lift, on Velika Planina, there are two mounds on each side of the road: mass graves Kopisce one and two. Buried in them are military and civilian prisoners of Croatian and Montenegrin nationality who were captured while retreating towards the Austrian border. They were held captive in the camp at Kamnik.

Around the bottom station of the cable lift on Velika Planina lies one of the six hidden mass graves in the surroundings of Kamniska Bistrica, where a large number of Croatians and Montenegrins were killed after an unsuccessful attempt to retreat to the Austrian border over Crnivec Pass.

Nearby, at Simnov the Plaz location, there is a mass grave north of the Stahovica–Kamniska Bistrica road. The mound near the edge of the forest is easily noticeable and is marked by a small wooden cross. It was there that an entire truckload of Croatian soldiers were massacred on 10 May 1945, and are possibly buried.[16]

Kočevski Rog

From a camp in Sentvid, north of Ljubljana, Croats, Serbs, Slovenes and others were taken by train to Kočevje, and then further by truck to the ravine at Kočeski Rog. Its most famous two pits are: *Jama ispod Krena*, (Pit under Krena) and *Jama ispod Macesnove* (Pit under Macesnove). A third ravine *Usiva jama* has yet to be discovered by researchers. The bones of up to 30,000 people lie in these graves, which is the largest mass grave site in Slovenia.[17]

---

16. Boze Vukošić, *Bleiburg memento*, 110–116.
17. Bože Vukušić, *Bleiburg memento*, 145–149. Josip Jurčević, *PSiG,* 32.

On the eastern edge of Kočevski Rog, besides the Roska road, human remains and clothes could be seen at the top of a dirt filled ravine. Based on eyewitness accounts, it was concluded that this was the location of the death of a large number of individuals who were brought by truck from the camp in Sentvid. Croatian prisoners of war were allegedly among them, and units of the Fourth Army committed this liquidation.[18]

The exact number of those killed at Kočevski Rog is uncertain. Simo Dubajac in a interview with Nikolaj Tolstoy, stated that 30,000 were killed at Kočevski Rog.[19] Five years later, to the weekly Globus, he confirmed:

> . . . I brought thirty thousand Ustaha to Kočevski Rog. There is even a document in English. Tito made the decision that they were to be eliminated; I just completed the task . . . As far as I know there were no women and children. Earlier, before Kočevski Rog, when we received from the English, Croatian, that is Ustasha and Domobrani, prisoners and after that we sent them in convoys to Yugoslavia. We only received soldiers . . .[20]

This same Simo Dubajac later said: 'I do not regret that I killed thirty thousand Croatians'.[21] The Black Book of Communism states: '. . . as many as thirty thousand were killed.'[22] According to Belgrade newspapers, when Simo Dubajac's health was deteriorating and he realised he was dying, he became very remorseful for the crimes he participated in at Kočevski Rog.

Konfin

On 26 September 2007, the Slovene commission for the discovery of graves confirmed that up to eighty-eight bodies of men aged between sixteen and twenty-five were exhumed from a forty metre pit near Konfin. Of the exhumed bodies, there were sixty Slovenes, twenty-six Croats and two Serbs, all of whom were taken from a Ljubljana

---

18. Bože Vukušić, *Bleiburg memento*, 155. Martina Grahek Ravančić, op. cit. p. 228.
19. Martina Grahek Ravančić. *BiKP*, 254 from Belgrade, *Duga* 1990.
20. ibid, 254. From *Globus*. Zagreb, 3 February 1995.
21. ibid, 254.
22. *The Black Book of Communism*, 326. Also Nikolai Tolstoy, *TMatM*, 176–207.

hospital on the evening of 24 June 1945.[23] There also exists a hospital register that enabled identification of the victims. On. the basis of other documentation, it is concluded that there are up to 200 victims in this grave.[24]

Krakovsko

Graves have recently been discovered near Kostanjevic on the river Krk, just six kilometres from the Croatian border; the exact place is known as the Krakovska forest. The burial place consists of two long tank trenches, and it is estimated that there are up to 6,000 bodies in the area.

A witness to the massacre of over sixty-five years ago is a local, Pavao Supanchich, who says that the Slovene police did not allow anyone to enter this area right up to 1999, even to chop wood. Talking about that time he stated: 'They called me to work and to bring a shovel. We found a heap of bones. There were bones of little children. We were told to dig pits. We didn't dig deep. They ordered us that when we returned to the village, we were not to say anything.'

When reporters approached the place of burial, he pointed to the place and turned his head away. On top of the heap were bones of children and skulls. We saw a walking stick with engraved plated words: *Bog i sHrvati* (God and Croatians).

When asked about these events, Supanchich said: 'From some of the guards we learnt that they were saying the prisoners were told they would be returning to Croatia and all were quite content, until the order was given that they were to be shot.' It is estimated that in this vicinity up to 6,000 bodies lie buried.[25]

Lepu Bukva

According to witnesses at Lepu Bukva, near Maceljski mountain, prisoners were designated for the thirteenth battalion. 'They were tied with wire in twos. They were lined up in two large circles. The guards shot one after the other or they were hit on the head with

---

23. Martina Grahek Ravančić. *BiKP,* 254–255. From M Ferenc, *The graves of Croatians on Slovene soil in 'Suffering in War and peace'*, 115.
24. Matina Grahek Ravančić. *BiKP,* 255–256
25. Hrvatski Tjednik, *Slobodna Dalmacia*, 13 January 2011, 8.

a blunt instrument; after which they would fall in the pit and pull their fellow sufferer with them.'[26] According to details of various excavations before 1992, up to twenty-six graves have been dug up with a total of 1,164 corpses, which is on average forty-four corpses per grave.'[27]

Maribor

The Yugoslav Army took Croatian soldiers and civilians captured near Bleiburg to Maribor. Several thousand were killed in the anti-tank trench in Tezenska Forest, while others were forced by 'The Way of the Cross' to other Yugoslav republics.

Between April 7 and June 22, 1999, during the construction of a motor way, workers excavated 70 metres of a former anti-tank trench, 4–6 metres wide and 3.5 metres deep.

Human remains were found at a depth of 1.5 to two metres, in a one-metre-deep layer. On average, eighteen bodies were excavated every metre, with 1,179 bodies in total. The upper and lower arm bones were tied with wire on most of the uncovered skeletons. With some, wire was used on the lower extremities as well. Injuries caused by firearms were visible on a number of skulls. Most of the skeletons and objects found with them belonged to men of the Croatian Armed Forces. About 80 objects have been preserved, including buttons with Independent State of Croatia and Ustasha symbols, Ustasha insignia, badges on pockets, wedding rings, wallets, spoons, shaving items and a gold coin, plus the wire used to tie up those killed. Bags with bones were laid to rest in Maribor's new cemetery in Dobrava.

Unfortunately, the remaining part of the trench has not yet been explored. The unconfirmed assumption is that this section of the trench, over one kilometre long, could contain a mass grave that is possibly the largest in Europe. At the end of the exploration work in 2004, a symbol in the form of a bronze cylinder was placed in the trench.[28]

According to Roman Leljak, Maribor and its vicinity contain the largest places of execution of Croatians.

---

26. Martina Grahek Ravančić. *BiKP*, 262.
27. Martina Grahek Ravančić, *BiKP*, 262–263 from Josip Jurčević, Bruna Esih, Bože Vukušić, *Cares of the memory of Bleiburg* Zagreb, 2005.
28. Bože Vukušić, *Bleiburg memento*, 126–130.

When St Pope John Paul II celebrated Mass at Maribor in 2001, he greeted the Croatian pilgrims in his homily:

> I extend a warm welcome to the pilgrims from neighbouring Croatia who have come to this sacred celebration. Their presence enables me to mention the innocent suffering of war and the totalitarian regime, especially those who were thrown into massive graves which were recently discovered near Maribor. May this dramatic event never be repeated! May God grant a precious peace to Slovenia, Croatia and all countries of Europe and the whole world.[29]

Maceljskoj Forest

At the beginning of June 1945, up to 210 soldiers were placed in 'three wagons of death', which went in an unknown direction. After their arrival they 'first took out all the prisoners from the first wagon, all seventy, half from the second wagon, that is thirty-five of them. It is assumed that these people were liquidated in the surrounding forests, while a portion of the prisoners who were in the third wagon managed to escape.' According to Slavko Ivankovich: 'I was on the Way of the Cross and on the way escaped from the shooting of the Croatian soldiers.'[30]

Mislinja

In the field between Loznica to the north, the water works pumps to the west and the Levec–Celje road to the south lies allegedly the mass grave of Croatian refugees, killed in May 1945.

South of the Abrsek estate near the 12,050 kilometres sign, perpendicular to the Velenje–Misljina road, is an anti-tank trench that is two metres wide and 1.5 metres deep. Ten to fifteen people are believed buried here, killed while retreating to the Austrian border.

The local inhabitants are also believed to have buried a large number of Croatian soldiers and civilians between 10 May and 15 May, 1945 in the anti-tank trench between the road and the railway below Mislinja gorge.

---

29. Roman Leljak, *Bleiburg memento*, 122
30. Martina Grahek Ravančić, *BiKP,* 262. From *Hrvatski Domobran* (Zagreb) Volume 2, 1996. Also Josip Jurčević, *PSiG,* 35. Dr Jozo Marević. *50 Godina Bleiburga*, 290, 292–293, 295.

Along the route of an abandoned railway track lie four mass graves with people of Croatian nationality, who were killed on the way to the Austrian border.[31]

Raduse

The mass grave in which human remains were uncovered covers ninety metres by between six to eight metres, and lies in a forest area of Jezevce in Zancani.

There are several assertions as to the origin of the mass grave because of the lack of written documentation and contradictory sources. It is most probable that it contains captured Croatians and perhaps Chetniks, who surrendered on the Bleiburg field on 15 May or who were captured after surrendering between 10 May and 14 May 1945. They were most likely killed around 20 May, or 28 May at the latest, when the first transfer of the Slovenian Home Guardsman from Bleiburg arrived. Collected police information estimates the number of victims at between 3,000 and 5,000 Croatian soldiers and possibly sixty to eighty *Kulturebund* (Cultural Association members) from Slovenj Gradec.[32]

Rogoški Gozd

On the road from Ptuja to Maribor, some four to five kilometres from Maribor, is the village of Rogoza. There were some anti-tank pits dug before the war by the Royal Yugoslav army, and these pits proved quite useful for the Partisans for they slaughtered up to 10,000 Croatian soldiers there where their bodies now lie.[33]

Špitalič

In Špitalič, close to Konjica, a witness Stanko Novak states:

> In this canyon in the main Croatians were killed, but of the numbers I will not mention as someone could have a heart attack. People say and some have showed me that with the bodies the Partisans firstly filled up the sixteen mines and in

---

31. Bože Vukušić, *Bleiburg memento*, 137–139.
32. Bože Vukušić, *Bleiburg memento*, 158.
33. Roman Leljak, *Buried Alive*, 122–125.

the surrounding area filled seventy large pits. When there was no longer any room they forced the German prisoners to dig graves in the forests as well as using all monastic towers and their wells for their purpose.[34]

Tezno

In the vicinity of Tezno, which is near Maribor, there are the remains of thousands of mainly Croatian bodies. In a three and a half kilometre long anti-tank bunker, of which only seventy metres has so far been dug up, as many as 1,179 bodies have been exhumed. Most of the bones were tied with wire and some had their lower extremities tied. The remains were found at a depth of 1.5–2 metres. On average, eighteen bodies were found for every metre of the bunker's length. There was a variety of identification signs found, which confirmed the nationality and status of the victims. There were military insignia, military shoes, items in pockets, rings ordinary and marriage, money and spoons, items for shaving and jewellery. With all this, it is concluded that the majority of the items belonged to members of the Croatian armed forces.[35] The Yugoslav Partisans in 1945 killed between 15,000 to 20,000 soldiers and civilians, mostly of Croatian nationality.

When this site was discovered, the slaughter was covered extensively in many newspaper articles in Slovenia and Croatia. Marinko Polich claimed that the minimum number killed was 12,000 Croatians. Branimir Kovachich, using mathematical calculations estimated 38,736 individuals.

In an article in the Croatian newspaper, Dragan Truhli writes of the arrival of these unfortunates at the Tezno forest on 13 May 1945 and almost immediately after this there was the separation of the Domobrani, Ustasha, officers and civilians. He quotes Alojzija Potochnik, whose home was nearby: 'They were shot here, near the waterworks'. Truhli writes that the trenches were dug by the victims

---

34. Martina Grahek Ravančić, *BiKP,* 226 (from an article by Stanko Novak, in *Večerni List*, Zagreb. 6 August 1999).
35. Ibid, 224 (Ivica Barelvica Barešic Tadić and Ivo Križanec were interviewed by the Slovene criminologist, Pavel Jamnik, as well as by Bojan Vidović both from the Slovene police department and Dr Mitja Ferenc from the commission of the Republic of Slovenia on 26 and 27 March 2008.) Roman Leljak, *MNSH,* 93-98.

themselves, into which 5,173 were thrown and another 4,000 victims into a 400 metre long trench not far from Maribor. The exact date of these killings is disputed, with the Slovenian government stating that it was on 9 May 1945 while Truhli claims it was between 13 May and 18 May 1945.[36]

A commission established by the government of Slovenia in 2007 to investigate the existence of the graves, confirmed the existence of three anti-tank trenches in the area. Matija Ferenc, who was a member of the commission, came to the conclusion that up to 15,000 victims lie in these trenches, although this number is disputed.[37]

Roman Leljak writes of the account by Zdenka Zavadlava, who was an officer of the Ozna at the time. Zavadlava describes how the trenches were filled with shot soldiers and how Tezno was 'a real slaughter house of Croatians'.[38]

Roman Leljak detailed an interview with Ivica Baresich Tadich and Ivo Krizanec, both of whom witnessed and participated in the killings of over 10,000 Croatian soldiers and civilians in a forest near Tezno, running east-west of the present Maribor-Ljubljana highway. Krizanec stated there were 36,000 Croatian soldiers liquidated: 'I was there, trucks would came in reverse to the pit, and when one was emptied, another was waiting to reverse, that was the case for the whole time ... at that time I heard there were up to 36,000.'

When asked were there any women and children, he stated there were no children but there were two truckloads of women who belonged to the Ustasha movement.[39]

Poljana

Near Poljana, in a trench of the Hasenbichlov mine and at the location intended for the sorting of waste rock, an unknown number of Croatian soldiers and civilians were killed, captured on the Frankolovo-Vitanje road, while retreating towards Austria. The entrance to the mine was destroyed after the war.

---

36. Martina Grahek Ravančić, *BiKP,* 226 (from an article by Stanko Novak, in *Večerni List*, Zagreb, 6 August 1999).
37. Martina Grahek Ravančić, *BiKP,* 226 (from an article by Stanko Novak, in *Večerni List*, Zagreb. 6 August 1999).
38. Roman Leljak, *MNSH*, 106.
39. Ibid, 96.

The mass grave lies in a two kilometre long belt along the Prevalje-Poljana road, and contains an unknown number of largely Croatian military members (and possibly some civilians) who were killed in concluding battles or liquidated after surrender on 15 May 1945. More accurate positions are not known; they probably lie in the area between the road and the Meza River.[40]

Sv Ivana

A former Slovene Partisan, Jaka Leber, witnessed the killings of mainly Croatian women and children in the Sv. Ivana valley. The civilians and soldiers were together, *"There came an order for them to take off their clothes and then they were liquidated by shooting or they were hit with hoes or axes".* According to Leber, there were up to 600 soldiers in the valley. *"The leader was Franc Oreshnik, who came from the Military Security Service and after him there was Jurij Klokochovnok. Present there was also Franc Smon, the district judge from Celj."*[41]

Tezen Forest

Just in this vicinity at least 15,000 prisoners, mainly Croatians, were killed.[42] As the main road was being built in April 1999, 70 metres of an anti-tank pit were dug out, and the bodies of 1,179 Croatian soldiers were unearthed. It was also discovered that the original anti-tank pit was some six kilometres in length and possibly held more bodies.[43]

Zgornje Hudini

One mass grave site lies in Zgornja Huinja, near Celje. During the war an anti-tank trench was dug there, and it was used in May 1945 as a mass grave for a yet-to-be determined number of victims.

In October 1996, during the examination of the mass grave sites in the field near the elementary school Frana Rosa, human remains

---

40. ibid (also 105–106, 127).
41. Martina Grahek Ravančić, *BiKP*, 226. (From Jaka Leber, in *Večerni List* (Zagreb), 19 August 1999.)
42. Mladen Sweitz, *BiH*, 96
43. Roman Leljak, *MNSH*, 127–128.

were found plus remnants of leather shoes and a piece of twisted wire. Excavations continued a year later and a large quantity of bones was found, belonging to thirty-seven men and three women. Researchers also found wire used to tie wrists, some just lying beside the bones of the upper limbs, which means that the victims were tied with wire before being killed. It is interesting that no shells were found during the excavation of the remains, although skull injuries indicates twenty-five people were killed as a result of injuries to the head or brain caused by firearms. This is confirmed by the claims of the local inhabitants that the victims were brought there from some other location.[44]

Mass Graves In Croatia

Dubrovnik's Daksa Island

Image of Daksa Island from the cover of Josip Sopta, *Daksa, Povijest Franjevačkog Samostana*, Matica Hrvatska, 1998.

---

44. Bože Vukušić, *Bleiburg memento*, 82–84.

Although the mass grave on Dubrovnik's Daksa island could be regarded as the beginning of the Bleiburg tragedy, it also symbolises the slaughter conducted by the Communists in the vicinity of Dubrovnik and its wider district. As the Partisans entered Dubrovnik unopposed on 18 October 1944, they immediately arrested up to 300 people, of whom 104 were killed by the end of the year.[45] From 25 October to 27 October 1944, up to fifty-three leading citizens of Dubrovnik were shot on Daksa island and their bodies now lie in a common grave next to the ruined former Franciscan monastery on the island which is just a kilometre away from Dubrovnik's habour. The victims included its mayor, Dr Niko Koprivica, one Orthodox priest and seven Catholic priests, one of whom was the Jesuit Father Petar Perica, who composed the popular Marian hymn, *Rajska Djevo* (Heavenly Virgin).[46] When we reflect on all the thousands of tourists who pour into Dubrovnik each week walking its medieval walls, very few are aware of or visit the graves of these leading figures of the Dubrovnik community who were put to death because they did not agree with Communist principles.

Gračani

Not far from Zagreb is the large village of Gračani, its population today being about 7,000 including the surrounding district. From 10 May 1945 until July 1945 the Partisans killed up to 6,000 people. The victims were mostly civilians and captured Croatian and German soldiers. All executions were conducted by the sixth Lika Proletarian Division under the command of Djoke Jovanicha and members of the Yugoslav secret police.[47] The first search of the graves was headed by Miroslav Haramija from the Department of Health in October 2012 with the assistance of some 600 locals. They discovered seventeen unmarked graves, although this had risen to twenty graves by 2018, with at least 783 bodies.[48]

---

45. Hrvoje Kačić, *DŽ*, 56.
46. Hrvoje Kačić, *DŽ*, 157–174, 319–320. Joško Radica, *IND*, 144–156, and *Hrvatski Mučenici i Žrtve iz Vremena Komunističke Vladavine*, 226–227.
47. Wikipedia, last accessed 11 November 2018.
48. Wikipedia, last accessed 11 November 2018

Harmica Near Zaprešić

It appears that members of the Slovene *Modre division* were killed here, as well as German soldiers and Croatian Ustasha.[49]

Jazovka

Seventy-five kilometres northwest from Zagreb, in the very picturesque district of Žumberak, near the village of Šošice, is a chasm called Jazovka.

As the war was coming to an end, Branko Mulich, who had been born and raised in Zagreb, arrived in Zagreb at the command of the tenth Partisan Corps. It was May 1945. As he had a driver's license, he was given the task of driving a bus which could carry up to twenty people. Two trucks also arrived, plus a Jeep full of Partisan soldiers, and they were to drive to the Holy Spirit Hospital in Zagreb. The wounded from the hospital were loaded onto trucks; those who were less seriously wounded went into the bus; and the more seriously wounded lay on straw on the two trucks. Branko Mulich heard that they were being transferred to another hospital, so he didn't pay much attention to where he was going. After an extended period of time, he realised that they were driving to the district of Žumberak, near the village of Šošice. There they parked in a field and the wounded were removed from the bus and trucks and were taken to a 1.5 metre-wide pit, where they were shot and thrown into the pit.

Mulich, who witnessed this machinery of massive evil, remembers the cries of these unfortunates. He distanced himself until the killings were over. He was fortunate that when he returned to Zagreb, his chief was sympathetic to him when he asked to be relieved of driving. Mulich believes that these killings continued for a number of weeks, since the trucks and bus continued to arrive at the square for a number of weeks.[50]

Jela Smiciklas, who lives in the village of Sopota, recalls:

> I don't know exactly where the pit is, but I know where they were passing. When I went to the fields, on the road there were prayer booklets, pictures and rosaries.

---

49. Mladen Schwarz, *BiH*, 39.
50. Zelimir Zanko & Nikola Solić. *Jazovka*, 16–18.

At that time I was of about thirty years of age. They would come down from the upper village and our field was close by. It was May, we were harvesting the corn. And they were passing day and night. There were columns of trucks; they would line up one after another like this for two weeks. We only saw bare feet which protruded from under the canvas. We were afraid of gathering anything from the road as we thought they could kill us. Later the Partisans gathered all this up and burnt it.

Our field was about fifty metres from the pit. We heard pitiful cries. When the trucks arrived at the turning which leads to the pit, they would send the people from the fields. We were told that we were to go away. Then we went to the top village. I don't know how I reached the top village. There was great fear, everyone was frightened. No one was to come close.

Two weeks after they left, there developed a very unpleasant smell so that in Sopotima in the morning windows were not to be opened. Some people went to look. There was talk that around the pit there was blood to one's knees. According to what was said they were tying them one to another like animals so that they pulled one another into the pit. The children they just killed. You knew this through the cries. We didn't see anything of this, but the cries were heard. Women, how they cried: 'O Lord have mercy when I come to die!' It is impossible to describe this. I immediately felt choked. That is impossible. No one was allowed to come close. People however secretly would go and have a look at the pit.

Later they were thinking how to disguise it all. They said that the pit needed to be covered with quicklime. Yes, quicklime! They did nothing to cement it in, they only rolled a stone over the entrance. There where they were unloading the people they hid behind trees so the people would not see or overhear. It is not known whether those killed were soldiers or civilians. But who will know? If anyone was prominent in the party, he would know, but it is for him to admit it. I can't remember his name. None of them are alive now.[51]

---

51. Želimir Žanko & Nikola Solić. *Jazovka*, 24–26.

Another villager from Šošica, Marko Tarac recalls: 'We all had to be silent, for we were under a ruthless Communism, and no one was allowed to approach the pit. The first few years after the war, people were sent away from their fields which were close to the pit and later, due to fear, no one would approach the pit.'[52]

Milan Smiciklas, who was president of the Žumberak Association in Zagreb, said at a speech to the Association:

> As an eight year old when the war ended, everything is engraved in my mind. I remember the arrival of all the armies who would replace one another as if on film. For us children all armies were good.
>
> As we were living near the pit, in neighbouring Sopotima, we heard clearly the trucks that brought the wounded. From 10 May to the end of June, every night the scene was the same: shooting, howling and crying. I was told that only soldiers were brought to Jazovka. That's a lie! We children would come to the pit. There, there was a piled heap of clothing. On one occasion, I, an eight year old, found children's shoes which I was able to put on.
>
> Who is responsible for this, it is hard to say. Every authority was working towards a clean slate. I think that was the main motive.[53]

Janko Badovinac, who came from the district of Žumberak, knew of the pit from 1955 when he was passing it with his father as a boy. He remembers his father saying:

> I will not live to see this, but you remember, here the flower of Croatia lost their lives. Don't forget this, and if you live to see it, make sure that people learn of it, but don't seek vengeance.
>
> Today there is an attempt to blame the people of Žumberak. They who did this evil are attempting to throw this mud on us. That is not the truth! The people of Žumberak are not guilty for what happened at Jazovka. Through history they showed they were not a vengeful people. Roman Catholics, Greek Catholics and Orthodox lived together and we received everyone with open arms."[54]

---

52. ibid, 26.
53. ibid, 26–27.
54. ibid, 27.

Zivko Kustich was a prominent priest journalist of the Eastern rite, thus married, whose early appointment was as pastor at Šošice. He recalls the following:

> In Šošice I learnt a lot from Stanko Visosevich, who was my predecessor there. He was the priest there before and after the war. The Partisan army burnt the monastery of the Basilian Sisters and the priest's house. Šošice was burnt, then Jazovka happened, and the priest, when he returned learnt that members of his family had finished up in the pit. He approached things quietly, gathering their prayer books and documentation which had been thrown amongst the trees. I was told he saved all this and left it in a church building, but I don't know where.
>
> My wife was told in confidence by other women so much about Jazovka. I knew almost everything, except the movement of the trucks. In spite of this, people knew that the trucks came from the direction of Karlovac. It was also known what Jela Smiciklas told the journalist, there was little shooting but much crying, screaming.
>
> It was known that, in the main, people were liquidated by axe, hit mainly in the back of the head and also many were thrown alive into the pit. It was also said that many people were tied together with wire and in this way thrown into the pit.[55]

The Jazovka pit is some forty-three metres deep, at the bottom of which there is a ledge where most of the bones of those killed lie. The ledge is some seventeen metres wide, at a roughly forty-five degree angle, at the end of which there is another dark drop down which no one as yet has explored. It is estimated that some 6,000 people were buried in the Jazovka pit.[56] This pit also includes the bodies of three religious Sisters of Mercy who worked in Zagreb Hospital. They were Geralda Jakob, Konstantina Mesar and Lipharda Horvat.[57]

---

55. ibid, 70–71.
56. ibid, 25, also Josip Jurčević, *PSiG*, 37, 150.
57. *Hrvatski Mučenici i Žrtve i Vremena Komunističke Vladavine*, 539, 546, 548.

Nikolai Tolstoy also gives a detailed account of a number of people who escaped the massacre at Kočevski Rog as well as filling in details of what happened.[58]

Serbia

With the collapse of Communism in the former Yugoslavia the burial sites of people killed by the Communists in Serbia were not in the public consciousness for almost twenty years. The situation changed greatly in June 2009 when the Belgrade newspaper *Večerne Novosti* carried an article on the importance of discovering the truth about the burial sites of those killed. In addition, an initiative was instigated by the Institute of Contemporary History in Belgrade compelling the government of the Republic of Serbia to establish a 'State Commission to research the existence of secret graves of those killed from September 1944'. For it was from September 1944 when the Communists took control of Serbia.

The Commission established two committees: The Committee of investigation and seeking evidence of secret grave sites and the Committee for exhumation. By the end of 2010 the Commission received 17,340 submissions, and evidence of 180 secret places of execution and graves were uncovered. Excavation of the burial sites was authorised and the establishment of dialogue with world-wide organizations of Germans from the Danube region (Swabians) began.

By 2012 up to 130 execution areas and burial sites had been discovered in Serbia proper. In Vojvodina, the Danubian region of Serbia, up to fifty execution and burial sites were found. The nationalities of the people executed were mainly German and Hungarian while those found near the village of Bela Crkva were Russian soldiers who fought with the Germans.[59]

---

58. Nikolai Tolstoy, *TMatM*, 176–207.
59. Josip Jurčević, *PSiG*, 190–195.

Chapter 8
Who is at Fault?

So who should be considered responsible for what I have written in the previous chapters.

I will argue that I believe the following are at fault.

- King Alexander Karagorgevich
- The British
- Josip Broz Tito
- Dr Ante Pavelich
- Rasovi
- Mara Pavelich
- The Withdrawal of the Croatian Army

King Alexander Karagorgevich

The fault for the mass slaughter of the Croatians, Slovenes, Montenegrens, Serbs and some Germans that began in Southern Austria on May 15, 1945, can be traced back to King Alexander Karagorgevich together with the ultra Serbian nationalists with whom he was closely associated, and his brutal regime that followed the assassination of the Croatian leadership in the Belgrade parliament in 1928.

On 6 January 1929, the King suspended the constitution, abolished parliament and, later that year, changed the name of the country from the Kingdom of the Serbs, Croats and Slovenes to Yugoslavia. The name Croatia therefore disappeared. His regime was extremely brutal, especially towards Croatians, Macedonians and Albanians and this ultimately motivated Dr Pavelich and the Ustasha's emergence.

King Alexander's brutality also caused a lasting division between the Croatian and Serbian peoples, the wounds of which have not yet been healed. Also, he antagonised liberal elements in the Serbian leadership and among the Serb people, causing some to gravitate to Communism. It could be reasonably argued that King Alexander's policy resulted ultimately in the Communists coming to power after the war and also causing enormous suffering on the Serbian people whose position in the new country he tried to enhance. Unfortunately, when the king implemented his oppressive measures no one at that time foresaw the approaching world economic depression, the rise of Hitler in Germany, or the eventual invasion and destruction of Yugoslavia and the enormous suffering of its people to which King Alexsander contributed.

The British

The British should bear a heavy share of responsibility for the Croatian-Serb division because their diplomacy supported the Karagorgevich regime and showed no understanding of the plight of non-Serb peoples under the Karagorgevich rule.

The British are also culpable for what happened at Bleiburg, because the war in Europe had ended by 8 May 1945, but one week later, they handed over thousands of soldiers and civilians fleeing the Communist Partisans. This was an unlawful act under international law. This culpability is reinforced by Milovan Djilas, who at that time was Vice President and a very important figure in Tito's government. In an interview he gave to Dr George Urban, Djilas expressed the view that the British acted immorally:

> To be quite frank with you, we didn't at all understand why the British insisted on the returning of these people. We believed in the ideological context prevailing at the time, that the British would have a good deal of sympathy for these refugees, seeing that they had fled Communism. We thought that the British would show 'class solidarity' with them, and some of us even feared that they would enlist them for future use against Communist governments, especially our own. Yet, to our great surprise, they did none of these things but delivered them into our hands. This was all the more astonishing because we knew that many Yugoslavs (Croats and others)

who found themselves in Britain as prisoners of war were considered quite safe from repatriation.[1]

Dr Urban then asked Djilas: 'So the British were guilty of a mixture of indifference, lack of political imagination, and plain imbecility?'

Djilas replied:

> Imbecility above all. They ought to have looked at the character of our government, such as it was at the time, and drawn their own conclusions. Yes, the British did completely do the wrong thing in putting these people back across the border, as we did completely the wrong thing in shooting them all. I make no secret of my view that these killings were senseless acts of wrathful revenge.

Dr Urban then asked if the British authorities responsible could have reasonably assumed that all the refugees would be massacred on their return.

Djilas answered:

> I think they ought to have had a pretty shrewd idea of what we would be doing with them. We had a British Military Mission attached to us. Its members could have entertained no doubt as to how the Ustasha and Chetniks were treating us, and how we were treating their captured men and, in fact, any one we remotely suspected of supporting them. But the British preferred to shut their eyes.[2]

In an earlier chapter it is stated that the key figure in the repatriation of these people was Harold MacMillan, and he virtually admitted this in his diary entry for 13 May 1945. The British had agreed to hand over any Cossacks who'd fought on the German side to Stalin's Russia in the Yalta agreement, and MacMillan was involved in this repatriation of the Cossacks. However there was no such agreement for the handover of fleeing Croats, Slovenes, Montenegrens, Serbs and Germans to Tito's Partisans.

---

1. Nikolai Tolstoy, *TMatM*, 356.
2. Nikolai Tolstoy, *TMatM*, 356.

Nikolai Tolstoy, who made a well respected analysis of the situation, in his book titled *The Minister and the Massacres,* is firm in acknowledging the decisive role played by Harold MacMillan. Tolstoy wrote:

> The role played by MacMillan now seems clear. The decision of enforced repatriation was a political one; MacMillan was the War Cabinet's highly experienced Political Adviser in the Mediterranean, a man in direct contact with the Prime Minister, Cabinet and the Foreign Office. His prestige was immense and unlikely to be questioned by a general in the field . . . It was MacMillan who advised Kneightley to hand over all the Cossacks. MacMillan sought McCreery . . . to back Kneightley's requests. It was MacMillan whose authority served to extract an order from General Robertson authorizing the hand overs and MacMillan who deliberately concealed what he was doing from the Foreign Office . . .[3]

> . . . There seems to be little question that it was MacMillan's initiative which prevailed in Klagenfurt. To Kneightley he could have acknowledged that existing instructions apparently left no option but to screen Soviet citizens and retain all the Yugoslavs. Nevertheless there were pressing reasons of state for circumventing those orders. What reasons MacMillan provided there is no certain means of knowing, but they must have been persuasive in the eyes of a not very intellectual or politically aware soldier of middle rank, all of whose energies up to the previous week had been devoted to commanding men in war.[4]

It can certainly be assumed that Harold MacMillan knew more about the Croats' plight than has been apparent. William Deakin, the first British representative for Tito's forces, was parachuted into Montenegro with some other officers on 27 May 1943, during the famous battle of Sutjeska. When his term of duty with Tito was completed, he was appointed to the staff of Harold MacMillan in Italy.[5] We will never know how Deakin's opinion coloured MacMillan's strategy.

---

3. Nikolai Tolstoy, *TMatM,* 84.
4. Nikolai Tolstoy, *TMatM,* 85.
5. William Deakin, *TEM,* 265.

Tolstoy continued: 'MacMillan's visit likewise resulted in the total reversal of established policy towards the surrendered Yugoslavs. Up to the time of the departure from Klagenfurt, General Kneightley had planned to dispatch them to safety in accordance with AFHQ order of 3 May.'[6]

General Sir Horatius Murray, who was commander of the Sixth Armoured Division, wrote an unequivocal letter to Tolstoy: 'I put the trouble where we were mainly with MacMillan, Minister for State to the Mediterranean for Winston Churchill.'[7]

Toby Low, later given the title Lord Arlington, played a big part in the handover of the Croats, Slovenes, Montenegrens and Serbs.[8] Although the bulk of the Croats had already been repatriated on the Bleiburg field on 15 May, Low's decision, negotiations and agreement had all been conducted in defiance of Alexander's order of 17 May and in the absence of any authority from the Eighth Army.[9]

Tolstoy wrote: 'Brigadier Low . . .to whom Kneightley had granted the "remit" to supervise the Yugoslav operations, can be shown beyond doubt to have engaged in elaborate deceptions, both of his superiors and of the refugees in his charge.'[10]

This is also true of Low's dealings with the Cossacks. Tolstoy accused him of being very deceptive.[11] He alleges that on 17 May Field-Marshal Alexander issued an order forbidding the return of the Yugoslavs. Despite this, Low issued an order on 17 May for the return of '. . . all Yugoslav nationals at present in the Corps area'. Tolstoy concluded: 'One is left with the overriding impression that Kneightley

---

6. Nikolai Tolstoy, *TMatM*, 81. Harold MacMillan was a very close friend of the brilliant English classicist and Biblical scholar Ronald Knox (1888–1957). When Ronald Knox became a Catholic in 1917, MacMillan himself contemplated converting to Catholicism, but refrained due to the opposition of his father. It is hard to understand how MacMillan, for whom the Christian faith was important, could send thousands of unarmed soldiers and civilians to be slaughtered by a ruthless Communism. Harold MacMillan refrained from speaking about it for the rest of his life, he never acknowledged it or expressed any remorse.[116] . . . (Conversation with Dr John Hill, The Entrence. NSW Australia. Monday 21 September 2020. The feast of St Matthew).
7. Nikolai Tolstoy, *TMatM*, 81.
8. Nikolai Tolstoy, *TMatM*, 140–142.
9. Nikolai Tolstoty, *TMatM*, 147.
10. Nikolai Tolstoy, *TMatM*, 154.
11. Nikolai Tolstoy, *TMatM*, 217–218.

and Low were acting in confident expectation of an imminent reversal of the Supreme Allied Commander's policy in these matters, though they made no effort at this time to respond to his intervention.'[12]

In an interview with English journalist and author, Nora Beloff, Low told her that neither he nor General Kneightley had the slightest idea that these people were being sent to their death. He told Beloff 'We assumed that the Yugoslav soldiers should go back to Yugoslavia, just as British soldiers should go back to Britain.'[13]

On 2 January 1984, BBC television broadcast a documentary on the Klagenfurt conspiracy, interviewing former officers who had been based in southern Austria and three Serbs who were saved from the repatriation. Low was interviewed as well, and defended the agreement. He cited its expediency for the British and the Partisans to withdraw from Koruske of their own accord, thus avoiding military conflict with them. A former officer in the British Army, Nigel Nicholson, said in the programme that, in his opinion, an agreement for the repatriation was made in Belgrade.[14]

Unfortunately Low refused to be interviewed when Tolstoy was writing his book on the repatriations, and Tolstoy concludes:

> The evidence indicates that it was Harold MacMillan, aided by one or two others, who enabled Stalin and Tito to achieve their ends . . . For their part, Stalin and Tito went to remarkable lengths in ensuring that no victim survived to tell the compromising tale.
>
> MacMillan's motives remain tantalizingly mysterious and may never be known. The explanations he has given are inadequate and inconsistent, documents have been tampered with and destroyed, and a forty year cover-up of extraordinary ingenuity and persistence have all but concealed a trail which has run cold. Perhaps the most disturbing factor, though, concerns not what lay behind the Minister Resident's actions in May 1945, but in what followed.[15]

---

12. Nikolai Tolstoy, *TMatM*, 223.
13. Nora Beloff, *TFLYatW*, 126.
14. Roman Leljak, *HJSCT*, 55–56.
15. Nikolai Tolstoy, *TMatM*, 399.

> The pattern of events shows clearly that the decisive intervention occurred on 13 May, when Harold MacMillan unexpectedly arrived at Corps Headquarters.[16]

> Before MacMillan's arrival the evidence indicates that the Fifth Corps had neither the intention nor the desire to hand anyone over to be maltreated or killed. Therefore a radical shift in policy occurred, which required extensive deception of the Allied command, to say nothing of the unfortunate prisoners.[17]

Referring to the Cossacks and by implication to the others, MacMillan stated that Kneightley agreed with the repatriation of the Cossacks for they presented a unsolvable administrative problem: 'What are we to do with all these people? Well, actually, we haven't the physical power to do very much . . .'[18]

Kneightley also had to concern himself with some 400,000 surrendered German soldiers who were not yet disarmed, and whom the British had to shepherd, feed and shelter.[19]

Tolstoy claims that General Robertson was frightened by the possibility that hundreds of thousands of panicking Croatian refugees would flood into southern Austria.[20]

Refering to General Sir Charles Kneightley, Commander of the Fifth Corps, Tolstoy writes:

> It was unfortunate for the Cossacks and the Yugoslavs that the commanding general into whose hands the chance of war had placed them was, while honest and able in his job, was also a man of restricted experience and narrow intellect. Of middle class upbringing and single minded military outlook, he lacked something of the broader perspective shared by commanders of the background of Alexander and Arbuthnott. In battle he was a first rate commanding officer: cool, confident and energetic. To Nigel Nicolson [an intelligence officer to The First Guards Brigade] he appeared

---

16. Nikolai Tolstoy, *A International Symposium in Zagreb 12–13 May 1995*, 216.
17. Nikolai Tolstoy, *A International Symposium in Zagreb 12–13 May 1995*, 216.
18. Nikolai Tolstoy, *TMatM*, 91.
19. Nikolai Tolstoy, *TMatM*, 96.
20. Nikolai Tolstoy, *TMatM*, 101.

a beau sabreur, tall, authoritative and decisive, as befitted an officer of the Fifth Dragoon Guards.[21]

Tolstoy exonerated Field Marshal Alexander, who was apparently unaware of possible ramifications for the repatriated soldiers and civilians, and put a halt to forced repatriation once he realised the brutality of Tito's soldiers. Tolstoy writes: 'On 17 May Field Marshal Alexander ordered a halt to forced repatriation of Yugoslavs, whatever their ethnic groupings.'

Field Marshal Harding once emphasised to Tolstoy that Alexander was mainly concerned with what he termed 'the etiquette of war'.[22] The Chief of the Imperial General Staff, Sir Alan Brooke, declared Alexander to be '... charming to deal with, never scheming or pulling strings. A soldier of the very highest principles ...'[23]

Tolstoy stated: 'It is a strange but seemingly an indisputable fact that Alexander remained wholly unaware of the existence of the order that personnel of established Yugoslav nationality... should be disarmed and handed over to Yugoslav forces until 21 May.'[24]

In a letter to Tolstoy dated 29 June 1984, Sir John Colville, who was private secretary to the Prime Minister, Winston Churchil wrote:

> ... I agree with you in thinking that it is improbable that Alex approved the handover. It would have been wholy untrue to his form. Whether Harold MacMillan was responsible I doubt if we shall ever know, for I expect the orders were never commited to paper and it seems clear that the COS, the FO and No 10 were not informed. But I doubt if General Kneightley would have taken such a step without higher authority.[25]

> ... It was not until some time later that we learned that the unfortunate Croats and Slovenians who had been expelled from Carinthia had been extensively slaughted by Tito's troops after crossing the Yugoslav frontier.[26]

---

21. Nikolai Tolstoy, *TMatM*, 85.
22. Nikolai Tolstoy, *TMatM*, 85.
23. Nikolai Tolstoy, *TMatM*, 119.
24. Nikolai Tolstoy, *A International Symposium in Zagreb 12–13 May 1995*, 219–220.
25. Nikolai Tolstoy, *TMatM*, 338.
26. Nikolai Tolstoy, *TMatM*, 337.

> ... since the incident was a disgraceful one the War Office should be asked to have enquiries made who was responsible for handing over to a certain and unpleasant death these unfortunate Croats, when the question of their future was still under consideration at a high level ... I think we can do no more than admit that a serious blunder did take place and that the story does not reflect well on the officers immediately concerned. It is no use trying to hush up an incident which is indefensible.[27]

Tolstoy believed there was a conspiracy of deception kept from Alexander about what happened. It would be difficult to believe that Harold MacMillan would have acted without instructions from the British Foreign Minister, Anthony Eden and Prime Minister Winston Churchill.

The souls of those who were slaughted, and the loved ones who survived them, cry out for acknowledgment of what happened. The time has come for the British Government to reveal all secret, classified or redacted documents relating to these shocking and obscene events, and enable a full analysis of this tragic and bloody chapter in British history.

Josip Broz Tito

Tito and the Partisan Communist leadership must bear the first and the greatest responsibility for the Bleiburg massacres. Although it is often said that Karl Marx saw Croatians as anti-social renegades, it was Fredrik Engels who wrote: 'a future world war will destroy the Croatian people and it will be a step forward.' The reason for Engel's negativity could be because of the Croatians' Catholic faith, and because they supported Ban Josip Jelachich in his defeat of the aggressive Hungarian nationalism led by Lajos Kossuth in 1848. Engel's negative writing on the Croatians greatly influenced the Communist movement worldwide in viewing Croatians negatively.[28]

When looking back, it is clear that the Communist Partisans were not fighting to liberate people. Instead, they were fighting to gain

---

27. Nikolai Tolstoy, *TMatM*, 338.
28. Jure Vujić, *ICoC*, 128–129. Also conversation with Mate Goreta, Sydney Australia. Monday 3 September 2018.

power and impose their ideology on people and they were prepared to use any means possible to achieve their aims. Christie Lawrence, who spent the first year of the war as a fugitive within villages of Serbia, wrote:

> The Partisans were by far the most unpopular of the three forces. They, of all, appeared to have the least regard for the good of the people. Their actions were indiscriminate; they killed a German officer here or a soldier there, irrespective of the subsequent reprisals. The occupation authorities had recently declared that, for every German killed by resistance forces of any denomination, three hundred Serbian hostages would be shot, and certainly for some months this policy was carried out. But the Partisans were in no way deterred by it ... they persevered in spite of the peoples suffering ... they were feared and hated, especially by the peasants, on whom they lived and depended for their supplies.[29]

Basil Davidson, a British officer with the Partisans who wrote sympathetically of the Partisans, described their attitude towards the enemy:

> The enemy they saw as a bloody murderer who must be destroyed in any guise he might adopt ... He would never be harmless until he was dead, for if he did not appear in one form he would do so in another. *Death to Fascism* they understood this in the literal sense of killing men who were corrupted beyond redemption. For people who had in mind brutal enemy reprisals they regarded as soft-hearted fools or party interested knaves.[30]

William Deakin, another British officer who experienced the most bitter fighting of Sutjeska, and must have witnessed extreme cruelty and brutality by the Communist Partisans, mentioned one incident which happened shortly after his arrival:

> The choice of horrors is wide. In one cave were ninety men, women and children huddled together. A German patrol approached within ten yards, without noticing the entrance.

---

29. Christie Lawrence, *IA*, 142–143.
30. Basil Davidson, *PP,* 29.

> At that time a new born baby began crying, and the mother sought to calm the child. The wailing continued, and panic seized hold of the people. A voice whispered to kill the baby, and the mother held out the infant in silent resignation. Even in terror no one had the will to commit the act. The mother strangled the infant.[31]

Dinko Suljak, who supported the Croatian Peasant Party and the ideals of Stjepan Radich, found himself near Karlobag on the Adriatic coast in November 1943. He relates a sad incident when he was amongst Partisans having a meal with a political commissar named Toplak. Suljak writes:

> While I was having the evening meal, I saw in one dark corner a soldier in German uniform. I asked who is that soldier. Toplak answered me: 'We caught this German soldier in the village of Smilčić.' And I innocently said: 'Give him something to eat, he will be hungry.' 'He doesn't need anything' Toplak answered. With that our conversation ended concerning this unfortunate German soldier. I don't think he was more then twenty three years of age. Early in the morning before dawn, I fell asleep, awaking sometime around eight. My first thought was to see that German soldier. He wasn't there. I saw a German uniform on one Partisan and I immediately concluded what had happened. To be certain I asked one of the "compassionate" ones what had happened to that German. The answer was silence, with his figure pointing to a heap of dirt, where the killed German soldier lay, with whom the previous evening I was exchanging compassionate glances.[32]

Fitzroy MacLean and other British representatives to Tito's headquarters must also have witnessed the brutality of the Partisans but, due to political expediency, placed Tito and his army in good light and refrained from telling the whole truth.

Stjepan Hojt remembers in 1944 coming across a Partisan pamphlet in which Tito called on the people to: 'Increase your hate for the enemy.' Hojt commented: 'Once a person hates they cease to be a human being.'[33]

---

31. William Deakin, *TEM*, 30.
32. Dinko Šuljak, *TSRH*, 185.
33. Coversation with Stjepan Hojt. 2 November 2003.

On October 18, 1944, Tito gave the order to punish and bring before the courts all who remained in enemy units after 15 October 1944. From that day, Tito's units were officialy allowed to eliminate the Ustasha, Chetniks and all enemies. Possibly one of the most significant archival documents concerning Communist crimes committed in Slovenia and Croatia in May and June 1945, was the order given by Alexander Rankovich on 9 April 1945. It was the order to completely liquidate the enemy.[34]

It is almost certain that Tito gave the order for the liquidation of these fleeing soldiers and refugees. On the 15 May 1945, he thanked the soldiers of the third army:

> Through quick and energetic assault the troops of our third army have cut the remains of the German Ustasha-Chetnik bandits and encircled them in the areas of Slone Gradec-Gustanj (Ravne)-Pliberk-Dravograd. After three days of heavy fighting they smashed them and forced them to capitulate . . . for this reason I thank the courageous troops of our third army under the command of Lieutenant General Kosta Nadj, Colonel Branko Petrichevich and Colonel Vukasina Subotich.[35]

In a speech in Ljubljana on 26 May 1945, Tito said:

> concerning the traitors, who were alone in the state . . . that is a matter of the past. The hand of justice, the hand of revenge of our people has already caught up with a large majority, and only a small number of traitors succeeded to escape through assistance outside our state. That minority will never see our glorious mountains and our blossoming valleys[36]

Ivo Rojnica met with Mate Mestrovich, the son of the famous sculptor, in Brugg, Switzerland in 1968. Mate Mestrovich had previously met Milovan Djilas, Tito's former deputy, and Djilas informed him that Tito was responsible for the slaughter of the Croatian army. Tito had personally given the order naming them as the enemy, who would always be in the way and needed to be liquidated. Rojnica commented: 'Is Djilas's version true or just a Serbian deceit?'[37]

---

34. Michael Portmann, *TDtBtSaSiCY 1944–1945*, 154–155.
35. Martina Grahek Ravančić, *BiKP 1945*, 93. Roman Leljak, *M:NSH*, 255 & 256.
36. Roman Leljak, *HJSCT*, 56.
37. Ivo Rojnica, *SiD*, Volume 2, 339.

Former diplomat and Universaty lecturer, Bogdan Radica, met Tito's former deputy, Milovan Djilas, in New York in 1968. Djilas said to him:

> I didn't participate in bringing about the decisions that the Ustasha, Domobrani and Chetnik groups be liquidated, nor did I participate in these slaughters. At that time I was in Montenegro. That was decided in Belgrade specifically under the chairmanship of Tito himself. I am not saying this just because I am wanting to exclude myself from all that, for had I been at that meeting I would have voted in support of it. It revolved around this: Stalin had decided to destroy all those forces amongst the Russians and amongst us, as an example to the followers of Vlasov, for he was afraid that the allies would arm them and send them to a crusade war against Communism. As an American soldier would not be passionately fighting Communism as these our enemies, it was held that at the most expedient time to liquidate them. I repeat, had I been in Belgrade I would have supported this decision.[38]

This same Milovan Djilas was in Montenegro on 15 May, and in 1977 he wrote about the capture and slaughter in Bleiburg:

> It was in Montenegro that I welcomed the end of the fighting: on 15 May 1945, the German forces, estimated at one hundred and thirty thousand, finally recognized us as a legal Allied army and laid down their arms. There were individual cases of retribution in the course of the disarming. The captured Germans were sent to camps and put to work. Along with the Germans, our enemies who collaborated with the invaders or bound their destinies to the fascist powers the Chetniks, the Ustasha, Home Guards and the Slovenian Home Guards also laid down their arms. Some of these groups got through to the British in Austria, who turned them over to us. All were killed, except for women and young people who were under eighteen years of age. We were told so at the time in Montenegro, and so I later heard from those who had taken part in these senseless acts of wrathful retribution.

---

38. Bogdan Radica, ŽinD, 578–579.

> Those killings were sheer frenzy. How many victims were there? I believe that no one knows exactly, or will ever know. According to what I heard in passing from a few officials involved in the settling of scores, the number exceeds twenty thousand, though it must certainly be under thirty thousand ... They were killed separately, each group on territory where they had been taken prisoner. A year or two later, there was grumbling in the Slovenian Central Committee that they had trouble with the peasants from those areas, because underground rivers were casting up bodies. They also said that piles of corpses were heaving up as they rotted in shallow mass graves, so that the very earth seemed to breathe.[39]

He further wrote:

> Who issued the order for this extermination? Who signed it? I don't know. It is my belief that a written order did not exsist. Given the power structure and chain of command, no one could have carried out such a major undertaking without approval from the top. An atmosphere of revenge prevailed. The Central Committee did not decide that. And what if it had? Doubtless the Central Committee would have gone along with those in power. There was never any voting anyway. And I would have agreed, perhaps with some reservation which would not have threatened my revolutionary resolve, my adherence to the party, and my solidarity with the leadership. As if there were no justice, truth, and mercy outside the ideology, the party, and around people, and around us leaders as their essence. We never spoke of it in the Central Committee or privately amongst ourselves. Once in a rambling conversation after the clash with the Soviet leadership in 1948, I mentioned we had gone too far then, because amongst the executed also were some fleeing for ideological reasons alone.

---

39. Milovan Djilas. *Wartime*, 446–447. Milovan Djilas, whose hands were covered in blood, knew very well that far more than 30,000 people were killed in these mass slaughters, but he did not want to admit the whole truth. His book *Wartime* wasn't written in the spirit of Croatian – Serb reconciliation. Its tone is very disparaging of Croatians.

> Tito retorted immediately, as if he had long since come to a final, though hardly comforting, conclusion: 'We put an end to it once and for all! Anyway, given the kind of courts that we had.'[40]

> Whether or not Tito had given direct orders no one knows. But certainly he was in favour of a radical solution for pragmatic reasons, as the British too, had pragmatic reasons for returning those refugees. Yugoslavia was in a state of chaos and destruction. There was hardly any civil administration. There were no properly constituted courts. There was no way in which the cases of twenty to thirty thousand people could have reliably been investigated. So the easy way out was to have them shot, and have done with the problem.[41]

When Ivan Mestrovich returned to Croatia on a visit in 1959, he was Tito's guest on the island of Brioni for almost a week. Mestrovich brought to Tito's attention the slaughter of the Croatian army, and Tito replied: 'That just couldn't be avoided. The Serbs just had to be allowed to be satisfied.'[42]

Nora Beloff wrote:

> Circumstances rule out the possibility that the killings were carried out in the spontaneous frenzy of civil war. According to the survivers, mass graves were prepared and reception centres organized before the train loads arrived. Prisoners were tied together by wire and marched in couples to be mowed down. In the massacre of the repatriated prisoners, Tito's personal responsibility can be in no more doubt than Stalin's. In neither case is there any documentary evidence and the orders were probably verbal. But by the time the killings took place, Tito, like Stalin, was in full control of the party and police and none of his well disciplined subordinates would have dared to operate on this scale without his approval.[43]

The brutality of the Communist regime in Croatia can also be seen from the diary of Dr Giuseppi Masucci, OSB, the secretary of the

---

40. Milovan Djilas. *Wartime*, 446–449.
41. Nikolai Tolstoy, *TMatM*, 357.
42. Hrvatska Revija, Year XX October 1970. Volume 3, 460
43. Nora Beloff, *TFLYatW*, 127.

Apostolic delegate to Croatia during the Second World War. In an extract from 17 June 1945, Masucci wrote:

> Communist measures against the Church are growing without end. The radio is continuing to broadcast vehment attacks on the Vatican and the Church. Many priests have been shot and a lot more are in prison. In the vacinity of Zagreb, the citizens are shot en masse. All Catholics are trembling before the new regime; they seek refuge and are in hiding. There is the expectation of even worse happening.[44]

In 26 November 1945, he wrote:

> Bitter tears are flowing without ceasing. Continuous new punishments, many people are being found and many people are being hanged. The whole land is flooded in a storm of tears. After the slaughter of hundreds of thousands of Croatian soldiers and civilians in the first months of the communist regime, shootings and hangings are happening from day to day. This is being committed by the new regime, and not by irresponsible elements. There is no one who doesn't grieve for someone.[45]

Dr Ante Pavelich

'Dr Ante Pavelich, the founder and head of the Ustasha, was so idolised, he became more a myth or a legend than a living person'. Thats how Mirko Zivkovich looked on Dr Pavelich in the 1930s before he ever saw him with his own eyes. Zivkovich qualified as a lawyer and became a secret member of the Ustasha movement in the autumn of 1932, mainly through the encouragement of his friends Ante Moshkov and Vladimir Singer who were very involved with the Ustasha movement. This is what Zivkovich wrote: 'I believe that it would be difficult to find in history a person who was so idolized by his followers as Dr Ante Pavelich. It will be rare that there will emerge a politician in the future who will have so loyal followers, ready for every sacrifice, as was his. Followers for whom loyalty and unconditional obedience was the highest law. Even in our dreams we

---

44. Guissepi Masucci, *MuH*, 206.
45. Guissepi Masucci, *MuH*, 234–235.

didn't allow, let alone publicly allow any criticism . . . of our leader.' In his writing, Zivkovich refers to Pavelich using the term 'Poglavnik', meaning chief or head. He continues:

> That's what Dr Ante Pavelich, the returning Ustasha Poglavnik, was to me right up to 13 April 1941. That day was the first time I laid eyes on him and immediately received a cold 'shoulder'. I was one of some sixty officers assembled within the buildings of some large army barracks in Karlovac, where there were waiting the representatives of the German and Italian army, the city elders of Karlovac and a group of Ustasha youth commanded by Reserved Lieutenant Colonel Franjo Mikshich. It was approaching dark when Dr Pavelich arrived. He first greeted the Germans, then the Italians and then the representatives of the city of Karlovac. He then turned to the Ustasha youth and Professor Mikshich spoke on their behalf. These young people were really young, for many of them would have been barely twenty years old. Dr Pavelich gave them a short speech, the summary of which was: '. . . with you young people I created this state and with you young people I will build it . . ." Then he turned away so that he didn't even look at us officers and there were amongst us people of rank from colonels to corporals.[46]

> This gesture of my much idolized Poglavnik I didn't like. It seemed to me that it wasn't politically wise or an act of a statesman. Why create opposition in people? With this act everyone was offended, especially the older officers. I left quite downcast and I was very bothered by this non-political act of the head of our state. Did he really think that he was going to build the state based on that youth? I couldn't understand or justify that attitude. The next day when I found my friend Moshkov I immediately informed him of my pain. He justified it by saying that the Poglavnik was offended by Serbian uniforms. In what uniforms did he want to see us on the first day? Is a uniform more important than Croatian men, who were in these uniforms through circumstances and had waited for him for hours?[47]

---

46. Mirko Živković, In Vinko Nikolić, *BUiP*, 311–312.
47. Mirko Živković, In Vinko Nikolić, *BUiP*, 311–312.

> When later disturbances began in the land, for me everyone was at fault except Dr Pavelich. I couldn't allow even the smallest doubt about him. It is difficult to lose faith in an idol. No matter how many doubts I received as to his person, because of the deterioration and the poor situation in the land. I justified it due to the unfriendly policies of the Italians towards us and their anti-Croatian politics which I immediately observed, for I was in service within their zone. In spite of the fact that I was Chief of Police, there were friends who knew that they could be honest with me without any fear and they would criticize the work of Dr Pavelich and his policies. Listening to this talk I found difficult and unpleasant, for it was hard not to believe these friends, for I knew they were good Croats, as I regarded myself. At that time I calmed myself with the thought they were poorly informed. I just couldn't allow questions about the patriotism of Dr Pavelich and I believed that he knew how and where he was leading us.
>
> On the other hand if I had come to a negative judgment of the Poglavnik, as I did later, what could I have done? Where and into which opposition could I go? The only alternatives were either the Partisans or the Chetniks. There wasn't a third! For me and for all those hundreds of thousands of Croatians who remained faithful to the end, there was no alternative! What else remained other than to be disciplined and more strongly give ourselves in work and struggle to save our state and bring her to a harbour of peace. When today I look back on our circumstances, not only its physical but also psychological aspect, it seems to me truly ghastly. I think there is nothing so hard and difficult to bear than to find oneself in a hopeless situation with no outlet, as we found ourselves at the end of 1944 and the beginning of 1945.[48]

Mirko Zivkovich also reflected on the character of Pavelich:

> One, and we could say the main characteristic of Dr Pavelich, was mistrust of everyone who had not emigrated with him. That mistrust was present towards his collaborators, towards the Croatian army, and also towards the Croatian people . . . he would hide the truth from his supporters and collaborators, especially from the people, with regard to Italy's aspiration to our country.

---

48. Mirko Živković, In Vinko Nikolić, *BUiP,* 313.

> The most dominating characteristic of Dr Pavelich was cunning and intrigue involving his closest collaborators. In this way he secured his position as an arbiter and his coworkers were resentful with one another for no reason, only because of the intrigues which would be sown by their chief. How is it possible to create a united purpose out of such a mistrusting and divided group, which he intentionally fostered?
>
> In bringing out this negative side of Dr Pavelich's character, it is also necessary to mention his lack of loyalty to his close collaborators. That lack of loyalty was clearly seen in his attitude towards the two Kvaterniks and especially towards Mladen Lorkovich and Ante Vokich.[49]

Zivkovich continued:

> Even during the withdrawal Pavelich's distrust towards the army came to the surface. When General Lohr, in the evening of 7 May 1945, returned to him the command of the Croatian army, he didn't place in command of the army an eminent Domobran General, but Maks Luburich. It is obvious he was afraid that the Domobran General would arrest him and prevent his escape which he had long before prepared.[50]

Zivkovich concluded his reflections on Pavelich: 'It is possible that not one Croatian, in Croatia's long history had such an oportunity to become a great historical figure as Dr Ante Pavelich. His lack of moral and intellectual qualities caused enormous sadness to us all.

The Croatians who lost their lives from April 1941 to May 1945, fell for the freedom of the Croatian people, defending the Croatian state. The Croatians who lost their lives at Bleiburg, died for nothing. Thats what makes Bleiburg, Bleiburg. Thats the core of the Bleiburg catastrophy.

Dr Ante Pavelich – to our enormous sadness-is the greatest and biggest link in the chain which led to the Bleiburg tragedy.'[51]

---

49. Mirko Živković, In Vinko Nikolić, *BUiP,* 314.
50. Mirko Živković In Vinko Nikolić, *BUiP,* 315.
51. Mirko Živković, *BUiP,* 320 Due to his disillusionment with Pavelich, Mirko Živković broke with Pavelich completely in 1947. During this convesation with the author Mirko Žvković became quite emotional. (Conversation with Mirko Živković, Buonos Aries, Argentina, Wednesday 24 June 1992).

Ivan Orshanich headed the Ustasha youth and worked closely with Pavelich during the war years, but broke with him after the war. He wrote:

> Due to a continuous fear that he might be liquidated, Pavelich wanted to be the direct chief of any Ustasha who had positions of any importance and wanted them to be be exclusively tied to him, so they would always trust him. Those who were Ministers or Generals or high Ustasha officials or in the Intelligence Service, were all under the direct control of Pavelich. Pavelich maintained authority over the whole organization. He allowed loyalty to himself and to no one else. Any friendship which developed among his underlings he perceived as a personal threat and dealt with accordingly.[52]

Ivo Rojnica related when, just before he left Zagreb on 6 May, he found himself at Kulina Square where he met the whole family of minister Dr Milovan Zanich who were saying goodbye to the servants. Rojnica asked Dr Žanich for any news, only to be told: 'Just hurry otherwise it will be too late.'

As he wept he added: 'We couldn't have expected any better with such a leadership and head of state.' They both departed weeping.[53]

Ante Moshkov was a very close and intimate colleague of Pavelich. He wrote:

> Pavelich was above all else a unique character: a personality which is constituted by some individuals . . . a strong will, an authoritarian manner, and a lust for power and cunning without regard for character.[54]

> With all that we must be aware that Pavelich never had trust in anyone. This is seen in the control he had on everyone and the way he manipulated his colleagues one against the other. He upheled some sort of permanent and latent enmity among individuals and cliques. That was his method and that served him well when he wanted to get rid of anyone whom he used.

---

52. Jure Kristo, *SS,* 28. From Ivan Oršanić, *MNi Ustastvo,* Republica Hrvatska, 25/1975. Also from Vinko Nikolić, *MBPiMH,* 54.
53. Ivo Rojnica, *SiD,* Volume 1, 231.
54. Jure Kristo, *SS,* 29. Quoting from *Pavelicovo Doba.*

Moshkov continued:

> The water had reached his neck, Pavelich played the refugee card. We needed to withdraw as many people from Croatia as possible. We decided to approach the Anglo-Americans with a hundred thousand soldiers and civilians and tell them: they are all for me. Then the Anglo-Americans must consider his person. That was just a game.[55] It was Franjo Dujmovich's understanding that Pavelich wanted to withdraw as many soldiers and civilians into southern Austria to show the British how many stood with him in the hope the British would use him in some way as a leader of the Croatian people. The more one reflects on it the more one comes to the conclusion that Dujmovich was right.[56]
>
> Jozo Tomasovich quoted Eugen Dido Kvaternik: 'But above all political mistakes, aberrations and human foibles–all greatly magnified in a period in which events were often stronger than men–the catastrophe of our Independent State of Croatia had a moral 'cause, which lay in the four year long and repeated transgression of all basic ethical principles. This transgression deprived many responsible people of the capacity for sound reasoning and in a way prevented them from reacting to the disasterous way in which the Croatian people were led.'[57]
>
> Looking at it from an Anglosaxon view there is another angle to it. As it was said to the author by Australians: 'What did Pavelich expect from the British? He had been an ally of Germany all through the war. When in 1943 and especially in 1944 it was obvious that Germany was losing the war he made no attempt to enter into dialogue with the British, he hung onto power right to the very end, then he withdrew the army into Southern Austria, hoping that the British would receive them as prisoners of war? It must be remembered that Tito and the Partisans were British allies. What could Pavelich expect.'[58] It is a very valid point.

---

55. Milan Basta, *RjZ7DK,* 321.
56. Coversation with Franjo Dujmović, Sao Paulo, Brazil, Thursday 18 June 1992.
57. Jozo Tomasovich, *WaRiY,* 781.
58. Colleen & Brian McCunnie. Stanhope Gardens. 9 April 2021.

Rasovi

The term Rasovi is used to describe the ultra-nationalist Croatians who were with Pavelich in Italy before the war and who comprised the core of the leaders of the Ustasha movement. A vast majority of Rasovi had no military training, yet Pavelich trusted them, and placed them in key positions, and their behaviour caused much harm in Croatia during the Second World War.

Ivo Rojnica, wrote about one of the Rasovi, General Ivo Herenchich:

> At around 11:00am General Ivo Herenchich and colonel Daniel Crljen went for talks with the English Command. They returned between 12:30 and 13:00 hours. It was heard straight after that the discussions had ended and that they had surrendered. After this final and fateful meeting with the English, they didn't call together the officers corps, nor did they openly state the true situation. This factual situation was passed on privately from person to person. General Herenchich and Colonel Crljen withdrew from this chaos and fled. This resulted in a limbo like situation for the army and civilians. The tragic result is known now to everyone.[59]

Rojnica then continued to reflect:

> After leaving Zagreb, fleeing and withdrawing, without any political preparation and without a true goal, the main Croatian army and a mass of civilians found themselves on the fields before Bleiburg, an Austrian town on the Slovene-Austrian border. They were stopped there by the English army. The person who made contact with them was the Ustasha General Herenchich, although he was the least suitable to negotiate with the English. Had there been at least an ounce of common sense and true patriotism on our side there should have been Domobrani generals, representatives of the regular army, who could have called on international norms in such situations. But, no, Herenchich wanted to be irresponsible to the end. When he was told that the Croatian army had only one hour to surrender, he disappeared, not even informing the army and the mass of people what awaited them. He was the first to flee.[60]

---

59. Ivo Rojnica, *SiD*, Volume 2, 48.
60. Ivo Rojnica, *SiD*, Volume 1, 236.

Rojnica continued:

> Herenchich and the rest of the 'Rasovi' are equally responsible for this, the greatest tragedy in Croatian history, in the first place because of incompetence, ignorance and irresponsibility. They didn't have the qualifications, either moral or expertise, to have such a high and responsible position. It is not enough to love one's country. One also needs wisdom, ability and a sense of moral and historical responsibility.[61]

General Ivo Herenchich wasn't a General Helmut Von Pannwitz, who after the Cossacks were repatriated, didn't flee but shared the fate of his troops. Herenchich ordered his troops to lay down their arms, leaving those under him to their fate and securing his own future through fleeing. Tolstoy wrote: 'General von Pannwitz himself declined to avail himself of any opportunity to escape, being resolved upon sharing the fate of his beloved Cossacks.'[62]

Ante Moshkov was also a Ras. Rojnica wrote of him as the army was approaching southern Austria. As they were nearing Klagenfurt they learnt that the Partisans were in the city: 'The column stopped. General Ante Moshkov changed into civilian clothes, sat in his "Tatra", turned on the ignition and without saying a word, nor passing on the command to anyone in the column, drove off to Volkermark and then to Wolfsberg. The column went in that direction although our first goal was Klagenfurt. Moshkov left his elite units and courageous fighters and simply fled. That was the sense of responsibility of our 'Rasovi', for whom Croatia was their exclusive property.'[63]

Mara Pavelich

Anecdotal evidence suggests Pavelich was influenced by his wife Mara, who was partly Jewish but there is no evidence she saved one Jewish person from their plight. When there was talk that Pavelich would need to relinquish his position due to the Lorkovich – Vokich

---

61. Ivo Rojnica, *SiD*, Volume 1, 236–237.
62. Nikolai Tolstoy, *TMatM*, 253. Quoting from General Helmut von Pannwitz und seine Kosaken, Oldendorf 1971. Lord Nicholas Bethal, *TLS*, 146, 220.
63. Ivo Rojnica, *SiD*, Volume 1, 236.

planned coup, his wife Mara said: 'Why would I want an Independent State of Croatia when in it the Poglavnik is no longer the Poglavnik.'[64]

It is interesting when Eugene Dido Kvaternik met Ernest Bauer in Vienna in 1944, Kvaternik said to Bauer:

> Be careful of Lady Mara Pavelich. When on 10 April 1941, my father Slavko proclaimed The Independent State of Croatia, I had no idea of what was happening, but in the late afternoon I came to Pavelich's villa in Pitoi where he was living at the time. Already at the staircase I was greeted by Lady Mara with a displeasing smile: 'Dido, don't you know that your father has proclaimed the Independent State of Croatia?!'. Dido then said to me that he had had enough, for it was clear to him that Lady Mara was glaring at him.[65]

Pavelich sent his family to safety to Austria in January 1945. Slavko Kvaternik related his experience:

> I arrived in Semmering in the Autumn of 1943 and stayed there till February 1945... During the month of January 1945 there arrived unexpectedly in Semmering Pavelich's whole family accompanied by the wife of the German ambassador to Croatia, Kasche, and the wife of the first secretary of the German embassy in Zagreb. With her there arrived the wife of General Prebeg, minister of the household with her two children, the wife of the medical doctor Mile Budak with two children, the master of ceremonies Crisomali, Colonel Lisak with a company of Ustasha, six private cars and twelve heavily laden trucks. I know all this from what I was told by the manager of the hotel, who told me that on those trucks were nailed boxes so heavy that one box could barely be carried by four men. According to what this manager told me, Mrs Pavelich did not allow these boxes to be carried by the personnel of the hotel, but only by the Ustasha who did this over a few days but always at night. On the floor of the hotel where the Pavelich family stayed armed Ustasha would keep guard day and night, until the other guests of the hotel

---

64. Bogdan Krizman, *UiTR*, 129. Also Dr Esther Gitman, *ASPoHR*, 206 & 297 affirms Mara Pavelić's Jewish background.
65. Ernst Bauer, *ŽJKS*, 172.

complained and then it was discontinued. The people of Semmering were angry that someone had at their disposal a whole park full of automobiles for their own personal use, when the whole district hadn't had any means to transport basic food necessities. The easy way of living of this woman and her family was compared to the modesty of the Prince of Wales, the former British king. I must admit that I was so ashamed that I didn't go out into the street. In the meantime I was told by a representative of the German government that I and my family were to leave for Bad Gastein, for Mrs. Pavelich was afraid for her life and for this reason she insisted on my leaving. This sort of behaviour in front of foreigners needs no commentary. It revealed the panic in which this despotic family lived. That's why I and my family had to move with little children in the severe winter cold on 15 February 1945 to Bad Gastein; this was arranged by the German Government.[66]

At the same questioning Kvaternik said: 'Pavelich didn't spare any deceit or crime in order to maintain power . . . He was served by a sick ambition and also his wife.'

Vladimir Djuro Degan in his study concluded: 'The blame for this Croatian tragedy falls on the Poglavnik Ante Pavelich. After declaring war on Britain and the United States in December 1941, before the end of that war he had led his forces to withdraw towards the British, who he assumed would welcome them as allies, would reorganize them and all together they would attack the Red army. In Rogaskoj Slatini on 8 May 1945, he changed into civilian clothes, abandoned and betrayed his army and the civilians in the retreat, and fled.'[67]

The head of state, the Poglavnik Ante Pavelich, during this critical moment, looked to the American zone for salvation just for himself. 'The captain didn't go down with the ship. He was the first to escape from the helm.'[68]

Vinko Nikolich, in his book *The Tragedy Happened in May*, reflected on this tragedy:

---

66. Bogdan Krizman, *UiTR,* 20. From records Slavko Kvaternik gave to the Yugoslav authorities after the war.
67. Vladimir Djuro Degan in Martina Grahek Ravančić, *BIKP 1945,* 95.
68. Vladimir Djuro Degan in Martina Grahek Ravančić, *BIKP 1945,* 94–95.

The Croatian army was destroyed by the Croatian government. Just like that! The Croatian government with its head of state! It wasn't destroyed by the Serbian Četniks, nor Yugoslav Partisans, under the so called name 'Peoples Liberation Army'. The army was left without its political and military leadership, and being overdependent on discipline, it waited for orders to no avail. Then there developed a general chaos. But such an undefeated army didn't deserve such a cruel and humiliating end. Throughout four years it fought heroically and wasn't defeated and here began a general self destruction. The army was left to itself and no one cared for anyone. From such heroic army units there emerged irresponsible individuals. This army was without an organized leadership or an organized rear, without any support and security, for nothing was forseen, nothing prepared, nothing organized. If then, the army was to leave its State, had it been done in an organized, military way, not only the English but the Partisans would have found themselves facing another difficult problem: who knows how all this would have ended? In this way we ourselves prepared all this, so that we could be more easily literally liquidated. If nothing else had happened many thousands would have been saved through successfully leaving the homeland; they wouldn't have been exposed to such a humiliating and cruel death. This tragedy was exacerbated, for in this fatal fleeing exodus there were very many civilians. The voice of Partisan terror stood out like some terrible black omen over the whole of Croatia, and this evil was exploited by the authorities and these leaderless masses of people had to serve as some sort of sad 'referendum', and also, in the masses of people those who were 'guilty' were easily lost. Having a general feeling of being guilty, many fled who had nothing to do with the regime and many of the young put on Ustasha uniforms for the first time for they were going into the forest, just for a short time. And that's how the bloodthirsty Partisans caught them, just this uniform pronounced them "criminals", which was paid for by death, without any questioning, without any trial.

O Good God, if there was the ability to penetrate into the feeling, thinking, into that endless pain, and even into that shame, into that humiliation of so many of our unfortunate people during the last moments of their tragic fate.

> For such a collapse of the Croatian State, for such a destruction of the Croatian Army, for such a tragedy of such a large section of the Croatian population someone must be held accountable!
>
> It is our thinking, that in the first place the Croatian government, with the military command, and Dr Ante Pavelich at its head, must be guilty.[69]

Nikolich also related what he was told while in a refugee camp in Italy after the war: 'The hardest thing is that we collapsed when in fact we were the strongest. The army was united, the people of one heart, the Church was with us, the youth was in good spirits, everything was ready for the final victory . . . just then.'[70]

Nikolich pointed out that Pavelich deceived the Croatian people, for on Thursday 3 May 1945 he gave a speech to *Zenske loze*, Women's Arm of the Ustasha movement. At this gathering some were taking the oath, becoming new members. Amongst other things Pavelich said:

> . . . We will not turn from the path we have taken and that is the path for the greatest development of the Croatian people and the Croatian state. For its development we are prepared to make any sacrifice.
>
> . . . Be convinced, we will use all our strength and might, all sacrifices to save even the smallest part of the Independent State of Croatia.
>
> . . . I can also tell you that we will continue to strengthen our forces which are involved in present battles, not limiting them but strengthening them.
>
> . . . One most important fact on which we can depend and on which we can build is the high morale and high spirits in all sections of our Croatian army, which in its organization, its spirit and preparedness is far in advance of what she was before one or two years ago.

---

69. Vinko Nikolić, *TsDuS*, Volume 1, 12–13.
70. Vinko Nikolić, *TsDuS*, Volume 1, 408.

> ... I believe that we will live, not us but the Croatian people not forty times four, but four hundred times four years of a happy and contented future of the Croatian state.

Nikolich read these words in a Croatian newspaper on 6 May, the day the order was given for the Croatian army to withdraw. The newspaper also stated: 'The Poglavnik's words were also received with great applause.'[71]

Pavelich was not a beacon of calm and surety; he did not show resolve and empathy.

It was not a sort of leadership that united distraught citizens in times of utmost stress and distress. He didn't rise to the occasion however horrible it was. He didn't say or do the right thing to assuage the wounds and calm the nerves. True leadership unites a nation in its darkest moments and inspires people to honour their shared humanity. It recognises that unity is stronger than division and hope can triumph over fear. When it was written:

> When during the early days of May 1945 the political leadership of the Independent State of Croatia resolved to flee from the country and to secure its flight with a massive movement of the Domobrani and Ustasha units, a huge number of civilians, among them women and children, went with them to the Slovene-Austrian border. The political leadership headed by Ante Pavelich saved itself but the army and the civilians were returned by the British and handed over to Tito's Partisans.[72]
> It was as simple as that.

Stjepan Buc in an article on Bleiburg concluded:"it was nothing more than the logical conclusion of the whole of Pavelich's fatal policy from beginning to end."[73]

It was as simple and as dreadful as that: Pavelich proved very cowardly. Although Tito always thought first of his own safety and that of his close collaborators, as attested to by Milovan Djilas, nevertheless while the battle of Sujeska was in progress where Tito and his army were almost completely encircled by the German army,

---

71. Vinko Nikolić, *TsDuS*, Volume 1, 64–65. Martina Grahek Ravančić, *BiKP 1945*, 52.
72. Marijan Karaula, *IBSSbf, 1944–1945*, 20.
73. Martina Grahek Ravančić, Stjepan Buc, *BiKP 1945*, 51.

Tito was very much in command.[74] The impression William Deakin had of Tito was that of a man of absolute authority who commanded operations in person.[75] This can't be said of Pavelich who all through the war never visited Split, Dubrovnik, Imotski, Mostar, Zenica, Sarajevo, Tuzla, or Vukovar and Osjek. Dragutin Kamber in a private conversation encouraged Pavelich to visit these regions but to no avail.[76] He never visited Croatian units in Bosnia or other parts of Croatia. On one occasion he did visit Banja Luka. Generally he kept himself within the safety of Zagreb and its vicinity.

---

74. William Deakin, *TEM*, 7–36.
75. William Deakin, *TEM*, 79–80, 87.
76. Dragutin Kambar, *Hrvatska Revija*, March 1981, 13–14. Also in conversations with Pavo Gagro. Dragutin Kamber, who was assistant vicar for all the Croatian military chaplains, wrote later that he approached Pavelich, saying to him: 'My dear Poglavnik, I am afraid to tell you this; possibly others are afraid to tell you. It concerns your presence at the battles that are happening in Croatia. You can see that Roosevelt, President of powerful America, gets into an aeroplane crossing the Ocean to go to Casablanca and Tehran. And Churchill although old, crosses oceans and comes to conferences and visits the front. And even Stalin is on the move . . . they all expose themselves to the danger of German fighters or antiaircraft guns. Draze Mihaljevich walks on tip toes through the mountains and Tito with his fighters has already been through half our mountains and towns . . . And you haven't been to one theatre of fighting. You still haven't been even for a few hours on a visit to Sarajevo, Osijek, Tuzla, Zemun, Mostar, Gospić and Dalmatia . . . You need to be seen at the front and with the people. You need by your presence even symbolically to take possession of Croatia and liven up and encourage our people. With your presence a new current of hope and encouragement would pass through our soldiers and people. I think you owe it due to your responsible position; you owe it to the people and to history . . . '
I spoke very calmly and with real respect. As I was talking to him, the Poglavik was looking at the floor and being very quiet, I felt that he was feeling uncomfortable . . . I felt I was taking a risk, but I resolved to go to the end. I added:
'Poglanik, I very much respect you and I love Croatia. I just can't accept the fact that you are less of a hero than any other hero in this war. As our towns and villages are burning and so many are suffering and being killed, I often read in the newspapers of Zagreb that you are visiting recreational places in the vicinity of Zagreb. I am afraid that others will develop similar feelings as I have and that it is not your place to go to recreational parks but to be amongst the soldiers. . . . . and that you are not giving of yourself what only you can give, you who are the head of government and the leading military commander.'
Kamber spoke calmly but he noticed Pavelich was finding it difficult to accept what Kamber was saying to him and there followed a prolonged silence, with Pavelich finally saying: 'This war has brought so many daily problems and work here in the office that I am unable to do what you say. I know I would have to do it.'

There were two views on him. Vinko Nikolich described the first as: 'He had overwhelming admiration and was loved by the people. The youth carried him with real fire in their souls, placing him in the most precious part of their hearts. His appearance would touch every Croatian within the depth of their being, full of feeling causing tears and the most divine sense of national pride. It is hard to describe. It can only be felt, and that feeling can never be forgotten. It was a divine feeling of love and respect towards his person as if he was an incarnation of our most beautiful and precious dreams. He was bigger than a man, bigger than a name. He was an expression of a great idea. This, combined with national adulation and love, no one in Croatia had ever received before. Those manifestations, those gatherings, meetings, concerts someone had to see and be overwhelmed. When one saw the scenes in Radničkoj komori, when he entered, one would be moved by those expressions of respect and patriotism.'

However Nikolich moved to the contrary view of Pavelich, on 9 May 1945, at near 13 hours, during the exodus at Rogaskoj Slatini, in Slovenia.

He arrived there in the Tatra automobile

'I was exhausted, unhappy and feeling mortally wounded within the depths of my soul. But my soul lightened up, it shook, when I saw him: new hopes were awakening.'

'He was walking defiantly, looking somewhere into the distance. He was walking restlessly in front of a house, in conversation. We thought he was conducting negotiations with regard to our movement or at least some recognition with the allies . . .'

'Then all at once we saw him entering the automobile. With him was his son Braco (nick name for Pavelich's son Velimir) and Colonel Lisak. Accompanying him was a column commanded by General Begich. Present also was the minister Mirko Puk. And our hopes, with everything completely evaporated, for there was no sign of brightness.'

Kamber could not accept Pavelich's answer and said to him quite openly: 'Poglavnik, I think there is no more important duty that you have than this what I have just told you.'

That was the end of the conversation and Kamber could not remember how they said goodbye to one another. (Dragutin Kamber. *Pavelićeva Baština*. Hrvatska Revija, March 1981, 13–14).

These two views of the man, in complete contrast, force the question: what is the Poglavnik now for us?[77]

In another section of his diary Nikolich wrote of their approach to Rogasku Slatinu:

The Withdrawal

In the end it seems that the end of the Second World War and the position of the victors was, to a certain extent, surprising to the government of the Independent State of Croatia. Evidence suggests that the political and military leadership of this state was not sufficiently aware of the situation at the time. And although it was obvious that the Communists were winning, Pavelich did nothing to prepare the people for an eventual Communist takeover. He did not look to the future or in any way try to ease the people's suffering when the Communists gained power. The British General and strategist, J.F.C. Fuller, said in 1929 that even in conventional war, negotiation with the enemy is unremarkable. 'In war, a grand strategist, general or statesman, does not fix his final object on the destruction of the enemy, but on establishing a condition from out of which a better peace can evolve.' Pavelich did not negotiate with the enemy to try to bring about the best possible outcome, there was none of that.

All Pavelich did was to hang onto the power of the sinking ship of state until he could hold on no longer. He then ordered the army and as many civilians as possible into southern Austria, with the hope that the British would accept their surrender, and after securing refugee status for himself and his family, he fled. Ivica Mandich recalled that when the order to withdraw to southern Austria was given, anyone who decided to stay behind in Croatia was regarded as treasonous[78]

---

77. Vinko Nikolić, *TsDuS*, Volume 1, 126.
78. Conversations with Ivica Mandić. Monday 11 June 2018. Ivo Rojnica, commenting on how Pavelich's Minister of Government, Vjekoslav Vranchich and Sea Captain Vrkljan were well received in Italy on the 7 May 1945, wrote when some of Pavelich's ministers and government officials were still alive:

> If he was well received on 7 May, how well would have he been received after the defeat at Stalingrad, the loss of Africa when it was obvious to every normal person that the Axis have lost the war. Or after the surrender of Italy? What did we do after the successful landing of the Allies in France? After the penetration of the Russians into Rumania, Bulgaria, Hungary, Czeckoslovakia and Poland, what did we attempt for our

Pavelich's government did consider establishing a final line of resistance named the 'Zvonimir Line', but nothing came of it. This thinking tied the government of the Independent State of Croatia to her ally, the Third Reich, right to the end. The later hope of changing sides to the western powers came too late. Many authors today question if the situation would have been different had the battle and resistance continued. Would the attitude of the Western Allies towards the Independent State of Croatia have changed? This was unlikely, considering the Western Allies did not recognise the Independent State of Croatia and as a result were not interested in her fate.[79]

The withdrawal was not accompanied by responsible political and military preparation and it quickly became obvious that it would be completed with great difficulty. The roads were blocked by large numbers of abandoned German trucks and heavy armour. The leadership of the Independent State of Croatia, headed by Pavelich, headed towards the American zone of occupation seeking refuge only for itself. "The captain didn't go down with the ship. He was the first to flee the wreck". These leaders lacked that psychological fibre with which armies and people could rely when the leadership shared their fate.

Pavelich's lack of character can also be seen a year or so after the Bleiburg disaster, when he encouraged a group of former Ustasha led by Bozidar Kavran to organise guerilla activity in Croatia with the hope achieving a revolution.[80] On the 10 April 1946 while in

---

salvation? Official sources could have given the initiative. Why were we not shaken and touched by the attempt of the Lorkovich – Vokich coup? Why were all partcipants in this failed coup shot? If Archbishop Stepinac and President Dr Machek were prepared to sacrifice themselves at the last moments to save the State and the Croatian people, why wasn't an attempt made earlier? What did the leadership of the government do or attempt to do that it does not come to this catastrophe? Why was the order given to withdraw? In all these factors, and certainly there were more, the Croatian public wants the responsible people to give an answer. These are questions so important that they can not remain unanswered. This is our common tragedy that we can not change, but knowing the reasons which brought about this tragedy will serve as an enlightenment to future generations. [119]
(Ivo Rojnica, SiD, Volume 1, 227–228)

79. Martina Grabek Ravančić, *BiKP 1945*, 93–94.
80. Bogdan Krizman, *PuB*, 165–194.

seclusion in the American zone of Austria Pavelich formed the 'Hrvatski Drzavni Odbor', Croatian State Committee, with the aim of liberating Croatia.[81]

Dr Krunoslav Draganovich was instrumental in saving Ante Pavelich from Tito's Communists after the war. He had arranged a passport for him from the Red Cross, in the name of a Hungarian engineer, Pal Aranyos, and an Argentine visa. He presented these to Pavelich in a monastery near Naples in the beginning of October 1948. Draganovich travelled to Naples with some foreboding.

He wrote:

> I went to Naples convinced that I was fulfilling my historical duty, which was dictated to me by my conscience. I was also

---

81. Bogdan Krizman, *PuB*, 177–194. Jozo Tomasevich, *WaRiY, 1941–1945*, 766. Martin Plananić, *TJIK*, 22. When he was in the American Zone of Administration of Austria, Pavelich on 10 April 1946 formed the *Hrvatski Narodni Odbor* (Croatian National Committee), with the aim of establishing a Croatian government, with Bozidar Kavran organizing resistance within Croatia. Kavran was a Croatian idealist, born in Zagreb in 1913 and he joined the Ustasha movement before the war. He had the confidence of Pavelich. Kavran organized up to a hundred and fifteen people, mostly former soldiers, into eighteen groups who were sent into Croatia through Hungary or Italy between July 1947 and June 1948. During this time Kavran had a number of meetings with Pavelich, informing him of developments.
After their capture and trial, forty two were sentenced to a cruel death, two were never to be released and twelve sent to imprisonments ranging from fifteen to twenty years. The rest avoided capture; three were communist informers who betrayed the plan. Due to the collapse of the plan and when he realized it was a catastrophic failure, Bozidar Kavran voluntarily gave himself up to the Communist Yugoslav authorities on 3 July 1948 (Martin Planinić, *TJIK*, 186. Ivan Prusac, *TKiD*, 266).
Someone involved in this venture with Kavran was Srechko Rover, who on three occasions led groups from Austria to a contact in Slovenia and who happened to be working for the Yugoslav secret service. Rover wrote there were up to nineteen groups, some entering Croatia through Hungary and the rest from Austria, with the total number being ninety one. Ivan Prusac, who was one of the participants and was captured, writes there were eighteen groups.
Ivo Rojnica, who migrated to Argentina, remembers receiving the news on 12 July 1948 of the trial of Kavran and his collaborators, ninety five of whom were captured. Rojnica himself was encouraged to participate in this action but he immediately saw its foolishness and stupidity. He stated that there were ninety five men sent into Croatia (Ivo Rojnica, *SiD*, 140–141)

convinced, knowing what I would tell him, and knowing his mentality at least from the angle that at that moment he would become my sworn, mortal enemy. Even from earlier days we were not the best of friends. In March 1942; I had a difficult conversation with him as Poglavnik of the Independent State of Croatia, a conversation which I regard as the most terrible in my life.

Some time at around eleven in the morning we met at the Jesuit monastery of Gesu Nuovo. I think it was a Sunday but I am unsure. At that time he was hidden in the seminary which was run by the Jesuit fathers at Possilipo. As soon as I came to the main door and introduced myself, Father Fiore, who I think was his 'guardian angel' came to me. Till then I had not known him.

Father Fiore took me to the room where the Poglavnik was present. The same Jesuit was a witness to our conversation. I intentionally spoke in Italian, which I thought was the logical thing to do and today I am grateful for this as I now have a living witness to this conversation, for this conversation was falsely reported in a article under the title:'Odlasak Poglavnika iz Evrope' (The Departure of the Poglavnik from Europe), which in my opinion was written by Ms Visna Pavelich, Pavelich's daughter. She said false things about me during the campaign against me by the Croatian Liberation Movement.

We shook hands. I entered immediately in medias res. I continually addressed him as 'Doctor' avoiding the word Poglavnik; this obiously displeased him. I could have even said, Former Poglavnik, but that would have been for him an insult. And so it was 'Doctor'.

After explaining to Pavelich that Draganovich had brought him his passport with a visa and a reservation on a cargo ship and other documents, Pavelich thanked him and Draganovich continued to tell him that which was so burdening his heart and pressuring him, even anticipating the former Poglavnik's reaction.

Draganovich then said:

But before this I have one request. You may accept it or reject it or in the end say nothing. Your salvation does not depend on the answer you give. You will certainly be saved whatever you answer. I ask you to accept my request not as if it is coming from me personally but as a request from the Croatian people, who ask this of you.

I now must explain this to you. You, Dear Doctor, have done more than any other person in the last eight hundred years for the establishment of the Croatian state and this the Croatian people will never forget. You were head of that state for four years and you did a lot of good but allowed a lot of evil. It is not for me now to pass judgement on all this. The Croatian people will judge you. In this as with most of the conversation I was looking at him straight into his eyes.

The life of the Croatian State has been broken. She could have continued to live naturally, but she drowned in a sea of blood. But one thing that hasn't drowned is the firm will and resolve of the Croatian people to again establish its freedom and state. The Croats will invest all their strength and bear all 'sacrifices' to achieve their goal. That, for now, is not within the aims or plans of international powers. We must rely on someone. Until now we have had the misfortune of always relying on those who lost the war.

Draganovich went on to mention that the Axis powers had lost the war and all their leaders had been killed. He then continued:

The only exception is the Head of the Croatian State and we Croatians are proud that we have saved him . . . I think concerning Russia and the Communist states every true Croat has no intention of having anything to do with them to save Croatia. After the collapse of the Independent State of Croatia the Communists spilt a sea of innocent blood in our homeland and wrapped in black almost everyone of our homes.

There remain only the Western Allies. They are the winners. They, and especially the United States of America, are the strongest power in the world. They represent for us the most suitable ideology. The Croatians must go with them to achieve their freedom and state. He then added–These Western Allies, dear Doctor, don't want you. They reject you, for you are on their black books. Every struggle for Croatia led in the name of

Pavelich is rejected and condemned from the start. And you, I regret to say, are an obstacle to Croatia's national struggle. And for this reason, once you are safe and have got to Argentina, firstly thank the Good God for saving you, and then lift your hands from Croatian politics. The whole bloodied, martyred Croatian people deserve the fullest consideration.

Draganovich then concluded: There is something more, and please don't misunderstand me. This doesn't mean that those who followed you, the Ustasha, amongst whom were truly good and noble patriots, are not to struggle further for Croatia. Furthermore, give them the encouragement to struggle to the last drop of their blood, but no longer under your leadership.

I understood how piercing these words were for him. They were piercing but not as I wished contra spem sperans (Hoping against hope). He remained calm, an outer calm, while everything was boiling within him. He revealed this by his later words and more so by his actions. He looked at me with a dark, scowling look and began to answer my 'request'.

Draganovich reflected further:

I understood his rage. I expected it and I firmly believed after my request that I would develop the most bitter enemy in my life. No one knows Pavelich who doesn't know his deepest lust, which captivated him. He drank from the sweetest cup of his life, the cup of power and he remained drunk from it. And now there is found one who is an insolent priest, who is prepared to deeply touch this, touch that, without which his whole life would not have any purpose. I wanted to persuade him, to prove to him, convince him, blackmail him, that if he renounced that power, if he withdraw from politics, for which he lived he would be safe and could live a better life. Possibly, who knows, he wanted to hold that place of power and let no one else take it from him.

He was fired up with 'anger of a justified person', against an insolent and crafty attacker, who had him in his grip as in chess. He, the Poglavnik of the Independent State of Croatia, controlled himself in an icy manner; he didn't like the conversation which brought about an explosive anger within him, but he retained his cool, while within him everything was in flame.[82] After this Pavelich travelled to Argentina.

Vinko Nikolich, who was with Pavelich every day when Pavelich arrived in Buenos Aires, affirms that Pavelich refrained from delving into Croatian politics. In the first meetings he had with him, Pavelich would often repeat and convincingly tell him: That they have begun their national aims well, in gathering the Croatian people together, and encouraged them to continue, and that he would no longer be involved in Croatian politics, for he has done his part. Then he added: If you need any advice from me, you know where I am.[83]

Pavelich's character can also be seen by the fact he almost certainly ordered the execution of Dr Mladen Lorkovich. Lorkovich collaborated very closely with Pavelich for twelve years before the war and was his Minister of Government during the war. It is almost certain that Pavelich also ordered the execution of Ante Vokich, Minister of the Army.

The Croatian historian Jure Kristo concluded that:

> The leadership of the newly created Croatian state completely failed the test of history.... What is tragic and inconceivable is that the political representatives organized the country and its main institutions so that they themselves became the source of antagonism. Laws were passed which were directed against part of the people and contrary to the fundamental principles of humanity. Just that was the behaviour of the persons, who due to the war, sheer chance, political meanderings and a combination of historical circumstances, came to the head of the Croatian state.
>
> The aim of this book is not to pass judgement about who is most to blame for such a sorry state. However, in a strictly hierarchically organized system, like the state administration, it is always the one on the top who is responsible.[84]

---

82. Mijo Ivurek, *ZiDKD*, 205–208. Vinko Nikolić's shorter version, *TsDuS*, Volume 1, 13–14. Bogdan Krizman. *Pavelić* u Bjekstvu, 206–207.
83. Vinko Nikolić, *TsDuS*, Volume 1, 14–15. Conversation whith Vinko Nikolić, Zagreb, 10 Tuesday February 1992.
84. Jure Kristo, *SS*, 430.

The Croatian American historian Jozo Tomasovich quoted Rev. Dragutin Kamber, a Catholic priest who was also present in southern Austria at the time:

> Many people when they look back today on our war time Independent State of Croatia, see only the aspect of evil that it brought to our present and future. Without any doubt there was evil, unfortunately too much of it. A considerable number of those who directed our human destinies during the war showed, unfortunately, that they were not qualified to administer a more advanced establishment of livestock husbandry, let alone steer in a responsible, politically wise and statesman like manner the ship of state through the tempest of war and Balkan and world upheaval.[85]

Tomasovich also provides his own analysis:

> Considering the development that contributed to the ever narrowing base of the Ustasha regime, it is difficult to understand why Pavelich did not try to enlarge its support by concessions to the Machek centre of the Croatian Peasant Party . . . The fact that Pavelich made no serious offer to the party . . . reflects a complete absence of political acumen and responsibility and bears out the supposition that the uppermost consideration in his mind was to hold onto as much personal power as possible.[86]

Pavelich's close collaborator Ante Moshkov under interrogation gave his impression of Pavelich during his flight: 'The whole attitude of Pavelich and his flight left a terrible, painful impression: not only was he in a great panic but also a coward. That impression was also held by others and I remember a lieutenant who was in our company turning to me saying: "What am I to do, everyone is insane?" I feel sorry for the men, I would rather stay with you here on the road.' Moshkov continues: 'I saw that in the midst of Pavelich's flight and attitude he was very disillusioned. It was then for the first time that the thought came to me: It is sad for Croatia when we are led by people like him.'[87]

---

85. Jozo Tomasovich, *WaRiY*, 782. Dragutin Kamber, *PB* Hrvatska revija, March 1981, 5.
86. Jozo Tomasovich, *WaRiY*, 356.
87. Bogdan Krizman, *PuB*, 18.

The commander of the Croatian Airforce, Vladimir Kren recalled a meeting with Pavelich in Rogaska Slatina, Slovenia. To everyone's surprise Pavelich was already in civilian clothes addressing a group of thirty officers in the town square, saying:

> Gentlemen! We find ourselves outside the borders of our state. As Germany has surrendered and the whole army of General Lohr is handing itself to the Partisans, we will not surrender to the Partisans but change into civilian clothes and move ourselves to where we feel best suits us. It's best that you give yourselves up to the English or Americans but not to the Russians or Partisans.
>
> But what if they hand us over to the Partisans? one questioned
>
> Then they will hand you over, he answered coldly.
>
> Then amongst the officers there was a general and angry disillusionment. Most were numb, some swore and others complained. We felt lost. After the first blow eased, we started asking advice and sought what to do. In the meantime the Poglavnik was not amongst us. He didn't seek leave of anyone.[88]

A real leader adds value by being there in a crisis, showing solidarity and confidence to inspire the troops, demonstrating compassion for victims, setting a calm tone and signaling to the world the seriousness of the situation. It is during times of crisis that real leadership is put to the test and revealed. Leadership makes a big difference, without leadership there is just confusion and a vacuum results. Not any style of leadership, but one which is co-operative, collaborative and collective, bringing all together rather than setting them against each other. It is here that Dr Pavelich failed.

To me, the author, it seems there was something in Pavelich's character that did not make him a good head of state. He was a politician but not a statesman. And he left his people when they most needed him.

Vinko Nikolich said that: 'When one spoke with him, everything seemed good and above board, but when one looked at the actions they were the exact opposite.'[89] When one reflects on it, Pavelich

---

88. Bogdan Krizman, *PuB*, 16–17. Vinko Nikolic, *TsDuS*, Volume 1, 241–243.
89. Conversation with Vinko Nikolić, Zagreb, Tuesday 10 February 1992.

modelled himself on the German Fuhrer, the Italian Duce, giving himself the title Poglavnik (The Head) instead of simply President. The salute in Croatia was the Nazi salute and it need not have been.

Ivo Rojnica wrote of the experience of the Croatian industrialist Leon Grivichich, who supported Pavelich and the Ustasha movement before the war, using much of his resources for the Croatian cause. During the war years the Grivichich and Pavelich families were very close to one another *and Grivichich believed in Pavelich only to discover that he was deeply disillusioned in Pavelich, who was not sincere with him.*[90]

Despite his previous promises not to do so, when Pavelich found himself reasonably secure in Peron's Argentina, he started involving himself in Croatian politics. On 7 April 1951, he announced the creation of a Croatian government 'in exile' with himself as head, and its ministers were mainly his ministers during the war who had managed to avoid being returned to Tito's Yugoslavia. Over a period of time, he would dismiss some ministers and add others, but his government 'in exile' was really unable to do anything, was more symbolic than practical, and became divisive among the Croatian diaspora, especially in the United States, Western Europe, Australia and South America. In 1956 he also established the Croatian Liberation Movement, with himself as head, causing further division in the diaspora.[91]

Franjo Dujmovich wrote of Pavelich that: 'power rocked him into a deep dream, which even held him in Argentina.'[92] After an attempt on Pavelich's life and wounding on 10 April 1957, his future in Argentina became uncertain. He was accepted by General Francisco Franco's Spain on the condition that he refrain from all political involvement. The last few months of his life his health deteriorated rapidly. He was admitted to the German hospital in Madrid, on 18 December 1959 he confessed his sins to a priest, receiving Holy Communion as well. On the 27 he received the Holy Annointing of the church and he died in the early hours of 28 December, with Father Branko Marich and daughter Vishnja by his side.[93] His grave is in Madrid's San Isidor cemetery.

---

90. Ivo Rojnica, *SiD*, Volume 2, 53–57.
91. Bogdan Krizman, *Pavelič u Bjegstvu*, 245–247, 363–368
92. Franjo Dujmović, *HnpkS*, 128.
93. Bogdan Krizman, *Pavelić u Bjekstvu*, 436–438.

During the fourteen years that he lived after the war, Pavelich never once expressed any anguishing remorse or sorrow for the thousands of soldiers and civilians he had led into southern Austria, and who were slaughtered. Any normal human being would feel enormous regret, sorrow and anguish for leading one innocent human being to their suffering and death. Strangely and tragically, there was no such expression of anguish or sorrow from Pavelich after the war.

Pavelich lacked the moral character of Dr Joseph Tiso, the leader of Slovakia during the war years, who always in extremely difficult situations would choose 'the lesser of two evils'. Referring to Tiso's Slovakia, Dr Franjo Tudjman wrote: 'With respect to the Jews, the situation in Tiso's Slovakia was decidedly different from that of Pavelich's Croatia or Nedich's Serbia. Because of this, in that period there were instances of individual and group rescues, and even emigration of Jews from "Hitler's fortress".'[94]

In his book *On the Psychology of Military Incompetence*, Norman Dixon, Professor Emeritus of Psychology at University College London, and himself a former British military officer, concluded that 'military incompetence is more a product of personality characteristics than of intellectual short comings'.

Dixon asserts that the authoritarian nature of military structure made it prone to particular types of personality characteristics, including: '. . . a need for approval, fear of failure, being deaf to unwelcome information, an inclination to internal codes of acceptable behavior, anti intellectualism and sensitivity to criticism.'

He broadly groups these as symptoms of 'ego weakness', which creates:

> neurotic paradox in which the individual's need to be loved breeds on the one hand, an insatiable desire for admiration with avoidance of criticism, and, on the other, an equally devouring urge for power and positions of dominance. The paradox is that these needs inevitably result in behavior so unrealistic as to earn the victim the criticism which he has been striving so hard to avoid.

---

94. Franjo Tudjman, *HoW*, 120–121.

According to Dixon, another characteristic of this mindset is a disregard for the welfare of the lower ranks; that so long as the officers were comfortable, they'd be content to see the troops suffer and die.

One of the better British commanders, Field Marshal Lord William Slim stated: 'There are no bad regiments, only bad officers.'

The authoritarian mindset does not welcome creativity or differences of opinion. Dixon writes: 'When all that is natural, creative, flexible, warm and outgoing in the human spirit becomes crushed and constricted, such qualities as compassion, bold decisions and military flair give way to conformity, sycophantism, indecision and a fear of failure.'

He goes on: 'It's a sad feature of authoritarian organizations that their nature inevitably militates against the possibility of learning from experience through apportioning blame.'

They are, he says, 'past masters in deflecting blame. They do so by denial, by rationalization, by making scapegoats . . . the net result is that no real admission of failure or incompetence is ever made by those who are really responsible.'

This is certainly true of Pavelich, who also placed his most trusted people into key positions in government and the military purely on the basis that they were loyal to him.

Where Croatia was concerned, I believe the soldiers and civilians were not to blame: they were the victims of an incompetent leadership lacking in moral courage and showing the aforementioned 'ego weakness'. There was no reconnaissance. There was a lack of preparation for the withdrawal. There was no maintenance of communication, and when severe crisis arrived, they divested themselves of all responsibility from their failings.

One of the characteristics of incompetent commanders which Dixon drew from the British experience from the Boer War was: An apparent imperviousness . . . to the loss of life and human suffering amongst the rank and file, or . . . irrational and incapacitating lack of compassion[95].

Pavelich was reluctant to relinquish power for the good of the Croatian people. One must ask the question how could he lead the army and people to such a catastrophe?

---

95. Norman Dixon, *OtPoMI*, 67

He was, as Dixon described some of the British generals: 'Vain, devious, scheming and dishonest. Indecisive, secretive, sensitive to the criticism of others. Terrifyingly insensitive to the sufferings of others'. Wellington repeatedly refused to sacrifice lives unnecessarily. He left nothing to chance.[96]

Montgomery said: "'a commander must think two stages ahead.'"[97] One military officer wrote of his meeting Montgomery: "that air of peace and calm which he carried with him was so strong that after a moment my panic and alarm began to die away: it was something which one felt was incongruous in a soldier.'"[98]

In his study of highly competent versus incompetent commanders, Dixon came to the belief that ego, weakness and authoritarianism rather than stupidity, underlined military ineptitude.[99]

In contrast, we have the behavior of such men as Wellington, Zhukov, and Montgomery, whose enormous energy and attention to detail might well have appeared obsessive but was in fact a deliberate and much needed policy of arranging to meet every contingency and of leaving nothing to chance–in short, good planning.[100]

'If the trumpet gives forth an uncertain sound, who shall prepare himself for battle.' This was his favorite text when Bernard Law Montgomery was a lecturer at the British Staff College at Camberley in the 1920s, before he became Field Marshal in the Second World War. The greatest British soldier since Wellington, he was disliked by most of his peers but deeply revered by his troops.

Pavelich's authoritarian attitude can be seen in his attitude to the Croatian Sabor or Parliament. It was opened with great expectations on 23 February 1942; it sat right up to September 1942 before being recalled at the beginning of 1943, at which time it was dissolved, with Pavelich announcing that he was to take full responsibility himself in running the country and no one else.[101]

Pavelich sacrificed a lot for Croatia and in his early career he showed courage, particularly when he defended the Macedonian patriots in Skoplje on 7 December 1927. He was the only Zagreb

---

96. Norman Dixon, *OtPoMI*, 155.
97. Norman Dixon, *OtPoMI*, 212
98. Norman Dixon, *OtPoMI*, 241–242.
99. Norman Dixon, *OtPoMI*, 395.
100. Norman Dixon, *OtPoMI*, 273.
101. Bogdan Krizman, *PiHiM*, 260, 262

lawyer who volunteered to do so. His speech in their defence, at a time when the Serbian authorities were particularly brutal towards the Macedonians, showed real courage.[102] After the assassination of Stjepan Radich and two of his colleagues in the Belgrade parliament in 1928, which was followed by the imposition of the brutal dictatorship of King Alexander, Pavelich left Croatia to form the Ustasha movement.

It was only when Pavelich became head of state of the Independent State of Croatia, that the limited power began to corrupt him. One is reminded of Lord Acton's famous phrase: 'Power corrupts and absolute power corrupts absolutely.' Not that Pavelich had absolute power, he was always beholden to the Germans and for the first two years, the Italians. Stejpan Hojt said: 'Had Dr Pavelich stood up to Hitler he would not have been head of the Croatian state for ten minutes.'[103] But the power which he did have he did not use properly. It is power which tests a person's character as Abraham Lincoln said: 'Almost all people will withstand an enormous amount of suffering, if you want to judge a person's character give them power.' It is here where Dr Pavelich failed. He didn't give up power even when he did not possess it in Argentina.[104]

Cardinal Stepinac had an understanding of Pavelich, although Pavelich caused him much pain. Stepinac took account of the war situation: the state was born during the most difficult of times; foreign armies were on Croatian territory; a civil war made it impossible to have peaceful control over people and events. Stepinac didn't take sides where party politics were concerned and this was also the case with Pavelich. He looked at the rights of the Croatian people for their legitimate state. In principle Pavelich' stood for this and that was his very strong and positive point.[105]

---

102. Ante Pavelić, *PHDP*, 246–258.
103. Conversation with Stjepan Hojt Sydney, Australia 2 November 2003.
104. Stjepan Hojt relates: 'I was a guerrilla after the war with a group of others on the slopes of Velebit mountain and I asked myself: where is the Poglavnik ? That was the first time I started to have doubts about Pavelich. Hojt also stated: Whatever we say about Dr Pavelich, he was ours. He wanted a free, independent state, which we all wanted. Tito, although biologically Croatian, was a hardened Communist internationalist, who had no Croatian feeling in him and that's the difference. Dr Pavelich was ours' (Conversation with Stjepan Hojt. Sydney, 2 November 2003).
105. Josip Vraneković, *Dnevnik,* 809.

Vinko Nikolich also puts blame on Dr Jure Krnjevich and Ban Dr Ivan Subashich who were leading figures in the Croatian Peasant Party based in London during the war, working towards the establishment of the Royal Yugoslav Chetnik government, thus against the Croatian state. Nikolich wrote:

> They, through all the four years of war were leading a policy against the Croatian State and for the reestablishment of the Royal Chetnik Yugoslavia. They were not leading a struggle against the Ustasha regime, nor against the Ustasha (as for example a Nazi) ideology, but they attacked Croatia itself, for Croatia was where through many ages she grew: our Croatia and only Croatia, whatever her regime. Nikolich went on: And so their co-fault be greater and more manifiest, let us say this, that these same party politicians did not at the moment of the tragedy take on the protection of their own people, many of whom were Croatian peasants, members of the Croatian Peasant Party, who lost their lives from Partisan bullets and knives and the leadership of the Croatian Peasant Party didn't raise its voice in protest. Nor did its leadership try to use its status on the side of the victors to save the poor Croatian man ... At every cry for help, it was said: They are the Ustasha, as if the Ustasha were not Croatian! Together with the Ustasha there were many, many thousands of non Ustasha killed. Why did the leadership of the Croatian Peasant Party remain silent so long after the 'liberation': did they hope that the Communists would share power with them? It can be seen, they did not know Communism: the Communists shared power with no one!
>
> The catastrophic Croatian politics during the war, the Ustasha regime at home, as well as the opposition from the Croatian Peasant Party, placed the Croatian people into the blood thirsty hands of the Yugoslav Partisans, like sheep to the slaughter. The English were just intermediaries and they as intermediaries are morally accused for the Tragedy.[106]

Although there appears a lot of truth in what Nikolich writes, Dr Krnjevich had direct contact with Prime Minister Churchill, but by the time Krnjevich knew what had happened at Bleiburg it was

---

106. Vinko Nikolić, *TSDuS*, Volume 1, 15–16.

already too late. It is also true that Ban Ivan Subashich joined Tito's government, becoming its Foregn Minister in 1944, doing much work to gain support for Tito among Croatian emigrants in the United States and Canada. Subaschich was just a naïve tool whom Tito used and when after the war he had no more use of him, he discarded.

So, who is at fault?

The ultimate blame for the slaughter that happened in southern Austria and Northern Yugoslavia straight after the war, falls on Tito and the leadership of the Communist party.

Although Communism in theory seems very humane, just and fair to all humanity, there is something brutal and heartless in its implementation. As The Black Book of Communism states . . . 'it claimed that its intention was to create an egalitarian society in which justice, fraternity, and altruism would be the key values . . . it produced a tidal wave of selfishness, inequality, and irrationality. To survive, people were forced to cheat, lie, steal, and turn their hearts to stone'. Communism reached its most extreme form in Cambodia where the Khmer Rouge slaughtered a million and a half of their own people out of a population of six million. When their leader Pol Pot disappeared in the Cambodian jungle in 1963, he did nothing to get back in touch with his family, even after 17 April 1975 when the Khmer Rouge gained power. His two brothers and his sister-in-law were deported along with everyone else. One of them died quite quickly. Only much later did the two survivors realize, thanks to an official portrait, who Pol Pot really was, and they never let on that they even knew him.[107]

Tito was very much a Stalinist. His colleague Milovan Djilas wrote: 'In 1937, at the time of the Soviet purges, the Comintern designated Tito as the head of the Yugoslav Communist party . . . he could not have been appointed to that position, with the right to veto all decisions had he not been personally checked out, his loyalty to the Soviet leadership tested, or, rather his disloyalty to the factionalists within his own party confirmed. Many other Communists had been checked out in that same fashion and they had not survived.'[108]

---

107. *The Black Book of Communism*, 603–604. From David P Chandler, *Brother Number One: A Political Biography of Pol Pot*. (Boulder: Westview Press, 1992), 172–175.
108. Milovan Djilas, *Tito*, 26.

Djilas admits bluntly: 'If Tito had not been loyal to . . . Stalin, how could he have survived'?[109] He also recorded a conversation he had with a Polish Communist in 1946 to whom Stalin praised Tito, saying: 'Tito is a tower of strength . . . he wiped them all out.'[110]

When Tito broke with Stalin in 1948, he turned against the Stalinist faction of the Yugoslav Communist party, men and women who had carried the Communist cause through the most bitter fighting of the Second World War. Tito eliminated them with a ferocity more ruthless than he used against the Ustasha. There were some fifteen thousand of them who were killed or sent to the notorious prison of Goli Otok.

Milovan Djilas recalled having a conversation on this subject with Aleksander Rankovich, on 28 June 1948,: 'Now we are treating Stalin's followers as he treated his enemies.' Rankovich retorted: 'Don't say that! Don't talk about it.'[111]

The reader will find it interesting to know that when Tito underwent a gall-bladder operation on 19 April 1951, it was performed by a Slovene surgeon, Doctor Lavrich, in Slovenia who had a Catholic nun working for him. It was this Catholic nun who cared for Tito during his convalescence, together with Jovanka Budisavljevich whom a year later Tito married.[112] It was at a time when Tito not only had Catholic and Orthodox priests in his prisons, but also Catholic nuns.

This is reminiscent of Fidel Castro of Cuba. After being arrested in 1953, Castro's father approached the Archbishop of Santiago de Cuba, Monsignor Perez Serantes, imploring him to intercede on behalf of his son, and so Fidel was saved mainly through the intervention of the Archbishop.[113] One can see the lack of shame in some of these Communist leaders who became world figures.

Although it could be quite reasonably argued the main responsibility falls on Pavelich due to his lack of responsibility and care, ultimately fault must be put on Tito and the leadership of the Yugoslav Communist party.

Despite the ideals of Communism, Communism has no concept of forgiveness and mercy. Although Tito possessed a brilliant mind and

---

109. Milovan Djilas, *Tito*, 28.
110. Milovan Djilas, *Tito*, 39.
111. Milovan Djilas, *Tito*, 84.
112. Milovan Djilas, *Tito*, 146–147.
113. *The Black Book of Communism*, 650–651.

brilliant organising abilities, he was extremely ruthless and heartless. He was also a master of manipulation and intrigue, Cardinal Stepinac described Tito as being: 'A true Zagorac (a region of Croatia where Tito comes from) but well lathered with every kind of oil'.[114]

Tito manipulated the leadership of the various nationalities of the former Yugoslavia, particularly the mistrust between the Croatians and Serbs, which he masterfully used and through which he was able to maintain power. He also manipulated world leaders, portraying himself as a world stateman. What kind of a statesman is that, when everything he lived for and fought for collapses ten years after one's death? During the thirty-five years of his rule he did nothing to bring about a reconciliation of the peoples of the former Yugoslavia, particularly that of the Croatians and Serbs, for he knew if he did bring it about he would lose the power for which he had a deep lust. Tito was no Nelson Mandela.

While the fault mainly lies at the feet of Tito, there are others who have blood on their hands, primarily the British for handing over these unfortunates to their certain death. Pavelich bears an enormous guilt. He is a good example of what happens so often in history. When he was entrusted with a position of power and responsibility, when he should have exercised great caution, when it was incumbent upon him to conduct governemnt in a collaborative and consultative manner, he instead abused his authority and worked to amass power to himself. He determined the destiny of Croatia and its people: he led it to the catastrophy of Bleiburg. May we all learn from his failings, most particularly those in government and positions of power and responsibility. He is a good example on how not to lead.

---

114. Related to the author by the Cardinal's nephew Juraj Mrzljak, Krašić, Croatia 8 July 2003. According to the Croatian author Dr Drago Simundza, Tito's government, from 1945 to 1950, killed up to half a million people from all nationalities of the former Yugoslavia. This does not include those returned by the British from Southern Austria immediately after the war. It was Tito's policy, that if anyone potentially would turn against you, to eliminate them (Conversation with Dr Drago Šimundza, Split, Croatia, Friday 3 August 2018)

Reconciliation: from:www.mindworks.org

Chapter 9
Reconciliation, Forgiveness and Peace

An Introduction

On this day, Sunday 11 November, in the year of our Lord, 2018, I commit these words to paper and to history. This day, the centenary of Armistice Day, marking the end of the First World War, The Great War. It was a great and terrible war meant to end all wars. And yet, just twenty-one years later, the world was cleaved once more by a war far more brutal and devastating. It wasn't the only horror of the twentieth century: a century which also introduced humankind to the shocking term *ethnic cleansing,* a term unheard of in previous ages.

Today, in a moving ceremony, German Chancellor Angela Merkel and French President Emmanuel Macron embraced one another at Aisne–Marne cemetery in Belleau, France. It was a ceremony to mark the centenary of Armistice Day which took effect at the eleventh hour, on the eleventh day, of the eleventh month, 1918. Pictures may tell a thousand words, but that thousand is buried beneath millions of bodies. They say we can look forward in hope as well as back in horror. Despite the inhumanity of war, there is another side to human nature that can forgive and find love.

What are we to make of it all, these brutalities, these cruelties, this slaughter? What has humankind made of itself, in this beautiful world we all share and inhabit? Will we ever learn to live in peace and harmony with one another, sharing the abundant resources for the betterment of one another and the development of humankind?

Can we ever find definitive answers to such huge questions? Perhaps not, but we have seen. We have suffered. And that suffering can bring about greater awareness; it can bring us together as one people bound to one another, and create people more committed to the betterment of humanity. Suffering has a role to play in life;

it has its effects, certainly apparently not positive, but, nevertheless beneficial in the development of the human person. St Augustine says: *he who isn't exposed to suffering, knows nothing.* Humankind has lost this view while facing adversity and, consumed with sorrow, finds it is ever a hard truth to bear.

Lessons Learned from History

There were those who discouraged me from writing this book. Their views were: why bring back the suffering and horrors of the past, leave the past to the past and move on. I found the words of Charlotte Delbo encouraging: "Do something, something to justify your existence ... because it would be senseless after all for so many to have died while you live doing nothing with your life."[1]

World history, the history of peoples, is tragic and painful. Throughout history flow rivers of blood, and human nature is its cause. The truth of history's tragedy must be faced with the hope that it never be repeated again. Rabbi Harold Kushner, in wrestling with the question of the suffering of the innocent, quotes a German theologian, Dorothee Soelle, who says that we are to ask not "where does the tragedy come from but where does it lead".[2]

The Spanish philosopher, Jose Ortegas Gasset, wrote on the importance of history: 'A knowledge of history is the first-class way of upholding and continuing the advancement of civilization. Not only because it gives positive solutions to new life conflicts, but also because life is so different from what it was, because we avoid the naïve mistakes of past ages'.[3]

The suffering that Bleiburg symbolizes is something that did happen, and it has never been acknowledged by the western world. A characteristic of all tyrannies is that they try to abolish the memory of their victims as if they never existed, were of no value and are best forgotten. But covering up and completely denying the crime is possibly a worse offence. Denying the crime is in some cases justifying it, and in many ways, it symbolically continues the crime. As LM Montgomery wrote: 'No one is really lost to us as long as we remember them' or as Elie Wiesel wrote: 'To forget would be the enemy's final triumph.'

---

1. Charlotte Delbo, *A-WP-HSwFRJ*, 95.
2. Harold Kushner, *WBtHtGP,* 150.
3. Vinko Nikolić, *BTHN,* 467–468.

Erase memory and you wash away the blood of the perpetrator's hands. You undo the done deed, and make it disappear from history. Erase memories of atrocities and you could provide future perpetrators with immunity. Inversely, remember the misdeeds and you erect a barrier against future misdeeds. As Wiesel said: 'The memory of death will serve as a shield against death. Forgetfulness is damnation, memory is redemption.'[4]

It is important to remember. Remembering enables us to open the past in the direction of the future–a better future. Remembrance is not the eternal emphasizing of victimhood, but a 'memory of a promise', a memory for a better future. At its best, remembering is a creative process in which negative emotional energy is transformed into positive energy that opens up a better future. Reconciliation requires a culture of remembrance that does not allow the victims of the past to be forgotten. And it allows us to learn from each other and from our experiences, uniting to ensure past sins will not be committed again. Solidarity with the victims is solidarity in time and back in time, as well as strengthening us that such evil will never happen again.

Forgiveness is the opposite of an escape into forgetting. One of the most unfortunate sayings is 'Just forgive and forget'. But the relationship is not one of forgiving and forgetting. One can only forgive things that cannot be forgotten. As Emmanuel Levinas writes: 'Forgetting cancels the relationship with the past, while forgiving shifts the past into a purified present.'[5]

Fratelli Tutti

Pope Francis wrote an Encyclical letter, titled *Fratelli Tutti*. This phrase was a favorite saying of St Francis of Assisi; it means 'Brothers and Sisters all'. Pope Francis wrote of St Francis's of Assisi's attitude as: 'a love that transcends the barriers of geography and distance, and declares blessed all those who love their brother "as much when he is far away from him as when he is with him".[6] In his simple and direct way, Saint Francis expressed the essence of a fraternal openness that

---
4. Miroslav Volk, *E&E*, 234.
5. Emmanuel Levinas, *A-WP-HSwFRJ*, 60–61.
6. *Admonitions*, 6. English translations in *Francis of Assisi: Early Documents*, Volume 1, New York, London, Manila (1999), 131.

allows us to acknowledge, appreciate and love each person, regardless of physical proximity, regardless of where he or she was born or lives.'[7]

Pope Francis continues in *Fratelli Tutti*: 'It is moving to see forgiveness shown by those who are able to leave behind the harm they suffered, but it is also humanly understandable in the case of those who cannot. In any case, forgetting is never the answer.'

He goes on:

> 'The Shoah must not be forgotten. It is 'the enduring symbol of the depths to which human evil can sink when, spurred by false ideologies, it fails to recognize the fundamental dignity of each person, which merits unconditional respect regardless of ethnic origin or religious belief'.[8] As I think of it, I cannot help but repeat this prayer" Lord remember us in your mercy. Grant us the grace to be ashamed of what we men have done, to be ashamed of the massive idolatry, of having despised and destroyed our own flesh which you formed from the earth, to which you gave life with your own breath of life. Never again Lord, never again'.[9]

Forgiving but not Forgetting

He then writes of the importance of remembering:

> Nowadays, it is easy to be tempted to turn the page, to say that all these things happened long ago and we should look to the future. For God's sake no! We can never move forward without remembering the past; we never progress without an honest and unclouded memory. We need to 'keep alive the flame of collective conscience, bearing witness to succeeding generations to the horror of what happened', because that witness 'awakens and preserves the memory of the victims, so that the conscience of humanity may rise up in the face of every desire for dominance and destruction'.[10] The victims themselves–individuals, social groups and nations- need to do so, lest they succumb to the mindset that leads to justifying

---

7. *Fratelli Tutti*, 7–8.
8. *Arrival Ceremony, Fratelli Tutti*, Israel (25 May 2014)
9. *Visit to the Yad Vashem Memorial*, Jerusalem (26 May 2014).
10. *Message for the 2020 World Day of Peace* (8 December 2019)

> reprisals and every kind of violence in the name of the great evils endured. For this reason, I think not only of the need to remember atrocities, but also all those who, amid such great inhumanity and corruption, retained their dignity and, with gestures small and large, chose the part of solidarity, forgiveness and fraternity. To remember goodness is also a healthy thing.
>
> Forgiving does not mean forgetting. Or, better, in the face of a reality that can in no way be denied, relativized or concealed, forgiveness is still possible. In the face of an action that can never be tolerated, justified or excused, we can still forgive. In the face of something that cannot be forgotten for any reason, we can still forgive. Free and heartfelt forgiveness is something noble, a reflection of God's own infinite ability to forgive. If forgiveness is gratuitous, then it can be shown even to someone who resists repentance and is unable to beg pardon.

He goes on to say that forgiveness is a decision or choice and at times it requires real effort.

> Those who truly forgive do not forget. Instead, they choose not to yield to the same destructive force that caused them so much suffering. They break the vicious circle; they halt the advance of the forces of destruction. They choose not to spread in society the spirit of revenge that will sooner or later take its toll. Revenge never truly satisfies victims. Some crimes are so horrendous and cruel that the punishment of those who perpetrate them does not serve to repair the harm done. Even killing the criminal would not be enough, nor could any forms of torture prove commensurate with the sufferings inflicted on the victim. Revenge resolves nothing.
>
> This does not mean impunity. Justice is properly sought solely out of love of justice itself, out of respect for the victims, as a means of preventing new crimes and protecting the common good, not as an alleged outlet for personal anger. Forgiveness is precisely what enables us to pursue justice without falling into a spiral of revenge or the injustice of forgetting.

> When injustices have occurred on both sides, it is important to take into clear account whether they are equally grave or in any way comparable. Violence perpetrated by the state, using its structure and power, is not in the same level as that perpetrated by particular groups. In any event, one cannot claim that the unjust suffering of one side alone should be commemorated. The bishops of Croatia have stated that, 'we owe equal respect to every innocent victim. There can be no racial, national, confessional or partisan differences'.[11]

Personally I am very happy that Pope Francis quoted the bishops of Croatia, for the suffering that Croatian people went through during the last hundred years is unknown in the west It is also true that the British press portrayed them very negatively in the wars of the early 1990s.

What does Forgiveness mean?

Human forgiveness is necessary because some things cannot be forgotten. Giving and receiving forgiveness releases neither the perpetrator nor the victim from remembrance. The victim is not released from memory but from the weight of resentment and hate: *The victim's wound, however, remains as an everlasting scar.*[12]

The past leaves a mark on society, and so it should. We continually recreate the past and its meaning. And while the past is past, it is also present. Therefore, the broken promises of the past can call upon us today to watch for those blemishes of the past in the present and to bear witness to them. In our very being we are affected by history. Our being is also constituted by the ability to act, that is, to respond to the situation we live in. We act in the present because we want to shape the way the world looks. But we do this in the context that carries the very physical and emotional scars of the past and against the broken promises of earlier generations. The human being is summoned to remember the past because remembering is a condition of the possibility of acting responsibly and creatively towards the future. Memory gives meaning to the past, especially in light of a future that one can shape.[13]

---

11. Croatian Bishops Conference, *Letter on the Fiftieth Anniversary of the End of the Second World War* (1 May 1995)
12. Didier Pollefeyt, *A-WP-HSwFRJ*, 61.
13. Britta Frede-Wenger, *A-WP-HSwFRJ*, 121.

If our past is lost, our future flounders aimlessly. Drawing from Carl Gustav Jung's discoveries of human psychology: a tribe's basic set of stories constitutes its psychic life. A tribe disintegrates and falls to pieces when it loses its mythological heritage. As Jung said: 'A tribe's mythology is its living religion, whose loss is always and everywhere, even amongst the civilized, a moral catastrophe.' Without myths, there is no link with the past and no basis for orientation toward the future. One is indeed lost[14]

Since every evil touches and endangers the network of humanity itself, forgiveness pertains to the totality of humanity. Reconciliation is not possible without forgiveness. It is not God who will punish them; they will punish themselves when they confront the love of God. Salvation consists not only in what we remember but also in what we do with what we remember.

But merely telling the truth will not suffice, one must *do* the truth. The truth must be faced, however painful it might be, if there is to be any hope of genuine reconciliation. It is to be a truth, but with love. Eberhard Arnold says: 'Truth without love kills, but love without truth lies.'

Words play an important part in all human relationships, but the acts that support and express the relationship are even more fundamental. Essentially, it must be a relationship founded on truth about what happened and a willingness on both sides to build on that truth. To be sincere it must be a *commitment* to a new beginning. We perpetrate the crime of ignorance through apathy to the past.

One incident struck me and will stay with me. The manager of a funeral home said to the cleaner: 'See this man lying there, he was found dead under a bridge, destitute. See the man lying next to him, he had property to the value of one hundred million dollars.' What a powerful lesson! In the normal way of thinking, the destitute man's life was a failure while the wealthy one's was a success and yet they lie beside one another in death. This image keeps close quarter in my thoughts. The destitute may have been mentally ill through no fault of his own, while the wealthy could have made his wealth through deceit and exploitation. I will never know. Both had worth. Both had valued lives to those who will remember them. We hope that both were loved.

---

14. Wallace B Clift, *J&CTCtR*, 60.

Faith in a Just and Supreme God

As believers, we believe the dead are not lost to us. Even the dead create a national strength; they are in solidarity with us. If the living do not express their memory, all the sufferings of the dead go unacknowledged. The dead speak through the living.

We must build a better future by acknowledging the past and learning from it. From this is derived our vitality, our strength, our heroism. The dead pass onto us not only their ideas, their knowledge, their discoveries; they simply continue to live in us, as grandparents live in their grandchildren. For this reason, we can be comforted by the millions who were killed last century. They now live in us, but their costly sacrifice was too dear a price to pay. But pay they have, and now we are blessed with hindsight and the incorporation of their combined spirits into ourselves.

Life is so sacred and unique, and we must have the deepest reverence for it. Protect the life of those close and those in the family of humanity, as there can never be any greater evil than to take another's life. Life is of the greatest value, more sacred than the most beautiful cathedral, more wondrous than any discovery in science.

Our belief must be in the human person. When we reflect on the human person, we marvel at our ingenuity and creativeness. Alone of all creatures, the human person has spread over the whole earth, able to adapt to all climates and environments. Over the past 65,000 years Australia has experienced major climatic and environmental changes, including during the last Ice Age, where not a blade of grass was left on the eastern side of Australia, and yet Indigenous Australians have survived. I marvel at them.

Humanity is the supreme value, more valuable than race, nationality and language. We all need more heart and soul. Humanity depends upon it. The Jewish scholar David Patterson writes:

> As all humanity was gathered into Adam, so is all humanity gathered into each human being. That is why the Talmud compares saving a single life to saving the world. That is why panim, the Hebrew word for 'face', is plural: each person bears his own face as well as the face of Adam, the face of humanity.[15]

---

15. David Patterson, *A-WP-HSwFRJ*, 178–179.

What are we making of our own lives? What are we making of our world? These questions we need to reflect on and ponder. Our life. We all own it. We are conscious of our struggle, with the problem of evil plaguing humankind ever since we walked the earth. The Bible vividly expressed this when speaking of Eve, it says: 'The woman saw that the tree was good to eat and pleasing to the eye . . . so she took some of the fruit and ate it . . . She gave some to her husband . . . and he ate it . . . Then the eyes of both of them were opened and they realized they were naked.' (Genesis.3v.6-7)

They did something they knew was wrong, as we do. There is something in us which makes us capable of evil and it is expressed in so many different ways. Nicholas Thomas Wright writes: 'I regard the main function of postmodernity, under God, to be the preaching of the doctrine of the Fall (the truth of a deep and fatal flaw within human nature) to the modernist, post-eighteenth-century arrogance that supposes it has solved the world's problems.'[16]

We can believe in a lie and miss our flaw. But it hides in us. To face it, frees us. We exercise our human freedom well when we choose what builds rather than destroys; conversely, we misuse our freedom when we choose to denigrate life and damage relationships.

The first man, upon discovering his nakedness, put off his guilt with the explanation: 'The woman who you gave me to be with me, she offered the fruit and I ate it.' Meanwhile Eve promptly made her own projection, saying: 'The serpent tempted me, and I ate it.' Everyone else is at fault, except ourselves. We need the courage to confront our own evil and admit it: *It was my fault, I did it.* One of the hardest things in life is to accept and admit that I did wrong, that it was my fault. In her book *Dead Man Walking,* Helen Prejean wrote that the hardest thing for a criminal was to admit their crime, though once the crime is admitted there is hope of recovery. This is also true for Alcoholics Anonymous, which holds that once alcoholics admit their alcoholism, then they are on the way to being cured.

For the people of the former Yugoslavia, particularly the Croatian and Serbian people, it is important they confront their recent past This is also true for people of the world wherever there was, and is, violent conflict. Contemplating on the tragedy Bleiburg symbolizes, I am reminded of what the well-known Croatian Protestant theologian,

---

16. NT Wright, *EatJoG*, 14.

Miroslav Volf, was asked by the eminent German Protestant theologian, Jurgen Moltmann, during the time of the Croatian-Serb conflict in the 1990s.

Jurgen Moltmann asked Volf: 'But can you embrace a Chetnik?'

Volf answers:

> It was the winter of 1993. For months now the notorious Serbian fighters called 'Chetniks' had been sowing desolation in my native country, herding people into concentration camps, raping women, burning down churches and destroying cities. I had just argued that we ought to embrace our enemies as God has embraced us in Christ. Can I embrace a Chetnik— the ultimate other, so as to speak to the evil other? What would justify the embrace? Where would I draw strength for it? What would it do to my identity as a human being, as a Croat? It took me a while to answer, though I immediately knew what I wanted to say. 'No, I cannot but as a follower of Christ I should be able to.'[17]

Evil generates more evil, as evil-doers fashion their victims into their own ugly image. Once a war starts and the right conditions are maintained, an uncontrollable chain reaction begins its cycle.

Carl Gustav Jung, reflecting on World War II, wrote: 'It is a fact that cannot be denied: the wickedness of others becomes our own wickedness because it kindles something evil in our own hearts.' Evil engenders evil, and like pyroclastic debris from the mouth of the volcano, it erupts out of aggressor and victim alike.[18] There must be a continuous work of mutual 'making space for the other in the self' and of re-arranging the self in light of the other's presence.[19] And there must be a will to embrace the other; it is essential: 'The will to give ourselves to others and "welcome" them, to readjust our identities to make space for them, needs to come before any judgement about others, except that of identifying them in their humanity.'[20]

The more I worked on this chapter, the longer I wrestled with this question of reconciliation and forgiveness, the more I came to the

---

17. Miroslav Volf, *Embracing the Enemy*, 9.
18. Miroslav Volf, *Embracing the Enemy*, 87.
19. Miroslav Volf, *Embracing the Enemy*, 154.
20. Miroslav Volf, *Embracing the Enemy*, 29.

conviction of the existence of God and the necessity of a faith in a just God, as the ultimate source of forgiveness and mercy. We frail, weak, selfish human beings need the ultimate lover, God, who calls us to embrace the perpetrator, which for frail human beings is very difficult. God's grace offers reconciliation in order to supersede the cycle of crime and punishment.

Repentance expresses our recognition of the true meaning of our humanity, our sorrow at the impact of our inauthentic exercise of our freedom, and the renewed desire to live in accord with what is conducive to true freedom. We are living in an age when we are far more conscious of the social dimension of human life and have a sense of the interconnectedness of the physical world and humanity, as well as a universal responsibility for that interconnectedness. The very identity of each is formed through relation to others; the otherness of the other enters into the very identity of each. As the Jewish philosopher Martin Buber said: 'All real living is meeting.'

Everything and every person is a part of us. Fritjof Capra writes:

'Deep ecological awareness recognizes the fundamental interdependence of all phenomena and the fact that, as individuals and societies, we are all embedded in (and ultimately dependent on) the cyclical process of nature.'[21]

He goes on:

> All members of an ecological community are interconnected in a vast and intricate network of relationships, the web of life. They derive their essential properties and, in fact, their very existence from their relationships to other things. Interdependence–the mutual dependence of all life processes on one another–is the nature of all ecological relationships. The behavior of every living member of the ecosystem depends on the behavior of many others. The success of the whole community depends on the success of its individual members, while the success of each member depends on the success of the community as a whole.[22]

Capra concludes his book with some basic principles of ecology: interdependence, recycling, partnership, flexibility, diversity, and, as

---

21. Fritjof Capra, *TWoL*, 6.
22. Fritjof Capra, *TWoL*, 290.

a consequence of all those, sustainability. As we go forward to a new millennium, the survival of humanity will depend on our ecological literacy, on our ability to understand these principles of ecology and live accordingly.[23] What Capra writes of ecology is true of humankind: we are all to value the individual person as precious and realize that we are all interdependent. We belong together. And humankind is continually moving in this direction.

I was moved by what Katherine Kemp wrote in her marvelous essay on South Africa:

> In reading about South Africa, there is a word I come across constantly: ubuntu. Ubuntu (in the Nguni languages) or botho (in Sotho languages) serves as the spiritual foundation of African societies. It is a world view reflected in the Zulu maxim umuntu ngumuntu ngabantu, which means 'a person is a person through other people.' Other translations elaborate: 'To be human is to affirm one's humanity by recognizing the humanity of others in humanity's infinite variety of content and form' or 'A human being is a human being through the otherness of other human beings.'[24]

Universal ideals and ideas bind us, and mean we can recognize our own humanity through another's. Beautiful music and art are some such relatable tethers, essential to the human person, for they lift the mind and heart to realities beyond themselves. Music and art are universal languages. Beethoven's nineth Symphony is his great profession of the brotherhood and sisterhood of humankind and the harmony of creation. Behind the harmony of music, we see dimly the great harmony of humanity.

God–the ultimate beauty–also binds us.

The human spirit, expressed in those higher aspirations, is a part of our strivings. We see it in works of art, in a person's service of one's fellow human beings, or in the attempt to understand the workings of nature and its order.

It is the spirit which gives life, even if it is only found in tiny crumbs; it is the spirit which gives guidance on how we are to embrace this difficult life, how we are to react to it, no matter what

---

23. Fritjof Capra, *TWoL*, 295.
24. Katherine Kemp. Essay, *Ubuntu:Caught Up in the Bundle of Life*.

catastrophe is ours. With the spirit, we grow through it and overcome it. It is interesting how in the ugliest surrounds, a table setting can be nicely arranged.

It is a fact that prisoners, in the most difficult environments, out of the most ordinary pieces of wood, cardboard, of the simplest of materials, create such objects for their use or to beautify their surroundings that one is amazed. Some are true works of art, which of themselves create light in the dim surroundings, uplifting the spirits of the prisoners. One's spirit lives on these little crumbs. It is the gathering of these small crumbs of beauty which lift the spirit. When spikes cause pain to our feet, we look up to the stars. No matter how severe the winter storms, we hope in the sun. The winter is easier for we have joy in anticipating spring.

Miroslav Volf wrote:

> Did I not discover in oppressed Croatia's face some despised Serbian features? Might not the enemy have captured some of Croatia's soul along with a good deal of Croatia's soil?[25] No recognition or misrecognition can inflict harm, or can be a form of oppression, imprisoning someone in a false, distorted and reduced mode of being. Greater trust in God's presence enables me to share my vulnerability and see others as companions and not as threats.[26]

We human beings must learn to be reconciling and forgiving; it is the only way forward. It is summed up perfectly here:

> If a wound is open and remains so, then reconciliation is impossible and remains so. In my view, reconciliation is needed precisely because the wound cannot stay open for ever, lest it contaminate the body completely. Forgiveness and reconciliation are not cosmetics that hide the injury; they are healing processes that transform the wound into a scar. The Holocaust should become a scar on the twentieth century's face. One can live constructively with a scar, but can never forget or neglect the injury to which it bears witness.[27]

---

25. Miroslav Volf, *E&E*, 17.
26. Miroslav Volf, *E&E*, 19.
27. Didier Pollefeyt, *A-WP-HSwFRJ*, 105.

> Forgiveness would imply forgetting the guilt, whose burden paralyzes both the remembrance and the ability to draw upon perspectives for one's future in a creative manner. It is not the past event or the criminal act that is forgotten, but rather its significance and its place in the whole of the dialectic of historical consciousness.[28]

The oppressors are also children of God. They had a mother and father who received them with loving arms. They played as children with other children and then in the course of life, in moments of extreme violence they chose evil. Volf wrote:

> Just as the oppressed must be liberated from the suffering caused by the oppression, so the oppressors must be liberated from the injustice committed through the oppression.[29] God is vulnerable love. If the victims do not repent today, they will become perpetrators tomorrow who in their self-deceit, will seek to exculpate their misdeeds on account of their own victimization.[30]

> If the victims remember rightly, the memories of inhumanities past will shield them and all of us against future inhumanities; if the perpetrators remember rightly, the memory of their wrong doing will help to restore their guilty past and transform it into the soil on which a more helpful future can grow.[31]

Mary McAleese and Northern Ireland's Reconciliation

As Mary McAleese, who worked very hard for reconciliation in Northern Ireland wrote:

> The practice of exclusion is not just something that the evil and barbaric others out there do; exclusion is also what we the good and civilized people do right here . . . the tendency lurks in the dark regions of all our hearts, seeking an opportunity to find a victim . . . We must make space for the other in the self and rearrange the self in the light of the other's presence. Logic of purity.. . . . a logic which reduces, ejects and segregates . . . Become like us and you will be happy.[32]

---

28. Paul Ricoeur, *A-WP-HSwFRJ*, 125.
29. Miroslav Volf, *E&E*, 23.
30. Miroslav Volf, *E&E*, 117.
31. Miroslav Volf, *E&E*, 131.
32. Mary McAleese, *LiCSGatSoPiNI*, 44.

Being a person of deep religious faith and speaking of the all-embracing love of God, she continues:

> If God our Father and Mother, offers such an embrace to the 'other', what right do I have, in God's name, to dare to offer less? She speaks of the courage needed: . . . call to turn and face the hate and name it, to out it, to resolve it. Refuse to run away from it or from ownership of the task confronting it.[33]

> Our Word of God is not to be selectively edited and conveniently paraphrased so that it matches our political and cultural ambitions. The only way to be sure we are listening to and actually hearing the true word of God is to place ourselves in an environment where our vision of God's word is exposed to other visions and where we are challenged and can challenge in turn.[34]

> Can we say we are honouring the commandment to love one another if we refuse even to listen to one another? If we presume that we alone know the mind of God, have we not ceased to be his friend and become instead his self-appointed, sole agent?[35]

She quotes Allan Boesak's words from South Africa: 'Reconciliation is not holding hands and singing "black and white together." Reconciliation is not black and white going to summer camp together . . . and then returning to separate lifestyles. Reconciliation is not merely feeling good, but doing what is right.'[36]

Mary McAleese also encourages the small steps each individual makes in their own, obscure personal lives: 'Love also means looking out for the tiny green shoots of hope, seeing in them the presence of the God we believe in and giving them help to grow to fruition.'[37]

Inspiration also comes from a Belfast charity, Flax Trust, whose motto is: 'Building peace, one person at a time.' We need to make small successful steps of learning to live together even if we do not understand the other's language, instead of suppressing each

---

33. Mary McAleese *LiCSGatSoPiNI*, 5.
34. Mary McAleese, *LiCSGatSoPiNI,*, 112.
35. Mary McAleese, *LiCSGatSoPiNI*, 113.
36. Mary McAleese, *LiCSGatSoPiNI,*, 75.
37. Mary McAleese, *LiCSGatSoPiNI*, 78.

other's voices and clinging to our own possessions and robbing the possessions of others. The grand vision and the small steps will together keep us on a journey of genuine justice between cultures.

The value of small gestures

This is also echoed by Pope Benedict acknowledging that:

> 'love overflowing with small gestures of mutual care, is also civic and political, and it makes itself felt in every action that seeks to build a better world'.[38] For this reason, charity finds its expression not only in small and intimate relationships but also in "macro – relationships: social, economic and political"[39] Indeed its close relation to truth fosters its universality and preserves it from being "confined to a narrow field devoid of relationships"[40] Without truth, emotion lacks relational and social content. Charity's openness to truth thus protects it from 'a fideism that deprives it of its human and universal breadth'.[41]

Croatia is a small country in central Europe and where world powers are concerned, seemingly insignificant. The Croatian writer, poet and journalist, Vinko Nikolich, reflected on this as the war was coming to an end. He expressed his sadness at Croatia being overrun by Communists; while fleeing as a refugee, he reflected:

> But who listens to a small people? Who pays attention to an ant, which in the middle of the road carries its crumb to the ant bed? It remains on the road as a small people, squashed. Where is the right of an ant to live compared to that of a grown man? As if the life of an ant is not representative of the great life of nature, glorifying its greatness and that of the creator, who created the large and the small?[42]

I am encouraged by the words of the anthropologist Margaret Mead: 'Never doubt that a small group of committed people can change the world . . . Indeed it is the only thing that ever has.' Let us work

---

38. Encyclical Letter *Laudato Si* (24 May 2015)
39. Benedict XVI Encyclical Letter *Caritas in Veritate* (29 June 2009)
40. Benedict XVI Encyclical Letter *Caritas in Veritate* (29 June 2009)
41. Benedict XVI Encyclical Letter *Caritas in Veritate* (29 June 2009)
42. Vinko Nikolić, *Bleiburg*, 23.

together in the small circles where we live, locally; it is there where we start to build a tolerant and peaceful world. It starts now. And it starts in our home, and what we convey to our children.

Forgiveness and Reconciliation

We all struggle with forgiveness and reconciliation in our own personal lives. Let us look at our inner selves and gaze into our own homes, forgiveness is unconsciously practiced daily in family life, and then there are cases where family members are so bitter that they are not talking to one another. Multiplied, such divisions fracture humankind. As Britta Frede-Weger writes: 'Just as every generation must find its way of thinking about the past and acting towards the future, reconciliation is a process that demands continual attention, a process that is part of the construction of identity.'[43]

Forgiveness and reconciliation are the only answer for a wounded world. As the Belgian theologian and scholar, Didier Pollefeyt, writes: 'Forgiveness and reconciliation have to do with the way perpetrators and victims, as well as their heirs, relate to the evil events of the past and to each other.'[44]

He also recognizes how the pain of one generation can be passed on to the next generation:

> . . . it is not so illogical and incomprehensible that the heirs of the victims see the descendants of the perpetrators in the light of the crimes of their ancestors. Recognizing and understanding this reality seems to me to be a necessary condition for making reconciliation a real possibility.[45]

This question is something that Rabbi and Professor, Peter J Haas, wrestles with:

> How do I, as a child of survivors overcome the Holocaust and establish relations with a child of the perpetrators? What role can I or should I play in helping the two of us overcome the past? . . . Acts of contrition and reaching out are still

---

43. Britta Frede-Wenger, *A-WP-HSwFRJ*, 126.
44. Didier Pollefeyt, *Incredible Forgiveness Christian Ethics between Fanaticism and Reconciliation*, 135.
45. Didier Pollefeyt, *Incredible Forgiveness* 133.

important after the Holocaust, even if it is impossible to effect forgiveness for the Holocaust[46]

The challenge lies in the effort of forgiveness for the crimes. Love the criminal but hate the crime. Recognize the humanity even of the perpetrator. This is a question that Jewish academic, Rachel N Baum, also asks:

> Jews are a people of memory, but it is not an easy responsibility to keep both memory and compassion alive at the same time . . . Remembering the Holocaust does not bring me closer to humanity, but puts me in utter despair. If I am able to move beyond that condition, it is by effort alone, not because the narratives bear any deeper truth. This effort is at the heart of spiritual practice, which demands that we soften the parts of us that have been hardened through pain and hurt, and that we open our souls, despite all the reasons to leave them closed.[47]

She asks the question as a Jew:

> It touches the deepest issues of our Jewish existence, both as individuals and as a community: How will we respond to a world that hurt us so deeply? Can we hope and trust again after having been so wounded? How will our painful experience affect who we are?[48]
>
> At the same time, we can admit that anger and hatred are ultimately unsatisfying roads to Jewish memory. Are the murdered honored by our bitterness, by our hardness to others? Such emotions limit our ability to connect not only to other people but to God. Is this how we honour our murdered brothers and sisters, by the closing of our own souls?
>
> So the spiritual question for Jews must be one of memory: How do we remember without becoming embittered? How do we remember our sufferings without being defined by them? How do we carry memory into the present while also recognizing that today is not yesterday?

---

46. Peter J Haas, *A-WP-HSwFRJ*, 70–71.
47. Rachel N Baum, *A-WP-HSwFRJ*, 230.
48. Rachel N Baum, *A-WP-HSwFRJ,*, 226.

> These are questions for the spiritual path; they are not questions that have easy answers, and different people will find different ways down this path.[49]

And yet we all have a common humanity and this should bring us together. As David Paterson and John K Roth conclude: 'And yet a face is precisely what we seek in these post-Holocaust struggles with forgiveness, reconciliation, and justice: it is the face of our fellow human being.'[50] 'Reconciliation requires nothing less than each group's becoming fully present to the other'[51] and face the concreteness of history.

Each party to a conflict accepts its wounded state; each shows its wounds to another in the dialogical endeavor to heal them. In jointly confronting the brokenness of both narratives, conflicting parties escape the seeming inevitability of violent action and reaction; they create a 'third way' or 'creative middle': the authentic 'whole' of dialogue. As Leonard Grob concludes: Dialogue is more process than product, it is more a verb than a noun.[52]

Reconciliation is the answer but life is often unfair, and it is full of things that can never be excused.

It is hard work. It requires action and we human beings have no other choice than to go forward and confront the perpetrator of the crime. There is hope and let us look forward in hope, for we must be people of faith, love, and believe in miracles. As Didier Pollefeyt wrote: 'When, after terrible events, people extend a hand to each other and thus open a space for the future, this cannot be understood in terms of biological, psychological, or social interaction. It is no more and no less than a miracle.'[53]

My hope is that we can make Britta Frede-Wenger's words our own: 'I must also remember who I am, and what my task is: to make sure in my thoughts and actions that Auschwitz is not be repeated, that nothing similar ever happens.'[54] As Britta Frede-Wenger writes of Auschwitz, my hope is that Bleiburg be not repeated and yet tragically,

---

49. Rachel N Baum, *A-WP-HSwFRJ*, 231.
50. David Paterson & John K Roth, *A-WP-HSwFRJ*, 251.
51. Leonard Grob, *A-WP-HSwFRJ*, 202.
52. Leonard Grob, *A-WP-HSwFRJ*, 201.
53. Didier Pollefeyt. *IFCEBFR*, 136.
54. Britta Frede-Wenger, *A-WP-HSwFRJ*, 140.

similar crimes have been committed and the world seems to have stopped still. It is happening today as I write.

Speaking of miracles, I am reminded of an encounter I had in Croatia during Croatia's war of independence from 1991 to 1992. I was on the island of Korčula, where there were refugees who had fled from the Serbian Četniks when Vukovar fell. A grandmother was holding her grandchild as I spoke with her. She saw Serbian Chetniks being very cruel towards the captured Croatians. When I asked her how did she feel towards the Chetniks when she witnessed their cruelty? She said something surprising: 'I felt sorrow and pity towards them.' To me, that answer was the mingling of the Divine with the human. She felt no bitterness or hatred, only pity and sorrow. She told me that she prayed for the Chetniks and she still does. In Didier Pollefeyt's words, it was a miracle.[55]

Let me add to this section the agonizing words of Britta Frede-Wenger:

> Auschwitz is overwhelming, nothing can undo it. What must be undone is its paralyzing effect on future generations. How can I (from the perspective of a German Christian) remember what my people did and not lose the ground I stand on . . . It is a question of how the heirs of both the perpetrators and victims 'relate to this past and to each other'.
>
> It happens when . . . the crimes of the fathers are not held against the children – and at the same time are not forgotten. And it cannot be achieved by one side alone. I must make myself vulnerable.[56]

While individuals can be held responsible for their actions, nobody can be held responsible for someone else's actions. It is good for us to remember Elie Wiesel's words: *"Only the guilty are guilty, not their sons."*[57]

We as human beings must recognize that there is no future in hate. As Martin Luther King said:

---

55. Coversation on island of Korčula, Croatia, Sunday 10 May 1992.
56. Britta Frede-Wenger, *A-WP-HSwFRJ*, 140.
57. Elie Wiesel, *A-WP-HSwFRJ*, 225. From New York Times, 5 May 2001.

> Returning hate for hate multiplies hate, adding deeper darkness to a night already devoid of stars. Darkness can't drive out darkness; only light can do that. Hate cannot drive out hate; only love can do that. Hate multiplies hate, violence multiplies violence, and toughness multiplies toughness in a descending spiral of destruction. Hate distorts the personality and scars the soul. It is more injurious to the hater than the hated.[58]

Albert Camus said at the end of World War II: 'Tomorrow, the most difficult victory that we need to gain over our enemies will have to take place in ourselves, in this superior effort to transform hate into a desire for justice.'[59] This is true for all of us wherever we may be.

And in this theme, it is important to remember a Chinese proverb attributed to Confucius: *Who opts for revenge digs two graves.*

The Australian moral theologian, Dr Neil Brown, reflected:

> The first step in the process of reconciliation must be the emergence, in our own eyes, of the true humanity of those who have been wronged and the ways that their lives have been ravaged by what has been done to them. This does demand recognition of what has been done on the part of the agents of harm, but much more important is the reclamation on the part of the victims of their 'violated' dignity and of their ability to make their own distinctive voices heard by those who harmed them.[60]

As we reflect on it all, there is a flaw in our lives. We are capable of so much good and then so much evil. As the fourth century writer Gregory of Nyssa wrote: *We are children of our choices.* He also wrote: *We go from one beginning to another.* Every day for us is a new start; in many ways a whole lifetime can be put into a single day and in a single day a whole lifetime. We reinvent ourselves many times through our decisions. It is important for us always to take responsibility for the outcomes, whatever they may be, or in the words of Carl Gustav Jung: 'In this thine own breast dwells the stars of thine own fate'.

---

58. Quoted by JC Arnold, *WF*, 50–51.
59. Albert Camus, *A-WP-HSwFRJ*, 57.
60. Neil Brown, *AHFR*, 18.

There is something profoundly human in relating closely with someone else. When we do connect, we see that life is a gift, a grace. The word *gratia* means thankfulness, so let us live our lives with gratitude. In the words of Abraham Lincoln: 'With malice towards none, with charity towards all.' As Mahatma Gandhi said: 'Be the change you want to see in the world.' I can, we all can, become a saviour or a victim. Let's hope we all act in a saving way every day of our lives.

To do this, we must *embody* forgiveness into specific habits and practices. It's a way of life, something we learn and relearn. Forgiveness is not so much a word to be spoken as a life to be lived and an action to be acted out.

Thomas Keating writes of an interreligious workshop he attended where people who experienced the most horrific events of the twentieth century spoke. He mentions a Jewish lady who lost her parents in a concentration camp during the Second World War, and who established a humanitarian organization to prevent such horrors happening again. She remarked, 'I really could not do this work unless I was fully convinced that if this situation had been reversed, I could have done the same things that were done to my people.' Keating continues, 'saying that, his ears pricked straight up as she went on with her presentation: we know with great clarity that if the situation in our lives had been changed, we too would be capable of any evil.'[61]

Selfishness and ignorance of humanity in others damages us individually and as a whole.

Our very identity as human beings is bound to others. There needs to be a conversion of heart. Love draws us into relationships, enabling us and inviting us to remember and claim the past as our own. We all need forgiveness. Forgiveness is costly since it involves acknowledging and experiencing the painful truth of human evil at its worst. Forgiveness needs to become a habit that transforms. We need to truly hear each other's stories.

In a letter to the Croatian sculptor Ivan Meshtrovich, Cardinal Stepinac, who at that time was living under house arrest in Tito's communist Yugoslavia, wrote:

---

61. Thomas Keating, *FaGotS*, 100–101.

> You will understand how hard it is in these circumstances to love a bloodthirsty and merciless persecutor. But in spite of this we must and will, for this is Christ's command. But how then will we be better than our torturers? This is why I often encourage the priests that they don't allow themselves to be misled by sorrow and misfortune, but joyfully and constantly pray for the enemy. Vengeance doesn't belong to us, but to God. Let Him, then, reply to them as a Father, who joyfully receives back a lost son.[62]

Forgiveness at times calls for that supreme, heroic act. Scholar and retired Anglican Bishop, Nicholas Thomas Wright, writes:

> I am committing myself to work towards the point where I can behave as if it didn't happen. But it did happen, and forgiveness isn't pretending that it didn't, it looks hard at the fact that it did and making a conscious choice, a decision of the moral will, to set it aside so that it doesn't come as a barrier between . . . forgiveness presupposes that the thing which happened was indeed evil and cannot be simply set aside as irrelevant.[63]

Naim Ateek, a Palestinian priest in Jerusalem said: 'When people hate, its power engulfs them and they are totally consumed by it . . . Keep struggling against hatred and resentment. At times you will have the upper hand, at times you will feel beaten down. Although it is extremely difficult, never let hatred completely overtake you.'[64] For some people forgiveness is a daily struggle.

As Miroslav Volf writes: 'For us, sinful and limited human beings, following in the footsteps of the Crucified means not only making space in ourselves for others, but in creating space for them making also space for their perspective on us and ours on them.'[65]

Just as we need to develop good habits of health to counteract the forces of disease, so we need to develop good habits of forgiveness to counteract the forces of evil. If we are to change society, if we are to change our culture, we must begin by changing ourselves. It is

---

62. Juraj Batelja. *Pismo iz suzanjstva*, 327.
63. NT Wright, *EatJoG*, 100.
64. JC Arnold, *WF*, 43.
65. Miroslav Volf, *E&E*, 215.

difficult to confront undesirable or unnatural parts of our nature, or behavior that is far less honourable than we imagine ourselves to be. It is an attitudinal change that needs to take place. The very identity of us is formed through our relationship to others. Sustaining and renewing relationships between persons and groups requires us to make space for the other in the very self, and rearranging the self in light of the other's presence. People stand in relation to the shape of their identity.

To accept oneself in all one's wretchedness is one of the hardest tasks. If we really want peace on the planet Earth, we have to work for it. We have to reach into the deep recesses of our own hearts and ferret out all those ugly prejudices, biases, fears and hatreds that keep true peace from reigning in our hearts. George Orwell wrote about the 'moral effort' sometimes required to acknowledge unpleasant facts about one's self. Finding ways of integrating the negative tendencies of one's personality, one can find meaning in them and use them positively to energize life.

As Carl Gustav Jung wrote:

> To accept oneself may sound like a simple thing, but simple things are always the most difficult things to do. In actual life to be simple and straight forward is an art in itself requiring discipline, while the question of self-acceptance lies at the root of the moral problem and at the heart of a whole philosophy of life.

Let me add some thoughts of CS Lewis:

> To forgive for the moment is not difficult, but to go on forgiving, to forgive the same offence again every time it recurs to the memory, there's the real tussle.[66] Lewis also added: Real forgiveness means looking steadily . . . and seeing it in all its horrors, dirt, meanness and malice, and nevertheless being wholly reconciled to the person who has done it. That, and only that is forgiveness.[67]

---

66. L Gregory Jones, 237. From *Letters to* Malcolm, 29–39.
67. Quoted by JC Arnold, *WF,* 65.

I find these thoughts of Carl Gustav Jung very moving:

> 'What if I should discover that the least of the brethren and the very enemy himself, that all these are within me, and I myself stand in need of alms of my own kindness, and that I myself am the enemy who must be loved?' Loving the enemy relates first and foremost to self-acceptance of one's shadow side. It is the question of relating to and taking responsibility for the very worst in oneself.[68]

It is interesting how the Japanese architect Junichiro Tanizaki sees it reflected in architecture when he writes of the depth and resonance brought about by the creation and play of shadows. To me it symbolizes the shadows and light in our own lives. 'The beauty of a Japanese room depends on a variation of shadows, heavy shadows against light shadows . . . it is nothing else. Westerners are amazed at the simplicity of Japanese rooms, perceiving them as no more than ashen walls bereft of ornament. Their reaction is understandable but it betrays a failure to comprehend the mystery of shadow.'

One of the challenges in forgiving is recognizing these shadows in ourselves; it is easier to blame than to look within. This is reflected in what JC Arnold writes:

> In my experience the strongest motivation for forgiveness is always a sense of having received forgiveness ourselves . . . or an awareness that, like everyone else in the human race, we are imperfect and have done things we need to be forgiven for.[69]

Our shadow needs to be integrated into the conscious life of our personality as much as possible. A Jewish Hasidic text expresses this perfectly: *'Thou shall love thy own evil as thyself.'*

The Catholic tradition of Christianity holds to the doctrine of Original Sin and there is some merit in this concept of evil, for: 'Original sin is not just a theoretical idea referring to a mythological past but is a fact that, as an individual, I am immediately and inevitably contaminated by evil . . . by very concrete forms of evil, both on the interpersonal level (as in the case of an unfair inheritance in my

---

68. Marvin J Spiegelman, *CaJP,* 190.
69. JC Arnold, *WF,* 34.

family) and on a collective level (as in the case of the racist policies of my country). The state of original sin is not due to my intentional faults but to my concrete existence.'[70]

We all know the power of evil. As N.T. Wright writes:

> Evil is alive and powerful, not least where mighty empires vaunt themselves and imagine they can do as they please, even if it means turning gardens into deserts and deserts into grave yards.[71] He goes on: Evil is the force of anti-creation, anti-life, the force that opposes and seeks to deface and destroy God's good world of space, time and matter, and above all God's image-bearing human creatures.[72]

'Evil isn't simply a philosopher's puzzle, but a reality which stalks our streets and damages people's lives, homes and property.[73]'

Proper mourning for the dead, and acknowledgement of the horrors that others have suffered, are a part of human life properly lived. How do we ponder suffering and loss on such a scale? And how can we conceive of those who commit such evil? How can one comprehend the thinking, motives and attitudes of those who perpetrated such evil, being confronted by the world's silence? The mind boggles.

Evil is irrational. And it is worse when one attempts to explain how sin and evil make sense. Perhaps we should say that evil is unintelligible. How do we think about unimaginable evils? Not thinking about them is easy enough. We can become immune, slot them away in some way, explain them as that is how things are and have peace of mind. But buying peace of mind in that way comes at unconscionable cost.

The 'problem of evil' is not simply or purely a cosmic thing; it is also a problem *about me*. I am not 'guilty' of World War II, but I *am* culpable in the sense that the effects of the war continue to mar my relations with others, making me complicit in the continuing scarring that defiles the memory of the lost we are all enmeshed in various histories and circumstances, and the result is that we can't evade the

---

70. Didier Pollefeyt, IFCEBFR, 133–134.
71. NT Wright, EatJoG, 38.
72. NT Wright, EatJoG, 55.
73. NT Wright, EatJoG, 98.

truth that we all invariably diminish and destroy others in the ways we ourselves live.

Human beings are filled with the possibility of goodness and the capacity for great destruction. If such commitments to memory are to be sustained, they require supportive friendships, practices and institutions that enable the unlearning of destructive habits and the cultivation of holy ones. Theologian, L Gregory Jones, writes: 'It takes only a moment to destroy lives through violence, but it takes a lifetime to cultivate alternative patterns and practices of forgiveness, of trust and of love'.[74] We cannot change the past but we are responsible for the way we shape the future.

Dietrich Bonhoeffer saw the importance of private confession:

> As the open confession of my sins to a brother insures me against self-deception, so, too, the assurance of forgiveness becomes fully certain to me only when it is spoken by a brother in the name of God. Mutual brotherly confession is given to us by God in order that we may be sure of divine forgiveness.[75]

The Catholic and Orthodox tradition of Christianity have the practice of confessing one's sins to God through an intermediary, a priest through whom one's sins are forgiven. The German theologian Karl Rahner writes: the individual can still feel and experience very vividly that he is coming to the Holy Church of Christ when he goes to the priest ... he is accusing himself ... that the sin he is confessing ... that he has sinned against the body of Christ ... In making his confession ... the sinner can experience ... that he is freed from his sins in the eyes of God.[76]

As the Australian theologian Dr David Coffey writes:

> For that repentance to be sincere and complete, and for it to move beyond merely private and to attain social reality and expression it needs to be expressed in confession and satisfaction ... Even if such a person approaches Christ in

---

74. L Gregory Jones, 76.
75. L Gregory Jones, 18.
76. Karl Rahner, *Penance and Reconciliation with Church*, Theological Investigations, Volume 10, 147–148.

private prayer, if this is all they do they are still laying down their own terms of forgiveness, for Christ has given us the Church and the sacrament of reconciliation for that very purpose...

He continues that confession 'is a counter-cultural exercise . . . in which we put ourselves on the line.'[77]

It is implicit in the writings of both these theologians that confessing one's wrongs to another, namely a priest, has real value.

To admit our wrongs to someone else, whether the person we have hurt or to someone we trust, defines a willingness to acknowledge our guilt and thus we are far more likely to find redemption. Forgiveness is not an occasional act; it is a permanent attitude when given with full grace. Forgiving is not a one-time decision; you live it every day. Every person moves at their own pace, and there are different paths to the same destination.

We see the freedom of forgiveness:

> Once you are able to let go of wrongs that have been done to you, it changes everything. It will change your relationships, your attitudes, your emotional make up, your whole approach to living. It will give you a better life. Plus, you'll find that when you forgive, you're always a winner. You don't lose a thing. Because it is not a sign of weakness to love somebody who hurts you. It's a sign of strength.[78]

To me the way forward for humanity is set by the example of the South African Truth and Reconciliation Commission (TRC). Not that South Africa has solved all its problems, it has a long way to go, but its example is the way forward. The TRC asked those who committed crimes during the white dominated regime to acknowledge their crimes before those whom they had offended, express their sorrow and move forward. Those who did so were granted amnesty and were not punished in any way. As Dr Kevin McDonnell wrote to me:

> Some leaders of the African National Congress were in prison on Robben Island together. There were about one thousand five hundred prisoners there, mostly political prisoners

---

77. Dr David Coffey, *The Sacrament of Reconciliation*, 77, 104, 109.
78. Steven D McDonald, X–X1. In JC Arnold, *WF.*

but some were common criminals. It was in this very harsh setting that the members of the African National Congress saw that violent revolution was not the way forward for South Africa. They drew up a plan of how South Africa, which was very much a multi-cultural country, was to develop. Nelson Mandela was one of its leading figures. The members of the African National Congress saw that peace and reconciliation was the way forward for the country and it was essential that a truth and reconciliation commission be established.

When the African National Congress won the election in 1994, with Nelson Mandela as the new president, he quickly established a Truth and Reconciliation Commission which did not seek to punish those who had committed crimes against South Africa's Blacks during the apartheid regime. It introduced the possibility of amnesty, whereby perpetrators who were guilty of atrocities would come forward, meet their victims, acknowledge their crimes, express their sorrow and then get on with their lives. There was no retribution or punishment. Its essence was the acknowledgement of the crime. There were some moving experiences of encounters between victims and perpetrators.

All this was not done in isolation. The vision for a new South Africa was built on the Freedom Charter developed by the African National Congress and other groups in 1955. The Truth and Reconciliation Commission drew from the experience of truth commissions in some South American and other countries.

It is an extraordinary fact that Nelson Mandela, who spent twenty-seven years in prison, some of it in maximum security in the harsh surroundings of Robben Island, came out of prison without a trace of bitterness.[79]

Our requirements can be very small but my desire is to live in the world with an open mind. After so much suffering life to me is so much clearer and dearer and in freedom I resolve to live my life to

---

79. Conversation with Dr Kevin McDonnell, Monday 17 December 2018, Sydney, Australia. Dr McDonnell lived in South Africa from 1998 to 2012 working in the field of education.

the full. To work, create and love the world around me. To value and safeguard life as something most dear and precious, and promote it in so many different ways.

I am a Minister of Religion, I try to do what I can in developing good relations with ministers of all churches and religious faiths in the district where I live and work. My efforts at times seem insignificant, but I am encouraged by the words of Cardinal Newman:

> God has created me to do Him some definite service. He has committed one work to me which He has not committed to another. I have my mission. I have a small part in a great work. I am a link in a chain, a bond of connections between persons. He has not created me for naught. I shall do his work.[80]

Although our link in the chain might be small and seemingly insignificant, it is still a link and lets us go forward developing good will. 'Each one has a unique note in the universal symphony; no one else can strike yours except you'.

While a small country, East Timor's size does not determine the wisdom of its people. Their tradition for settling disputes and reconciling divided communities astonishes me. People there have a tradition of being pragmatic. The country experiences common village vendettas, where villagers burn one another's huts. Villagers realize the violence can't continue, so the people meet and elect a village chief, to arbitrate between disputing parties and restitution is made to the offended party to the satisfaction of both parties so ending the matter. East Timor is a good example of a small seemingly insignificant country, yet one with much practical wisdom.[81]

The South American country of Colombia is another example. A truce agreed between President Juan Manuel Santos's government and the left-wing militants of Farc (Revolutionary Armed Forces of Colombia) at a service of reconciliation held in the city of Villavicencio was witnessed by Pope Francis. Pope Francis heard testimonies from those caught up in the conflict. The most powerful testimony came from Pastora Mira Garcia, a sixty-one-year-old, who told the crowd that she had lost two of her children, her father and

---

80. Mary McAleese, *LiCSGatSoPiNI*, 82.
81. Conversations with Edwin Krsevan, Sydney, Australia, 27 December 2018 and 11 January 2019. Edwin Krsevan visited East Timor many times.

her husband in the violence. Yet, inspired by her faith, Mira Garcia said she had met and cared for her father's killer, who had been left sick and abandoned, and her son's murderer, who had been wounded. 'The unforgivable can be forgiven.'

Mira Garcia spoke beneath the gaze of the mutilated crucifix of Bojaya, which shows Christ without arms and legs. It had been seen as a symbol of violence in Columbia since it was damaged in 2002, when a bomb exploded in a church in which 300 people were sheltering. 'Christ broken and without limbs is for us ever more Christ,' the Pope told the crowd, 'because he shows us once more that he came to suffer for his people and with his people.'[82]

Conclusion

The more I ponder this question of reconciliation, forgiveness and peace, and investigate the selfishness of my life, I realise I must face up to my life. As James Baldwin wrote: 'Not everything that is faced can be changed but nothing can be changed unless it is faced.'[83] As I face up to my life, I find encouragement from the symbol of the cross: that important symbol challenges me to forget self and embrace the other.

It is true that in life we are at times discouraged, but the words of Martin Luther King are inspiring: 'The Arc of history bends slowly, but it bends towards justice.'[84]

After pondering the horrendous violent suffering that humanity endured during the twentieth century Pope Francis prayed:

> I ask God 'to prepare hearts to encounter our brothers and sisters, so that we may overcome our differences rooted in political thinking, language, culture and religion. Let us ask him to anoint our whole being with the balm of his mercy, which heals the injuries caused by mistakes, misunderstandings and disputes. And let us ask him for the grace to send us forth, in humility and weakness, along the demanding but enriching path of seeking peace.'[85]

---

82. *The Tablet,* 16 September 2017, 8.
83. NT Wright, *EatJoG,* 62.
84. NT Wright, *EatJoG,* 62.
85. Pope Francis, *Fratelli* Tutti, 124.

As I come to the end of this book, and particularly this chapter, I, together with you the reader, grapple with the meaning and purpose of all past suffering. Together with you we wrestled with these essential responses in our own personal lives and the wider world. As I question reconciliation, forgiveness and mercy and the cycle of growth in us as a whole, I come to my few concluding words.

Many people grab, grasp, live their lives as if life owes them something, taking as much as they are able out of life. Vanity shrouds selfishness and obscures humanity, keeping us separate from the individual. These limited perspectives can isolate and alienate us from those we share our lives with.

As we journey through life, let us learn to grow in solidarity with life. Let us love the future and embrace the future, certainly always learning from the past–but loving the future and moving forward with courage and a whole-hearted embrace of the future. When we join in the 'parade of life' by fostering, upholding, encouraging and supporting each other, we are uplifted and can rejoice, and celebrate life together. As we come to the end of this story, may we embrace life, and find the exuberance and fulfillment that comes with truly participating in the union with all people.

Let us walk together: aware that as human beings we have our shadows. We are a mixture: We are people of greed and generosity, of lust and purity, people of pettiness and magnanimity, of violence and peace, of hate and love. We must acknowledge our shadows: to affirm the positive and the work of reconciliation and forgiveness, which contributes to a lasting peace for humankind.

To achieve this: *We must bend our knee before our God asking for forgiveness and mercy*

Conclusion

One must wonder what we are to make of it all. One can't help but think of the enormous mistake Austria made in declaring war on Serbia; although it was with some justification given the Serbian leadership supported the Black Hand terrorist organisation whose aim was to provoke war. When war was declared, the youth enthusiastically volunteered thinking it would last a few months at most. No-one foresaw the prolonged senseless carnage that followed. It would have been far better for Austria to have worked diplomatically to set things right; it's much harder, much slower, very painstaking but much more effective.

Once peace was finally restored a few years later the world, and certainly Europe, was far worse off than it was before the war. It was a world ruled by dictators, where diabolically brilliant men used the chaotic situations to gain power and imposed their inhuman ideologies on those beneath them. This ultimately resulted in the suffering of millions. There are good examples of this in the twentieth century.

The famous Bolshevik revolution of 6 and 7 November 1917 was a *coup d'état* in which less than two per cent of the population, through brilliant and ruthless leadership, attained power and imposed its will on the balance of the population. This imposition was maintained for decades to follow. This is not unlike many other dictatorships.

The saddest part of the situation is that ordinary, innocent and blameless people were caught up in the whirlwind of events and suffered. Defenceless children, the old and infirm. It makes one weep. It's sufficiently shocking if one innocent person looses their life through violence, cut out from the web of life. It's equally heartbreaking that millions of people suffered. Think of the unfulfilled potential of these people and the contribution that they could have made to humankind, the children that would have been theirs, the future generations that would have developed the wellbeing of humanity. All cut short. The vast majority of human beings are decent people, who would assist their neighbours in need. It is only a tiny minority in any society who are nasty, and less still those who are evil.

I am thinking in particular of a Croatian lady who lost her father in this slaughter, he was in his early twenties at the time. She had never seen her father, he died before she was born. That longing she had for her father, waiting for him to come back, asking 'will he come back?' 'will she ever see him?' Those questions 'what happened?' 'how did his life end?' All gone into the unknown, he lost his life in a ghastly slaughter. This story is repeated by countless others.

With the loss of so many innocent lives and so much suffering, let us consider the hate that develops. Hate! Once a person hates, they cease to be a human being. Reflecting on Croatia's life from the First World War and onwards. It is very important to maintain the right path. Upheavals will happen, turmoil and much wrong will be done, it is the person who remains faithful to integrity of life who will prevail in the end. We must believe in truth, justice, goodness, doing what is decent for our fellow human beings. Religion plays a big part in this mission. Religion is a beautiful aspect of human life, we acknowledge that we are all children of the one heavenly Father, made in the image and likeness of God, we give God homage by doing what is decent to our fellow human beings. It is only when religion is abused that it becomes ugly. True religion is always an expression of love of God and neighbour; for the human being is precious. A genuine religious believer possesses a sense of spiritual growth that will guide people to embrace a sense of universal responsibility, to work for the common good and to promote the interiority of the greater community of life. A genuine religious leader will also encourage us to consider what legacies we wish to leave to future generations. Albert Einstein said 'The release of atomic power has changed everything except our way of thinking . . . the solution to this problem lies in the heart of man.' Religion touches the human heart, for it realises that evil actions are an expression of an inner disposition. Religion calls and inspires its adherents to a change of heart, a heart of forgiveness, compassion and love. For religious believers God is essentially and radically relational, and everything that contributes to the well being of of the human person is also contributing to humankind's salvation.

The United Nations recognises the importance that the world religions play in promoting peace and well being globally. In its preamble to the Earth Charter it states. 'The protection of the earth's vitality, diversity and beauty is a sacred trust.'

We are realizing more and more that everything is interconnected and interrelated. Human life is grounded in our relationship with our neighbour. The natural world is woven together and we are to learn to live with one another. Valuing each other. The Cosmologist William Stoeger writes of entities constituted by patterns of relationships that are nested upon one another, each entity is interrelated with, and dependent upon, the Sun and the solar system, the Milky Way Galaxy, our Local Group of Galaxies, Human fulfilment is radically relational, we grow more and mature more, to the extent that we enter into relationship.

This is why it is so important for the world's religions to come together and work for the wellbeing of humanity. It is integral that people of religious faith, work with all people of good will. We all have friends and acquaintances who have no religious faith but are nonetheless good living people concerned for the well being of their local community and wider world. Let's work with those people to inspire them to work towards a better world.

It is important that we acknowledge the past, with all of its nobility and horror. Our past is part of the tapestry of who we are. Forgiveness makes it possible to weave past sad experiences into this tapestry, so that we can be at peace with ourselves and with our fellow men and women.

Having completed this book, I feel close to you, the reader, who gained an insight into the suffering of the Croatian people during the twentieth century, the causes of the Croatian–Serbian conflict and what the peoples of the former Yugoslavia lived through. Let us commit ourselves to work towards a lasting peace. No more war. We start with ourselves in our families, our neighbourhood and the wider world. Supporting all humanitarian organizations that work for the betterment of humankind. At times it will be difficult, sometimes disappointing. At times we might feel like we have failed. Let us have realistic goals but unlimited hope for we know that truth, justice and goodness will prevail. Friedrich Nietzsche wrote: 'If you have a why, then you can cope with any how.' There is no more noble cause than working for the collective wellbeing of humanity. Let us move forward, embracing the future and loving the future with the knowledge and faith that we will succeed.

Bibliography

Akrap Dr sc Gordan, *Kardinal Stepinac u Dokumentima Gestapa i Ozne* (Cardinal Stepinac in the Documents of the Gestapo and Ozna) Published by the Societies of St Juraj, Glas Koncila & Laser plus, Zagreb 2016. ISBN Society of St Juraj: 978-953-96313-3-6. ISBN Glas Koncila: 978-953-241-509-4.

Alexander Stella, *The Triple Myth, A Life of Archbishop Alojzije Stepinac*, East European Monographs, No. CCXXVI. Columbia University Press, New York 1987. ISBN O-88033-122-4.

Andrew Christopher & Gordievsky Oleg, *KGB The Inside Story*, Hodder & Stoughton. First Published in Great Britain 1990. Printed by Butler & Tanner Ltd, Frome and London. ISBN 0-340-48561-2.

Arnold Johann Christoph, *Why Forgive?* Published by Orbis Books, Maryknoll, New York 10545, November 2012. ISBN: 978-1-57075-876-8.

Baković don Anto. *Svečenici Žrtva Rata i Poraca 1941–1945. Stradanja Crkve u Hrvata u Drugom Svjetskom Ratu* (Priests, The Suffering of the Church in Croatia during the Second World War 1941–45). Editor: don Anto Baković. Printed by August Šenoa, Ilica 35, Zagreb, Croatia. 1994.

Balfour Neil & Mackay Sally, *Paul of Yugoslavia Britain's Maligned Friend*, Hamish Hamilton, London, 1980. Printed by Ebenezer Baylis and Son Ltd, Trinity Press, London. ISBN: 0-241-10392-4.

Barnett Neil, *Tito*. Published in Britain in 2006 by Haus Publishing Limited, 26 Cadogan Court London SW3 3BX. ISBN: 1-904950-31-0.

Barbarić Ilija, *Nezavisna Država Htvatska Bilo Joj Pravo Ime* (The Independent State of Croatia Was Her True Name). Publishe by Bošković, Split. 2010. Printed by Grafotisak. ISBN: 978-953-263-126-5.

Basta Milan, *Rat je završen 7 dana kasnije* (The War Ended Seven Days Later). Edited by Milan L Gojković. The fourth, complete and expanded edition. Printed by GRO Liburnija, Rjeka. Published by Pres Kliping. Knez Mihajlova 2/1X street Belgrade, Croatia. 1982.

Batelja Juraj, Alojzije Stepinac, Nadbiskup Zagrebacki: *Propovijedi, Poruke, Govori. 1934-1940* (Sermons, Messages and Speeches). Priredio i pregovor napisao Dr Juraj Batelja. Tiskara Puljeko, Zagreb, Croatia. 2000

Batelja Juraj, *Crna Knjiga o grozovitostima Komunističke vladavine u Hrvatskoj* (The Black Book of the Cruelty of Communist Rule in Croatia). Published by Dr Juraj Batelja. Printed by Zrinski dd Cakovec. ISBN 953-97221-3-6. Zagreb, Coatia. 2000.

Batelja Juraj, *Pisma iz suzanjstva* (Letters from House Arrest) (1951-1960). Editor Dr Juraj Batelja. Printed and binding by Tiskara Puljko, Zagreb, Croatia. ISBN 953-97221-0-1.

Batelja J & Tomič C, Alojzije Kardinal Stepinac. *Propovjedi, Govori, Poruke* (Sermons, Talks, Messages). (1941-1946). Published by The Postulara for the canonization of the servant of God Cardinal Alojzija Stepinac, Zagreb, Kaptol 31, AGM, Zagreb, Mihanoviceva 28, Croatia. 1996. ISBN: 953 – 174 – 054 – 2.

Batelja Juraj, *Sluga Božiji Alojzije Stepinac* (The Servant of God Aloysius Stepinac). Publisher: Nadbiskupski Duhovni Stol in Zagreb, Kaptol 31, Croatia. 1995.

Bauer Ernest, *Slava i Tragika Hrvata* (The Glory and Tragedy of Croatians) Published by Harold Druck und Verlag, Vienna, 1973.

Bauer Ernest. *Zivot Je Kratak San Uspomene 1910-1985* (Life is a Short Dream Memories 1910-1985). Knjizica Hrvatske Revije. Barcelona – Munchen, 1986. Urednik: Vinko Nikolić. Printed in Spain. ISBN 84 – 599 – 6811-1. Deposito Legal. B. 25780-86. Egs – Rosario, 2-Barcelona, Spain.

Beljo Ante for the publisher, *Bleiburg 1945-1995. A International Symposium Zagreb 12*th- *13*th *May 1995*. Published by the Croatian Heritage Foundation. Editor In Chief: Aleksander Ravlić. Printed by Targa, Zagreb, Croatia. ISBN: 953-6525-07-0.

Beljo Ante, *Yugoslavia Genocide A Documented Analysis*, Northern Tribune Publishing. Sudbury 1985. Translated by D Sladojević – Šola, Cover Design: Berislav Fabek. ISBN: 0-919817-07-6.

Beloff Nora, *Tito's Flawed Legacy Yugoslavia and the West: 1939-84*. Published by Victor Gollancz Ltd, 14 Henrietta Street, London WC2E 8QJ. 1985. ISBN: 0-575-03668-0.

Benigar Aleksa, *Alojzia Stepinac, Hrvatski Kardinal* (Aloysious Stepinac, Croatian Cardinal). 11 popravljeno i prošireno izdanje (an updated and developed edition) Zagreb 1993. Edited Glas Koncila, Zagreb, Kaptol 8 and the Croatian Franciscan Province of St Cyril and Mythodius in Zagreb, Kaptol 9. Printed by Zrinski, Čakovac, Croatia.

Berkovits Eliezer, *With God in Hell: Judaism in the Ghettos and Deathcamps*, Sanhedrin Press, 80 Fifth Avenue, New York, NY 10011. Printed in the United States of America. 1979. ISBN: 0-88482-937-5.

Bilić-Erić Mirko, *Sluga Domovine život hrvatskog viteza Vjekoslava Maksa Luburića general Drinjanina* (The Servant of the Homeland the life of the Croatian Knight Vjekoslav Maxs Luburić the general from the Drina). Published by Mirko Bilić – Erić. Zagreb, Croatia. 2018. ISBN: 978-3-00-059584-4.

Bjelovučić Dr. Nikola Zvonimir, *Crvena Hrvatska i Dubrovnik* (Red Croatia and Dubrovnik) Published by Matica Hrvatska. MCMXXIX. (1929) Printed by *Narodnih Novina*, Zagreb, Croatia.

Bonifačić, Prof Antun F, Mihanovich, Prof Clement S *The Croatian Nation in its Struggle for Freedom and Independence*, A Symposium by Seventeen Croatian Writers. "Croatia" Cultural Publishing Center. 4851 Drexel Bulavarde, Chicago, Illinois. 1955. Printed in the United States of America.

Burnheim John, *To Reason Why From Religion to Philosophy and Beyond*, Darlington Press 2011. ISBN: 9781921364143 (Paper Back).

Capra Fritjof, *The Web of Life. A New Synthesis of Mind and Matter*. First published in Great Britain by Harper Collins, 1996. ISBN: 0 00 654751 6.

Carroll Warren H, *The Crises of Christendom*, A History of Christendom Series. Volume 6. Published in USA by Christendom Press. 134 Christendom Drive, Front Royal, VA 22630. 2013.

Clift Wallace B, *Jung and Christianity, The Challenge of Reconciliation*. Dove Communications Melbourne, Australia. 1983. ISBN: 0 85924 243 9.

Coffey David M, *The Sacrament of Reconciliation*, Lex Orandi Series. John D Laurence, SJ Editor, The Liturgical Press, Collegeville, Minnesota, USA, 2001. ISBN: 0-8146-2519-3.

Čović Bože, *Croatian Between War and Independence*. Published by The University of Zagreb and OKC Zagreb. Zagreb, November 1991. Printed by Durieux doo, Smodekova St Zagreb, Croatia.

Čović Bože, Editor, *Roots of Serbian Aggression*. Debates, Documents, Cartographic Reviews. Published by Centre for Foreign Languages, Zagreb, Croatia. Printed by Grafički zavod Hrvatske, 1993. ISBN: 953 – 174 – 001 – 1.

Courtois Stephane, Werth Nicolas, Panne Jean-Louis, Paczkowski Andrzej, Bartosek Karel, Margolin Jean-Louis, *The Black Book of Communism: Crimes, Terror, Repression*, Harvard University Press, Cambridge, Massachusetts, London, England. Third printing, 2000. ISBN: 0-674-07608-7.

Dabinović Antun, *Hrvatska Povjest* (Croatian History) Published by Bošković, Split, Croatia, 2002. ISBN: 953-98940-0-X.

Dallas Gregor, *Poisoned Peace, 1945, the War that Never Ended,* John Murray Publishers, Paper Back edition, London, 2006.

Davidson Basil. *Partisan Picture,* Bedford Books Ltd, Bedford. Printed in England by Diemer & Reynolds Ltd, Bedford, England, 1946.

Davie Michael. *The Diaries of Evelyn Waugh*, George Weindenfeld And Nicolson Limited. 11 St John's Hill, London, SW 11. 1976. ISBN: 0 297 77126 4.

Deakin F. William D, *The Embattled Mountain,* Oxford University Press, Ely House, London W1, 1971. ISBN: 0 19 215175 4.

Dedijer Vladimir, *Tito Speaks. His Self Portrait and Struggle with Stalin.* Weidenfeld and Nicolson, 7 Cork Street, London, W1, Printed by Jarrold and Sons Limited, Norwich. First Published 1953.

Dedijer Vladimir, *The Road To Sarajevo,* First published 1967 by Macgibbon & Kee Ltd. Printed in Great Britain by Cox & Wyman Ltd, London, Fakenham and Reading.

Dixon Norman, *On the Psychology of Military Incompetence,* Printed and bound by CPI Group (UK) Ltd. Croydon, CRO 4YY. Pimlico edition 1994. ISBN: 9780712658898.

Djilas Milovan, *Conversations with Stalin*, Rupert Hart-Davis Ltd, Soho Square London W1, 1962.

Djilas Milovan, *Memoir of a Revolutionary*, Harcourt Brace Jovanovich, Inc, New York, 1973. ISBN: 0-15-158850-3.

Djilas Milovan, *Parts of a Lifetime,* Harcourt Brace Jovanovich, New York and London, 1975. ISBN: 0-15-170969-6.

Djilas Milovan, *Wartime,* Harcourt Brace Jovanovich, Inc, First edition, 1977. Printed in USA. ISBN: 0-15-194609-4.

Djilas Milovan, *Rise and Fall*, Hardcourt Brace Jovanovic, Publishers, New York. 1983. ISBN: 0-15-177572-9.

Djilas Milovan, *Tito the Story from Inside*, First published in Great Britain in 1981 by George Weidenfeld and Nicolson Ltd, 1981. ISBN: 0 297 77885 4.

Dujmović Franjo, *Hrvatska na putu k Oslobodjenja* (Croatia on the Road to Freedom). ZIRAL (Zajednica Izdanja Ranjeni Labud). Roma – Chicago, 1976. Main editor: Prof Dr Vinko D Lasić, Knjiga 12. Tipografia A, Picchi – Villa Adriana – Tivoli, Italy.

Draganović Dr Krunoslav and Butorac Josip, *Povjest Crkve u Hrvatskoj* (The History of the Church in Croatia). Published by Hrvatsko Književno Društvo Sv Jeronima, Zagreb 1944. Printed by Milan Šufflaya printers in Zagreb, Croatia.

Esih Bruna prof, *Bleiburg Tragedy and Hope*, published by Glas Koncila, Kaptol 8, Zagreb, Croatia, 2008. ISBN: 978-953-241-133-1.

Eterovich Francis H & Spalatin Christopher, *Croatia, Land, People, Culture*. Volume 1, published by University of Toronto Press, Canada. 1964. ISBN: 0-8020-3122-6.

Eterovich Francis H & Spalatin Christopher, *Croatia, Land, People, Culture*, Volume 11. Published by University of Toronto Press, Canada. 1970. ISBN: 0-8020-3226-5.

Fotitch Constantin, *The War We Lost Yugoslavia's Tragedy and the Failure of the West*, published in New York by Viking Press, 1948. Printed by American Book-Stratford Press.

Gitman Dr Esther, *When Courage Prevailed. The Rescue and Survival of Jews in the Independent State of Croatia 1941–1945*. Published by Paragon House 1925, Oakcrest Avenue St Paul, MN 55113. 2011, USA. ISBN: 978-1-55778-894-8.

Gitman Dr Esther, *Alojzije Stepinac – Pillar of Human Rights*, published by Kršćansko sadašnjost d.o.o., Zagreb, Maruličev trg 14. ISBN: 978-953-11-1198-0 and Hrvatsko katoličko sveučiliste, Zagreb, Ilica 242, Croatia. January 2019. ISBN: 978-8014-27-7.

Goreta Thea, *Hrvatski Kočkasti Grb* (Croatian Chequered Coat of Arms). *Hrvatska Revija* (Croatian Review). Edited by Vinko Nikolić: Apartado de Correos 14030 – 08017 Barcelona, Spain, Volume 35, March 1985.

Gračanin Hrvoje, *Kratka Povjest Hrvatske za Mlade od Kraja 18og Stoječa do Početku 21og Stoljeca* (A Short History of Croatia for the Youth from the End of the 18th Century to the Beginning of the 21st Century). Published by Sysprint doo. Zagreb, Croatia. 2006. ISBN: 953-232-110-1.

Grahek Ravančić Martina, *Bleiburg i Križni Put 1945* (Bleiburg and the Way of the Cross 1945), published by the Croatian Institute of History, Zagreb, Croatia. 2009. Printed by Zelina printing, Sv Ivan Zelina. ISBN: 978-953-6324-79-8.

Grčić Marko, *Bleiburg Otvoreni Dossier* (Bleiburg Open Dossier). Published by Vjesnik, Zagreb, Croatia. Printed by Tisak revijalnih izdanja Avenue Bratsva and Jedinstva 4. Zagreb, Croatia.

Hastings Adrian, *Nationalism, Genocide and Justice*, 255–260. In *Priest and People*. The Tablet Publishing Company Limited. Clifton Walk, London. July 1999. Volume 13, No 7.

Hecimovic Joseph, *In Tito's Death Marches and Extermination Camps*. Translated and Edited by John Prcela. A Reflection book, Carlton Press, New York, USA. 1962.

Horvat Josip, *Politička Povjest Hrvatske* (Political History of Croatia) Volume 1 Second Edition. Published by August Cesarec, Zagreb, Croatia. 1990. ISBN: 86-393-0151-4. ISBN: 86-393-0152-2.

Horvat Josip, *Politička Povjest Hrvatske* (Political History of Croatia 1918–1929) Volume 2. Second Edition. Published by August Cesarec, Zagreb, Croatia. 1990. ISBN: 86-393-0151-4. ISBN: 86-393-0153-0.

Horvat Romana, *Represija i Zločini Komunističkog Režima u Hrvatskoj* (Repression and Crimes of the Communist Regime in Croatia) Published by Matica Hrvatska, Zagreb 2012. ISBN: 978-953-150-968-8. It contains two articles in this book. One by Vladimir Geiger. *Brojibeni Pokazatelji O Ljudskim Gubicima Hrvatske U Drugome Svjetskom Ratu i Poraću* (The Number of Human Croatian Losses in The Second World War and Afterwards). Second by Michael Portmann, *Nasilje Tijekom Izgradnje Države i Društva Komunističke Jugoslavije (1944–1946).* The Aggression During the Building the State and Society in Communist Yugoslavia (1944–1946).

Hrvatski Mučenići i Žrtve iz Komunističke Vladavine (Croatian Martyrs and Suffering During Communist Rule). By the Commission of the Conference of Catholic Bishops of Croatia and of Bosnia Hercegovina. Published by Glas Koncila Zagreb, Croatia. 2013. ISBN: 978-953-241-392-2.

Isaacson Walter, *Einstein His Life and Universe*. Published by Simon and Schuster. New York, USA. 2007. ISBN: 978-0-7432-6473-0

Ivurek Mijo, *Život i Djelo Krunoslava Draganovića 1903–1983* (The Life and Work of Krunoslav Draganović 1903–1983.) Published by the Croatian Cultural Society Napredak, Sarajevo, Croatia. 2013. ISBN: 978-953-7604-02-5.

Jareb Mario, *Ustaško-domobranski pokret od nastanka do travnja 1941 godine* (The Ustaša-homeguard movement from its beginning to April 1941). Published by Školska knjiga, d.d. Zagreb, Masarykova st. 28. Second edition, September 2007. Printed by Grafički zavod Hrvatske, doo. ISBN: 978-953-0-60817-7.

Jones L Gregory, *Embodying Forgiveness: A Theological Analysis,* Eerdmans, Grand Rapids, Michigan, USA. 1995. ISBN: 978-0-8028-0861-5.

Jonić Tomislav & Matijević Zlatko, *Hrvatsk Izmedju Slobode i Jugoslavenstva* (Croatia Between Freedom and Yugoslavianism). Symposium held in Zagreb on 8 & 9 January 2009. Published by Naklada Trpimir, Zagreb, Croatia. 2009. ISBN: 978-953-55421-1-7.

Jug Dr sc Damir, *Oružane Snage NDH Sveukupni Ustroj* (The Armed Forces of the Independent State of Croatia its General Structure). Published by Nova Stvarnost, Zagreb, Croatia. 2004. ISBN: 953-6562-23-5.

Jung Carl Gustav, MD, *Psychology and Religion*, Yale Universaty Press, New Haven and London. Copyright 1938. Printed in USA by The Vail-Ballou Press, Inc, New York, USA. ISBN: 0-300-00137.

Jurčević Josip, Esih Bruna, Vukučić Bože, *Čuvari Bleiburčke Uspomene* (Guardians of Bleiburg's Memories). Published by the Club of Croatian Returnee's, Stejpan Radić Square 3, 10000 Zagreb, Croatia. Second edition, 2005. ISBN: 953-97963-6-9.

Jurčević Josip PhD, *The Black Book of Communism in Croatia*, Publisher: The Croatian Herald, Melbourne, 1st May 2006. ISBN: 0 – 646 – 46046 – 3.

Jurčević Josip, *Prikrivena Stratišta i Grobišta Jugoslavenski Komunističkih Zločina* (Covered Places of Execution and Graves of Yugoslav Communist Crimes). Published by Grafički zavod Htvatske, Zagreb, Croatia. May 2012. ISBN: 978-953-95043-5-7.

Jurišić Fra Mario. *Lovrečki Mučenici.* (The Martyrs of Lovreć). Printed by Franjo Kluz d.d. Omiš, Croatia. 2006.

Kačić Hrvoje. *Dubrovačke Žrtve Jugokomunistički Teror Na Hrvatskom Jugu 1944 i Poratnim Godinama* (Dubrovniks Sacrifices Jugocommunist Terror on Croatia's South 1944 and Post War Years). Published by Gea, Zagreb, Croatia. 2009. ISBN 987-953-7604-03-05.

Kamber Dragutin (1901-1969). *Pavelićeva Baština.* (Pavelić's Inheritance). Hrvatska Revija. Edited by Vinko Nikolić. March 1981. Printed in Spain.

Karapandzich Borivoje M. *The Bloodiest Yugoslav Spring 1945 – Tito's Katyns and Gulags.* A Hearthstone Book. Carlton Press, Inc. New York. Printed in USA. 1980. ISBN 0-8062-1455-Y.

Katalinić Kazimir. *Argumenti NHD, BiH, Bleiburg i genocide* (Arguments, NDH, BiH and genocide.) Published by periodical 'Republika Hrvatska', Zagreb, Croatia. 1993. ISBN: 953-6155-00-1.

Karaula Marijan. *Iskušenja Bosne Srebrene Stradanja Bosanski Franjevaca 1944-1985.* (The Trials of Bosnia Argentina, Suffering of the Bosnian Franciscans 1944-1985) Pubished by Synopsis d.o.o., Zagreb. Synopsis d.o.o., Sarajevo, Croatia. 2014. ISBN. 978-953-7968-13-7 Zagreb. 978-9958-587-99-3 Sarajevo.

Karaula |Želko. *Maćekova Vojska Hrvastka Seljačka Zaštita u Kraljevini Jugoslaviji.* (Maćekć's Army The Croatian Village Diffence in Monachical Yugoslavia). Published by Despot Infinitus d. o. o. Zagreb, Croatia. 2015. ISBN: 978-953-7892-42-5.

Keating Thomas. *Fruits and Gifts of the Spirit.* Lantern Books, A Division of Booklight Inc. New York, NY 10003, USA. 2000. ISBN 1-930051-21-2.

Kemp Helen. *Ubuntu: Caught Up In The Bundle Of Life.* This Essay took the Silver Award in the Royal Dutch Shell Economist Essay Competition in 2002.

Kindermann Gottfried-Karl. *Osterrich gegen Hitler Europas erste Abwehrfront 1933-1938* (Austria against Hitler, Europes first Defence 1933-1938). Langen Muller. Printed by Wiener Verlag, Vienna, Austria. 2003. ISBN 3-7844-2821-5.

Kisić Kolanović Nada. *Muslimani i Hrvatski Nacionalisam 1941-1945* (Muslims and Croatian Nationalism 1941-1945). *Hrvatski Insitut Za Povjest* (The Croatian Institute for History). Published by Školska knjiga, d.d. Masarykova 28, Zagreb, Croatia. 2009.

Klaić Vjekoslav. *Povjest Hrvata* (The History of Croatians). Knjiga Prva (Volume 1) Published by Nakladni Zavod Matice Hrvatske, Zagreb, Croatia. 1988. Edited by Igor Zidić. Printed by Tiskara Rijeka, Croatia. ISBN 86-401-0051-9. and ISBN 86-401-0063-2.

Klaić Vjekoslav. *Povjest Hrvata* (The History of Croatians). Knjiga Druga (Volume 2). Published by Nakladni Zavod Matice Hrvatske, Zagreb, Croatia. 1988. Edited by Igor Zidić. Printed by Tiskara Rjeka, Croatia. ISBN 86-401-0051-9. and ISBN 86-401-0075-6.

Klaić Vjekoslav. *Povjest Hrvata* (The History of Croatians). Knjiga Treca (Volume 3). Published by Nakladni Zavod Matice Hrvatske, Zagreb, Croatia. 1988. Edited by Igor Zidić. Printed by Tiskara Rjeka, Croatia. ISBN 86-401-0051-9 and ISBN 86-401-0087-X.

Klaić Vjekoslav. *Povjest Hrvata* (The History of Croatians). Knjiga Cetvrta (Volume 4). Published by Nakladni Zavod Matice Hrvatske. Zagreb, Croatia. 1988. Edited by Igor Zidić. Printed by Tiskara Rjeka. ISBN 86-401-0051-9, ISBN 86-401-0099-3

Klaić Vjekoslav. *Povjest Hrvata* (The History of Croatians). Knjiga Peta (Volume 5). Published by Nakladni Zavod Matice Hrvatske, Zagreb, Croatia. 1988. Edited by Igor Zidić. Printed by Tiskara Rjeka. 1988. ISBN 86-401-0051-9 ISBN 86-401-0111-6

Kljaković Jozo. *U Suvremenom Kaosu Uspomene i Doživljaji* (In Contemporary Chaos Memories and life's experiences). Published by Matica Hrvatska, Zagreb, Croatia. 2011. ISBN: 978-953-150-947-3.

Knežović Dr Fra Oton. *Poviest Hrvata* (The History of the Croats) Volume 1. Publishers: Hrvatski Nakladni Zavod, Domovina. Madrid – Buenos Aires, Argentina. 1961. Deposito Legal: M. 4618 – 1961. No Rgtro. 5645 – 61.

Krišto Jure. *Sukob Simbola Politika, vjera i ideologia u Nezavisnoj Državi Hrvatskoj* (Clash of Symbols Politics, Religion and Ideology in the Independent State of Croatia). Edited by Jere Jareb. Published by Globus, Zagreb, Croatia. 2001. ISBN 953-167-133-8.

Krizman Bogdan. *Ante Pavelić i Uštaši*. (Ante Pavelić and the Ustaši). Second Edition. Published by Globus, Zagreb. Printed by Delo, Ljubljana, Croatia. 1983.

Krizman Bogdan. *Ustaši i Treči Reich* (The Ustaši and the Third Reich) Volume 2 Edited by Dragovan Sepic. Printed by Delo, Ljubljana, Croatia. Published by Globus, Zagreb, Croatia. 1983.

Krizman Bogdan. *Pavelić Izmedju Hitlera i Mussolinija* (Pavelic Between Hitler and Mussolini) Published by Globus, Zagreb. Printed by CGP Delo, Ljubljana, Croatia. 1980.

Krizman Bogdan. *Pavelić u Bjekstvu* (Pavelić in Flight). Published by Globus, Zagreb. Printed by CGP Delo, Ljubljana, Croatia. 1986. YU ISBN 86-343-0139-7.

Kumm Otto. *Prince Eugen. The History of the 7 SS Mountain Division Prince Eugen.* Published by JJ Fedorowicz Publishing Inc 106 Browning Blvd Winnipeg, Manitoba, Canada. 1995. Printed in the USA. ISBN 0-921991-29-0.

Kushner Harold S. *When Bad Things Happen to Good People.* Anchor Books, Random House, Inc New York, USA. 2004. ISBN: 1-4000-3472-8.

Lamb Christopher. *The Bruised Peacemaker. The Tablet*, 1 King Street Cloisters, Clifton Walk, London W6 OGY, UK. 16 September 2017.

Lawrence Christie. *Irregular Adventure.* Faber and Faber Limited 24 Russell Square London, UK. 1946.

Leljak Roman. *Huda Jama Strogo Čuvana Tajna* (Huda Pit a Strictly Kept Secret). Published by Hrvatsko Zrtvoslovno Društvo, Zagreb, Croatia. 2015. ISBN: 978-953-7817-10-7.

Leljak Roman. *Maribor: Največe stratište Hrvata* (Maribor: Largest Place of Execution of Croatian's). Published by Društvo ya rayiskovanje zgodovine, Kapelske cesta, 1, 2000 Maribor, Croatia. 2017. Printed by Letis doo Čakovec, Croatia. ISBN: 978-961-285-962-6.

Lepre George. *Himmler's Bosnian Division The Waffen –SS Handschar Division 1943-1945.* Published by Schiffer Publishing Ltd. 4880 Lower Valley Road, Alglen, PA 19310, USA. 1997. ISBN: 0-7643-0134-9.

Mačan Trpimir. *Povjest Hrvatskog Naroda* (The History of the Croatian People). Published by Nakladni Zavod Matice Hrvatske. Školska Knjiga (School Book) Zagreb Main Editor: Branimir Donat. Editor: Dubravko Horvatić. 1992. Printed by Hrvatska Tiskara doo Zagreb, Croatia. ISBN 86-401-0058-6.

Mačan Trpimir & Šentija Josip. *A Short History of Croatia.* Published with Croatian PEN Centre, Atlantik Papir and Matica Hrvatska. Zagreb, Croatia. 1992.

Maček Vladko. *Memoari* (Memoirs). Published by Hrvatsk Seljačka Strank. Zagreb 1992. Naklada Zavod Zagreb. Urednik: Zlatko Crnković, Croatia. Arranged by: ing Boris Urbić.

Macmillan Harold. *Tides of Fortune 1945-1955.* Macmillan Publishers, London, 1969.

Maclean Fitzroy. *Tito A Pictorial Biography.* A McGraw-Hill Co-Publication. United Kingdom. 1980. ISBN 0-333-31003-9

Maclean Fitzroy. *Eastern Approaches.* Published by J Cape. London, UK. 1949. ISBN: 9780141042848. (pbk)

Mandić Dr. Domenik. *Bogomilska Crkva Bosanski Krštjana* (The Bogomil Church of Bosnian Christians). Published by Ziral Chicago-Rome-Zurich-Toronto 1979. Printed by ESCA – Vicenza, Italy. Edited by Vinko D. Lasić

Mandić Dr Domenik. *Bosna i Hercegovina Povjestno- Kriticno Istraživanja* (Bosna and Herzegovina a Critical Historical Study). Published by the Croatian Historical Institute P.O. Box 8353, Chicago 80, Illinois, USA. 1960.

Mandić Dr Dominik. *Crvena Hrvatska u svjetlu povijesnih izvora* (Red Croatia in the Light of Historical Souces). Published by the Community of Ranjeni Labud (ZIRAL), Croatia. August 1972. Main Editor Vinko D Lasić.

Mandić Dr Domenik. *Hrvati i Srbi Dva Stara i Različita Naroda* (Croatians and Serbs Two Old and Different Peoples). Published by Hrvatska Revija in Barcelona, Spain on 13 March 1971. Printed by EGS, Rosario 2, Barcelona 17, Spain.

Mandić Domenik. *Hrvatske Zemlje u Prošlosti i Sadašnjosti* (Croatian Lands in the Past and Present). Published by Ziral. Chicago-Rome 1973. Second Edition. Editor Vinko D Lasić.

Mandić Domenik. *Za Hrvatstvo i Hrvatsku Drzavnost* (For Croatia and Croatian Statehood). Published by Hrvatska Revije, Munchen – Barcelona, Printed in Spain EGS – Rosario, 2 – Barcelona, Spain. 1973. ISBN: 84-399-0102-X.

Marević Dr Jozo. Editor. *50 Godina Bleiburga* (50 Years of Bleiburg). A collection of papers on Bleiburg and the Way of the Cross held at a International Symposium on Bleiburg held in Zagreb, Croatia. 14–15 May 1995. Printed by Croatiaprojekt, Croatia. 1995. ISBN: 953-6321-01-7.

Marjanović Professor Jovan with collaboration of Mihailo Stanišić MA. *The Collaboration of D Mihailović's Četniks with the Enemy Forces of Occupation 1941 – 1944.* Published by: Arhivski pregled, Belgrade, Karnedzijeva 2, Croatia. Printed by: Servis Saveza, Proleterska brigade 74. Belgrade, Croatia. 1976.

Marjanović Jovan. *Draže Mihailović izmedu Britanaca i Nemaca* (Draže Mihaljević between the British and Germans). Volume 1. Published by CGP Delo, Ljubljana, Slovenia, Croatia. 1979.

Marković Marko. *Jure i Boban Povijest Crne Legije* (Jure and Boban the History of the Black Legion). Published by MBF – Tomislavgrad, Bosnia-Hercegovina. April 2003.

Masucci Giuseppe Dr, OSB. *Misija u Hrvatskoj* (Mission to Croatia). Edited by Drinina Knjiznica. Apartado 5024 – Madrid, Spain. 1967. Printed by Drinapress, Apartado 1523, Valencia, Spain. Prepared for publishing: Marijan Mikac.

Matković Hrvoje. *Povjest Nezavisne Države Hrvatske* (The History of the Independent State of Croatia). Second edition. Published by Naklada Pavičić, Zagreb, Croatia, 2002.

McAleese Mary. *Love in Chaos, Spiritual Growth and the Search for Peace in Northern Ireland.* A Media Media Book. The Continuum Publishing Company 370 Lexington Avenue New York, USA. 1999.

Mestrović Ivan. *Uspomene Na Politicke Ljude i Dogodjaje* (Memories on Political People and Events). Published by Matica Hrvatska, Zagreb, Croatia. 1969. Printed by Ognjen Prica, Zagreb, Croatia. 1969.

Mestrović Maria. *Život i Djelo Ivana Mestrovića* (The Life and Work of Ivan Mestrovic). Published by Matica Hrvatska, Zagreb, Croatia. 2008. ISBN 978-953-150-876-6

Mijatović Anđelko. *Bleiburg 1945–1995. A International Symposium in Zagreb 12–13 May 1995.* Printed by Targa. Published by Hrvatska Matica Iseljenika 1997. ISBN 953-6525-07-0.

Mijatović Anđelko. *Bitka Na Krbavskom Polju 1493* (The Battle on the Krbavska Field 1493). Published by Školska Knjiga, Zagreb, Croata. 2005. ISBN 953-0-61429-2.

Moran Herbert M. *Viewless Winds, being the Recollections and Digressions of an Australian Surgeon.* Peter Davies Publisher, London. Printed in Great Britain at Windmill Press, Kingswood, Surry, UK. First Published in 1939.

Moore Gerard sm, Editor. *The Hunger for Reconciliation in Society and Church.* Published by St Pauls Publications, Sydney, Australia. 2004. ISBN: 1 876295 86 4.

Mužić Ivan. *Katolička Crkva, Stepinac i Pavelić* (The Catholic Church, Stepinac and Pavelic). Marjan Tisak, Split. 111 Izdanje, Croatia. 2003. ISBN 953-214-008-5.

Nevistić Franjo. *Za Slobodu Čovjeka i Hrvatskog Naroda* (For the Freedom of the Human Person and the Croatian People). Arranged by Blažena and Milan Blažeković. A Collection of Articles and Essays 1938–1984. Published by Knižnica Hrvatske Revije, Barcelona-Munchen, 1989. ISBN: 84-599-9882-7.

Nikčević Milorad Prof dr sc. *Josip Juraj Strossmayer i Nikola I. Petrović Njegoš u Korespondenciji i Dokumentima* (Joseph George Strossmayer and Nikola I. Petrović Njegoš in Correspondence and Documentation). Published by Nakladnik in Osjek, Croatia. December 2009. ISBN 978-953-7589-01-1.

Nikolić Vinko. *Stepinac Mu Je Ime* (Stepinac is his Name). Knjižica Hrvatske Revije. Munchen – Barcelona, 1978. Knjiga Prva. Printed in Spain. EGS – Rosario, 2- Barcelona, Spain. ISBN 84-399-9315-3.

Nevistić Franjo & Nikolić Vinko. *Bleiburgsa Tragedia Hrvatskog Naroda* (The Bleiburg Tragedy of the Croatian People). Knjižica Hrvatske Revije (A Book of the Croatian Revue) Munchen – Barcelona, Spain. 1976. Printed in Spain. ISBN: 84-399-5386-0.

Nikolić Vinko. *Tragedija Se Dogodila u Svibnju* (The Tragedy Happened in May) Volume 1. Knjižica Hrvatske Revije. Barcelona – Munich, 1984. Printed in Spain. ISBN 499-8066-6

Nikolić Vinko. *Tragedija Se Dogodila u Svibnju* (The Tragedy Happened in May). Volume 2. Knjižica Hrvatske Revije. Barcelona – Munich, Spain – Germany. 1985. Printed in Spain. ISBN 84-599-5507-9.

Nikolić Vinko. *Bleiburg: Uzroci i Posljedice* (Bleiburg: Causes and Consequences) Published by Hrvatska Revije. Munich – Barcelona, Germany – Spain. 1988. Printed in Spain. ISBN: 84-599-8605-5. (Tela)

Nikolić Vinko. *Mile Budak: Pjesnik i Mučenik Hrvatske* (Mile Budak: Poet and Croatia's Martyr). In Commemoration of the Centenary of His Birth 1889–1989. Published by Hrvatska Revije. Barcelona – Munchen, Spain – Germany. 1990. Printed in Spain. ISBN 84-599-4619-3.

O'Brien Anthony Henry, Count of Thomond. *Archbishop Stepinac The Man and His Case*. Standard House, Peace Street. Printed by Wood Printing, First published, March 1947. Dublin. Ireland.

Obhađaš Amir. *The Ustaša Army. The Armed forces of the Ustaša Movement in the Independent State of Croatia 1941–1945*. Photo Album. Published by Despot Infinitus doo, Zagreb, Croatia. 2016. ISBN: 978-953-7892-51-7.

Obhođaš Amir, Werhas Mario, Dimitrijević Bojan, Despot Zvonimir. *Ustaška Vojnica i Oružana sila Ustaškog pokreta u Nezavisnoj državi Hrvatskoj 1941–1945* (The Ustaša Army. The armed forces of the Ustaša movement in the Independent State of Croatia 1941–1945). The first book, Volume 1, April 1941- Rujan 1943. Published by Despot Infinitus doo. Zagreb, Croata. 2013. ISBN: 978-953-7892-10-4.

Obhodaš Amir Werhas Mario, Dimitrijević Bojan, Despot Zvonimir. *Ustaška Vojnica. Oružna sila Ustaškog pokreta u Nezavisnoj Državi Hrvatskoj 1941–1945* (The Ustaša Army. The Armed forces of the Ustaša movement in the Independent State of Croatia 1941–1945). Volume 2 from Rujan 1943- May 1945. Published by Despot Infinitus doo. Uskopska ulica 9. Zagreb, Croatia. 2013. ISBN: 978-953-7892-17-3.

Olson Lynne & Cloud Stanley. *For Your Freedom and Ours*. The Kosciuszko Squadron: Forgotten Heroes of World War 11. Published in United Kingdom by Arrow Books. 20 Vauxhall Bridge Road, London, SW1V 2SA, UK. 2004. Printed in UK by CPI Bookmarque, Croydon, CRO 4TD, UK. ISBN 9780099428121

O'Malley John W. *Vatican 1 The Council and the Making of the Ultramontane Church*. Printed by Belknap Press of Harvard University, USA. 2018. ISBN: 9780674979987.

Oršanic Ivan. *Vizija Slobode* (Vision of Freedom). Edited by Professor Kazimir Katalinić. Published by Dubrovnik publications. Chicago, Il.60659. USA. 1990.

Omrčanin Ivo. *Hrvatska 1941* (Croatia 1941) Volume 1. Printed by IVOR PRESS. 700 New Hampshire Avenue, NW Washington, DC 20037, USA. 1989. ISBN 0- 9613814-7-7.

Omrčanin Ivo. *Hrvatska 1941* (Croatia 1941). Volume 2. Printed by IVOR PRESS. 700 New Hampshire Avenue, NW Washington, DC 20037, USA. 1989. ISBN. 0-961384-8-5.

Omrčanin Ivo. *Hrvatska 1942* (Croatia 1942). Published by Ivo Omrčanin, Pantovčak 123. Zagreb, Croatia. Printed by Zagrebačka Tiskara, Preradovićeva 21–23. Zagreb, Croatia.

Omrčanin Ivo. *Hrvatska 1943* (Croatia 1943). Published by Ivo Omrčanin. Pantovčak 123. Zagreb, Croatia. Printed by Zagrebačka Tiskara, Preradovićeva 21–23. Zagreb, Croatia.

Omrčanin Ivo. *Hrvatska 1944* (Croatia 1944). Published by IVOR PRESS. 700 New Hampshire Avenue, NW, Apt 701. Washington, DC 20037, USA. 1990. ISBN 1-878716-01-8.

Omrčanin Ivo. *Hrvatska 1945* (Croatia 1945). Published by IVOR PRESS. 700 Hampshire Avenue, NW, Apartment 701. Washington, DC 20037, USA. 1991. ISBN 1-878716-05-0.

Omrčanin Dr Ivo. *Seed of Blood*. Printed by ANPRINT Co, Sydney, Australia. *Nihil Obstat*: JJ McGovern, *Imprimatur*: E McAuliffe: 28 July 1961.

Patterson David and Roth K John. *After Words Post-Holocaust Struggles with Forgiveness, Reconciliation, Justice*. University of Washington Press, Seattle and London, UK. 2004. ISBN: 0-295-98406-6.

Pavelić Dr Ante. *Putem Hrvatskog Državnog Prava Članci, Govori i Izjave 1918–1928* (On the Road of Croatian Statehood, Articles, Speeches and Announcements 1918–1928). Published by Domovina, Buenos Aires – Madrid, Spain. Edited by Višna Pavelić. Printed by Suc. De Vda, de G. Saez-Meson de Panos, 6. Madrid 13, Spain. 1977. ISBN 84-399-6000-X. ISBN 84-399-6001-8. ISBN 84-399-6002-6. ISBN 84-399-6003-4.

Pavelić Dr Ante. *Hrvatska Pravoslavna Crkva* (The Croatian Orthodox Church). Edited by Višna Pavelić. Printed by Taravilla – Meson de Panos, 6 – 28013 Madrid, Spain. 1984. ISBN: 84-499-7253-1.

Perić Dr Miljenko. *Bleiburg 1945–1995 Svjedočanstvo* (Bleiburg 1945–1995 Witness). Published by the author. Printed by Kerschoffset, Zagreb, Croatia. May 1995.

Pintarić Nedjeljko. In conjunction with Dragčević Zvonko & Kutleša Ante. *Bleiburg Tragedy and Hope.* Published by Glas Koncila, Kaptol 8, Zagreb, Croatia. 2008. ISBN: 978-953-241-133-1.

Planinić Fra. Martin. *Tko Je Izdao Kavrana?* (Who Betrayed Kavran?). Published and printed by Tomislavgrad's ilitary newspaper Trn. Issued in Zagreb, Croatia. 1994.

Pollard F John. *The Unknown Pope Benedict XV (1914–1922) and the Pursuit of Peace.* First published by Geoffrey Chapman, New York, USA. 1999. First paperback 2000. ISBN 0-225-66891-2.

Pope John Paul 11. *Redemptor Hominis* (The Redeemer of Man). Encyclical. A Saint Paul Publication. 60 – 70 Broughton Road Homebush NSW 2140, NSW, Australia. 1979.

Pope John Paul 11. *The Theology of the Body Human Love in the Divine Plan.* Pauline Books and Media, 50 St Pauls Avenue, Boston, MA 02130, USA. 1997. ISBN 0-8198-7394-2.

Pope Francis. *Fratelli Tutti* (Everything for the Brothers) Encyclical Letter on Fraternity and Social Responsibility. Published by St Pauls Publications, 35 Meredith St Strathfield, NSW 2135, NSW, Australia. 2020. ISBN: 978 1 925494 66 2.

Prcela John, MA and Guldescu Stanko, PhD. *Operation Slaughterhouse, Eyewitness Accounts of Postwar Massacres in Yugoslav.* Dorrance & Company, Philadelphia, USA. 1970. Standard Book Number: 8059-1406-4. Printed in the United States of America.

Prejean Helen. *Dead Man Walking.* Fount Paperbacks, Harper Collins Publishers. 77–85 Fulham Palace Road, London W6 8JB, UK. First published in Great Britain 1994. ISBN 0 00 628003X.

Prusac Ivan. *Tragedija Kavrana i Drugova Svjedočanstvo Preživjelog* (The Tragedy of Kavran and Companions a Witness of One who Survived). Printed in Salzburg, Austria by Salzburger Druckerei und Verlag, Bergstr. 12. Salzburg, Austria. 1967.

Radica Bogdan. *Živjeti i Nedoživjeti* (To Live and Not to Be Fulfilled). Volume 1. Published by Hrvatska Revija, Barcelona, Spain. Printed by EGS, Rosario 2, Barcelona, Spain. 1982. ISBN: 84-499-8544-7.

Radica Bogdan. *Živjeti i Nedožvjeti* (To Live and not be Fulfilled). Volume 2. Published by Hrvatska Revija, Barcelona, Spain. Printed by: EGS, Rosario 2, Barcelona, 17, Spain. 1984. ISBN 84-499-9979-0.

Radica Joško. *Istine Nikad Dosta* (There is Never Enough Truth). New Discoveries of Crimes Committed by the Yugo-Communist in Southern Croatia. Published by Matica Hrvatska – Dubrovnik section, Croatia. 2014. ISBN 978-953-7784-34-8.

Rahner Karl, SJ. *Theological Investigations.* Volume 2. Published by Darton, Longman & Todd Ltd London, UK. 1963. ISBN: 232 48245 4.

Rahner Karl, SJ. *Theological Investigations.* Volume 10. Published by Darton, Longman & Todd Ltd London, UK. 1973. ISBN: 0 232 51187 X.

Rahner Karl, SJ. *Theological Investigations.* Volume 15. Published by Darton, Longman & Todd Ltd London, UK. 1983. ISBN: 0 232 51232 9

Ravančić Martina Grahek. *Bleiburg i Krizni Put 1945* (Bleiburg and the Way of the Cross 1945). Published by Hrvatska Institut Za Povijest, Croatia. Printed by Tiskara Zelina dd Sv Ivan Zelina, Croatia. 2009. ISBN 978-953-6324-79-8.

Remak Joachim. *Sarajevo The Story of a Political Murder.* Criterion Books, Inc New York, USA. 1959.

Ridley Jasper. *Tito.* Published by Constable and Company Limited, 3 The Lanchesters, 162 Fulham Palace Road, London, UK. 1994. ISBN: 0 09 471260 3.

Rojnica Ivo. *Susreti i Doživljaji 1938–1945* (Encounters and Life Experiences 1938-1945). Volume 1. Published by Hrvatska Revije, Munchen 1969. Printed by Lohos, GmbH, Buchdruckeri u Verlag, Munchen 19, Bothmerstr, 14, Germany.

Rojnica Ivo. *Susreti i Doživljaji 1945–1975* (Encounters and Lives Experiences 1945–1975), Volume 2. Published by Hrvatska Revije. Munchen-Barcelona, Spain. 1983. Printed in Spain. ISBN 84-499-9313-X.

Rogers S Lindsay. *Guerilla Surgeon.* Collins Clear-Type Press: London and Glasgow. Printed in Great Britain. 1957.

Rootham Jasper. *Miss Fire The Chronicle of a British Mission to Mihailovich 1943–1944*. Chatto & Windus, London, UK. Printed by T and A Constable Ltd. At University Press, Edinburgh, UK. 1946.

Rover Srečko. *Svjedočanstvo i Sječanja* (Witness and Memories). Published by Protektor, Zagreb, Croatia. 1995. ISBN: 953-96176-3-4.

Rulitz Florian Thomas. *Bleiburška i Vetrinjska Tragedija* (The Beliburg and Vetrinja Tragedy). First published in German by Bleiburger Ehrenzug / Klagenfurt. Translated from German by Ivo Pomper. Edited by Josip Jurčević. Zagreb, Croatia. May 2012. ISBN 978-953-7379-03-2.

Rusinović Dr Nikola. *Moja Sječanja Na Hrvatsku* (My Memories of Croatia). Biblioteka: Svjedočanstva, Knjiga V Meditor, Tiskara Puljko. Zagreb, Croatia. 1996. ISBN: 953-6300-08-7.

St Isidore of Seville. HTTPS://www.britannica.com/biography/saint-isidore-of-sevillia.

Schwartz Mladen. *Bleiburg i Haag* (Bleiburg and The Haag). Published by IuvenaliS Samizdat. Zagreb, Crotia. 2009. ISBN: 978-953-98181-6-8.

*Serbian Voice Newspaper.*122 Snell Grove, Oak Park, Victoria 3026, Australia. 12 January 2018 edition.

Singer June K. *Boundaries of The Soul The Practice of Jung's Psychology*. Anchor Books. Anchor Press, Doubleday Garden City, New York, USA. 1973. ISBN: 0-385-06900-6.

Spiegelman J Marvin, PhD. *Catholicism and Jungian Psychology*. Falcon Press, Phoenix, Arizona, USA. 1988.

Stuparić, Darko. Dizdar, Zdravko. Grčić, Marko. Ravlić, Slaven. *Tko Je Tko u Nezavisnoj Državi Hrvatskoj 1941–1945* (Who is What in the Independant State of Croatia 1941–1945). Published by Minerva, Zagreb, Croatia. 1997. ISBN: 953-6377-03-9.

Supek Ivan. *Povijesne Meditacije* (Historical Meditations). Published by AGM, Mihanovičeva 28, Zagreb, Crotia. 1996. ISBN: 953-174-053-4.

Srkulj Stjepan. *Hrvatska Povjest u devetnest karata* (Croatian History in Nineteen Maps). Published by Tipografia DD. Dionično Društvo u Zagrebu, Croatia. (Shareholders Society of Zagreb) Easter 1937.

Srkulj Dr Stjepan & Lučić Dr Josip. *Hrvastka Povjest u Devetnest Karata & Hrvatska Povijest u Dvadeset Pet Karata* (Croatian History in Nineteen Maps and Croatian History in Twenty Five Maps). A Wider and More Developed edition. Printed by KERSCHOFFSET, Zagreb, Crotia. Published by AGM. The Croatian Information Centre. Trsat, Zagreb, Croatia. 1996. ISBN 983-174-030-5.

Šanjak Franjo. *Krscanstvo Na Hrvatskom Prostoru* (Christianity On Croatian Territory). Krščanska Sadaštnjosti. Second edition. Printed by Krščanskoj Sadišnosti, Zagreb, Croatia. 1996. ISBN 953-151-103-9.

Šidak Jaroslav. *Kroz Pet Stoljeća Hrvatske Povijesti* (Through Five Centuries of Croatian History). Školska Knjiga (School Book) – Zagreb, Croatia. 1981. Edited by Blagota Drašković. Prepared by Boris Dogan. Printed by Grafitski Zavod Hrvatske, Zagreb, Frankopanska 26, Croatia.

Šimić Pero. *Tito Fenomen Stoljeća Prva Politička Biografija* (Tito Phenomenon of the Century First Political Biography). Published by Večernji posebni proizvodi doo, Slavonska avenue 4, Zagreb, Croatia. 2009. ISBN: 978-953-7313-40-1.

Šišić Ferdo. *Pregled Povijesti Hrvatskoga Naroda* (Overview of the History of the Croatian People). Štamparia *Vjesnik*. Chief editor Jakša Ravlić assisted by Dr Jaroslav Šidak. Published by Matica Hrvatska, Zagreb, Coatia. 1962.

Šinović Marko. *Nezavisna Država Hrvatska u Svjetlu Dokumenta* (The Independent State of Croatia in the Light of Documents). Edicion Del Autor. Buenos Aires. Impreso en la Argentina. Republika Argentina. Queda hecho el deposito marca. La Ley 11. 723. Copyright by Autor. 27 Siegnja 1950.

Štir Ivan pukovnik. *Elementi i Metode Komunističkog Gerile* (Elements and Methods of Communist Guerrilla). Editor: Drinine Knjiznice. Madrid, Spain. 1964.

Štir Ivan Pukovnik. *Izmedju revolucionarnosti i oportunizma u borbi za Hrvatsku Državu* (Between Revolution and Optimism in the Struggle for the Croatian State). Published: Drinina Knjižnica. Madrid, Spain. 1966. Printed: Drina Press, Valencia, Spain.

Šuljak Dinko. *Trazijo Sam Radičevu Hrvatsku* (I Searched for Radich's Croatia). Published by Hrvatska Revije, Barcelona-Munchen, Spain – Germany, 1988. Printed in Spain. ISBN: 84-599-9079-6.

Šuvar Mira. *Vladimir Velebit Svjedok Historije* (Vladimir Velebit Witness of History). Biography, published by Razlog doo. Zagreb, Croatia. Palmoticeva Street 70/11. 2001. ISBN: 953-6985-00-4.

The Jewish Encyclopedia. Funk and Wagner Company. New York and London/USA and UK. Copyright 1905, 1909, 1912, 1916. Volumes 1 & 1V.

Tolstoy Nikolai. *The Minister and the Massacres*. Published by Century Hutchinson Ltd. Brookmount House, 62–65 Chandos Place, London WC2N 4NW, UK. 1986. ISBN: 0-09-164010-5.

Tomasovich Jozo. *Četnici u Drugom Svjetskom Ratu 1941–1945* (The Četniks in the Second World War 1941–1945). Published by the University of Zagreb publishing house Liber. Printed by >Ognjen Prica< Karlovac. Zagreb, Croatia. 1979.

Tomasovich Jozo. *War and Revolution in Yugoslavia, 1941-1945. Occupation and Collaboration*. Stanford University Press. Stanford, California. Printed in the United States of America. 2001. ISBN 0-8047-3615-4.

Tudjman Franjo. *Hrvatska U Monarhistickoj Jugoslaviji 1918-1941* (Croatia In Monarchical Yugoslavia 1918-1941). Volume 1. 1918-1928. Hrvatska Sveučilišna Naklada. Zagreb, Croata. 1993. ISBN 953-169-000-6

Tudjman Franjo. *Hrvatska U Monarhistickoj Jugoslaviji 1918-1941* (Croatia In Monarchical Yugoslavia 1918-1941). Volume 2. 1928-1941. Hrvatska Sveučilišna Naklada. Zagreb, Croata. 1993. ISBN 953-169-001-4.

Tudjman Franjo. *Horrors of War Historical Reality and Philosophy*. M Evens and Company, INC New York, USA. 1996. ISBN: 0-87131-838-5.

Trotsky Leon. *The Defence of Terrorism*. George Allen & Unwin, London, UK. 1920.

Vnuk Frantisek. *This is Dr Jozef Tiso*. Published by Friends of Good Books. Cambridge, Ontario, Canada, 1977. Printed in Canada. NSBN: 0-920150-04-0.

Volf Miroslav. *Exclusion and Embrace A Theological Exploration of Identity, Otherness and Reconciliation*. Abingdon Press, Nashville, USA. 1996. ISBN-13: 978-0-687-00282-5.

Vrančić Vjekoslav. *Branili Smo Drzavu* (We Were Defending the State). Volume 2. Published by Hrvatska Revije. Barcelona – Munich, Spain – Germany.1985. Printed in Spain. ISBN 84-599-5775-6.

Vrančić Vjekoslav. *U Službi Domovine* (In the Service of the Homeland) which included the books *S Bjelom Zastavom Preko Alpa* (With a White Flag Over the Alps). *Postrojenje i Brojčano Stanje Hrvatskih Oruzni Snaga* (The Units and Numbers of the Croatian Armed Forces). Published by the author. Printed by Talleres Graficos Vilkos, rI, Estados Unidos 425, Buenos Aires, Argentina 1977.

Vraneković Josip. *Dnevnik Život u Krašiću zasuznjenog nadbiskupa i kardinala Alojzija Stepinac 5th December 1951-10th February 1960* (Diary, Life Under House Arrest in Krasič of Archbishop Cardinal Stepinac 5th December-10th February 1960). Editor Dr Juraj Batelja. Printed by Denona, Zagreb, Croatia. 2011. ISBN 953-7441-01-6.

Vukušić Bože (Executive Editor). Zivić Dražen Dr sc (Editor) *Hidden Croatian Mass Graves in the Republic of Slovenia*. Publisher: Bleiburg Honoury Guard, Zagreb, Croatia. 2007. Co-Publisher: Rados Damir, Burlimgame, USA. ISBN 978-953-7379-01-8.

Vukušić Bože. *Bleiburg Memento*. Second Edition published by Počasni bleiburgski vod Zagreb, Croatia. 2009. ISBN: 978-953-7379-02-5.

Werhas Mario – Božidar Mikulčić. *Handzar Borbeni Put 13. SS. Gorske Divizije.* (Handzar the Path of Battle of the 13 SS Mountain Division). Published by Despot infinitus d.o.o., Zagreb, Croatia. 2018. ISBN: 978-953-8218-03-3.

West Rebecca. *Black Lamb and Grey Falcon: A Journey through Yugoslavia.* Macmillan Publishers Limited, London, UK. First published 1942. Reprinted 1984. Printed in Hong Kong. ISBN: 0 333 38551 9.

Wright Nicholas Thomas. *Evil and the Justice of God.* Published by Society for Promoting Christian Knowledge in Great Britain 2006. ISBN: 13: 978-0-281-05788-7.

Žanko Želimir & Solić Nikola. *Jazovka.* Published by Vjesnik, Slavonska Ulica 4. Zagreb, Croatia. 1990.

Žanko Dušan. *Svjedoci* (Witnesses). Published by Hrvatska Revija. Printed in Spain. 1987. ISBN: 84-599-7400-6.

Živojinović Dragan R. *America, Italy and the Birth of Yugoslavia. 1917–1919.* Published by Eastern European Quarterly, Boulder distributions, Columbia University Press, New York 1972.

Znameniti i Zašluzni Hrvati Te Pomena Vrijedna Lica u Hrvatskoj Povijesti od 925–1925 (Distinguished and Worthy Croatians in Croatian History from 925–1925) Published by the Committee Commemorating One Thousand Years of the Croatian Kingdom. It was arranged and printed by the Croatian Printing Zavod DD in Zagreb. Co-editors: Dr Ante Cividini, Ancica Idzakovic, Antonija Kassowitz-Cvijić, Rev Ante Milosević, Rev Andelko Posinković OP, Rev Antun Zaninović OP, Dr Janko Božić, Dr Božidar Sirola, Cvjetko Skarpa, Dr Dane Gruber, Dr David Karlović, Rev Davorin Krmpotić, Emilij Laszowski, Dr Franjo Bucar, Rev Klement Basić, Rev Gavro Cvitanović, Rev Jure Božitković, Rev Pavao Dragičević, Rev Karlo Evetović, Rev Dr Stanko Petrov, Dr Fran Suklje, Hamdija Kresevljaković, Dr Ivo Pevalek, Dr Ivan Bojničić Kninski, Jeronim Borac, Rev Janko Barle, Josip Poljak, Rev Dr Julian Jelenić, Dr Josip Nagy, Josip Tomičić, Slava Franic, Martin Lovrenčević, Stevo Petrović, Lina Bogdan, Ljubomir Mastrović, Milan Krasović, Mirko Breyer, Milorad Gavazzi, Dr Miroslav Hirtz, Dr Niko Bjelovučić, Dr Oton Franges, Rev Oton Knežović, Pavao Butorac, Dr Petar Karlić, Rudolf Franjin Magyer, Dr Rudolf Horvat, Rudolf Strohal, Safvet beg Basagić, Stevo Petrović, Stjepan Szavits-Nosan, Stjepan pl Platzer, Stjepan Sirola, Dr Velimir Dezelić, Vjekoslav Klaić, Dr Vale Vouk, Vjekoslav Norsić, Vjekoslav Spiničić. 26 July 1925. Administrative Committee: Aleksandar pl. Ballogh, Stjepan pl Ballogh, Olga pl Ballogh, Anka pl Ballogh, Stjepan Banović, Kresimir Biljan, Ivan Hecimović, Nikola Host, Ivan Majstorović, Milan Poljugan, Stanka Poljugan, Ivan Schwechler, Gjuro Turkalj. The introduction was written by Emilij Laszowski on behalf of the editors together with Aleksandar pl Ballogh on behalf of the administrators in Zagreb dated 26 July 1925. The book is extremely rear and valuable, the author is grateful to Mrs Thea Goreta for lending it to him.

Zovko Jure. *Križni Put i Dvadeset Godina Robije* (The Way of the Cross and Twenty Years of Servitude). Published by Nakladni Zavod Globus, Zagreb, Croatia. 1997. ISBN 953-167-091-9.

Index of Names

A

Akrap, Gordan, 120, 351.
Arnold, Eberhard, 321, 327, 337, 338, 339, 342, 351.

B

Babich, Ivan, 13, 17, 24, 28, 36, 67.
Balfour, Neil, 72, 74, 351.
Baničević, Don Božo, 10, 11, 233.
Baserichek, Djuro, 49, 52.
Basta, Milan, 94, 106, 107, 108, 109, 124, 127, 129, 285, 351.
Batelja, Juraj, 118, 127, 337, 352, 368.
Bauer, Ernest, 83, 288, 352.
Bazala, Albert, 61.
Bekovac, Ante, 127.
Beljo, Ante, 92, 94, 126, 352.
Beloff, Nora, 91, 124, 270, 279, 352.
Benedict XV, Pope, 38, 41, 44, 364.
Benedict XVI, Pope, xii, 38, 41, 44, 364.
Benigar, Aleska, 37, 38, 39, 41, 48, 53, 60, 61, 62, 63, 65, 66, 70, 77, 78, 79, 80, 84, 86, 87, 88, 89, 90, 91, 92, 94, 97, 101, 116, 117, 352.
Berkovits, Elizer, xxiv, 353.
Bethel, Nicholas, 109, 129.

Bjelovučić, NZ, 3, 4, 11, 226, 228, 229, 232, 369.
Bjelovučić, NZ, 3, 4, 11, 226, 228, 229, 232, 353, 369.
Blum, Leon, 46.
Bonifačić, Antun F, 1, 39, 43, 88, 353.
Bozidar, Marko, 195–204.
Brguljanin, Martin, 21.
Bridjachich, Karl, 65.
Buc, Stjepan, 292.
Budak, Mile, xi, 67, 80, 85, 247, 288, 362.

C

Campbell, Ronald, 73.
Capra, Fritjof, 325, 326, 353.
Capistrano, John, Friar, 13.
Carroll, Warren H, 26, 353.
Chamberlain, Neville, 69.
Charles V, Emperor, 17.
Chernozemski, Vlado, 60.
Chicherin, Georgy, 46.
Chubranovich, Andrija, 11.
Churchill, Winston, 68, 73, 74, 87, 102, 105, 110, 124, 269, 273, 293, 309.
Churchin, Milan, 61.

Clift, Wallace, 321, 353.
Ciliga, Ante, 48.
Cincar-Markovich, Alexsander, 76.
Clement VII, Pope, 16.
Coffey, David, 342.
Crljen, Daniel, 102, 104, 105, 106, 107, 108, 139, 144, 145, 146, 286.
Cvetkovich, Dragisha, 36.
Cvijich, Duro, 51.
Cvijich, Jovan, 30.

D

Dabinović, Antun, 36, 354.
Dallas, Gregor, 101, 354.
Davidovich, Ljuba, 49.
Davidson, Basil, 122, 123, 124, 274, 354.
de Chateaubriand, Francois-Rene, xxi.
Deakin, William, 52, 121, 122, 123, 125, 126, 268, 274, 275, 293, 354.
Dedija, Vladimir, 127, 129.
Delbo, Charlotte, 316.
Dixon, Norman, 305, 306, 307, 354.
Djilas, Milovan, 50, 51, 52, 66, 122, 123, 124, 125, 205, 244, 245, 266, 276, 277, 278, 279, 292, 310, 311, 354.
Dozich, Gavrilo, 74.
Draganovich, Krunoslav, 50, 51, 88, 128, 232, 239, 240, 297, 298, 299, 300, 372.
Dragoljov, Fedor, 98.
Drashkovich, Janko, 23.
Drljevich, Sekula, 68, 146, 234.
Drzich, Marin, 11.
Dubajac, Simno, 160, 161, 250.
Dujmović, Franjo, 28, 31, 37, 38, 39, 40, 42, 43, 53, 69, 71, 72, 73, 76, 78, 79, 80, 86, 96, 98, 112, 285, 304, 354.

E

Efenko, Ivan Kovachich, 106, 107.
Einstein, Albert, 56, 57, 348, 356.
Eterovich, Francis, H, 5, 355.

F

Ferdinand, Franz, Archduke, xvii, 31.
Ferdinand, King, 14, 16, 17, 19, 14.
Filipovich, Joseph, 28.
Francis, Pope, xxv, 317, 318, 320, 330, 344, 364.
Frankopan, Bernadin, 13, 14, 15.
Frankopan, Krsto, 13, 18, 19.
Frede-Weger, Britta, 331.

G

Gagro, Pavo, xxvi, 113, 183, 188, 293.
Gaj, Ljudevit, 23.
Garashanin, Ilija, 30.
Gasparri, Pietro, 41, 44.
Gavrilovich, Milan, 49.
Gazzari, Julije, 40.
Gitman, Esther, 53, 63, 72, 117, 119, 120, 288, 355.
Gordievsky, Oleg, 50, 351.
Gorkich, Milan, 50, 51, 58.
Gregorich, Ilija, 17, 103.
Gregory, Pope, 5.
Grol, Milan, 69, 70.
Gruber, Wendel, 219, 220, 221, 222, 223, 224.
Gubec, Matija, 17, 18.
Guldescu, Stanko, 2, 3, 4, 5, 6, 12, 27, 32, 33, 92, 96, 97, 106, 108, 109, 134, 135, 136, 137, 138, 140, 164, 167, 176, 180, 364.
Gundulich, Ivan, 11.

H

Hastings, Adrian, 29, 355.
Herenchich, Ivo, 88, 103, 104, 105, 106, 107, 108, 109, 138, 139, 144, 145, 146, 147, 185, 286, 287.
Herron, George, 41.
Hitler, Adolf, 37, 58, 59, 60, 67, 71, 72, 75, 76, 77, 78, 79, 80, 81, 87, 91, 110, 111, 113, 116, 119, 266, 305, 308, 358, 359.
Hojt, Stjepan, xxv, 121, 131, 275, 308.
Horvat, Ban Ivan, 11.
Horvat, Josip, 23, 25, 26, 27, 40, 42, 43, 45, 47, 356.
Horvat, Lipharda, 263.
Horvat, Romana, 219.
Hunyadi, Janos, Prince, 13.

I

Innocent, Pope, 7.
Ivurek, Mijo, 50, 51, 232, 233, 234, 240, 301, 356.

J

Jelachich, Josip, 24, 25, 140, 273.
Jenko, Valerian, 213, 214.
Jones, L Gregory, 338, 341, 356.
Jovanovich, Stjepan, 28, 141.
Jug, Damir, 110, 128, 129.
Jurčević, Josip, xxi, 64, 91, 94, 98, 99, 101, 213, 216, 217, 244, 248, 252, 253, 263, 264, 357, 366.
Jurkovich, Josip, 98.

K

Kaima, Hasan, 21.
Kambar, Dragutin, 293, 294.
Karadzich, Stefanovich, 29, 30, 233.
Karagorgevich, Alexander, King, xix, 35, 43, 44, 54, 215, 265.
Karagorgevich, Paul, Prince, 36, 60, 72, 73.
Karagorgevich, Peter, King, 31.
Karapandich, Borivoje, 209, 210, 211, 212.
Karaula, Zelko, 114, 115, 292, 357.
Karpandzich, Borivoje, 167.
Kasche, Siegfried, 80, 91, 123, 288.
Kemp, Katherine, 326, 358.
Kisic-Kolanovich, Nada, 70, 81, 85, 86, 110, 113, 358.
Klaić, Vjekoslav, 2, 3, 4, 5, 6, 7, 12, 13, 15, 16, 17, 18, 24, 358, 369.
Kljakovich, Jozo, 85, 86, 115, 116.
Kneightley, Chalres, 106, 271.
Knezović, Oton, 1, 3 4, 5, 6, 7, 8, 9, 10, 11, 12, 13, 15, 16, 17, 18, 19, 23, 24, 28, 30, 234.
Knezović, Oton, 1, 3, 4, 5, 6, 7, 8, 9, 10, 11, 12, 13, 15, 16, 17, 18, 19, 23, 24, 28, 30, 234, 358.
Knopfelmacher, Frank, 32.
Korosec, Anton, 38, 68.
Koshchak, Tom, 22.
Koshutich, August, 69.
Kossuth, Ludvik, 23, 24.
Kosutich, August, 56.
Kozul, Marko, 81.
Krašić, Stjepan, 2, 22, 32, 312, 368.
Krasich, Bartol, 23.
Krishovich, Vinko, 114.
Krnjevich, Juraj, 56, 309.
Krsevan, Edwin, 344.
Kruzich, Peter, 16.
Kulenovich, Dzafer, 70, 76, 85.
Kum, Otto, 224, 225, 359.
Kushner, Harold, 316, 359.
Kvaternik, Dido, 55, 86, 93, 111, 285.
Kvaternik, Dido, 93, 285.

Kvaternik, Eugene, 26.
Kvaternik, Eugene, 26, 55, 93, 111, 285, 288, 289.
Kvaternik, Slavko, 77, 78, 288.
Kvaternik, Slavko, 77, 78, 86, 92, 118, 283.

L

Lawrence, Christie, 110, 274, 359.
Lazar, King, 11.
Leljak, Roman, 247, 248, 252, 253, 254, 255, 256, 257, 270, 276, 359.
Leon, Pope, 14.
Lepre, George, 130, 131, 359.
Lorkovich, Mladen, 93, 94, 126, 283, 287, 296, 301.
Luchich-Bogoslavich, Teronim, 21.
Ludovic, King, 16.
Lukas, Filip, 86, 114.

M

Mačak, Vladko, 52.
McAleese, Mary, 328, 329, 344, 361.
McDonnell, Kevin, xxvi, 342, 343.
Macan, Trpimir, 1, 2, 3, 4, 6, 7, 8, 10, 11, 12, 13, 15, 16, 18, 19, 22, 23, 24, 25, 26, 27, 28, 29, 37, 39, 42, 43, 45, 47, 49, 53, 55, 56, 57, 58, 359.
Machek, Vlatko, 36, 55, 56, 57, 59, 60, 61, 62, 63, 65, 67, 69, 70, 71, 72, 73, 74, 75, 76, 78, 82, 86, 87, 110, 111, 114, 296, 302.
Mackay, Sally, 72, 74, 351.
MacMillan, Harold, xviii, 96, 101, 102, 126, 267, 268, 269, 270, 271, 272, 273, 360.
Mahnich, Anton, 38.
Makanec, Julia, 120.

Mandić, D, 2, 3, 4, 5, 6, 7, 8, 9, 10, 12, 15, 16, 17, 18, 19, 21, 22, 23, 25, 27, 29, 31, 32, 42, 43, 45, 53, 54, 55, 56, 60, 69, 74, 75, 113, 226, 228, 229, 230, 232, 360.
Mandich, Nikola, 84, 85, 96, 126.
McDonald, Steven, 342.
Mandich, Ivica, xxvi, 295.
Mann, Heinrich, 56, 57.
Mann, Thomas, 56, 57.
Marjanović, Jovan, 73, 360, 361.
Markovich, George, 138.
Markovich, Sima, 50, 51.
Martich, Pero, 176–180.
Masucci, Giuseppe, 92, 93, 94, 97, 98, 100, 101, 279, 280, 361.
Matković, Drago, 11.
Matković, Hrvoje, 126, 361.
Matković, Stjepan, 57.
Maximilian, King, 18.
Mazuranich, Ivan, 26, 27.
Mestrovich, Ivan, 29, 37, 39, 40, 48, 49, 60, 61, 74, 83, 86, 118, 119, 234, 279.
Mestrovich, Mate, 276.
Mihanovih, Clement, 1, 39, 40, 43, 88, 353.
Milinovich, Nedo, 220, 221.
Minich, Mihajilo, 237.
Moshkov, Ante, 183, 280, 281, 284, 285, 287, 302.

N

Napulski, Ladislav Anjou, King, 12.
Nicolson, Nigel, 212, 271.
Nikolić, Vinko, 40, 90, 95, 96, 99, 100, 109, 110, 121, 128, 142, 159, 195, 204, 207, 209, 210, 213, 214, 218, 219, 237, 239, 240, 281, 282, 283, 284, 291, 292, 295, 301, 303, 309, 316, 330, 352, 355, 357, 362.
Njaradija, Dionizij, 62.

O

O'Malley, John W, 26, 363.
Obrenovich, Alexander, King, 31, 53, 72.
Obrenovich, Draga, Queen, 31, 53, 72.
Omrcanin, Ivo, 73, 74, 78, 86, 91, 93, 94, 112, 115, 126, 128, 130, 363.
Orshanich, Ivan, 284.

P

Pasanac, Ivan, 17, 18.
Pasich, Nikola, 38, 39.
Paul III, Pope, 16, 17.
Pavelich, Ante, 35, 53, 54, 55, 64, 68, 78, 79, 83, 84, 85, 86, 87, 88, 89, 90, 94, 98, 100, 111, 112, 113, 116, 117, 118, 119, 121, 126, 128, 185, 190, 265, 280, 281, 282, 283, 284, 285, 286, 291, 292, 293, 295, 297, 300, 302, 303, 304, 305, 306, 311, 312.
Pavelich, Mara, 287, 288, 289.
Pazman, Josip, 45.
Petričević, Mate, xxvi.
Petrovich, Dimitrija, 235, 237.
Pollard, John, 41, 44, 364.
Pollefeyt, Didlier, 320, 327, 331, 333, 334, 340.
Popovich, Pavao, 37, 123, 191, 218.
Portman, Michael, 219, 276, 356.
Prcela, John, 92, 95, 97, 106, 108, 109, 134, 135, 136, 137, 138, 140, 164, 167, 176, 180, 355, 364.
Prebeg, Vladimir, 45.
Protulipac, Ivo, 90, 121.
Puk, Mirko, 81, 294.

R

Radica, Bogdan, 111, 123, 277, 365.
Radica, Joško, 259, 365.
Radich, Stjepan, 29, 42, 44, 45, 46, 47, 48, 49, 52, 56, 111, 125, 275, 308, 367.
Rankovich, Alexander, 101, 276, 311.
Ravancic, Martina, 97, 98, 99, 109, 127, 212, 244, 245, 246, 248, 250, 251, 252, 253, 255, 256, 257, 276, 289, 292, 296, 355, 365.
Ricoeur, Paul, 328.
Ridley, Jasper, 49, 52, 53, 58, 123, 124, 127, 131, 365.
Rodgers, Lindsay, 123, 206, 208, 365.
Rojnica, Ivo, xxvi, 69, 99, 100, 126, 127, 276, 284, 286, 287, 295, 296, 297, 304, 365..
Rusinovicch, Nikola, 31, 82, 87, 88, 366.
Russell, John, 32.

S

Schober, Johann, 46.
Šentija, Josip, 2, 3, 4, 6, 12, 13, 16, 19, 23, 24, 25, 26, 37, 39, 42, 45, 47, 49, 53, 359.
Šentija, Josip, 2, 3, 4, 6, 12, 13, 16, 19, 23, 24, 25, 26, 37, 39, 42, 43, 45, 47, 49, 53, 359.
Shimovich, Dushan, 72, 73, 74, 75, 76.
Shufflay, Milan, 56.
Shuljak, Dinko, 125.
Simich, Pero, 51.
Šišić, Ferdo, 3, 4, 6, 7, 8, 9, 11, 12, 13, 16, 17, 18, 19, 23, 25, 26, 27, 28.
Srkulj, Stjepan, 1, 3, 5, 10, 12, 13, 16, 79, 366.

Spiegelman, Marvin, 339, 366.
Stalin, Joseph, 50, 52, 58, 87, 141, 218, 220, 267, 270, 277, 279, 293, 311, 354.
Stancer, Slavko, 104, 109, 127, 148.
Starchevich, Ante, 26, 27.
Steed, Wickham, 46.
Stepinac, Aloysius, xix, 37, 38, 39, 41, 48, 60, 61, 62, 63, 65, 66, 70, 77, 78, 79, 80, 81, 83, 84, 86, 87, 88, 89, 90, 91, 92, 94, 97, 98, 100, 101, 116, 117, 118, 119, 120, 121, 308, 312, 336, 351, 352, 355, 361, 362, 368.
Stojadinovich, Milan, 36, 62, 63, 64, 65, 67, 68, 70.
Stojanovich, Nikola, 30, 84.
Strossmayer, Josip Juraj, 25, 26, 362.
Suljak, Dinko, 125, 275, 367.
Supek, Ivan, 125, 366.
Supilo, Franjo, 37, 38.
Šuvar, Mira, 123, 124, 205, 234, 367.
Schwartz, Mladen, 128, 257.

T

Tartaglia, Ivo, 61.
Tito, Josip Broz, 49, 50, 58, 71, 109, 127, 265, 273.
Tjednik, Hrvatski, 251.
Todorovich, Branislav, 190–195.
Tolstoy, Nikolai, 96, 102, 167, 195, 212, 213, 250, 264, 267, 268, 269, 270, 271, 273, 279, 287, 367.
Tomashevich, Stjepan, 13.
Tomasovich, Jozo, 75, 76, 121, 125, 126, 128, 214, 218, 285, 302, 367, 368.
Trinjsich, Dinko, 40.
Trogrančicč, Franjo, 11.
Trumbich, Ante, 29, 37, 39, 40, 41, 48, 54.

Tudjman, Franjo, xxii, xxiii, 29, 30, 31, 37, 38, 39, 40, 41, 42, 46, 47, 49, 50, 52, 53, 55, 56, 57, 59, 60, 61, 62, 64, 65, 66, 69, 70, 73, 74, 75, 76, 111, 183, 305, 368.
Tvrtko, King, 11, 12.

V

Varnava, Patriach, 56, 66.
Vasich, Dragisha, 73.
Vetranovich, Mavro, 11.
Vojnovich, Luja, 37.
Volf, Miroslav, 317, 324, 327, 328, 337, 368.
Von Herran, Viktor, 76.
Vranchich, Anton, 18.
Vranchich, Faust, 23.
Vranchich, Vjekoslav, 96, 126, 128, 295.
Vujić, Jure, 52, 273.
Vukoslavich, Petar, 21.
Vulchich, Hrvoj, 12.
Vukušić, Bože, 246, 247, 249, 250, 252, 254, 258, 368.

W

Watson, Seaton, 46.
West, Rebecca, 26, 52, 369.
Wilson, Woodrow, 41.
Wright, NT, 323, 337, 340, 345, 369.

Z

Zanich, Milovan, 86, 99, 284.
Žanko, Dušan, 3, 114, 226, 369.
Zivkovich, Mirko, xxvi, 121, 122, 280, 281, 282, 283.
Zivkovich, Petar, 52, 53, 62, 73.
Zivojinović, Dragan, R, 40, 234, 369.
Zlatarich, Dinko, 11.

Printed in the USA
CPSIA information can be obtained
at www.ICGtesting.com
JSHW020852241223
54126JS00003B/125